RAGNARÖK

Volume 8:
Revenge of the Valkyrie

By
Myung-Jin Lee

English Version
by
Richard A. Knaak

TOKYOPOP®

Los Angeles • Tokyo • London

Translator - Lauren Na
Copy Editor - Tim Beedle
Retouch and Lettering - Tina Fulkerson
Cover Layout - Anna Kernbaum

Editor - Jake Forbes
Managing Editor - Jill Freshney
Production Coordinator - Antonio DePietro
Production Manager - Jennifer Miller
Art Director - Matt Alford
Editorial Director - Jeremy Ross
VP of Production - Ron Klamert
President & C.O.O. - John Parker
Publisher & C.E.O. - Stuart Levy

Email: editor@TOKYOPOP.com
Come visit us online at www.TOKYOPOP.com

A  Manga

TOKYOPOP Inc.
5900 Wilshire Blvd. Suite 2000
Los Angeles, CA 90036

ISBN: 1-59182-207-6

First TOKYOPOP printing: October 2003

10 9 8 7 6 5 4 3 2 1

Printed in the USA

Bonus Supplement

RAGNARÖK
Players Handbook

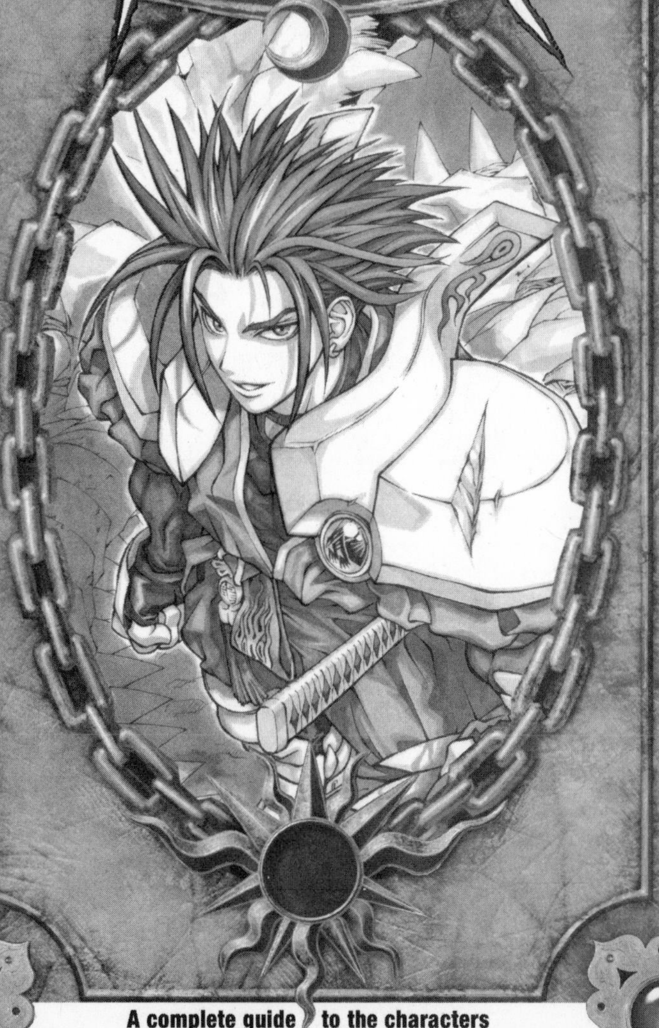

A complete guide to the characters
and story for novice adventurers.

HEROES

NOTE: THE FOLLOWING STATISTICS ARE INSPIRED BY THE MANGA, BUT DO NOT REFLECT ANY OFFICIAL RAGNAROK RPG. – EDITOR

NAME: Chaos
Class: Rune Knight (Dragon Knight?)
Level: 10 (Level up!)
Alignment: Chaotic Good
STR: 17
DEX: 10
CON: 15
INT: 12
WIS: 14
CHR: 16

Equipment:
Vision- Enchanted sword- STR +2

Rune Armor- AC -4, 20% bonus
saving throw vs. magical attacks.

Notes:
The reincarnation of the fallen god Balder,
Chaos has been told by his divine mother,
Frigg, that the fate of the world rests in his
hands. He may also be tied to the legendary
"Dragon Knights."

NAME: Iris Irine
Class: Cleric
Level: 6 (Level up!)
Alignment: Lawful Good
STR: 7
DEX: 12
CON: 9
INT: 13
WIS: 16
CHR: 16

Equipment:
Chernryongdo- Enchanted dagger-
STR +1, DEX +1, 1D4 damage if
anyone but she touches it.

Pronteran Leather Armor- AC -3,
DEX +1

Notes:
Iris would have become the new leader of the city
of Fayon... that is, if it weren't destroyed by her sister, the Valkyrie Sara Irine. She now follows her
close friend Chaos.

HEROES

NAME: Fenris Fenrir
Class: Warlock
Level: 10 (Level up!)
Alignment: Neutral Good
STR: 14
DEX: 15
CON: 13
INT: 16
WIS: 12
CHR: 14

Equipment:
Psychic Medallion: Magic compass
which leads its bearer to whatever
his or her heart most desires.

Laevatein, Rod of Destruction- STR+1, extends
to staff on command.

Warrior's Hanbok- AC -4.
Notes:
The reincarnation of the Wolf God, Fenris
helped Chaos to realize his identity. She now
follows him on his quest.

NAME: Loki
Class: Assassin
Level: 10 (Level up!)
Alignment: Lawful Neutral
STR:14
DEX: 18
CON: 12
INT: 12
WIS: 14
CHR: 10

Equipment:
Sword of Shadows: + 4 to hit, damage +2

Bone Armor- AC -5, STR +2

Notes:
Greatest of the Assassins, Loki's anonymity
is a testament to his skill at going unseen.
An enigma himself, his curiosity and respect
for the even more mysterious Chaos caused
him to join the Rune Knight for as long as
they follow the same road.

HEROES

ENEMIES

NAME: Lidia
Class: Thief
Level: 3 (Level DOWN! heh heh...)
Alignment: Neutral Good
STR: 8
DEX: 15
INT: 13
WIS: 10
CHR: 15

Equipment:
Treasure Hunter's Bible: 50% chance of
identifying magical items

Follower- Sessy, Cat o' Two Tails: +50%
saving throw to pick pockets

Notes:
An "expert treasure hunter" by trade,
Lidia "borrows" whatever she can get her
hands on while she looks for bigger
hauls. She was last seen leaving the city
of Prontera. She's currently en route to
Geffen in search of the treasures of
Alfheim.

NAME: Sara Irine
Class: Valkyrie
Level: 8 (Level up!)
Alignment: Chaotic Neutral
STR: 14
DEX: 12
CON: 13
INT: 14
WIS: 15
CHR: 17

Equipment:
Haeryongdo, Sword of Retribution-
STR+2

Enchanted Parchments x24

Notes:
One of the 12 Valkyries of Valhalla,
Sara was once the heir to Fayon until
the village elders cast her out in favor
of her sister, Iris. Sara returned to
Fayon and destroyed everything,
including her parents. She was last
seen leaving Prontera in possession of
Ymir's heart.

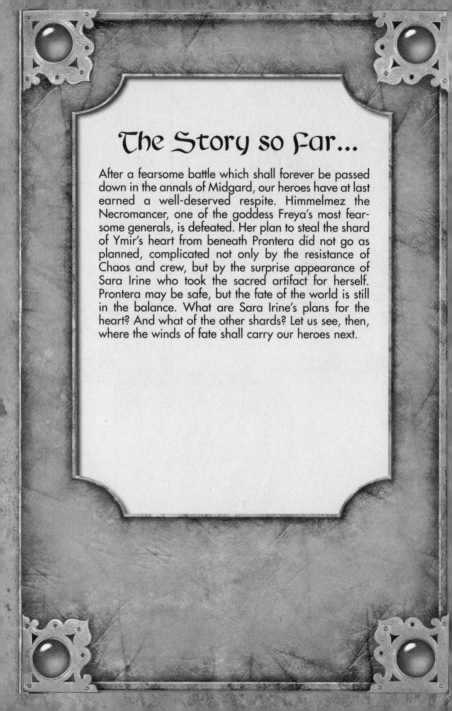

The Story so Far...

After a fearsome battle which shall forever be passed down in the annals of Midgard, our heroes have at last earned a well-deserved respite. Himmelmez the Necromancer, one of the goddess Freya's most fearsome generals, is defeated. Her plan to steal the shard of Ymir's heart from beneath Prontera did not go as planned, complicated not only by the resistance of Chaos and crew, but by the surprise appearance of Sara Irine who took the sacred artifact for herself. Prontera may be safe, but the fate of the world is still in the balance. What are Sara Irine's plans for the heart? And what of the other shards? Let us see, then, where the winds of fate shall carry our heroes next.

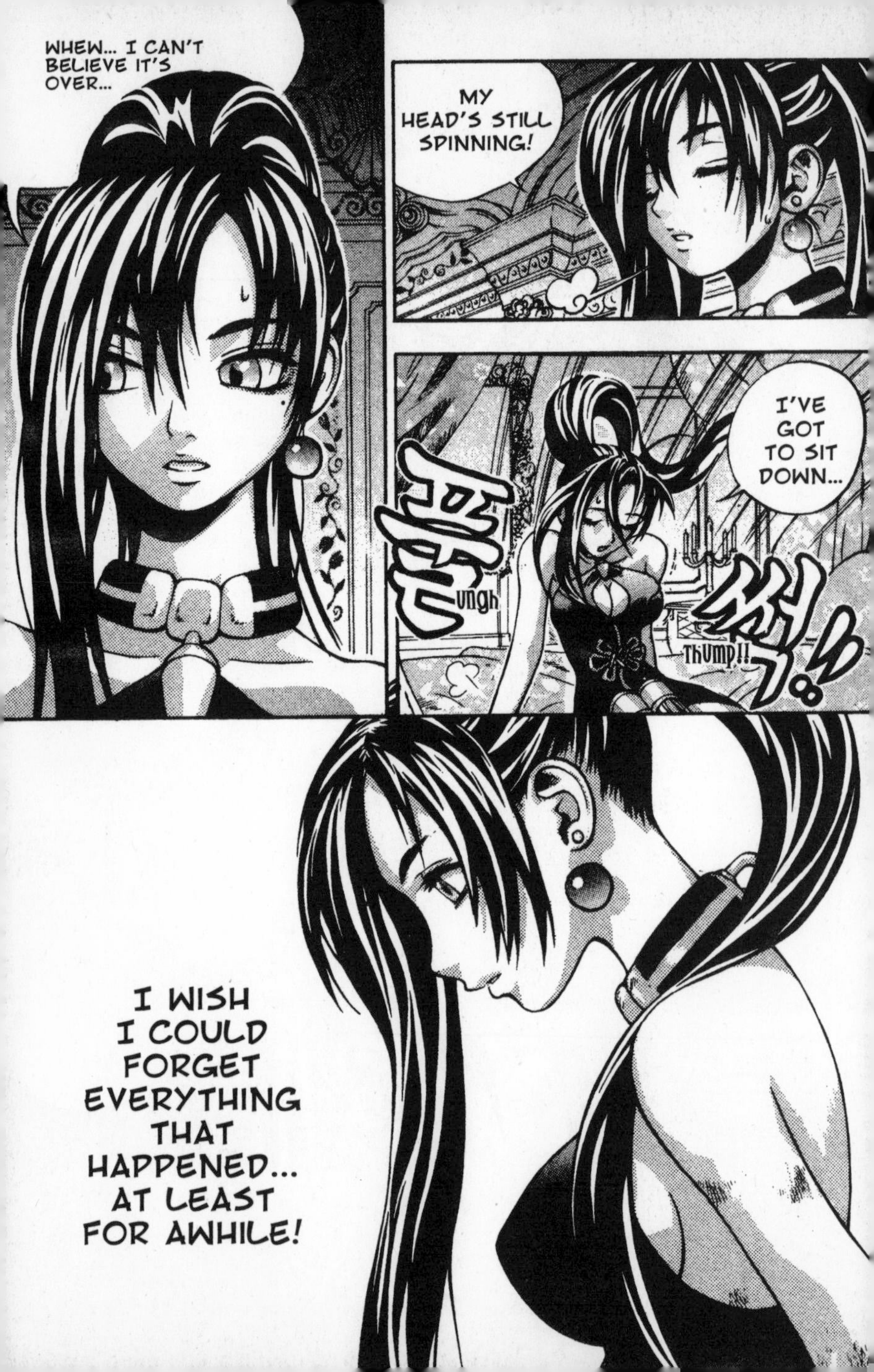
WHEW... I CAN'T BELIEVE IT'S OVER...
MY HEAD'S STILL SPINNING!
I'VE GOT TO SIT DOWN...
UNGH
THUMP!!
I WISH I COULD FORGET EVERYTHING THAT HAPPENED... AT LEAST FOR AWHILE!

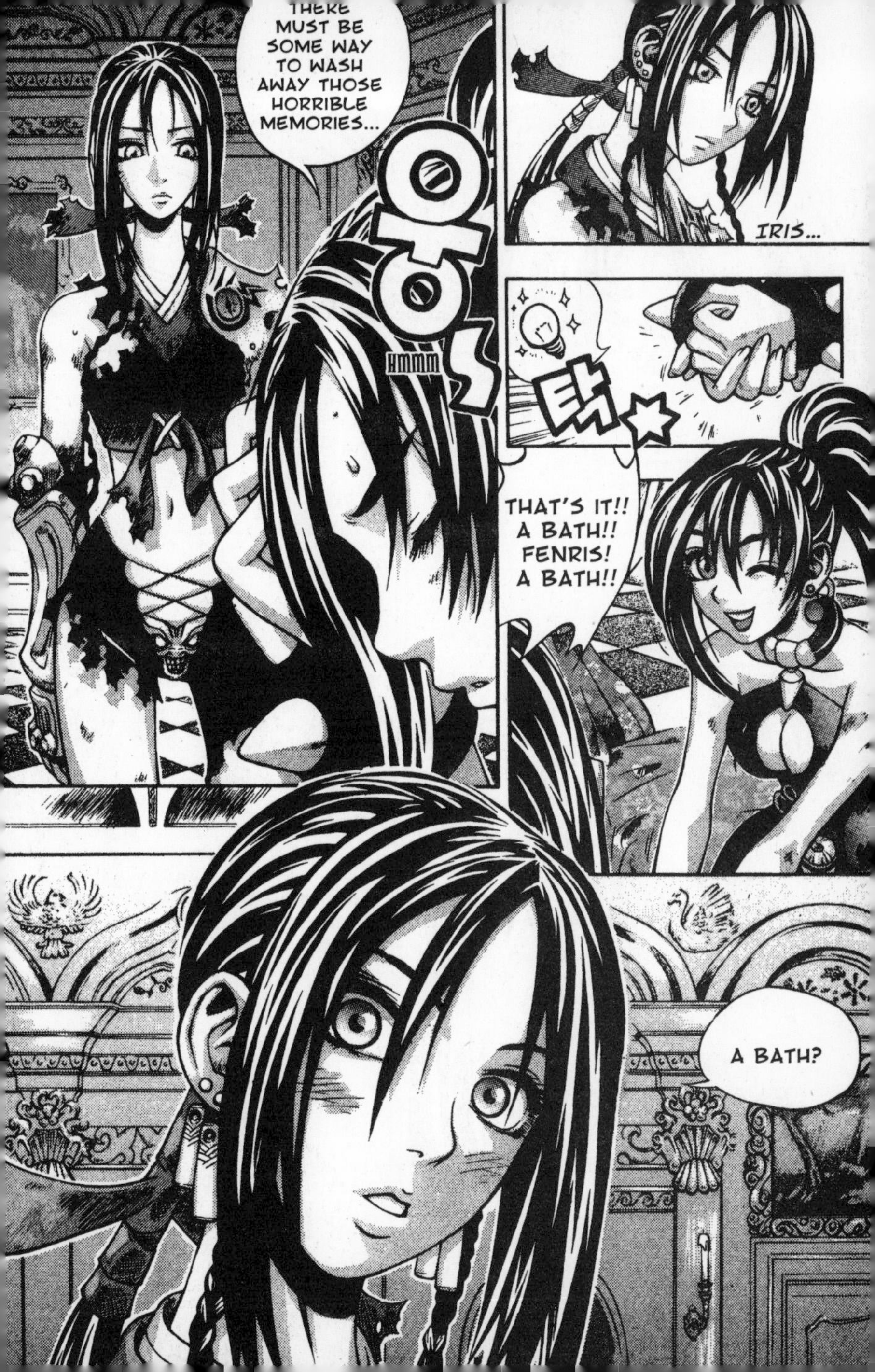
THERE MUST BE SOME WAY TO WASH AWAY THOSE HORRIBLE MEMORIES...
HMMM
IRIS...
THAT'S IT!! A BATH!! FENRIS! A BATH!!
A BATH?

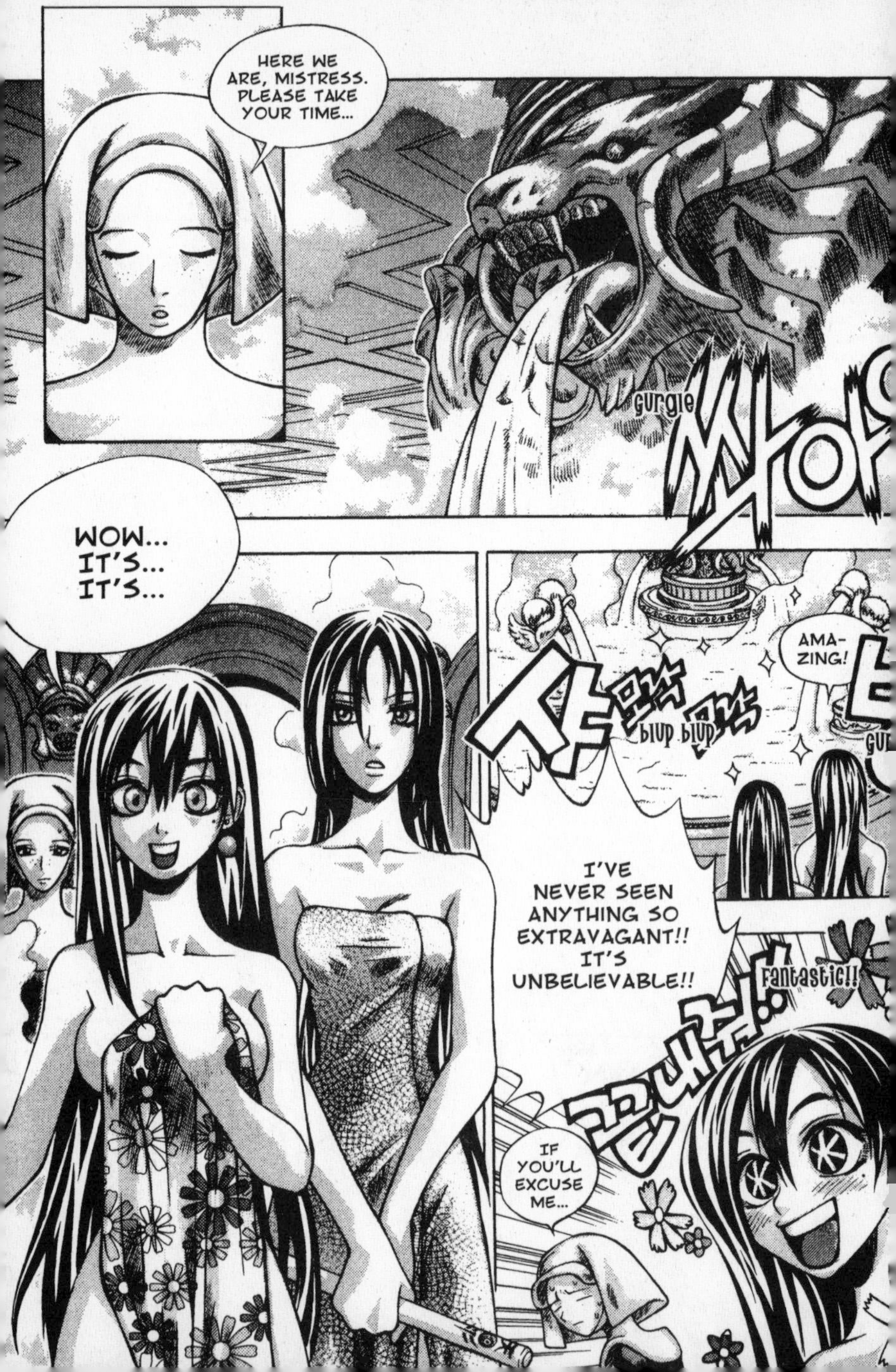
HERE WE ARE, MISTRESS. PLEASE TAKE YOUR TIME...
gurgle
WOW... IT'S... IT'S...
AMA-ZING!
blup blup
I'VE NEVER SEEN ANYTHING SO EXTRAVAGANT!! IT'S UNBELIEVABLE!!
Fantastic!!
IF YOU'LL EXCUSE ME...

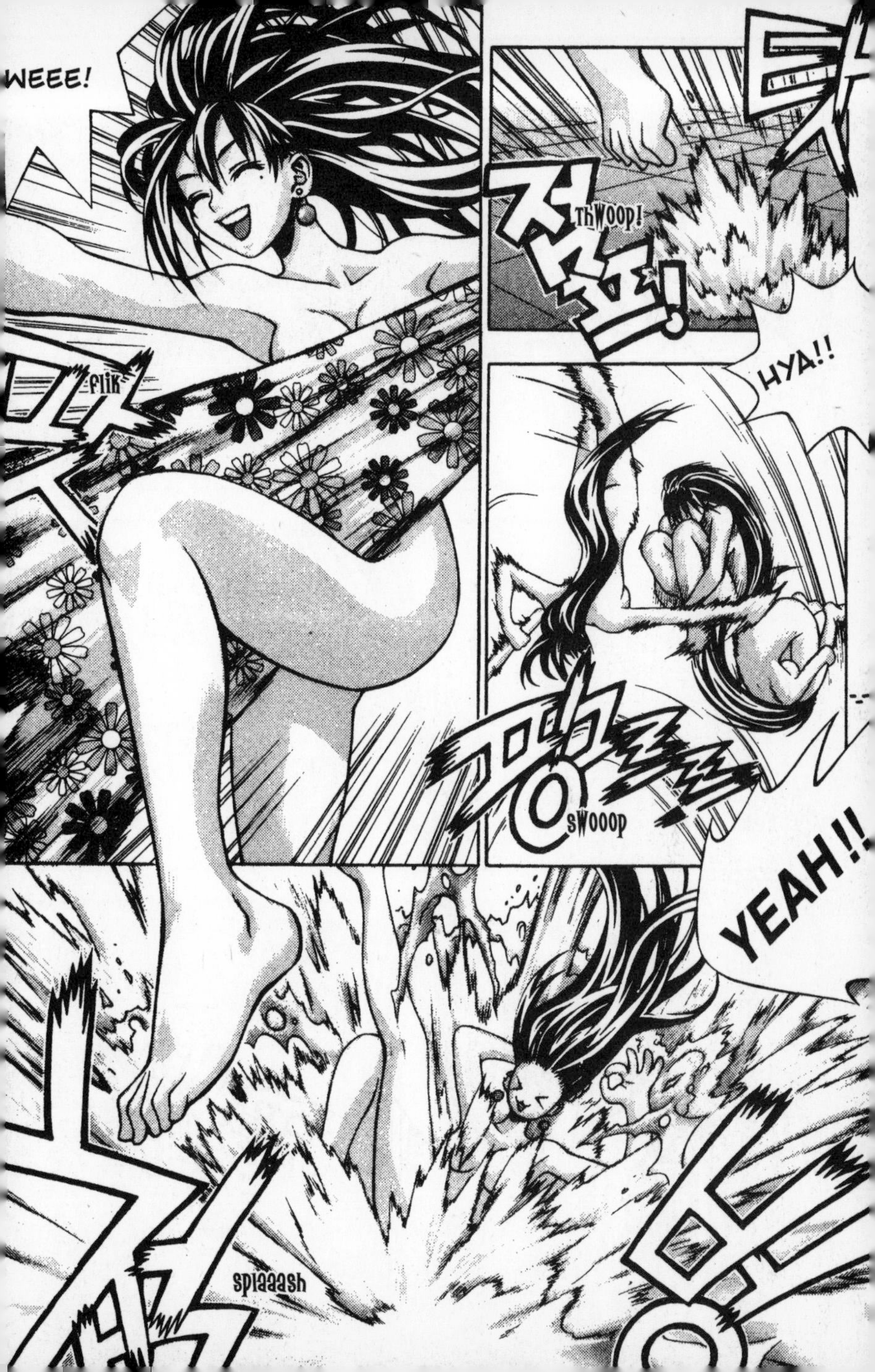
ThWOOP!
HYA!!
sWOOOP
WEEE!
flik
YEAH!!
splaaash

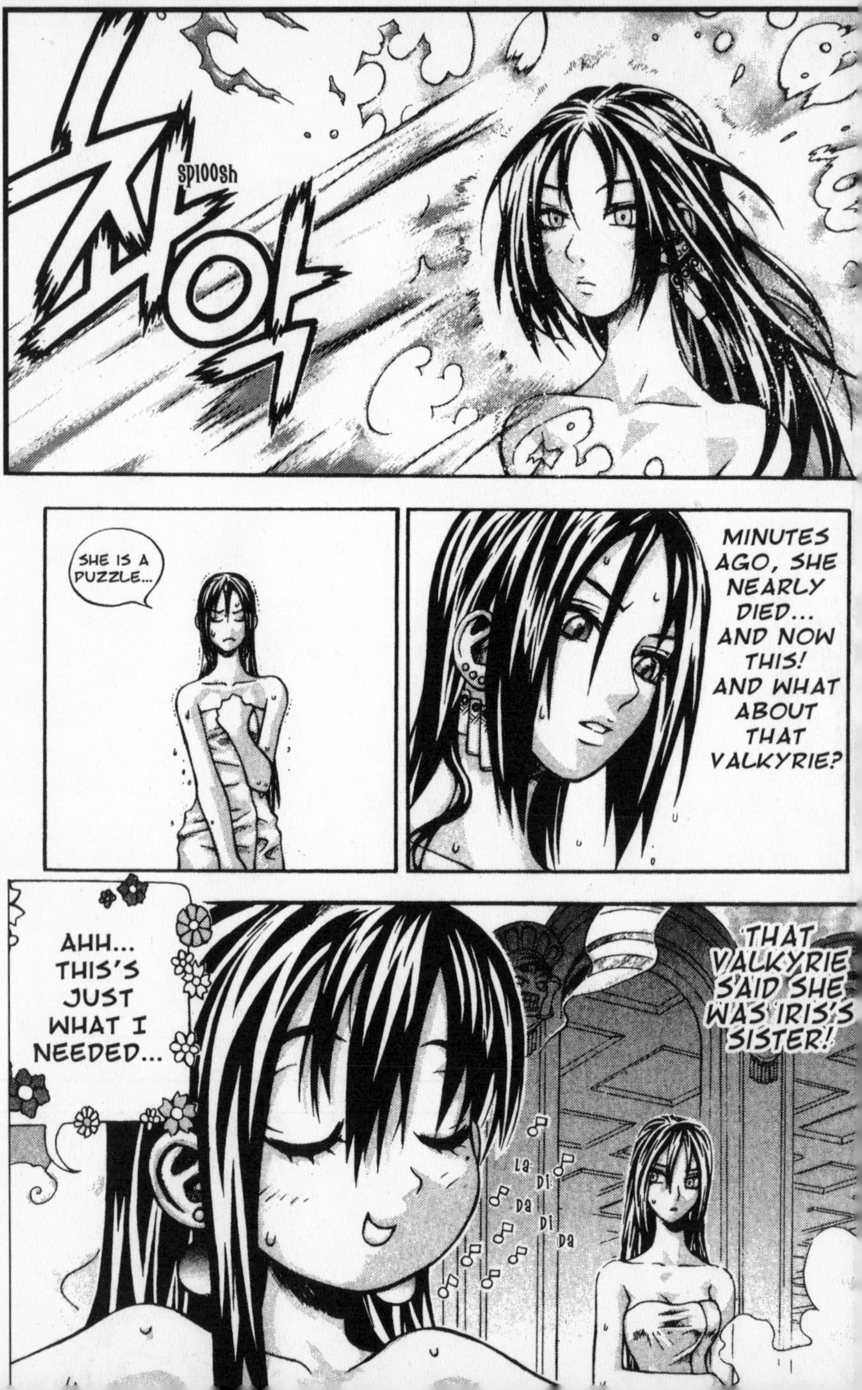
SPLOOSH
SHE IS A PUZZLE...
MINUTES AGO, SHE NEARLY DIED... AND NOW THIS! AND WHAT ABOUT THAT VALKYRIE?
AHH... THIS'S JUST WHAT I NEEDED...
THAT VALKYRIE SAID SHE WAS IRIS'S SISTER!
LA DI DA DI DA

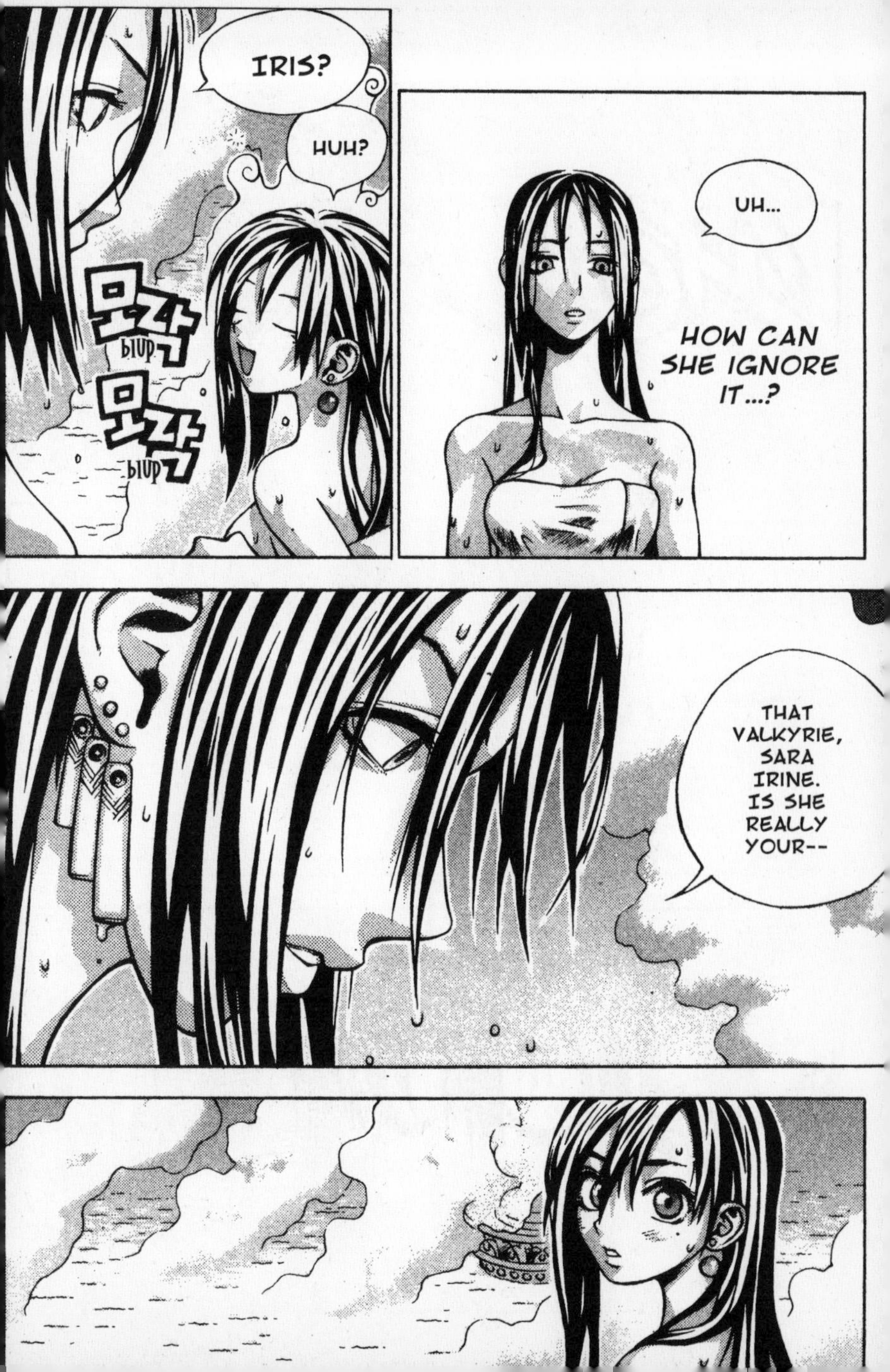

IRIS?
HUH?
blup
blup
UH...
HOW CAN SHE IGNORE IT...?
THAT VALKYRIE, SARA IRINE. IS SHE REALLY YOUR--

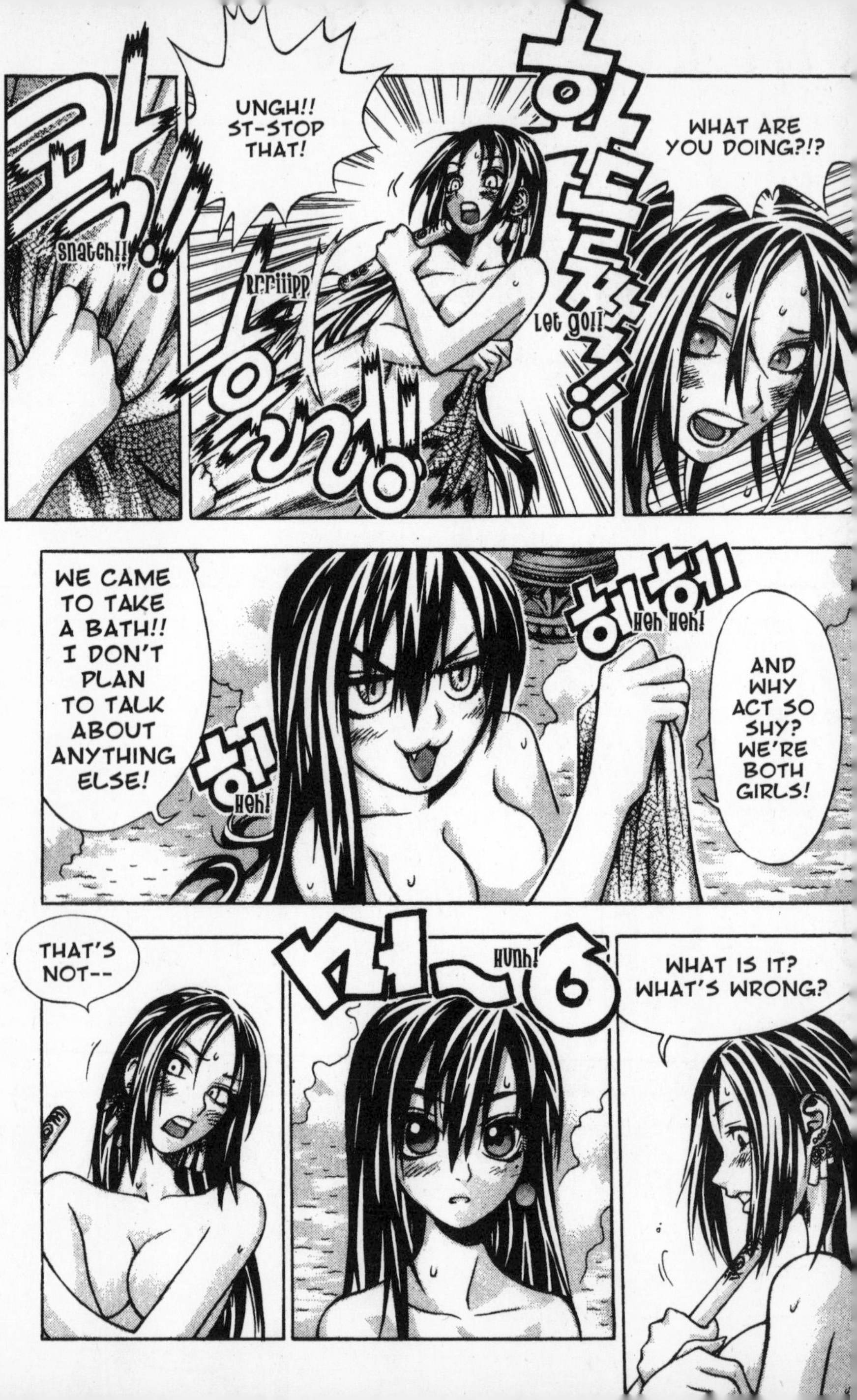
snatch!!
UNGH!! ST-STOP THAT!
RRRIIIPP
Let go!!
WHAT ARE YOU DOING?!?
WE CAME TO TAKE A BATH!! I DON'T PLAN TO TALK ABOUT ANYTHING ELSE!
Heh!
Heh heh!
AND WHY ACT SO SHY? WE'RE BOTH GIRLS!
THAT'S NOT--
HUNH!
WHAT IS IT? WHAT'S WRONG?

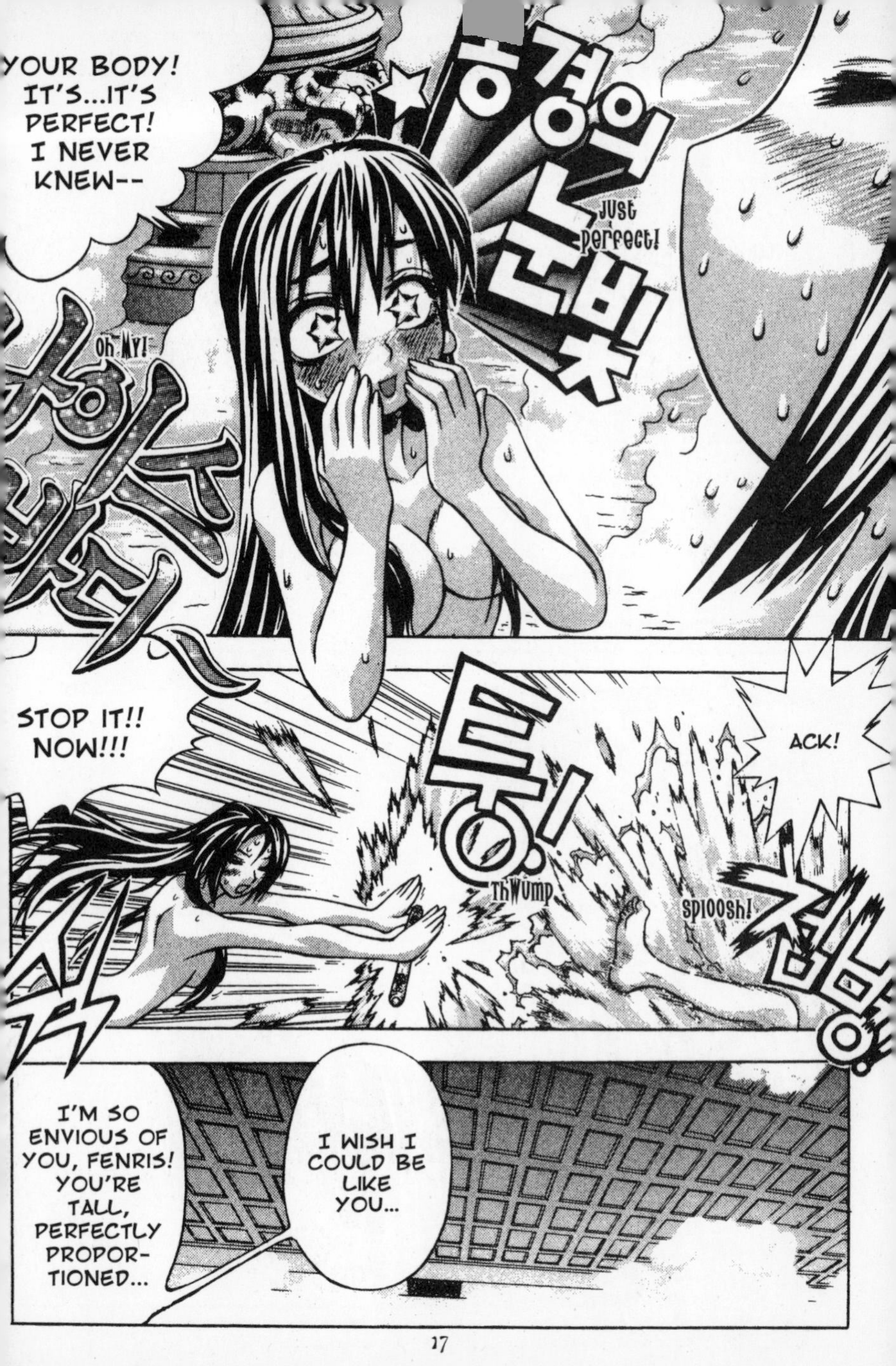
YOUR BODY! IT'S...IT'S PERFECT! I NEVER KNEW--
Oh My!
Just perfect!
STOP IT!! NOW!!!
ThWump
Splooosh!
ACK!
I'M SO ENVIOUS OF YOU, FENRIS! YOU'RE TALL, PERFECTLY PROPOR-TIONED...
I WISH I COULD BE LIKE YOU...

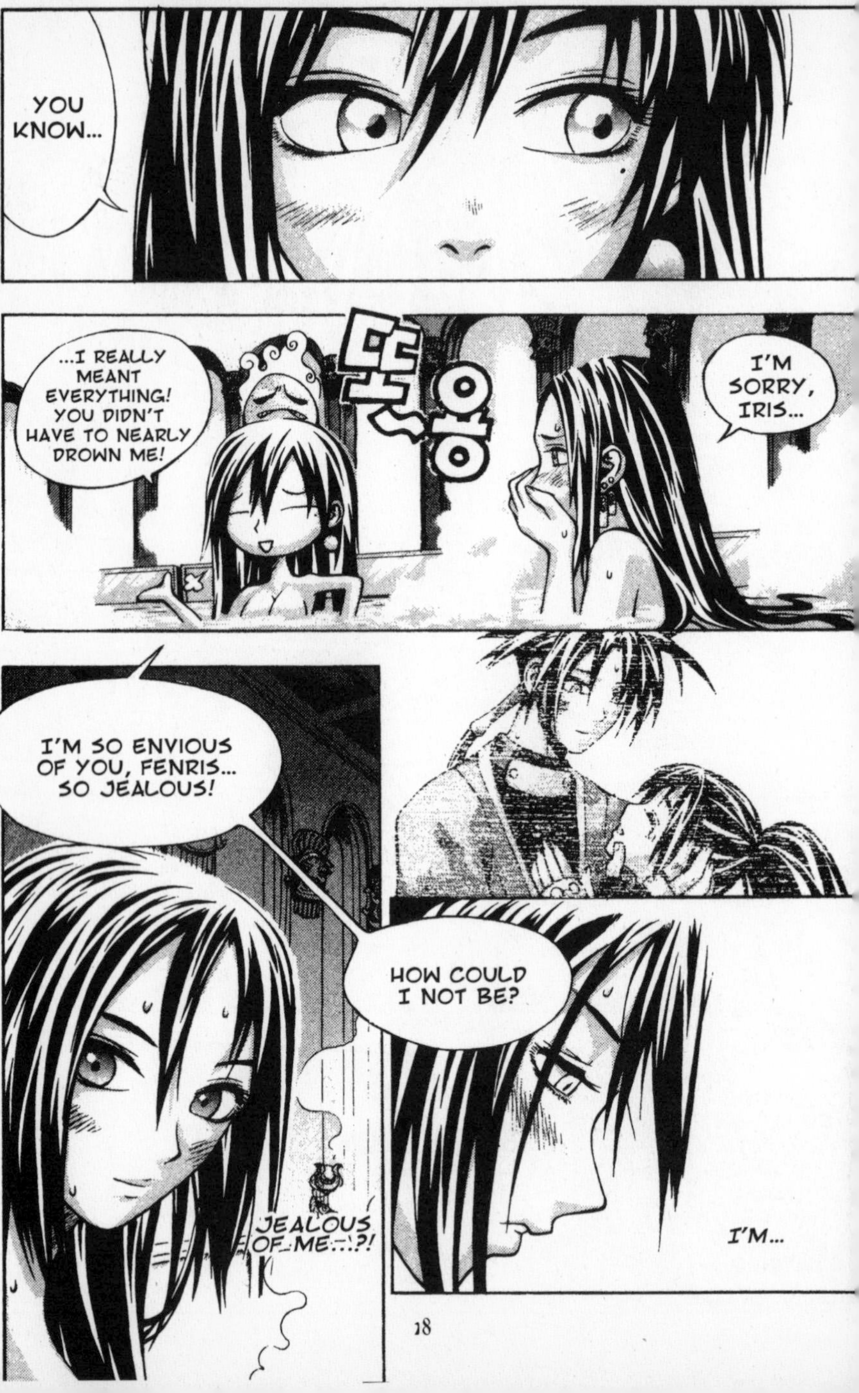
YOU KNOW...
...I REALLY MEANT EVERYTHING! YOU DIDN'T HAVE TO NEARLY DROWN ME!
또옹
I'M SORRY, IRIS...
I'M SO ENVIOUS OF YOU, FENRIS... SO JEALOUS!
HOW COULD I NOT BE?
JEALOUS OF ME...?!
I'M...

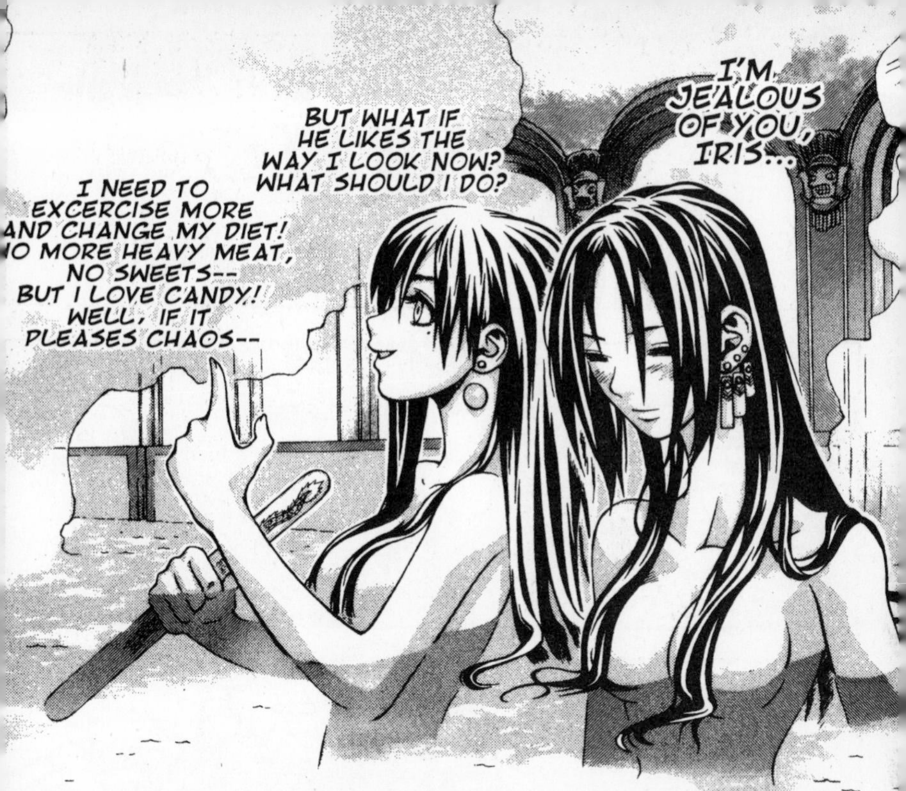
I'M JEALOUS OF YOU, IRIS...
BUT WHAT IF HE LIKES THE WAY I LOOK NOW? WHAT SHOULD I DO?
I NEED TO EXCERCISE MORE AND CHANGE MY DIET! IO MORE HEAVY MEAT, NO SWEETS-- BUT I LOVE CANDY! WELL, IF IT PLEASES CHAOS--

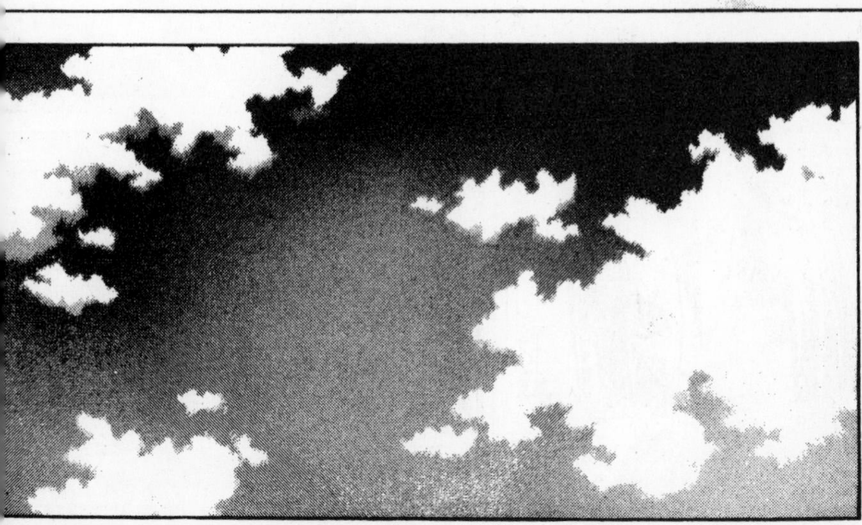

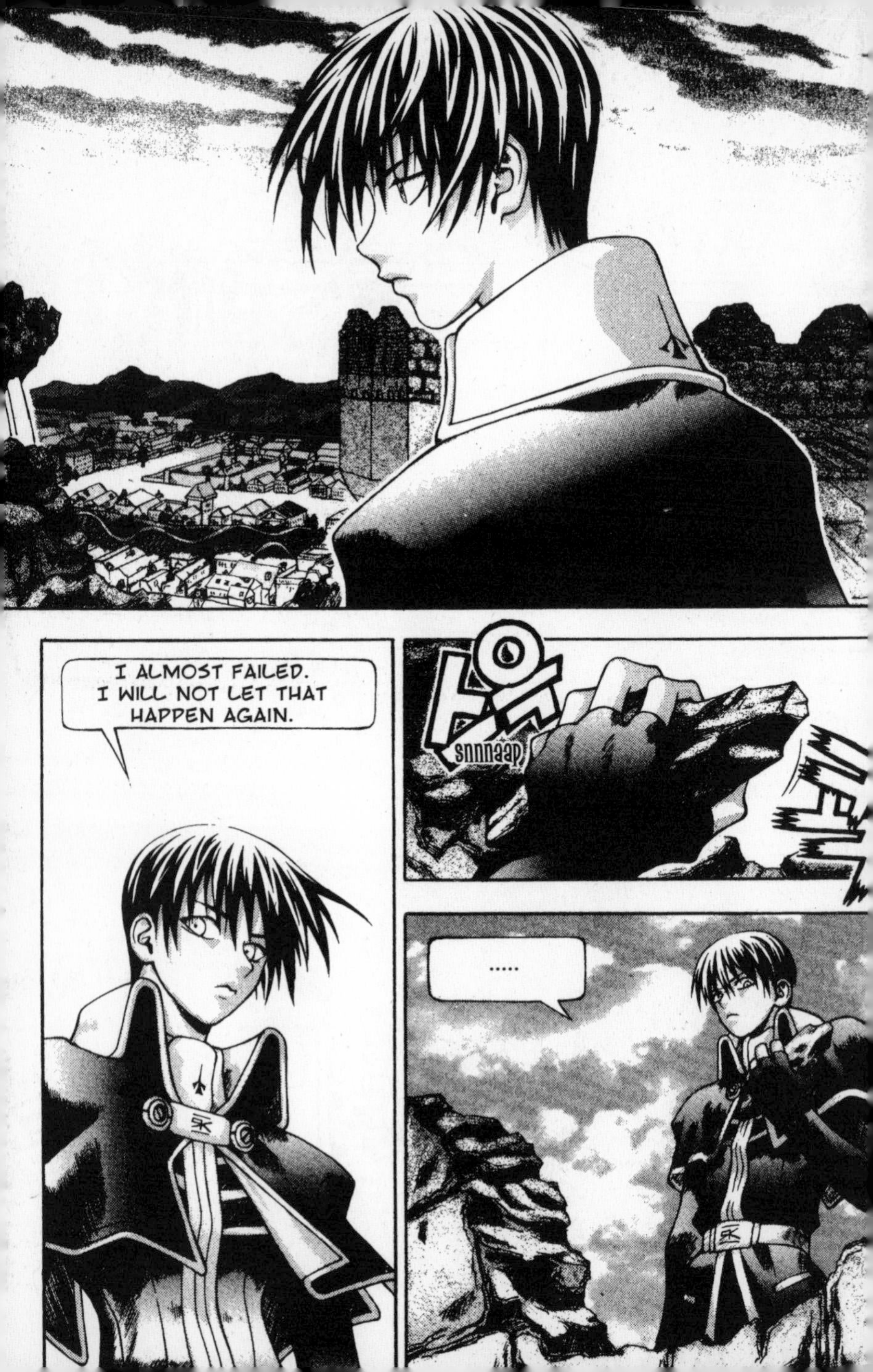
snnnaap
......
I ALMOST FAILED.
I WILL NOT LET THAT
HAPPEN AGAIN.

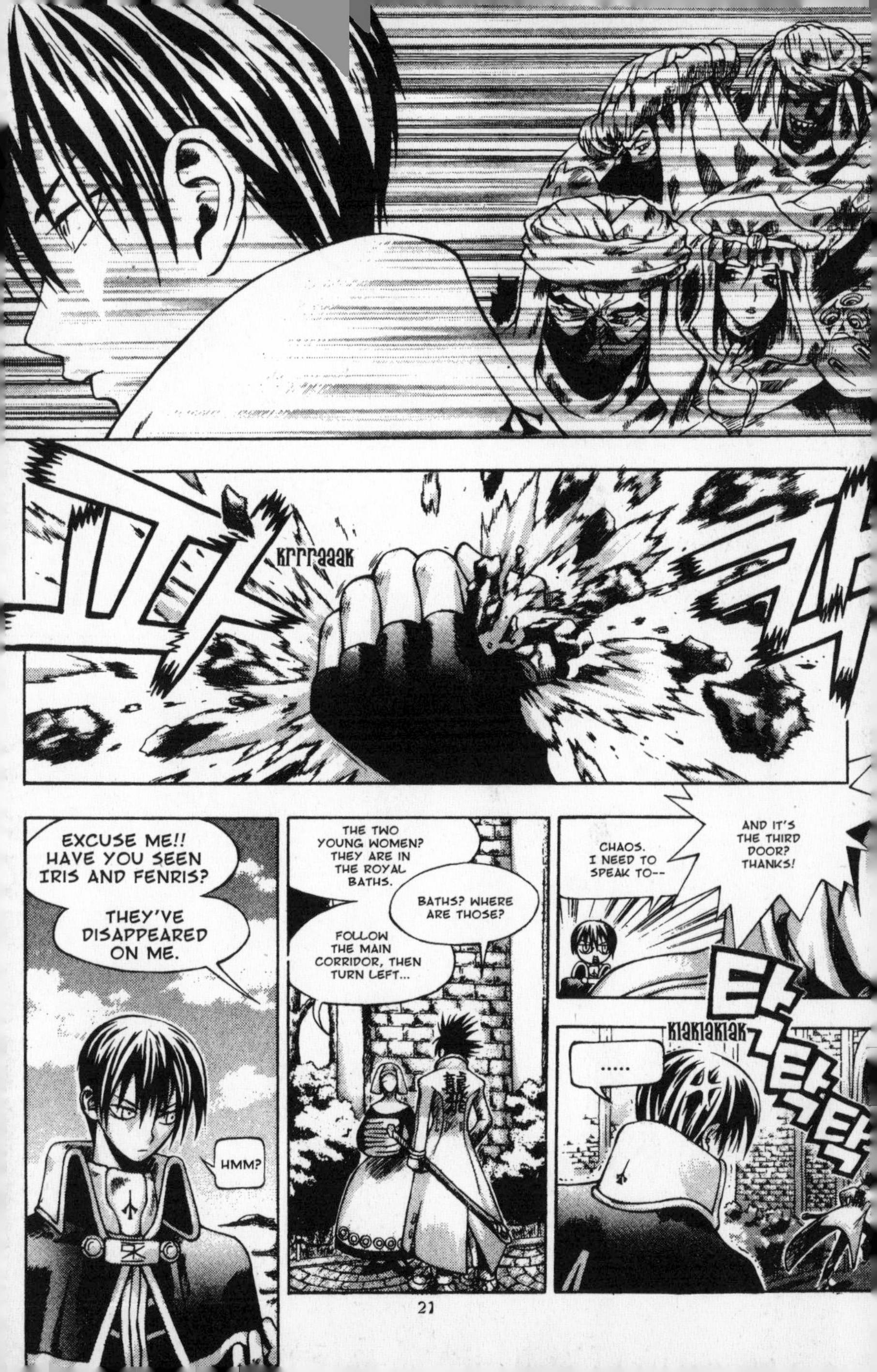
KRRRAAAK
EXCUSE ME!! HAVE YOU SEEN IRIS AND FENRIS?
THEY'VE DISAPPEARED ON ME.
HMM?
THE TWO YOUNG WOMEN? THEY ARE IN THE ROYAL BATHS.
BATHS? WHERE ARE THOSE?
FOLLOW THE MAIN CORRIDOR, THEN TURN LEFT...
CHAOS. I NEED TO SPEAK TO--
AND IT'S THE THIRD DOOR? THANKS!
KLAKLAKLAK
......

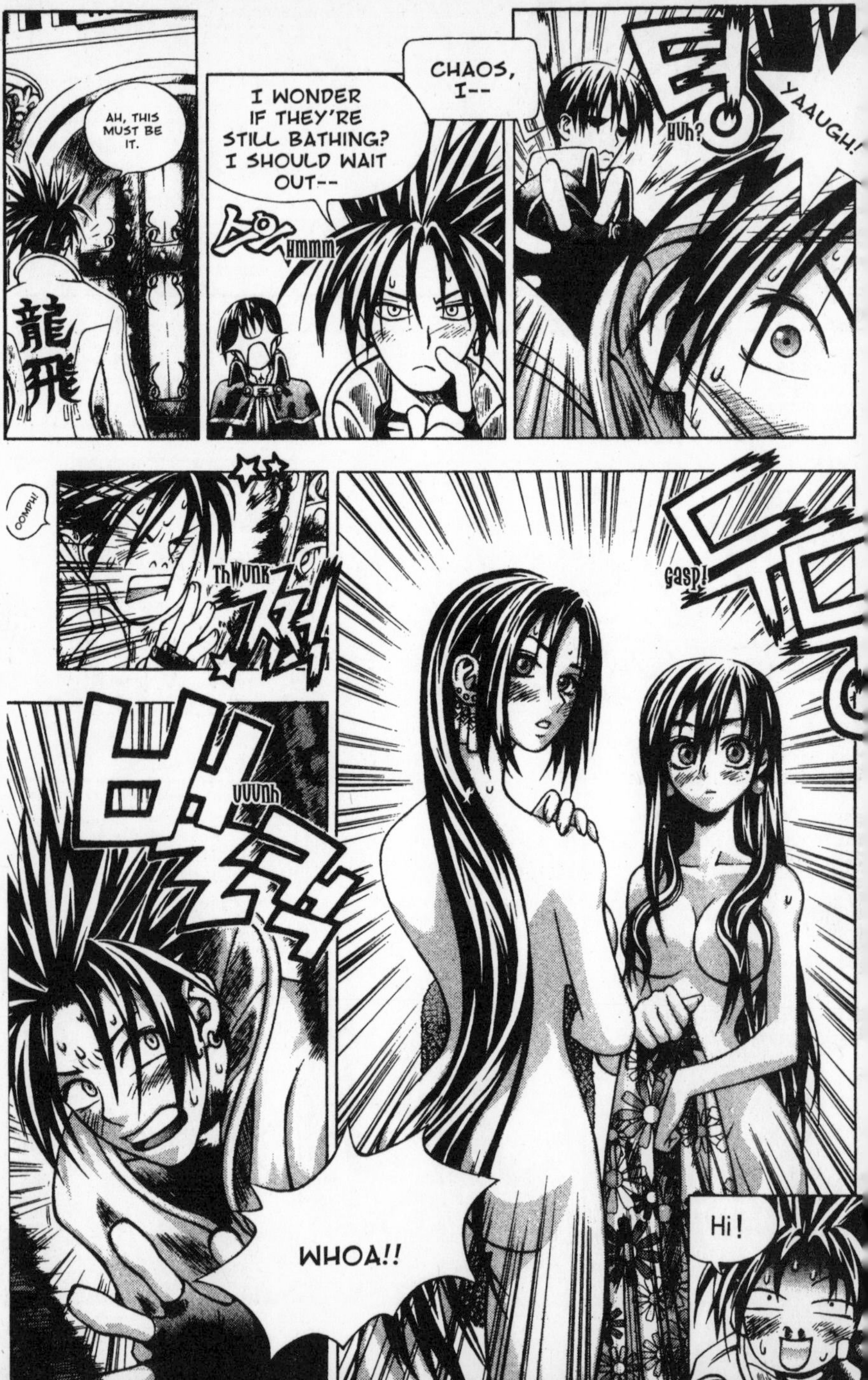
AH, THIS MUST BE IT.
I WONDER IF THEY'RE STILL BATHING? I SHOULD WAIT OUT--
HMMM
CHAOS, I--
HUH?
YAAUGH!
OOMPH!
THWUNK
GASP!
VVVNH
WHOA!!
Hi!

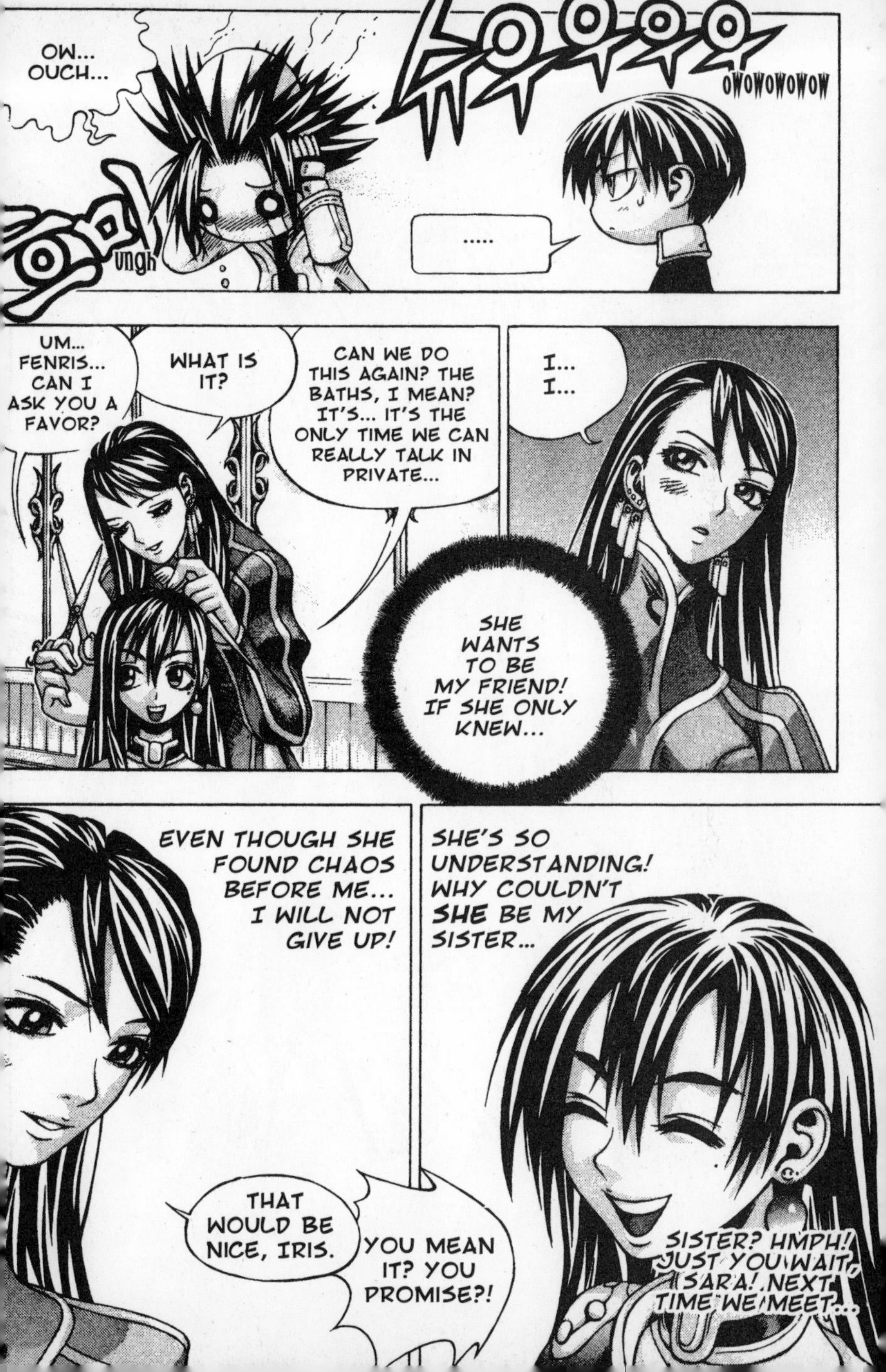
OW... OUCH...
UNGH
OWOWOWOWOW
.....
UM... FENRIS... CAN I ASK YOU A FAVOR?
WHAT IS IT?
CAN WE DO THIS AGAIN? THE BATHS, I MEAN? IT'S... IT'S THE ONLY TIME WE CAN REALLY TALK IN PRIVATE...
I... I...
SHE WANTS TO BE MY FRIEND! IF SHE ONLY KNEW...
EVEN THOUGH SHE FOUND CHAOS BEFORE ME... I WILL NOT GIVE UP!
THAT WOULD BE NICE, IRIS.
SHE'S SO UNDERSTANDING! WHY COULDN'T SHE BE MY SISTER...
YOU MEAN IT? YOU PROMISE?!
SISTER? HMPH! JUST YOU WAIT, SARA! NEXT TIME WE MEET...

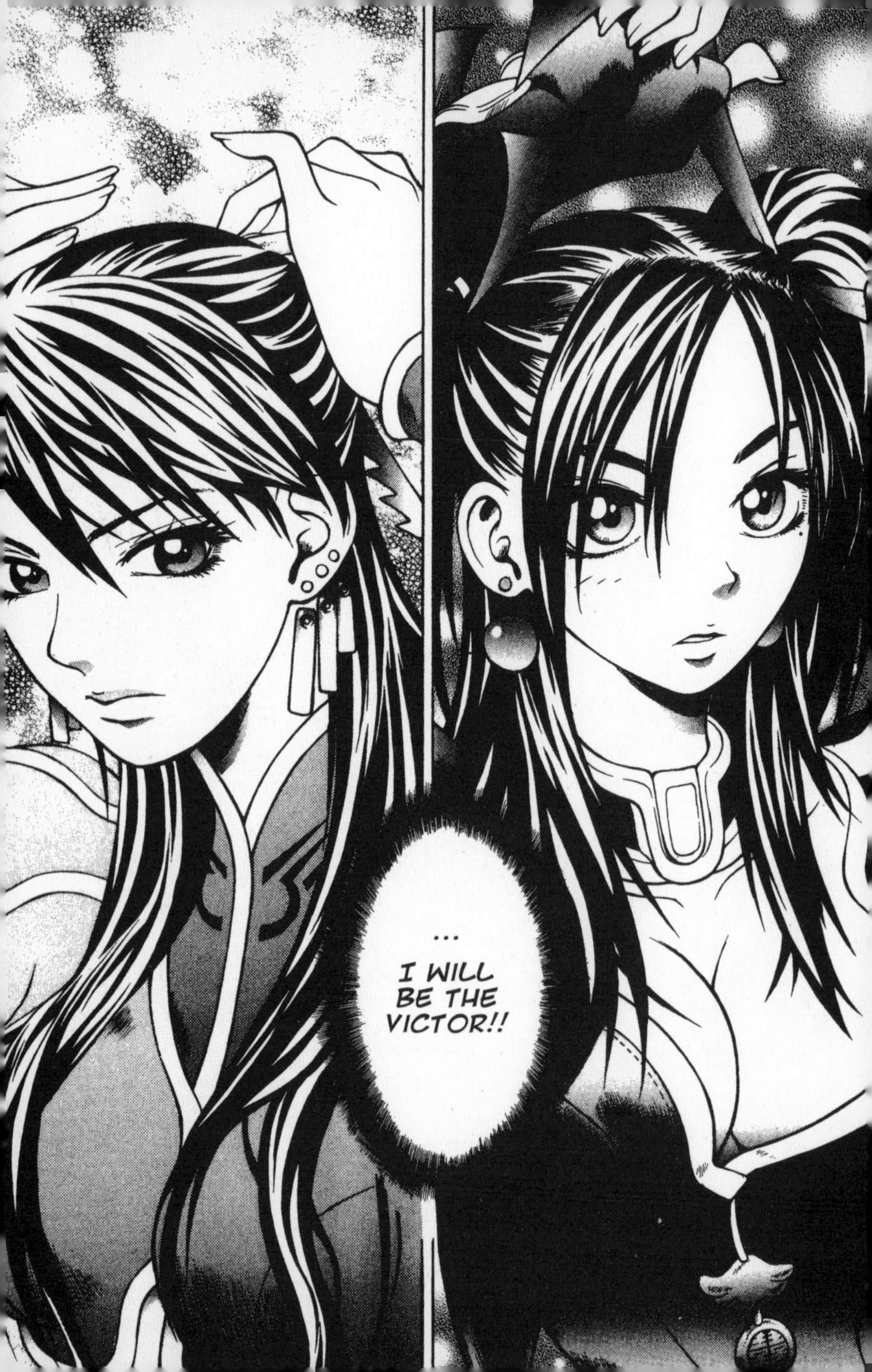
... I WILL BE THE VICTOR!!

RAGNAROK
라그나로크
IN TO THE ABYSS

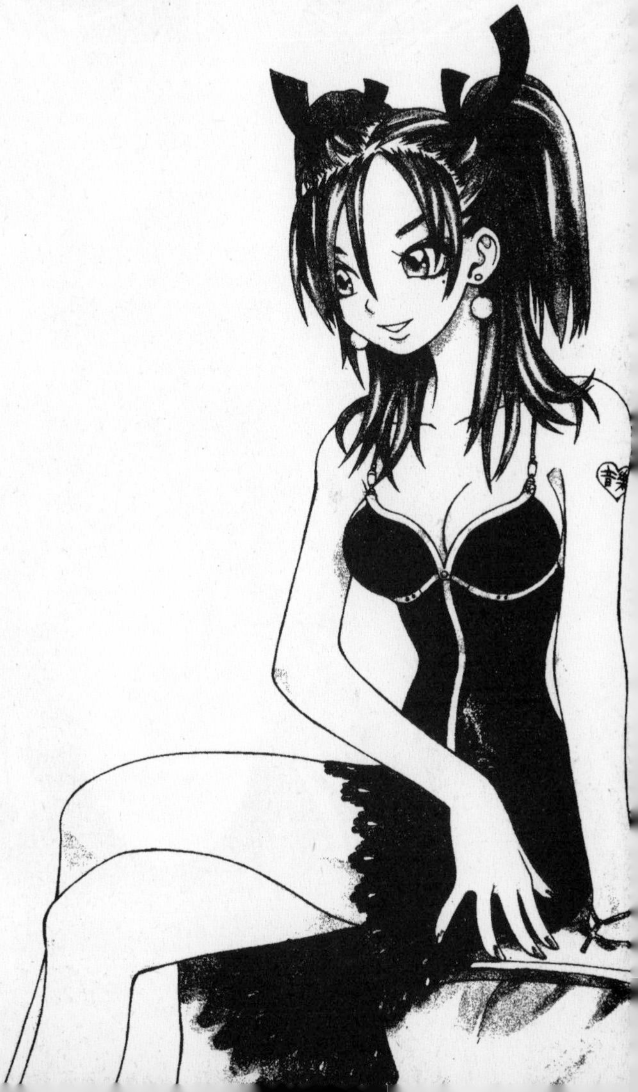

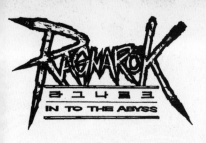

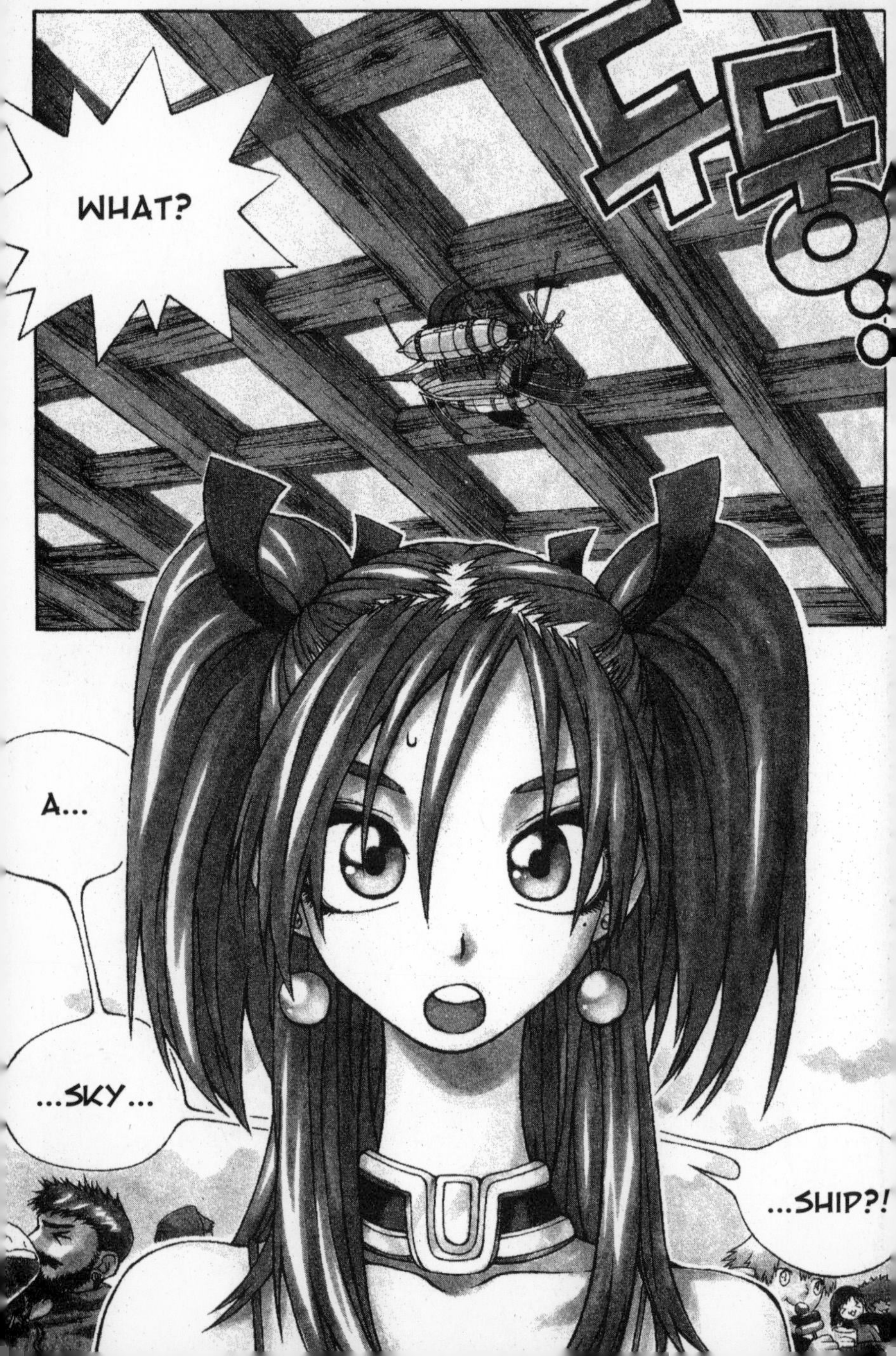
WHAT?
A...
...SKY...
...SHIP?!

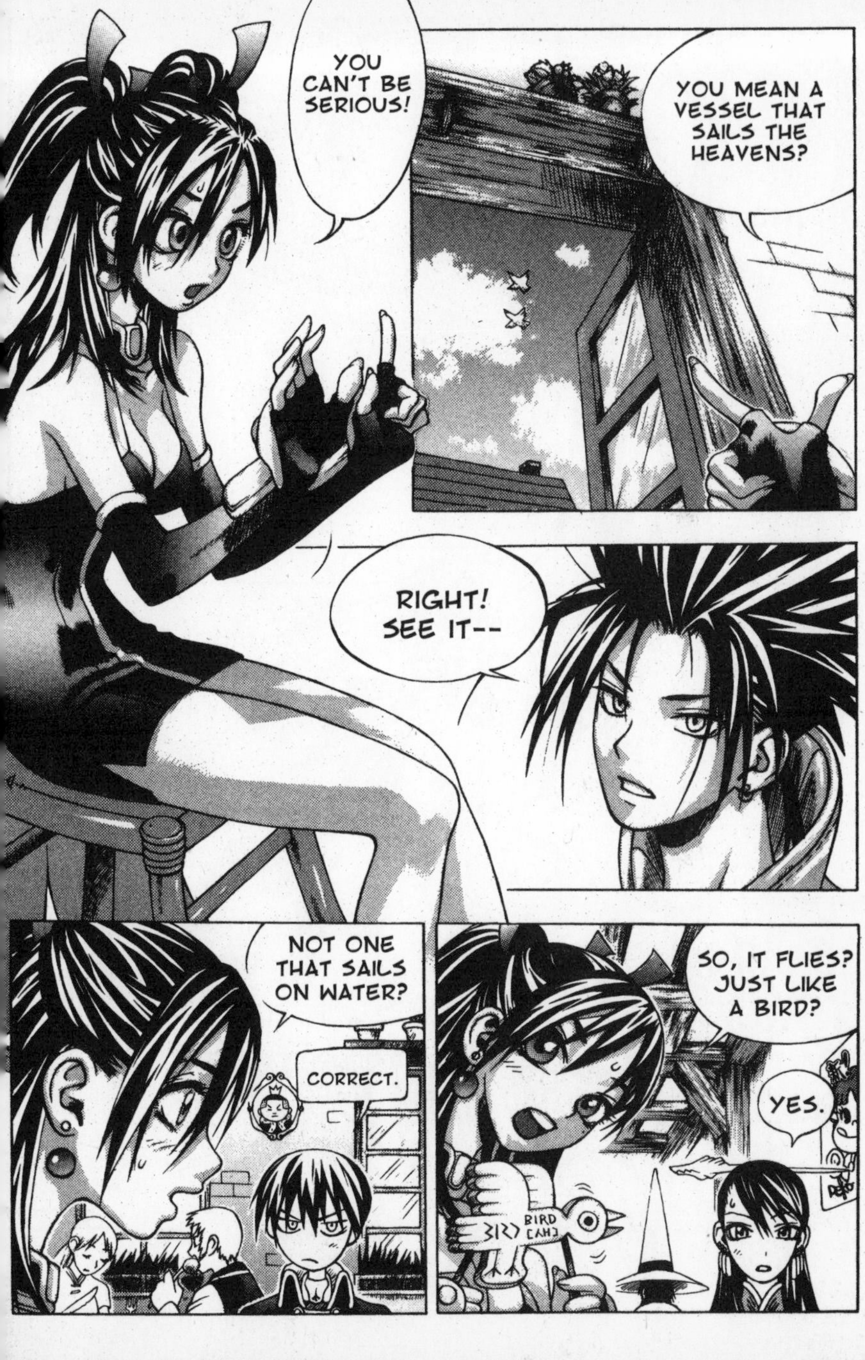
YOU CAN'T BE SERIOUS!
YOU MEAN A VESSEL THAT SAILS THE HEAVENS?
RIGHT! SEE IT--
NOT ONE THAT SAILS ON WATER?
CORRECT.
SO, IT FLIES? JUST LIKE A BIRD?
YES.
BIRD [AH]

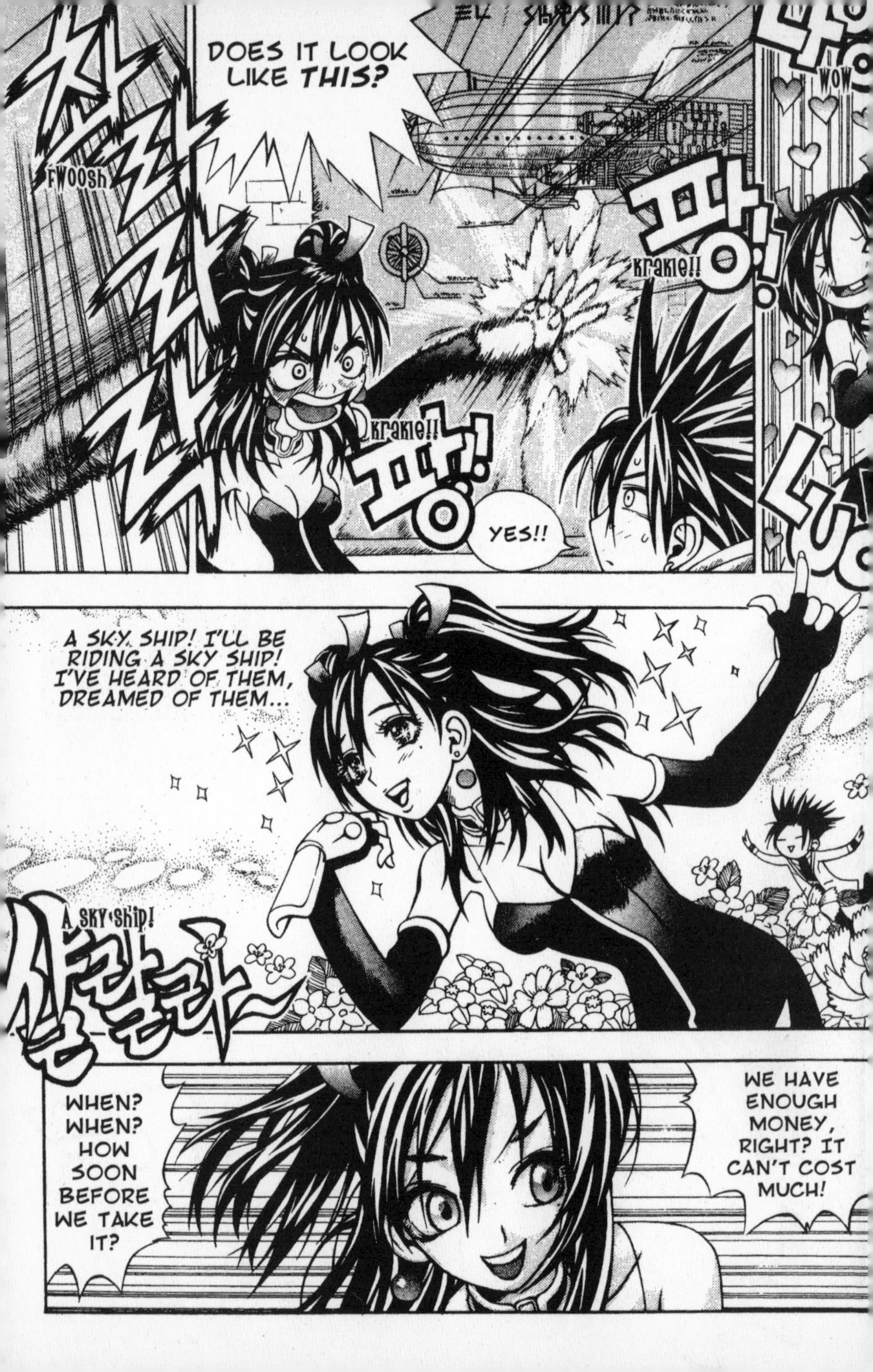
FWOOSH
DOES IT LOOK LIKE THIS?
KRAKLE!!
KRAKLE!!
YES!!
WOW
A SKY SHIP! I'LL BE RIDING A SKY SHIP! I'VE HEARD OF THEM, DREAMED OF THEM...
A SKY SHIP!
WHEN? WHEN? HOW SOON BEFORE WE TAKE IT?
WE HAVE ENOUGH MONEY, RIGHT? IT CAN'T COST MUCH!

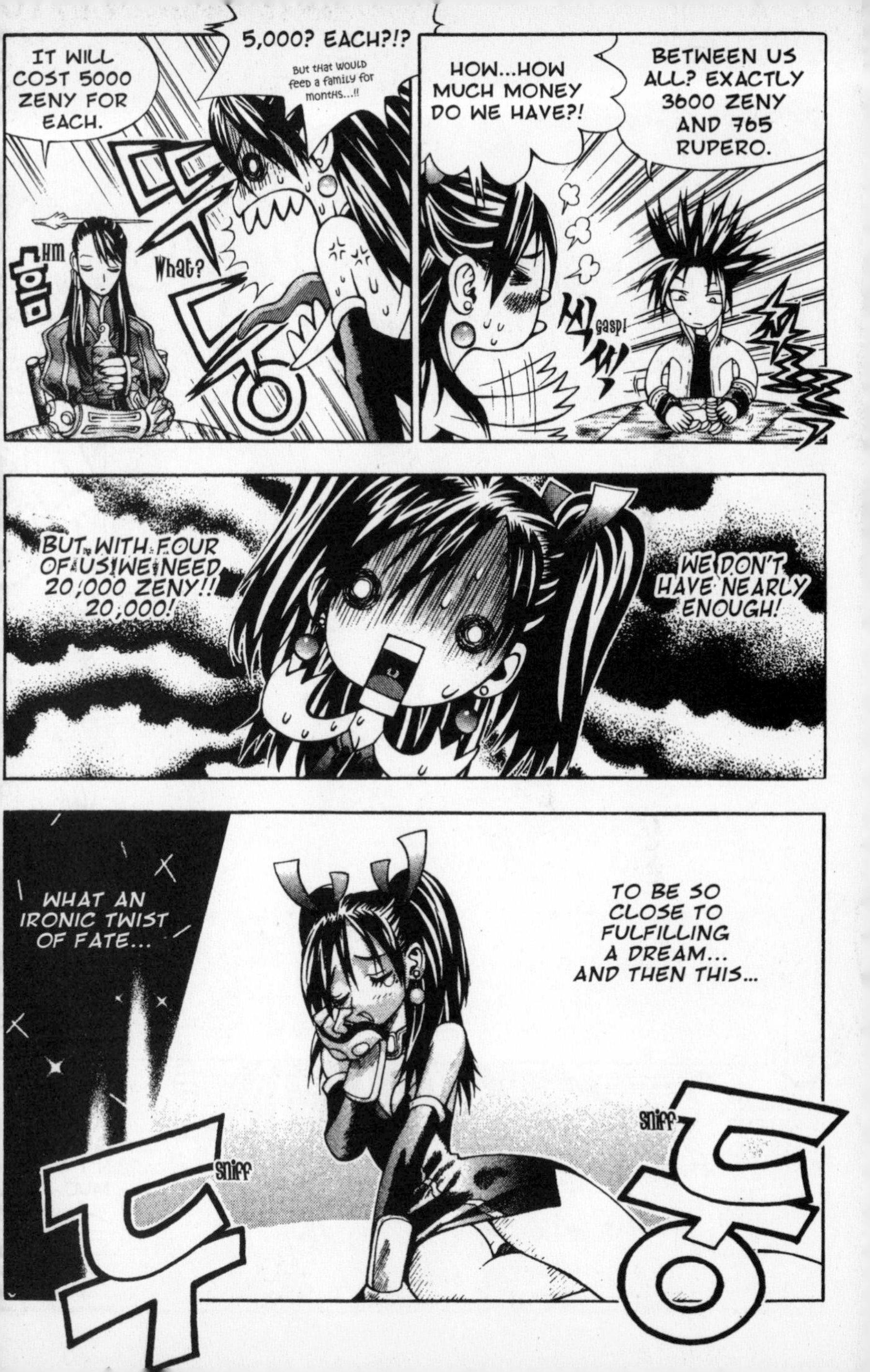
IT WILL COST 5000 ZENY FOR EACH.
HM
5,000? EACH?!?
But that would feed a family for months...!!
What?
HOW...HOW MUCH MONEY DO WE HAVE?!
BETWEEN US ALL? EXACTLY 3600 ZENY AND 765 RUPERO.
GASP!
BUT WITH FOUR OF US WE NEED 20,000 ZENY!! 20,000!
WE DON'T HAVE NEARLY ENOUGH!
WHAT AN IRONIC TWIST OF FATE...
TO BE SO CLOSE TO FULFILLING A DREAM... AND THEN THIS...
sniff
sniff

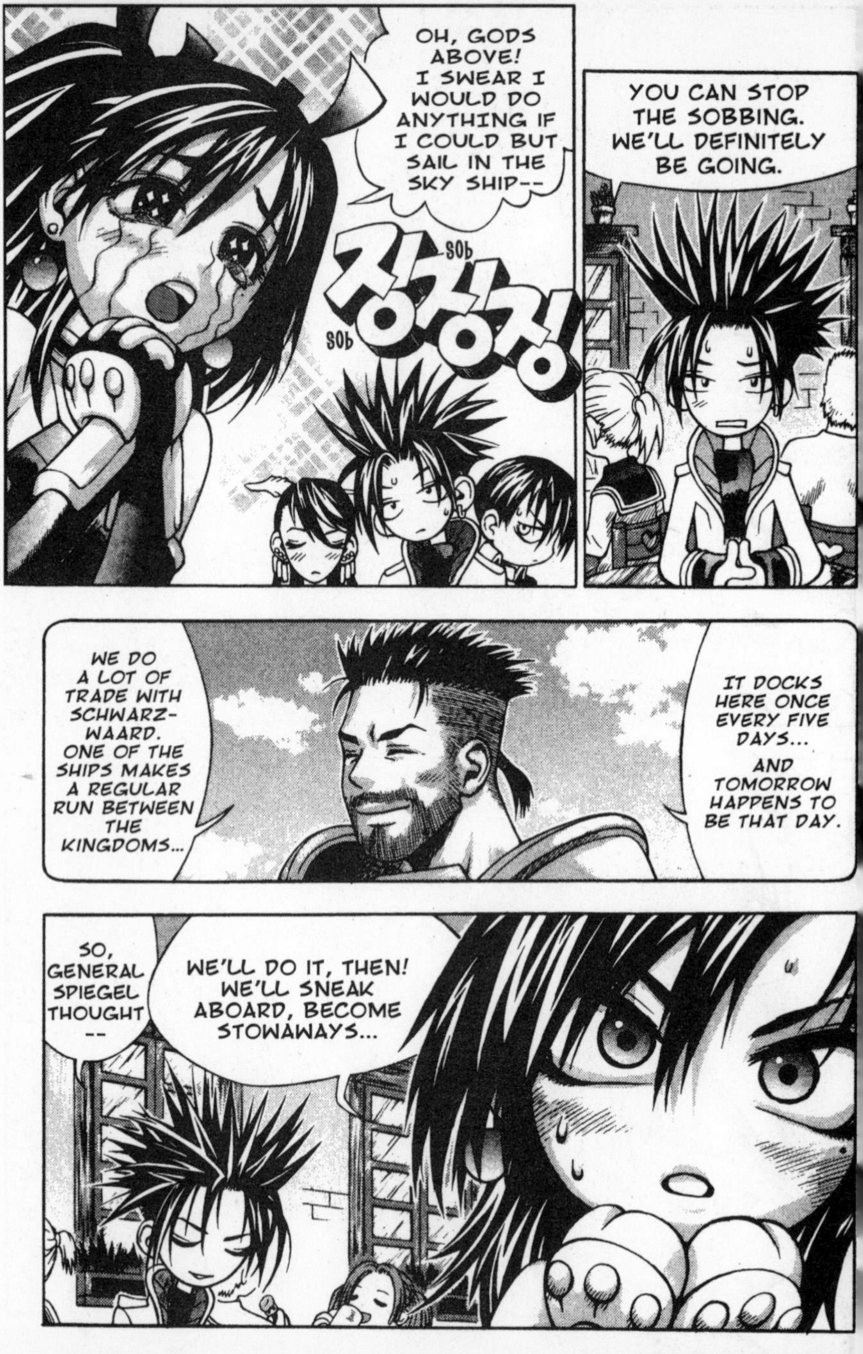
OH, GODS ABOVE! I SWEAR I WOULD DO ANYTHING IF I COULD BUT SAIL IN THE SKY SHIP--
SOb
SOb
YOU CAN STOP THE SOBBING. WE'LL DEFINITELY BE GOING.
WE DO A LOT OF TRADE WITH SCHWARZ-WAARD. ONE OF THE SHIPS MAKES A REGULAR RUN BETWEEN THE KINGDOMS...
IT DOCKS HERE ONCE EVERY FIVE DAYS...
AND TOMORROW HAPPENS TO BE THAT DAY.
SO, GENERAL SPIEGEL THOUGHT --
WE'LL DO IT, THEN! WE'LL SNEAK ABOARD, BECOME STOWAWAYS...

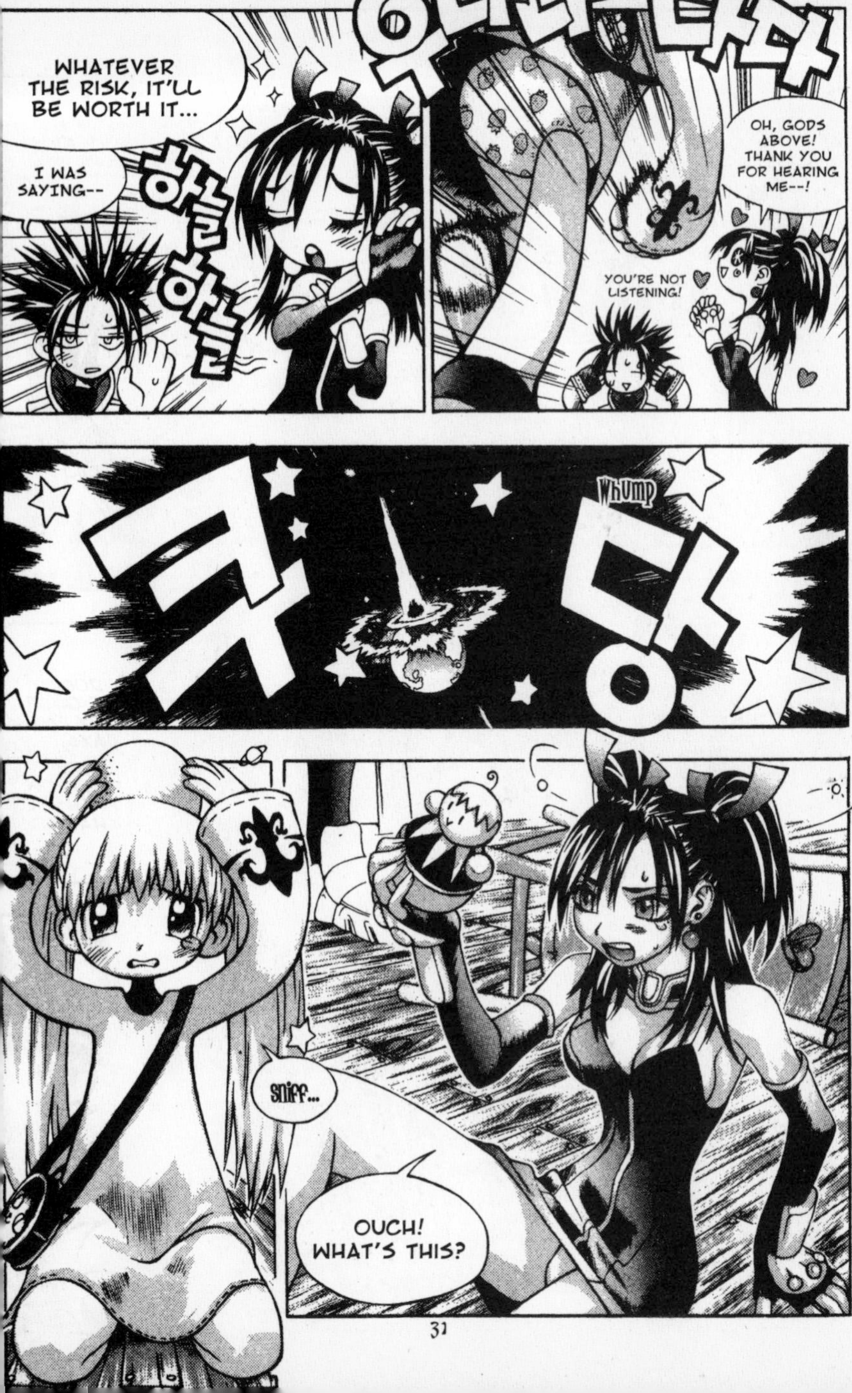
WHATEVER THE RISK, IT'LL BE WORTH IT...
I WAS SAYING--
하늘하늘
OH, GODS ABOVE! THANK YOU FOR HEARING ME--!
YOU'RE NOT LISTENING!
WHUMP
SNIFF...
OUCH! WHAT'S THIS?

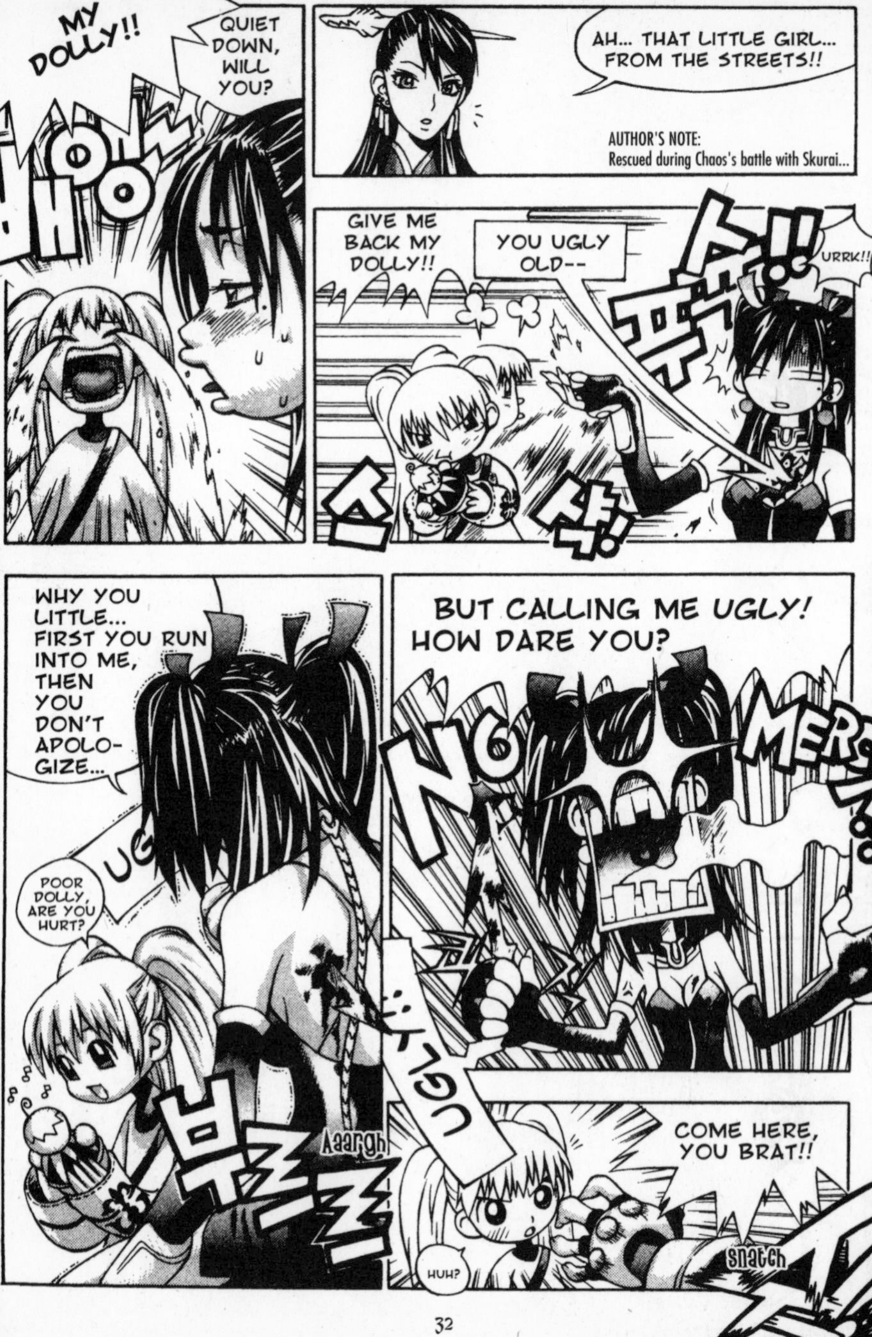
MY DOLLY!!
QUIET DOWN, WILL YOU?
AH... THAT LITTLE GIRL... FROM THE STREETS!!
AUTHOR'S NOTE:
Rescued during Chaos's battle with Skurai...
GIVE ME BACK MY DOLLY!!
YOU UGLY OLD--
URRK!!
WHY YOU LITTLE... FIRST YOU RUN INTO ME, THEN YOU DON'T APOLO-GIZE...
POOR DOLLY, ARE YOU HURT?
Aaargh
BUT CALLING ME UGLY! HOW DARE YOU?
COME HERE, YOU BRAT!!
HUH?
snatch

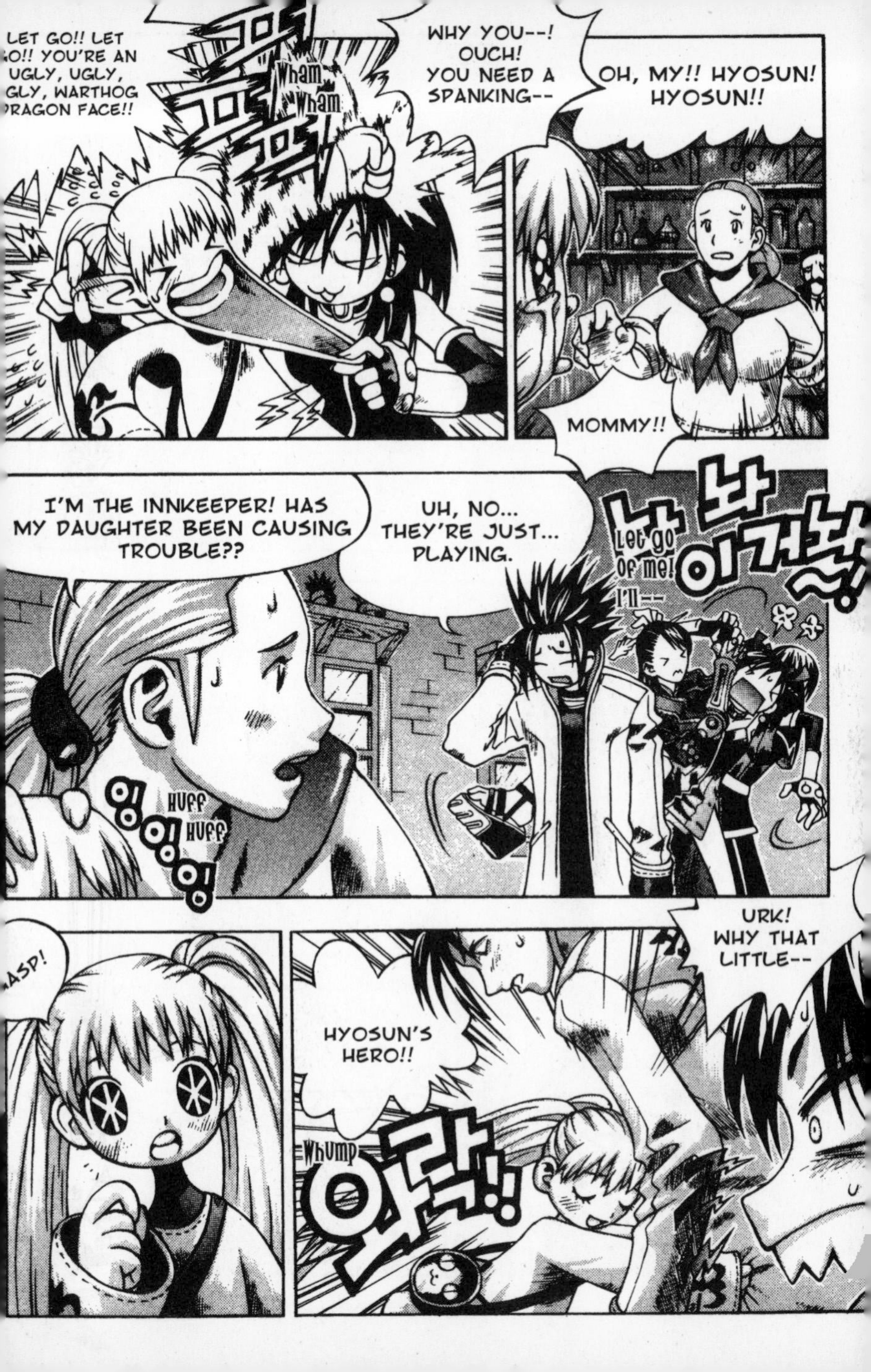
LET GO!! LET O!! YOU'RE AN UGLY, UGLY, GLY, WARTHOG RAGON FACE!!
Wham Wham
WHY YOU--! OUCH! YOU NEED A SPANKING--
OH, MY!! HYOSUN! HYOSUN!!
MOMMY!!
I'M THE INNKEEPER! HAS MY DAUGHTER BEEN CAUSING TROUBLE??
HUFF HUFF
UH, NO... THEY'RE JUST... PLAYING.
Let go of me! I'll--
ASP!
HYOSUN'S HERO!!
Whump
URK! WHY THAT LITTLE--

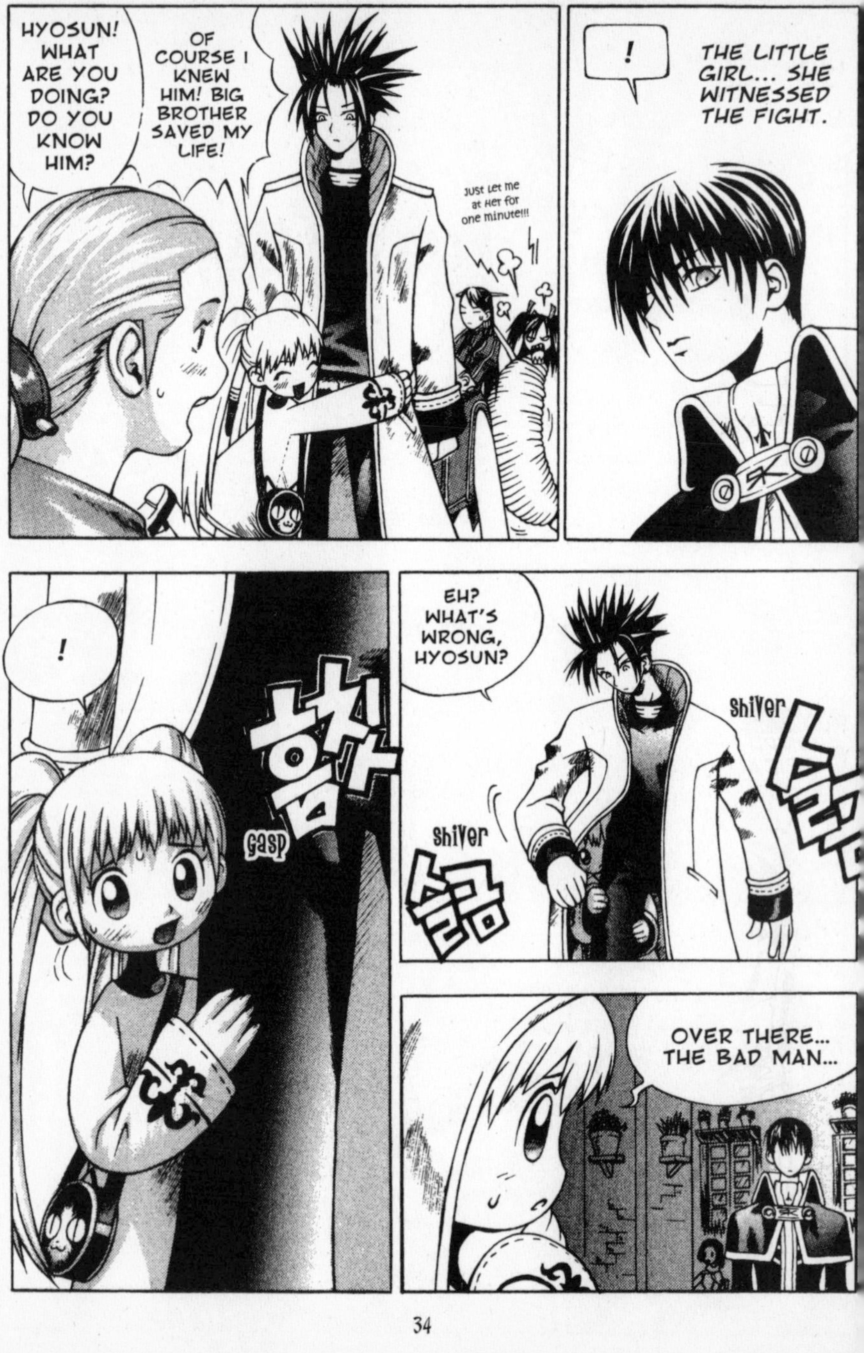
HYOSUN! WHAT ARE YOU DOING? DO YOU KNOW HIM?
OF COURSE I KNEW HIM! BIG BROTHER SAVED MY LIFE!
Just let me at her for one minute!!!
!
THE LITTLE GIRL... SHE WITNESSED THE FIGHT.
!
흠칫
gasp
EH? WHAT'S WRONG, HYOSUN?
shiver
슬금
shiver
OVER THERE... THE BAD MAN...

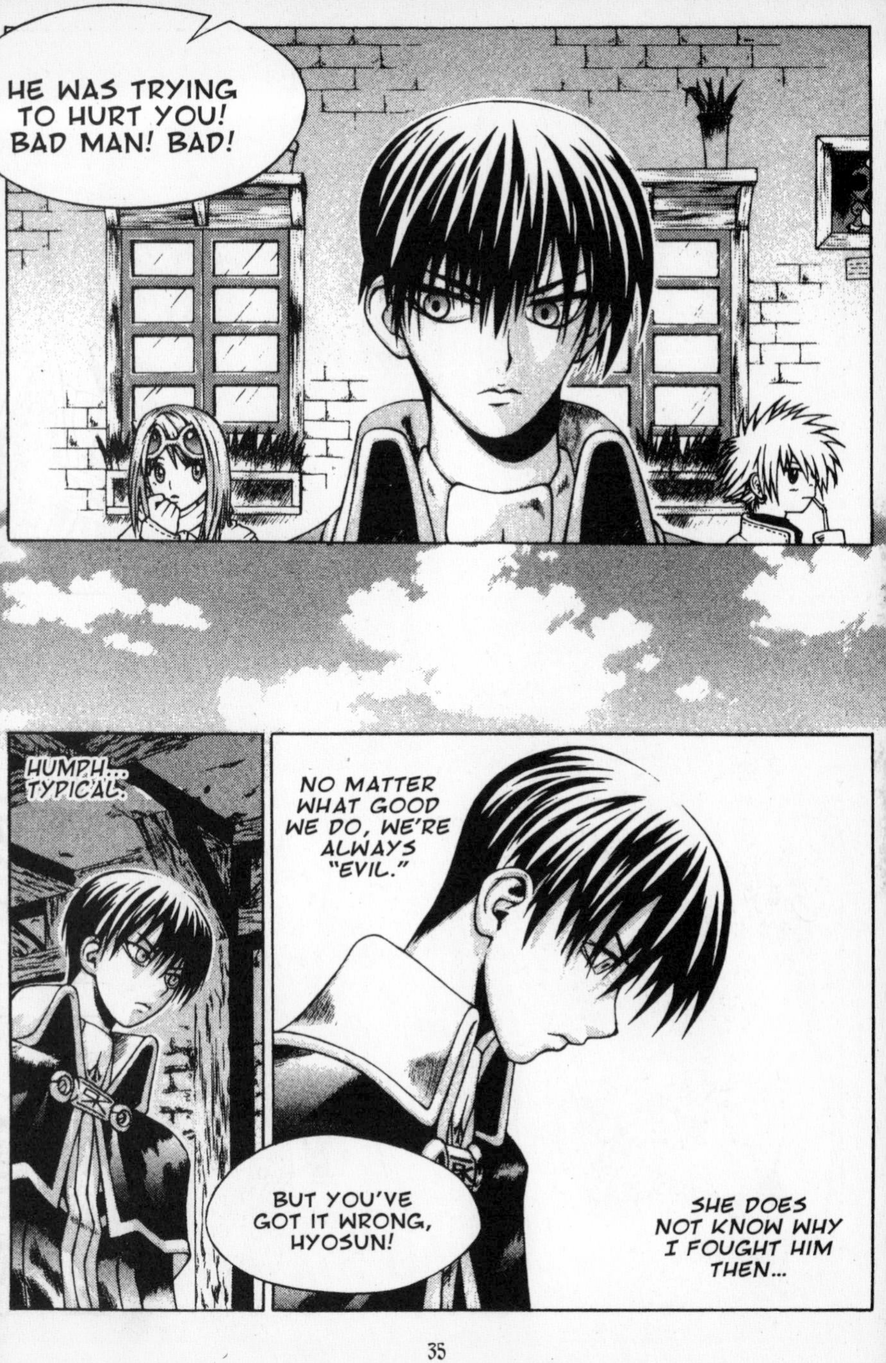
HE WAS TRYING TO HURT YOU! BAD MAN! BAD!
HUMPH... TYPICAL.
NO MATTER WHAT GOOD WE DO, WE'RE ALWAYS "EVIL."
BUT YOU'VE GOT IT WRONG, HYOSUN!
SHE DOES NOT KNOW WHY I FOUGHT HIM THEN...

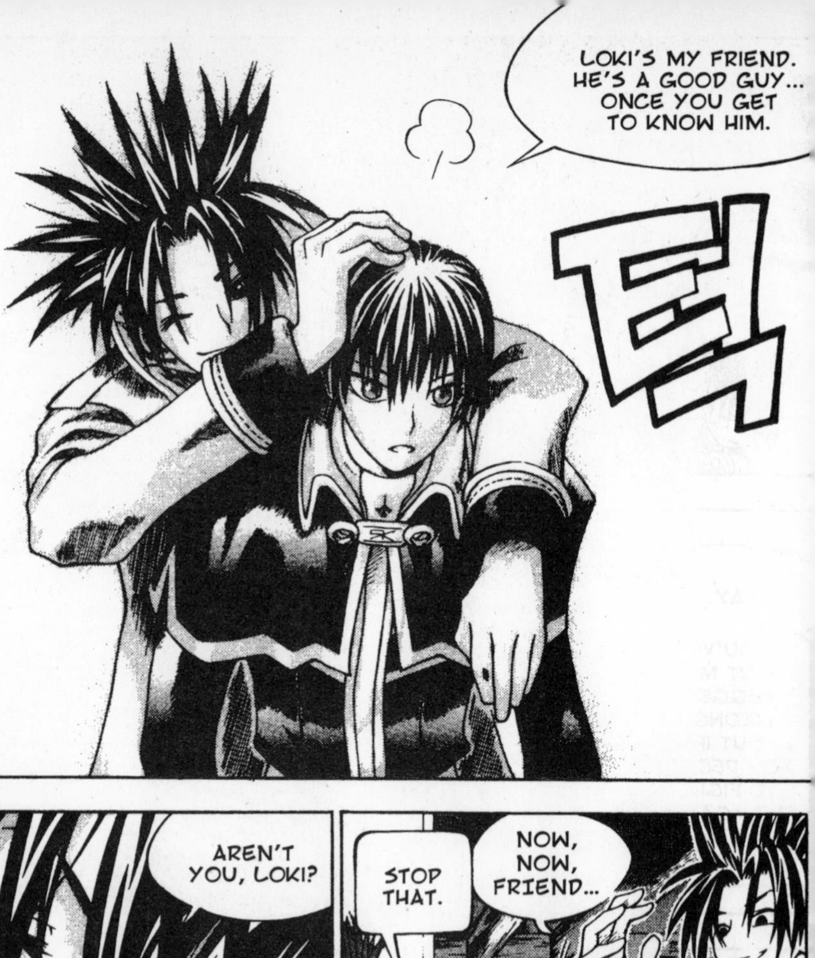
LOKI'S MY FRIEND. HE'S A GOOD GUY... ONCE YOU GET TO KNOW HIM.
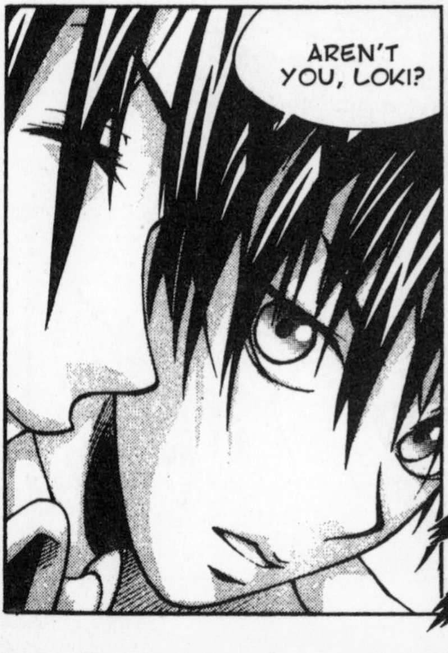
AREN'T YOU, LOKI?
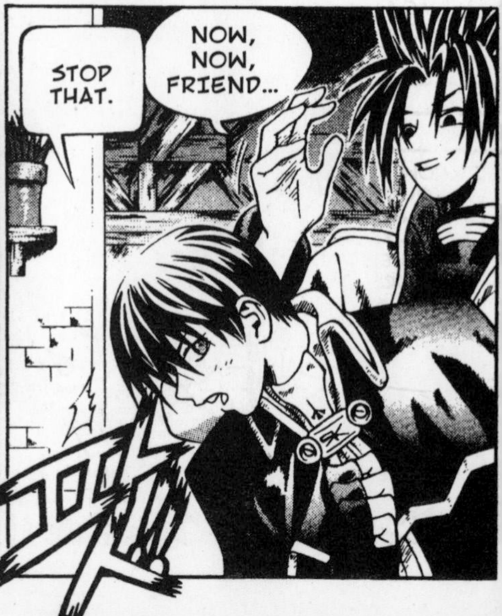
STOP THAT.
NOW, NOW, FRIEND...

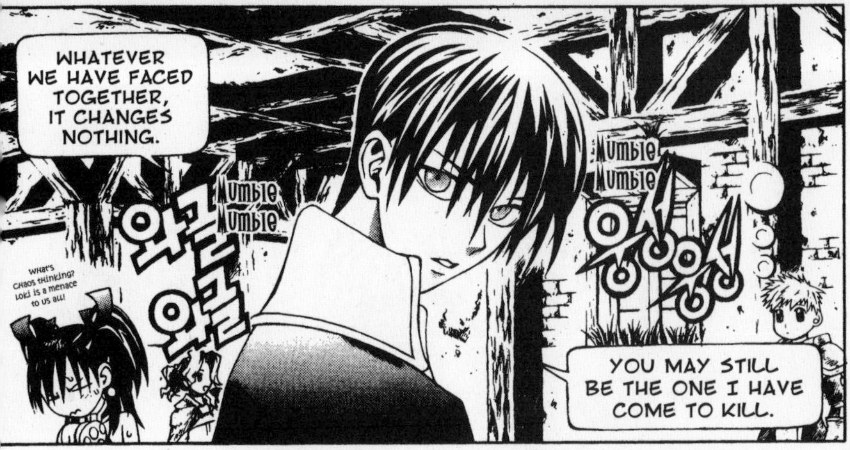
WHATEVER WE HAVE FACED TOGETHER, IT CHANGES NOTHING.
Mumble Mumble
What's Chaos thinking? Loki is a menace to us all!
Mumble Mumble
YOU MAY STILL BE THE ONE I HAVE COME TO KILL.

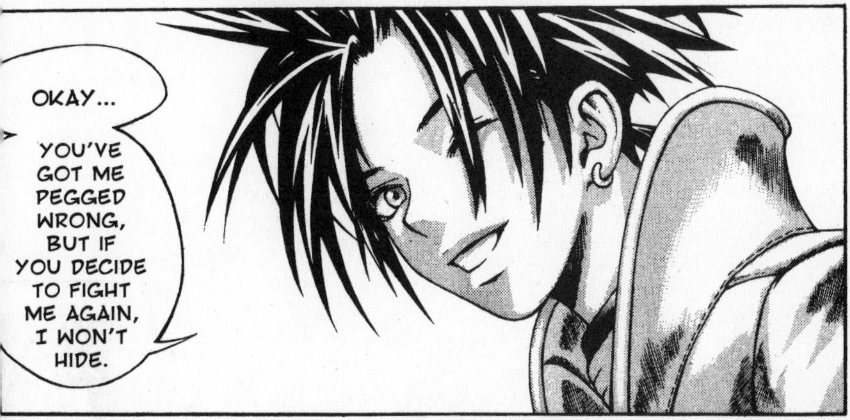
OKAY... YOU'VE GOT ME PEGGED WRONG, BUT IF YOU DECIDE TO FIGHT ME AGAIN, I WON'T HIDE.

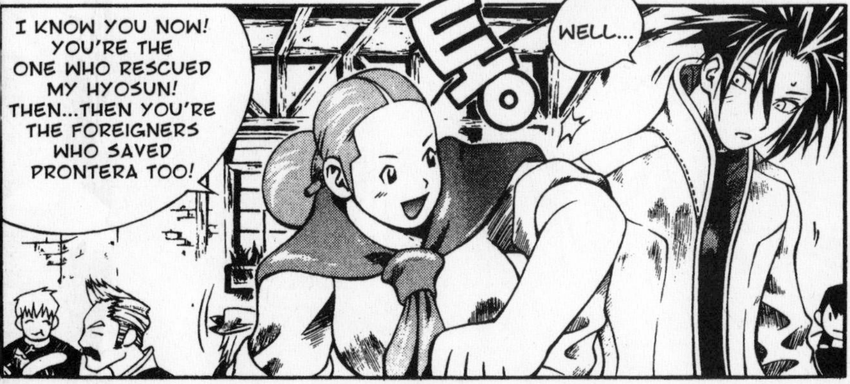
I KNOW YOU NOW! YOU'RE THE ONE WHO RESCUED MY HYOSUN! THEN...THEN YOU'RE THE FOREIGNERS WHO SAVED PRONTERA TOO!
WELL...

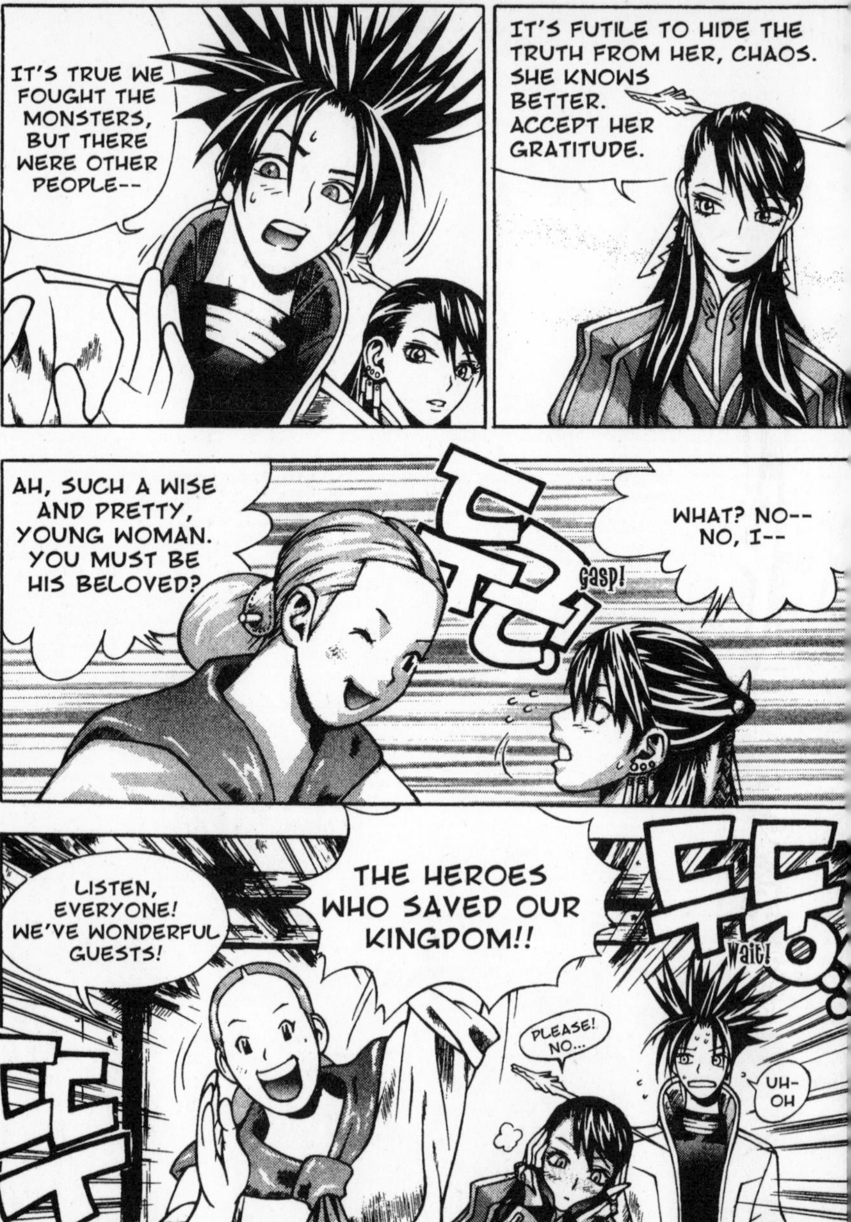
IT'S TRUE WE FOUGHT THE MONSTERS, BUT THERE WERE OTHER PEOPLE--
IT'S FUTILE TO HIDE THE TRUTH FROM HER, CHAOS. SHE KNOWS BETTER. ACCEPT HER GRATITUDE.
AH, SUCH A WISE AND PRETTY, YOUNG WOMAN. YOU MUST BE HIS BELOVED?
GASP!
WHAT? NO-- NO, I--
LISTEN, EVERYONE! WE'VE WONDERFUL GUESTS!
THE HEROES WHO SAVED OUR KINGDOM!!
WAIT!
PLEASE! NO...
UH- OH

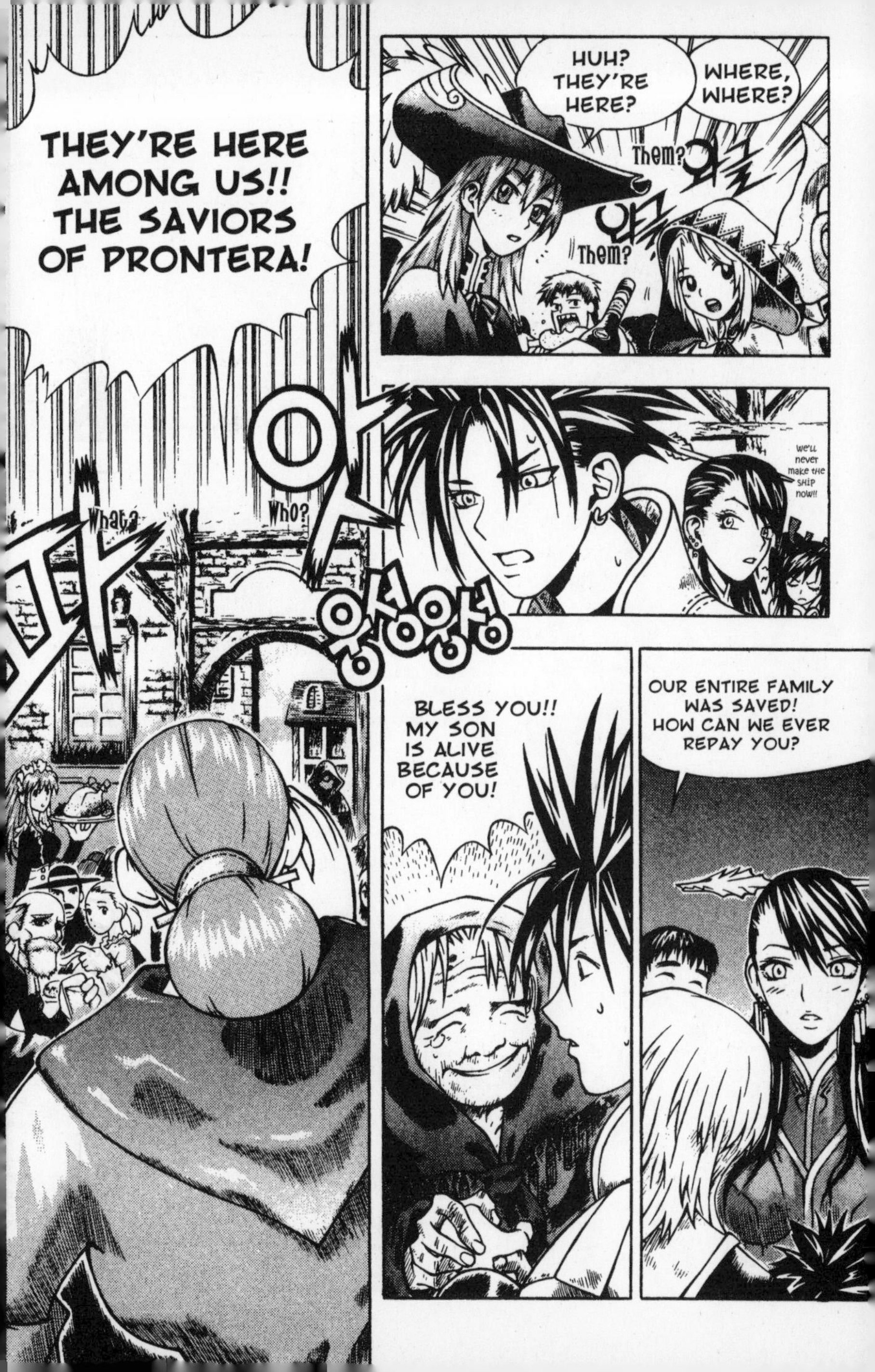
THEY'RE HERE AMONG US!! THE SAVIORS OF PRONTERA!
What?
Who?
HUH? THEY'RE HERE?
WHERE, WHERE?
Them?
Them?
We'll never make the ship now!!
BLESS YOU!! MY SON IS ALIVE BECAUSE OF YOU!
OUR ENTIRE FAMILY WAS SAVED! HOW CAN WE EVER REPAY YOU?

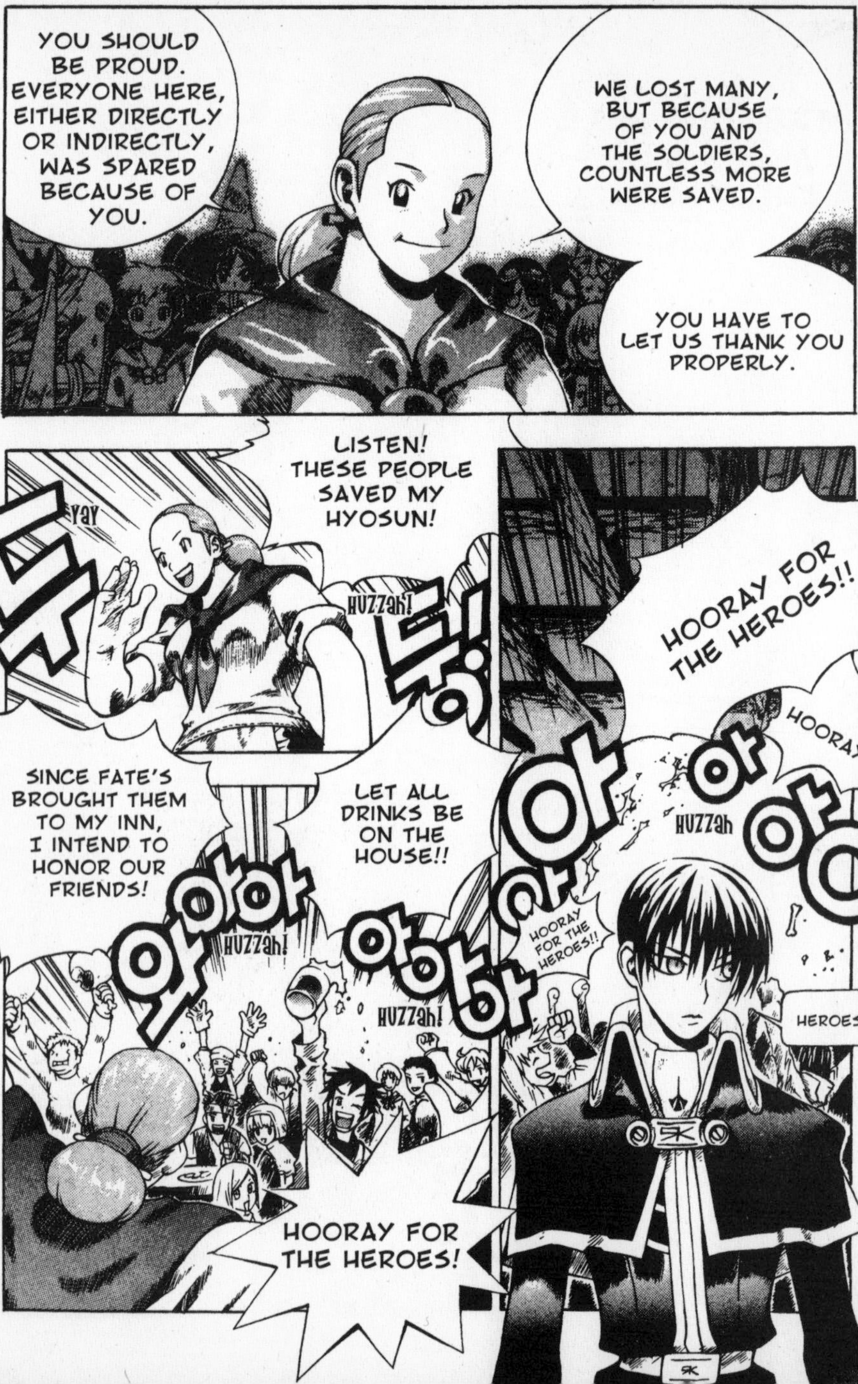
YOU SHOULD BE PROUD. EVERYONE HERE, EITHER DIRECTLY OR INDIRECTLY, WAS SPARED BECAUSE OF YOU.
WE LOST MANY, BUT BECAUSE OF YOU AND THE SOLDIERS, COUNTLESS MORE WERE SAVED.
YOU HAVE TO LET US THANK YOU PROPERLY.
YAY
LISTEN! THESE PEOPLE SAVED MY HYOSUN!
HUZZAH!
HOORAY FOR THE HEROES!!
HOORAY.
HUZZAH
SINCE FATE'S BROUGHT THEM TO MY INN, I INTEND TO HONOR OUR FRIENDS!
LET ALL DRINKS BE ON THE HOUSE!!
HUZZAH!
HOORAY FOR THE HEROES!!
HUZZAH!
HOORAY FOR THE HEROES!
HEROES.

RAGNAROK
라그나로크
IN TO THE ABYSS

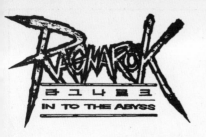

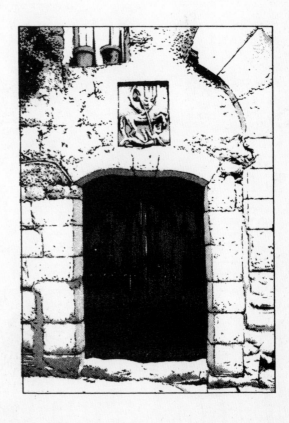

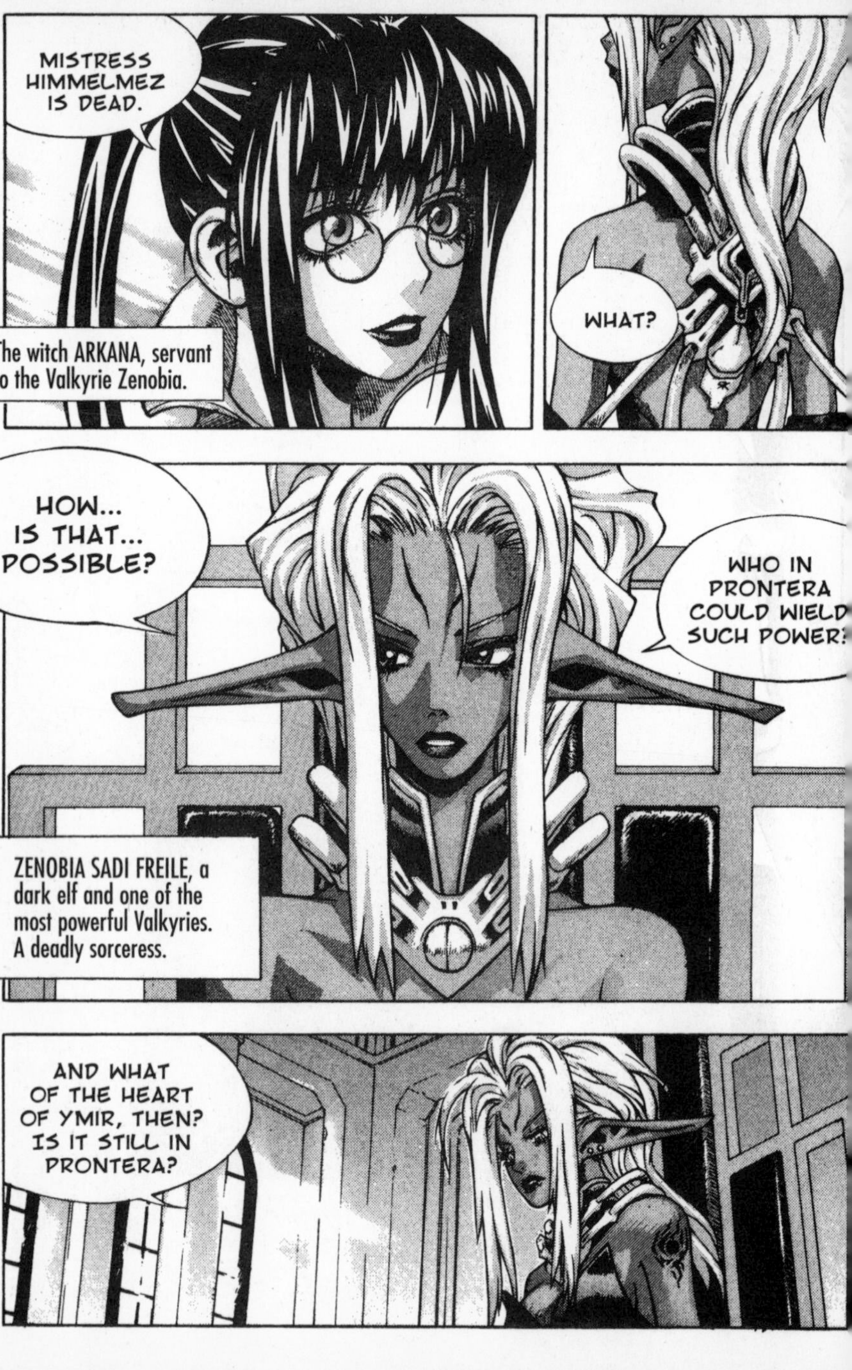
MISTRESS HIMMELMEZ IS DEAD.
The witch ARKANA, servant to the Valkyrie Zenobia.
WHAT?
HOW... IS THAT... POSSIBLE?
WHO IN PRONTERA COULD WIELD SUCH POWER?
ZENOBIA SADI FREILE, a dark elf and one of the most powerful Valkyries. A deadly sorceress.
AND WHAT OF THE HEART OF YMIR, THEN? IS IT STILL IN PRONTERA?

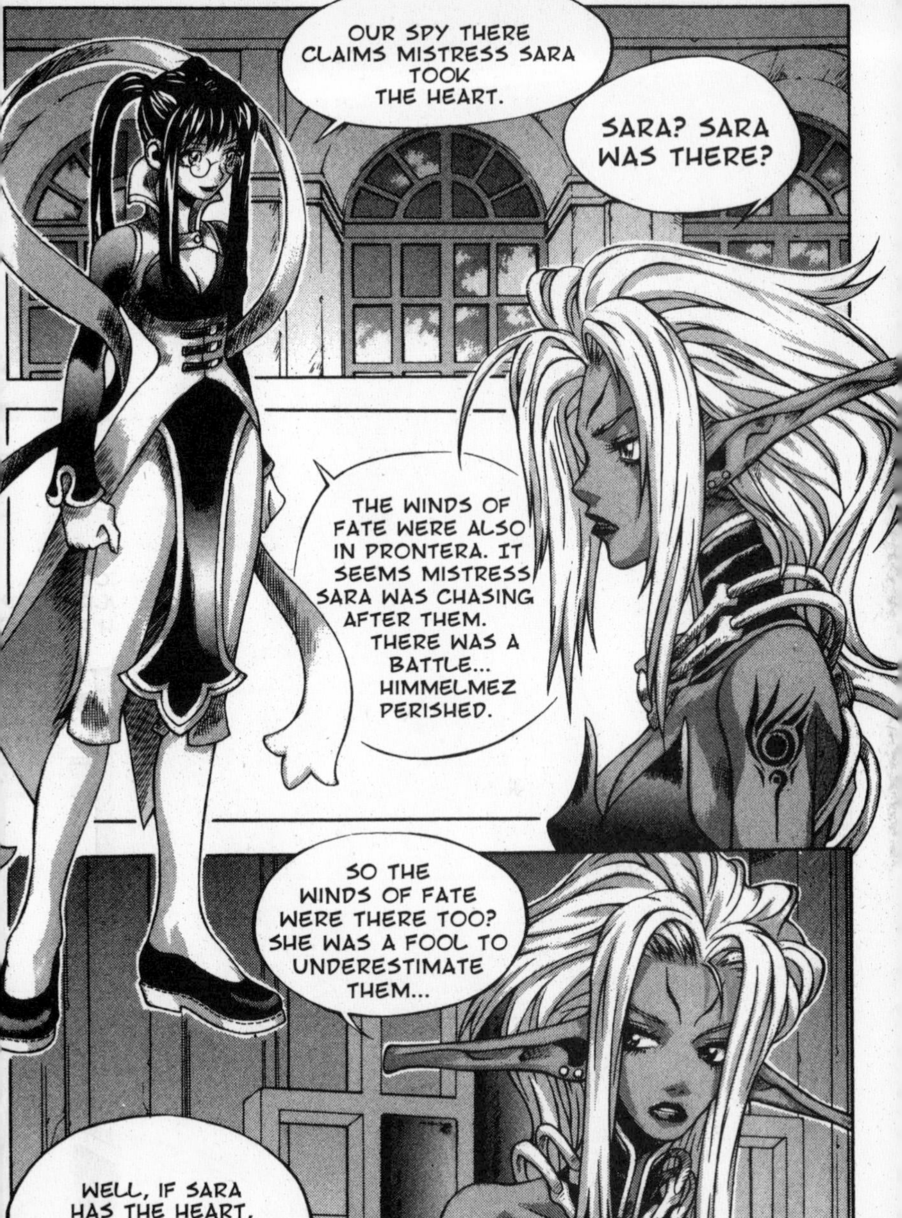
OUR SPY THERE CLAIMS MISTRESS SARA TOOK THE HEART.
SARA? SARA WAS THERE?
THE WINDS OF FATE WERE ALSO IN PRONTERA. IT SEEMS MISTRESS SARA WAS CHASING AFTER THEM. THERE WAS A BATTLE... HIMMELMEZ PERISHED.
SO THE WINDS OF FATE WERE THERE TOO? SHE WAS A FOOL TO UNDERESTIMATE THEM...
WELL, IF SARA HAS THE HEART, IT MUST BE IN VALHALLA BY NOW.

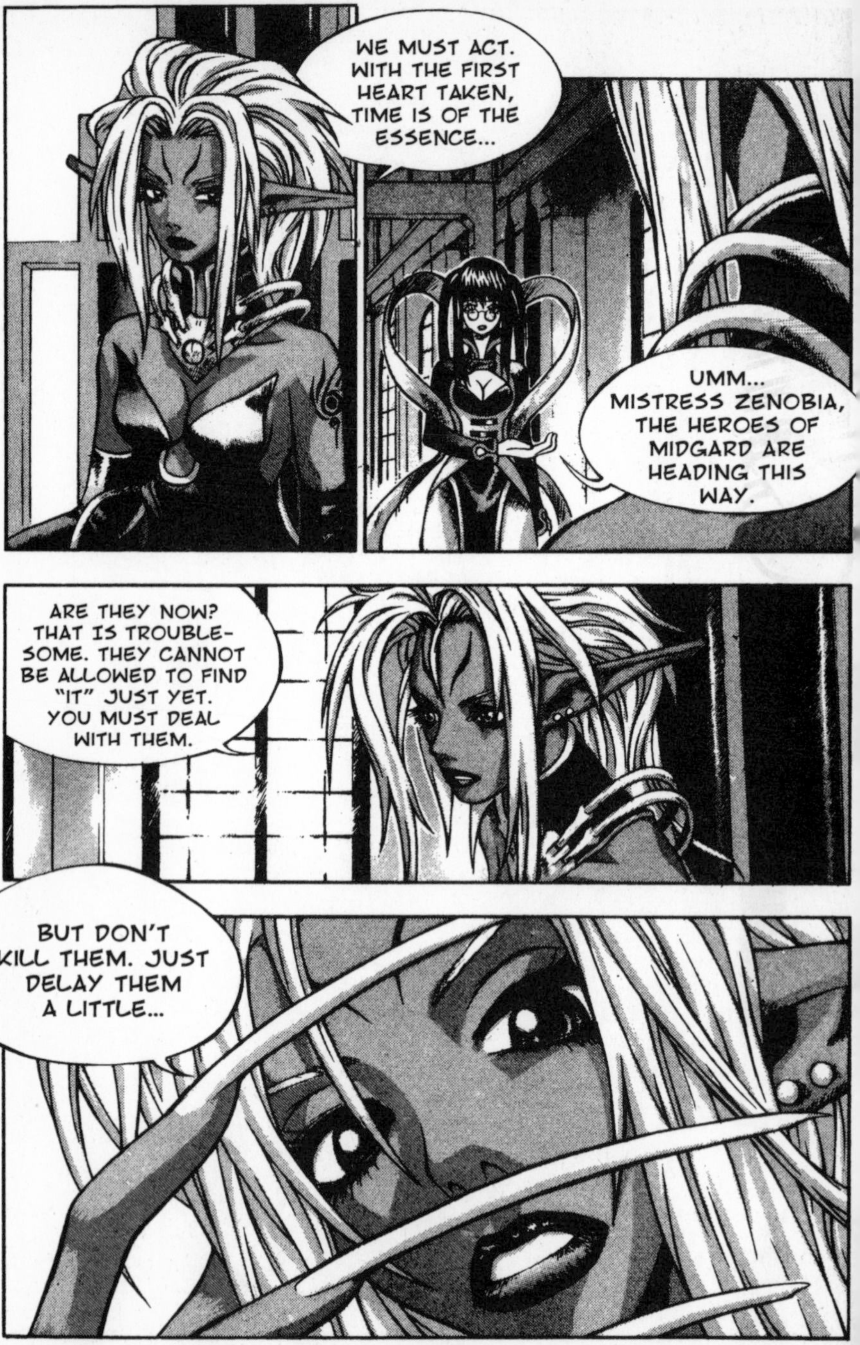
WE MUST ACT. WITH THE FIRST HEART TAKEN, TIME IS OF THE ESSENCE...
UMM... MISTRESS ZENOBIA, THE HEROES OF MIDGARD ARE HEADING THIS WAY.
ARE THEY NOW? THAT IS TROUBLE-SOME. THEY CANNOT BE ALLOWED TO FIND "IT" JUST YET. YOU MUST DEAL WITH THEM.
BUT DON'T KILL THEM. JUST DELAY THEM A LITTLE...

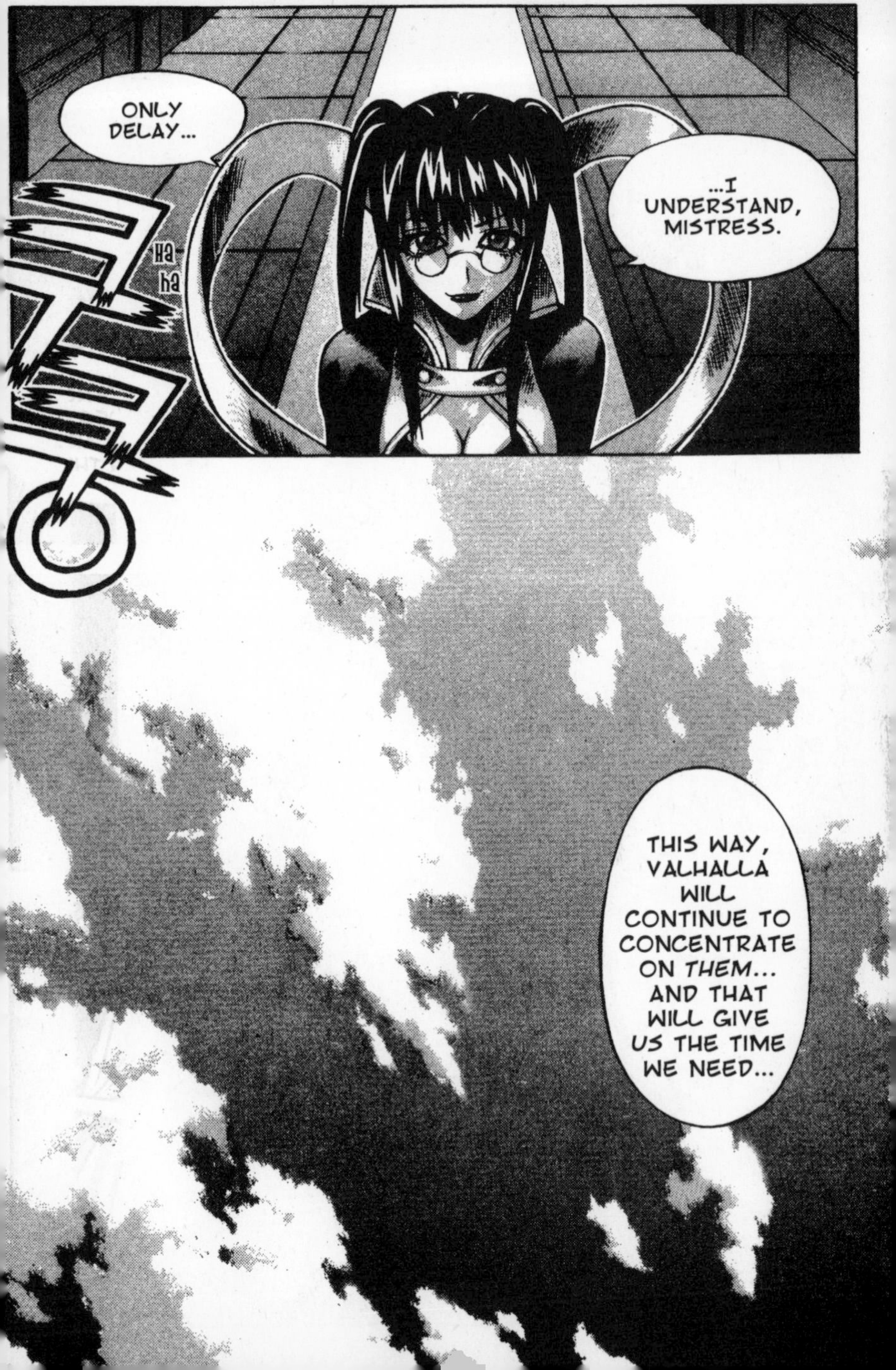
ONLY DELAY...
...I UNDERSTAND, MISTRESS.
HA HA
THIS WAY, VALHALLA WILL CONTINUE TO CONCENTRATE ON *THEM*... AND THAT WILL GIVE US THE TIME WE NEED...

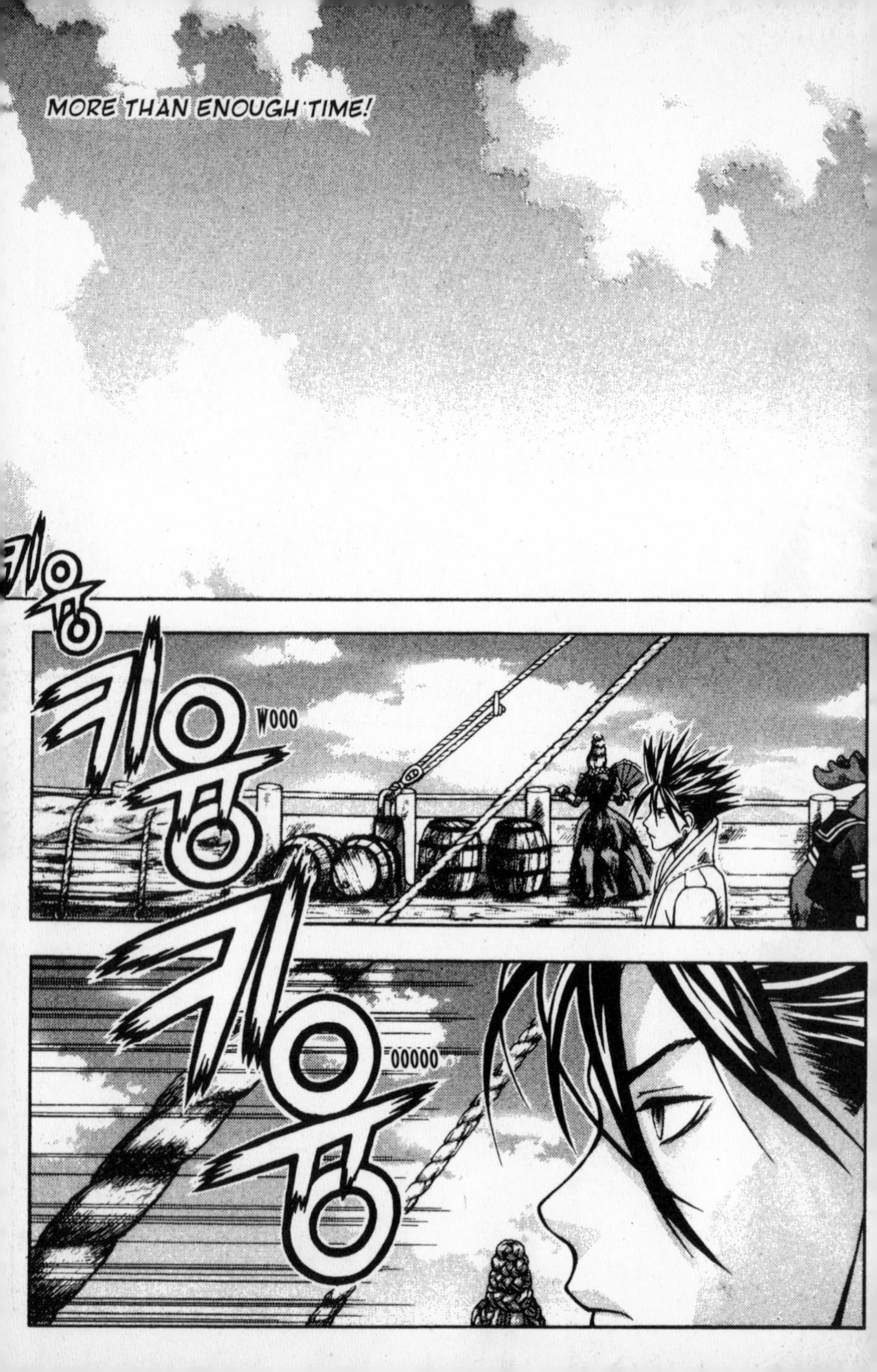
MORE THAN ENOUGH TIME!
WOOO
OOOOO

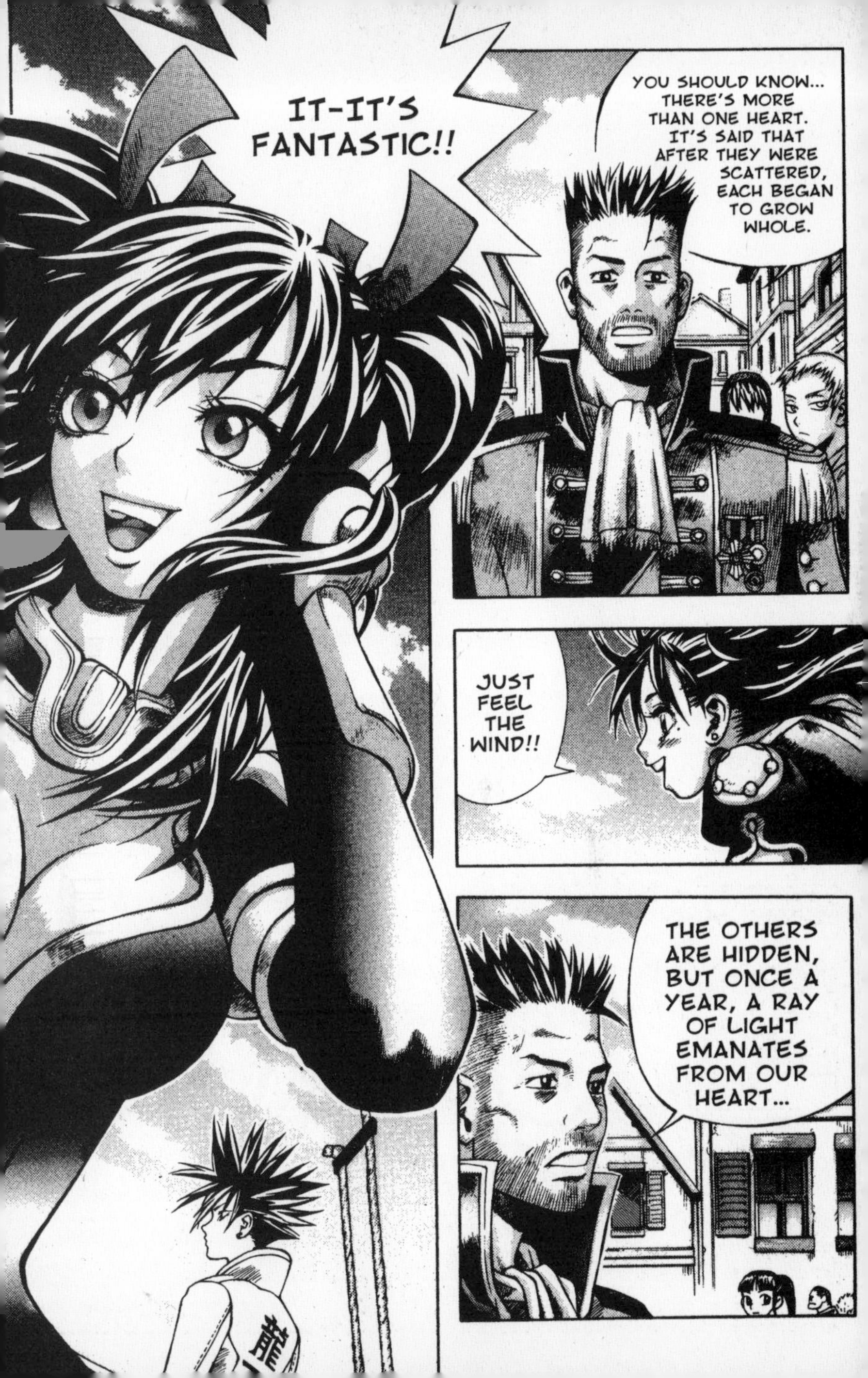
YOU SHOULD KNOW... THERE'S MORE THAN ONE HEART. IT'S SAID THAT AFTER THEY WERE SCATTERED, EACH BEGAN TO GROW WHOLE.
JUST FEEL THE WIND!!
THE OTHERS ARE HIDDEN, BUT ONCE A YEAR, A RAY OF LIGHT EMANATES FROM OUR HEART...
IT-IT'S FANTASTIC!!

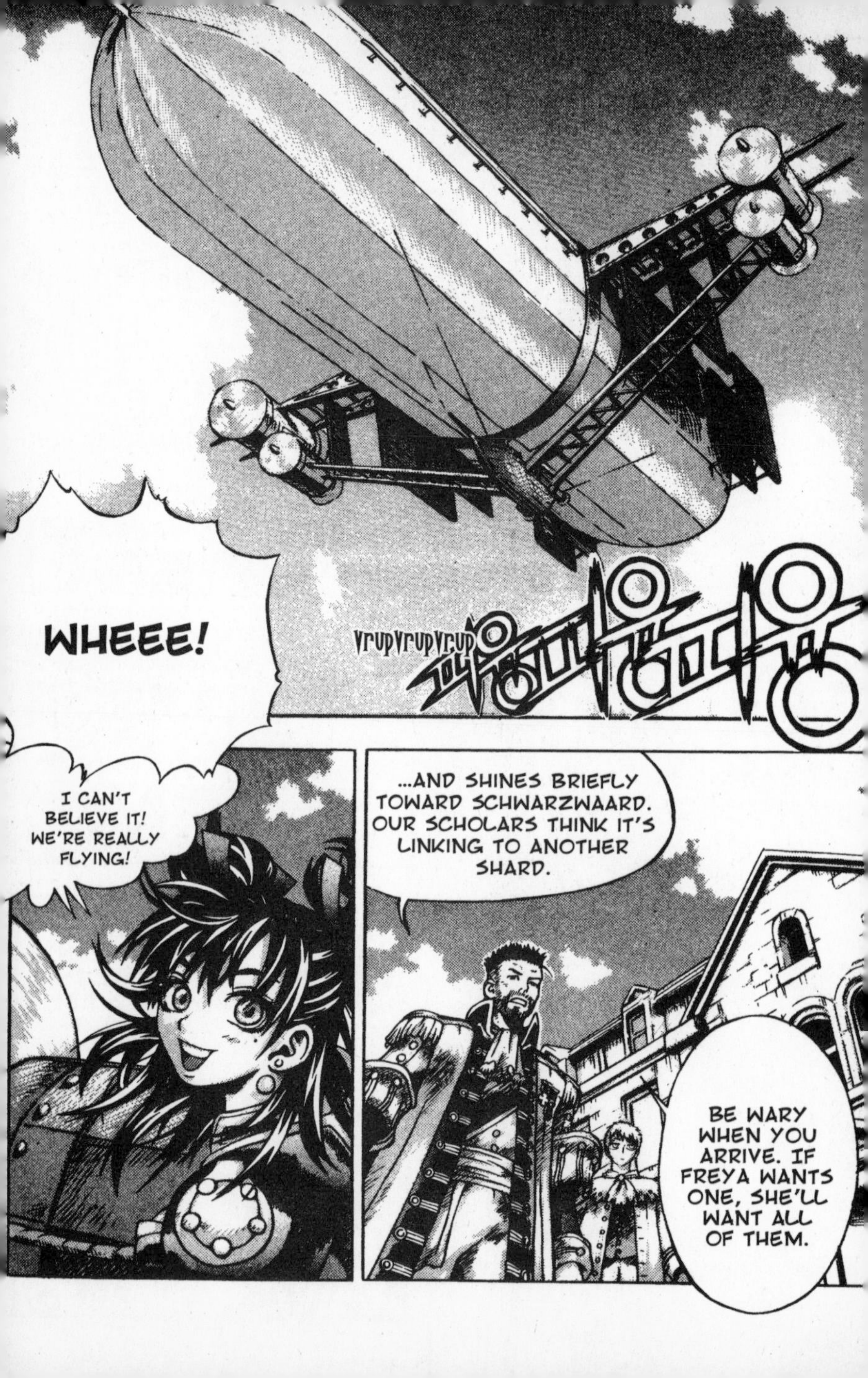
WHEEE!
VRUPVRUPVRUP
...AND SHINES BRIEFLY TOWARD SCHWARZWAARD. OUR SCHOLARS THINK IT'S LINKING TO ANOTHER SHARD.
BE WARY WHEN YOU ARRIVE. IF FREYA WANTS ONE, SHE'LL WANT ALL OF THEM.
I CAN'T BELIEVE IT! WE'RE REALLY FLYING!

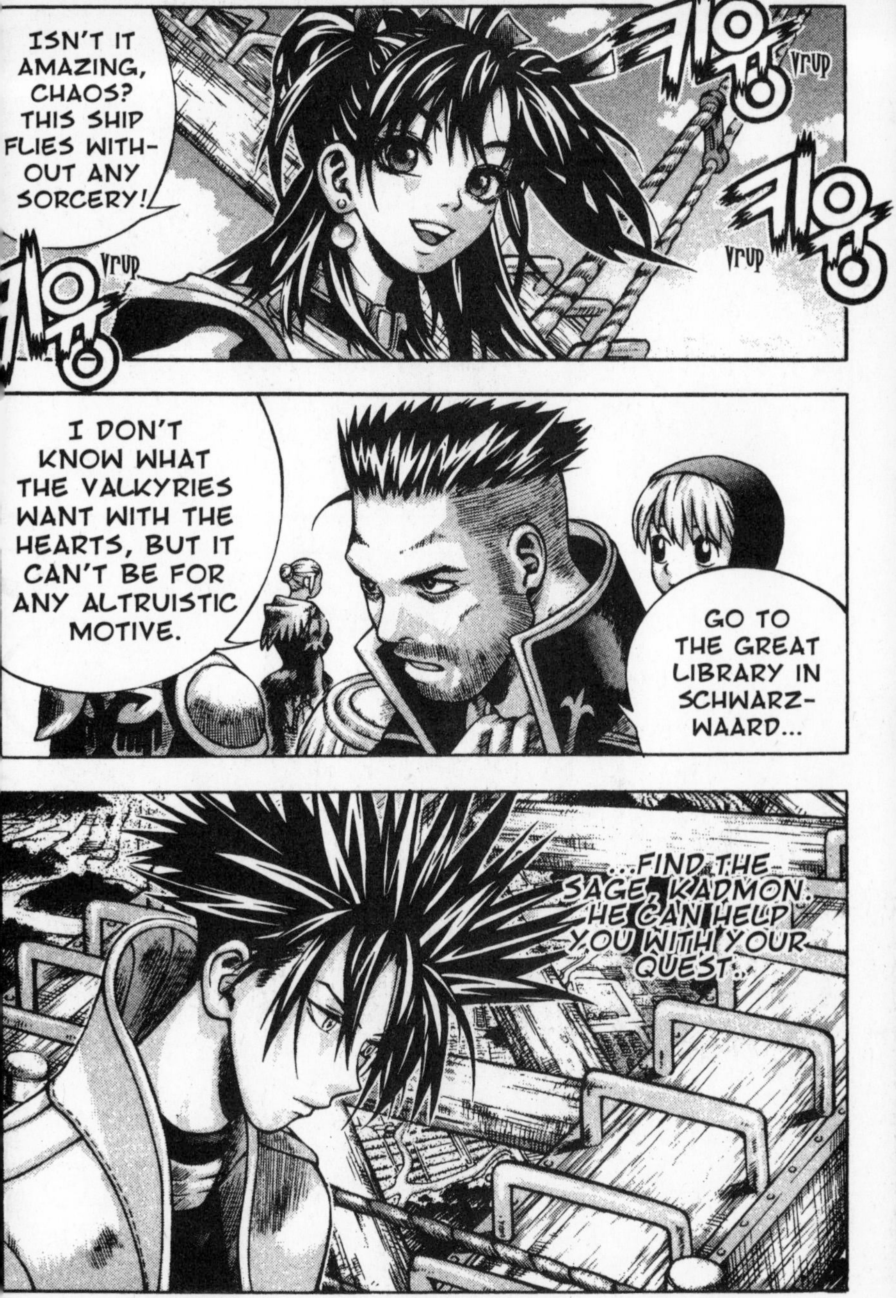
ISN'T IT AMAZING, CHAOS? THIS SHIP FLIES WITH-OUT ANY SORCERY!
VRUP
VRUP
VRUP
I DON'T KNOW WHAT THE VALKYRIES WANT WITH THE HEARTS, BUT IT CAN'T BE FOR ANY ALTRUISTIC MOTIVE.
GO TO THE GREAT LIBRARY IN SCHWARZ-WAARD...
...FIND THE SAGE, KADMON. HE CAN HELP YOU WITH YOUR QUEST...

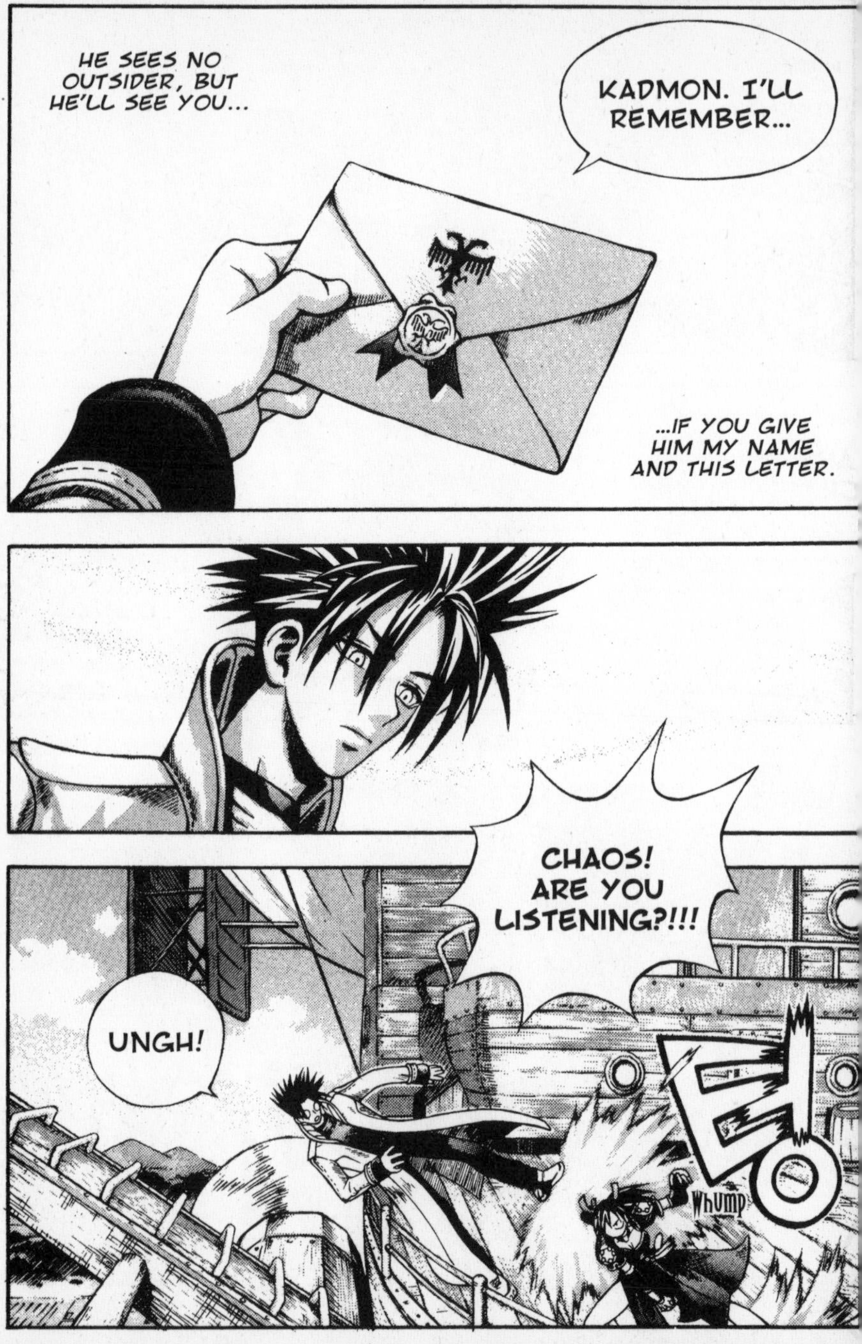
KADMON. I'LL REMEMBER...
HE SEES NO OUTSIDER, BUT HE'LL SEE YOU...
...IF YOU GIVE HIM MY NAME AND THIS LETTER.
CHAOS! ARE YOU LISTENING?!!!
UNGH!
Whump

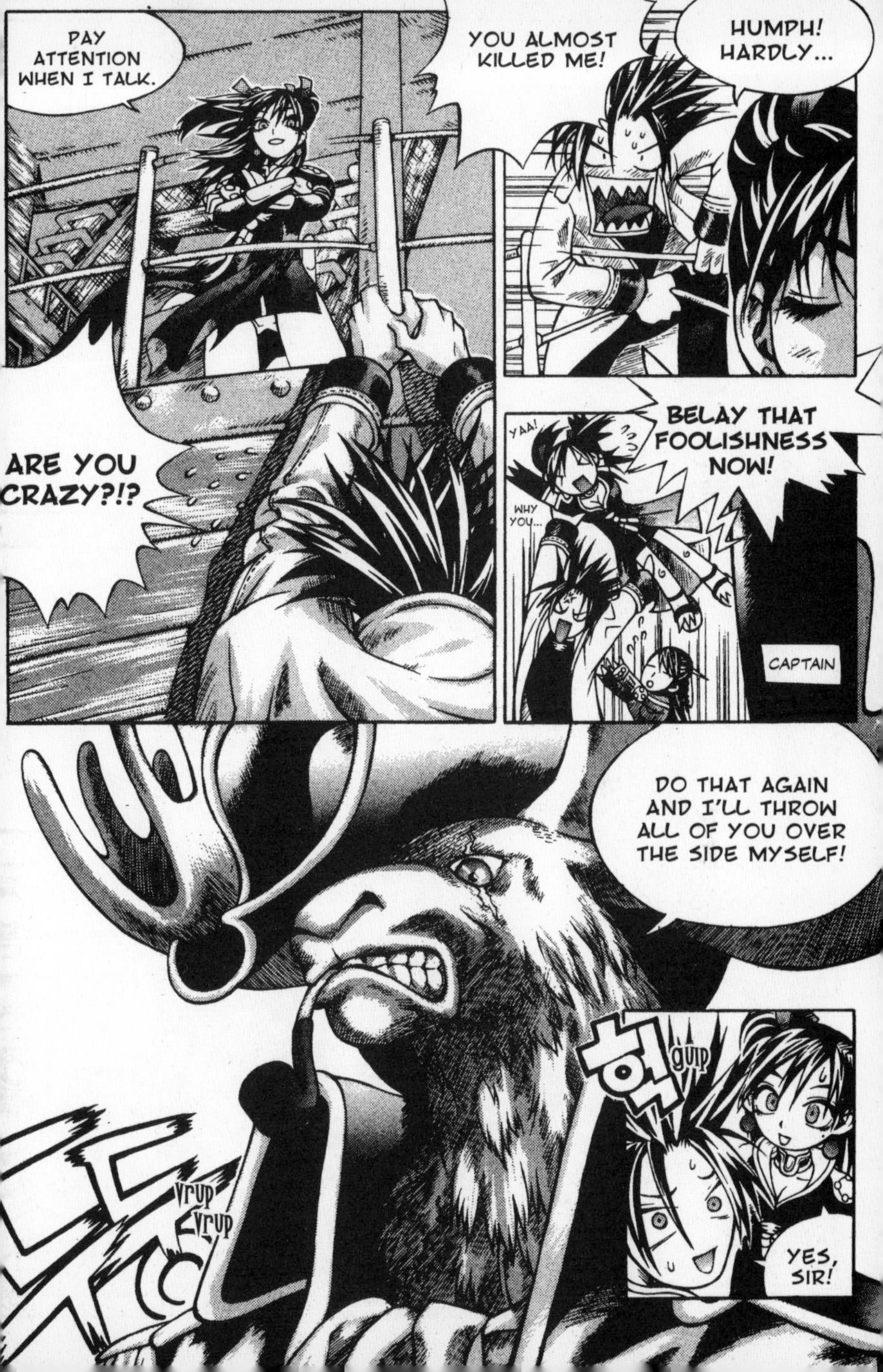
PAY ATTENTION WHEN I TALK.
ARE YOU CRAZY?!?
YOU ALMOST KILLED ME!
HUMPH! HARDLY...
YAA!
WHY YOU...
BELAY THAT FOOLISHNESS NOW!
CAPTAIN
DO THAT AGAIN AND I'LL THROW ALL OF YOU OVER THE SIDE MYSELF!
vrup
vrup
gulp
YES, SIR!

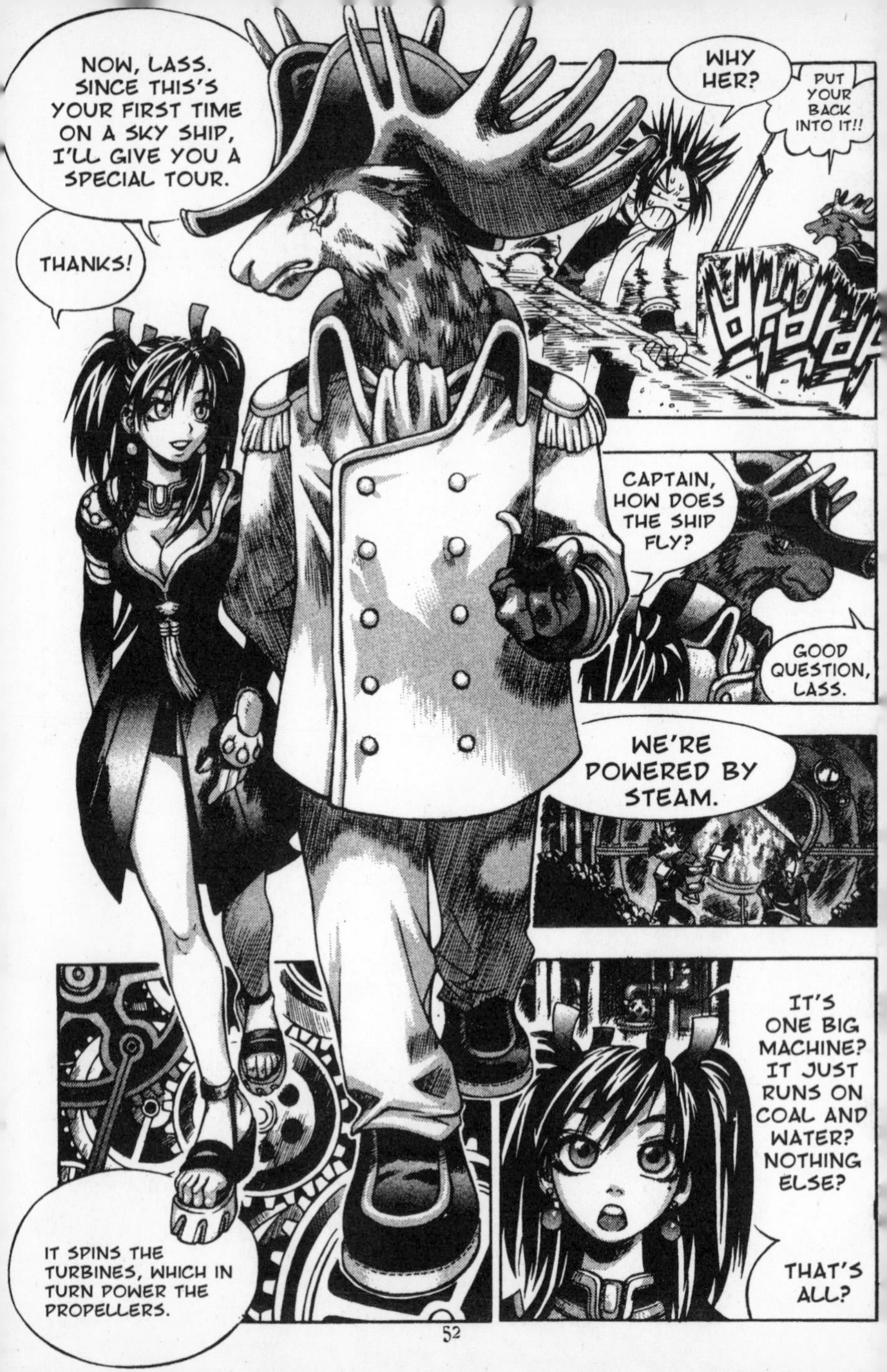
NOW, LASS. SINCE THIS'S YOUR FIRST TIME ON A SKY SHIP, I'LL GIVE YOU A SPECIAL TOUR.
THANKS!
WHY HER?
PUT YOUR BACK INTO IT!!
CAPTAIN, HOW DOES THE SHIP FLY?
GOOD QUESTION, LASS.
WE'RE POWERED BY STEAM.
IT SPINS THE TURBINES, WHICH IN TURN POWER THE PROPELLERS.
IT'S ONE BIG MACHINE? IT JUST RUNS ON COAL AND WATER? NOTHING ELSE?
THAT'S ALL?

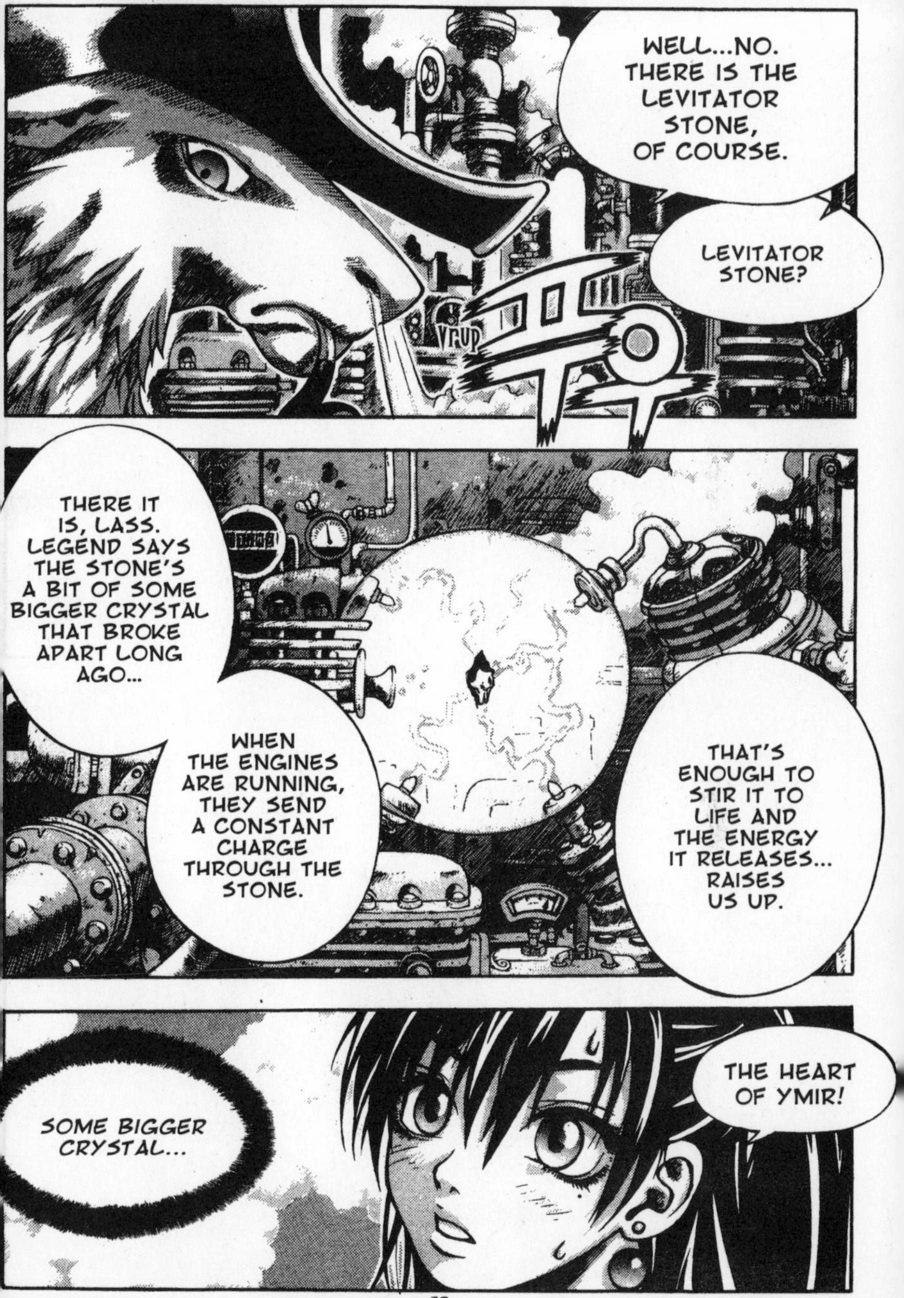
WELL...NO. THERE IS THE LEVITATOR STONE, OF COURSE.
LEVITATOR STONE?
VRUP
THERE IT IS, LASS. LEGEND SAYS THE STONE'S A BIT OF SOME BIGGER CRYSTAL THAT BROKE APART LONG AGO...
WHEN THE ENGINES ARE RUNNING, THEY SEND A CONSTANT CHARGE THROUGH THE STONE.
THAT'S ENOUGH TO STIR IT TO LIFE AND THE ENERGY IT RELEASES... RAISES US UP.
SOME BIGGER CRYSTAL...
THE HEART OF YMIR!

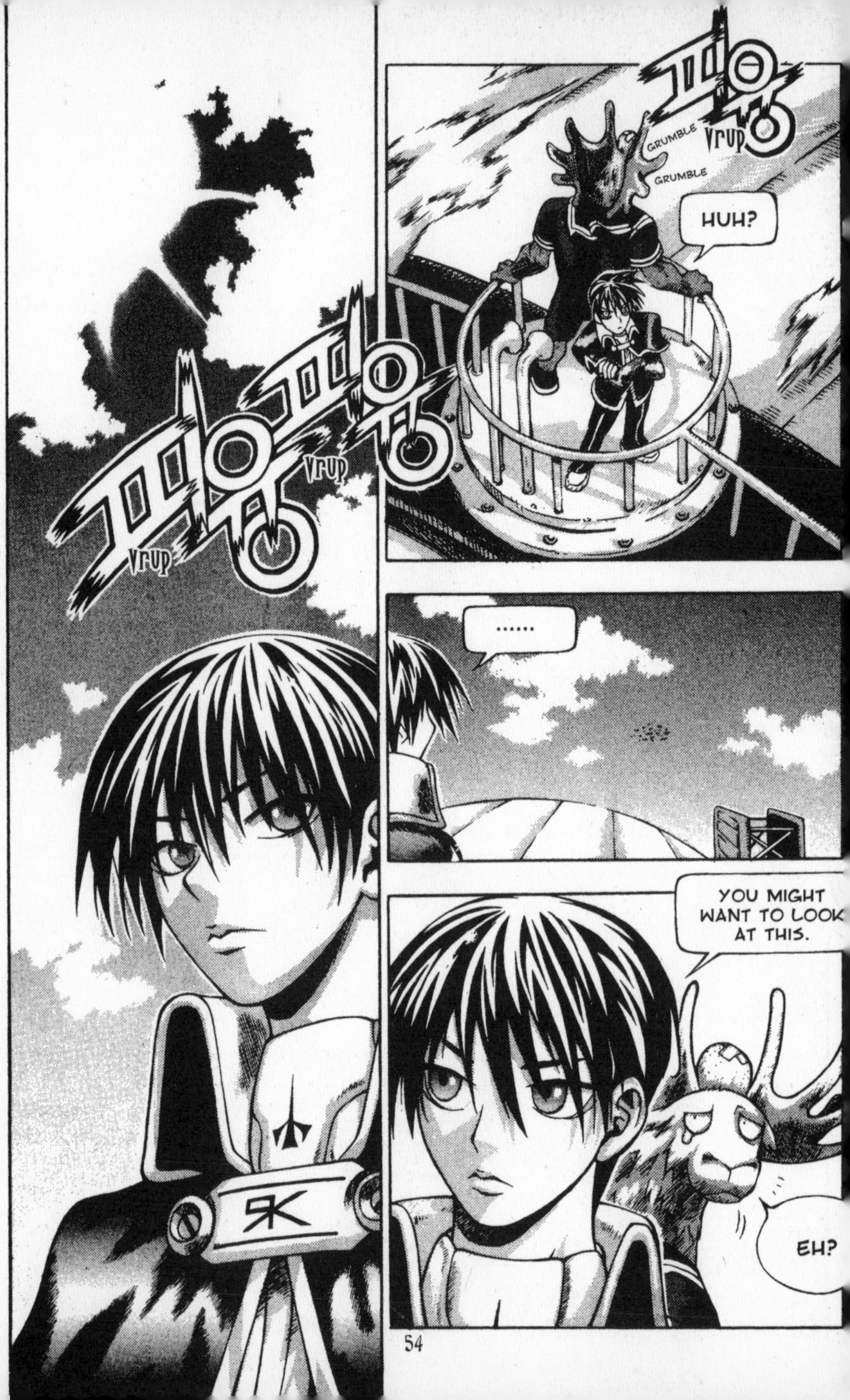
GRUMBLE
VRUP
GRUMBLE
HUH?
......
YOU MIGHT WANT TO LOOK AT THIS.
EH?
VRUP
VRUP

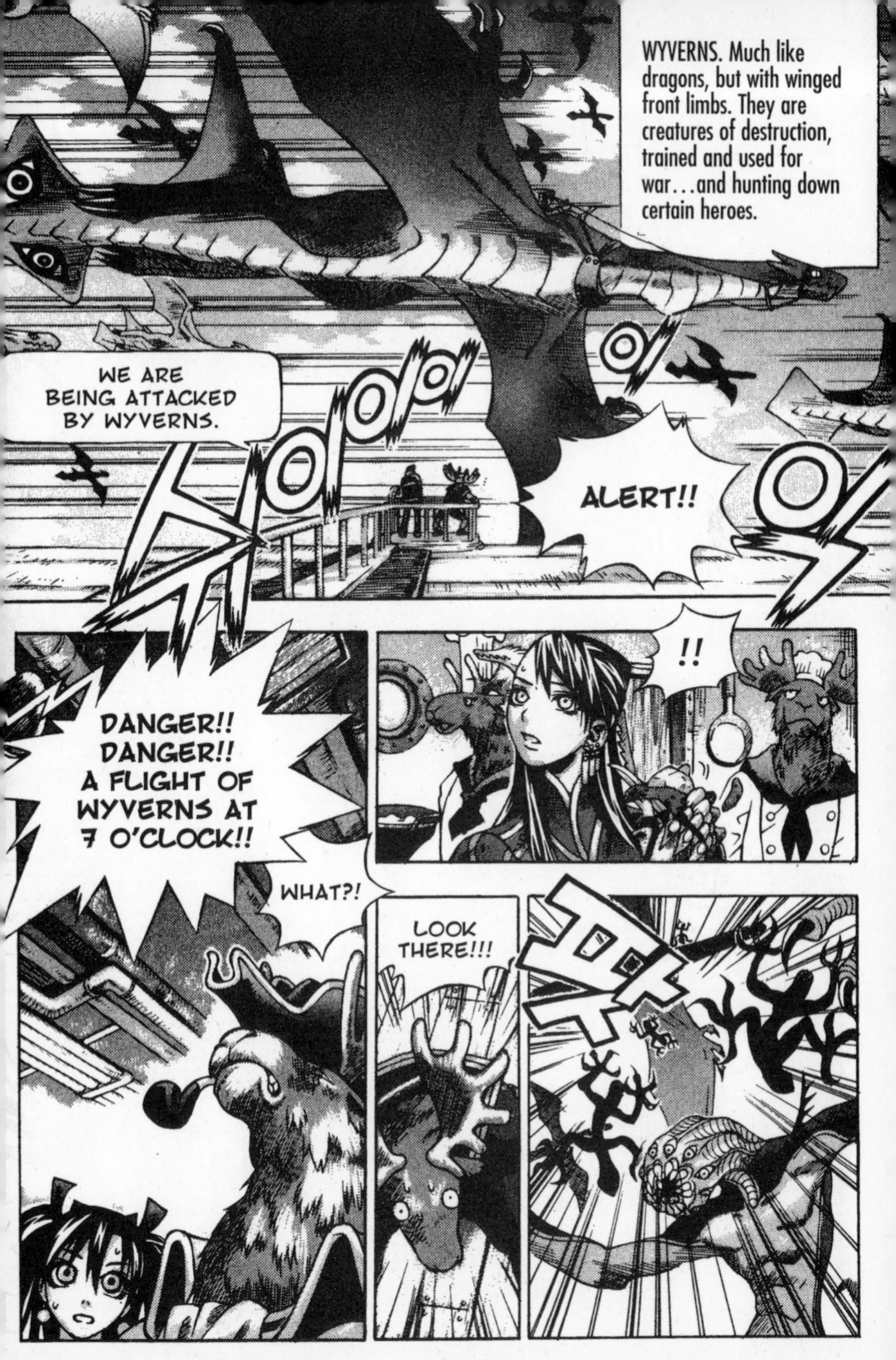
WYVERNS. Much like dragons, but with winged front limbs. They are creatures of destruction, trained and used for war...and hunting down certain heroes.
ALERT!!
WE ARE BEING ATTACKED BY WYVERNS.
!!
DANGER!! DANGER!! A FLIGHT OF WYVERNS AT 7 O'CLOCK!!
WHAT?!
LOOK THERE!!!

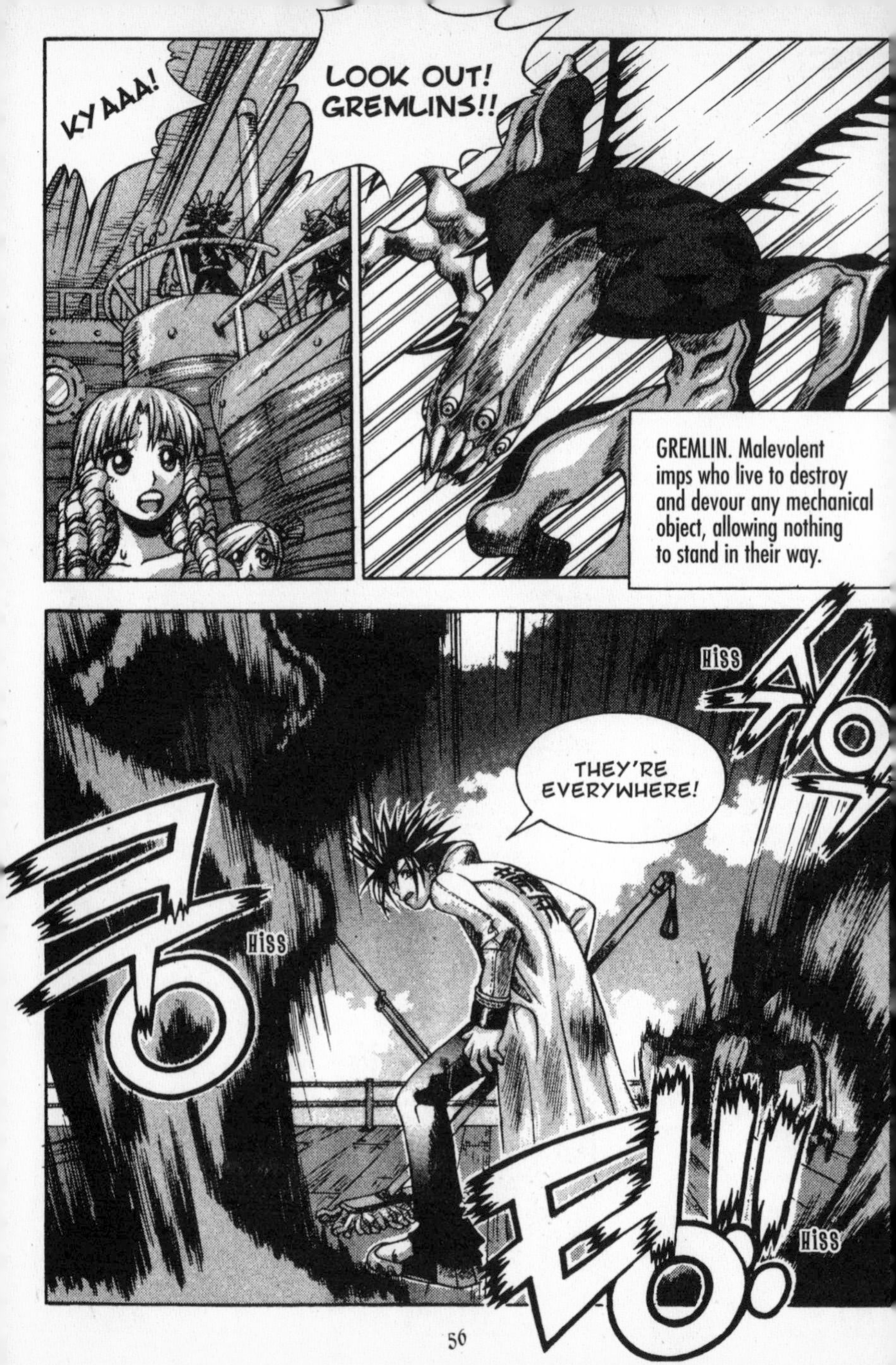
LOOK OUT! GREMLINS!!
GREMLIN. Malevolent imps who live to destroy and devour any mechanical object, allowing nothing to stand in their way.
KYAAA!
HISS
THEY'RE EVERYWHERE!
HISS
HISS

RAGNAROK
라그나로크
IN TO THE ABYSS

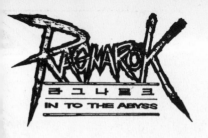

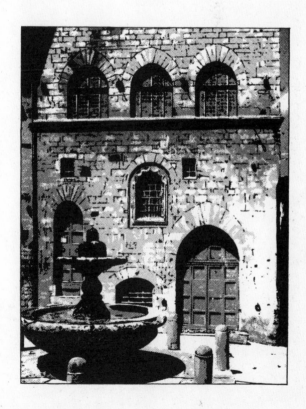

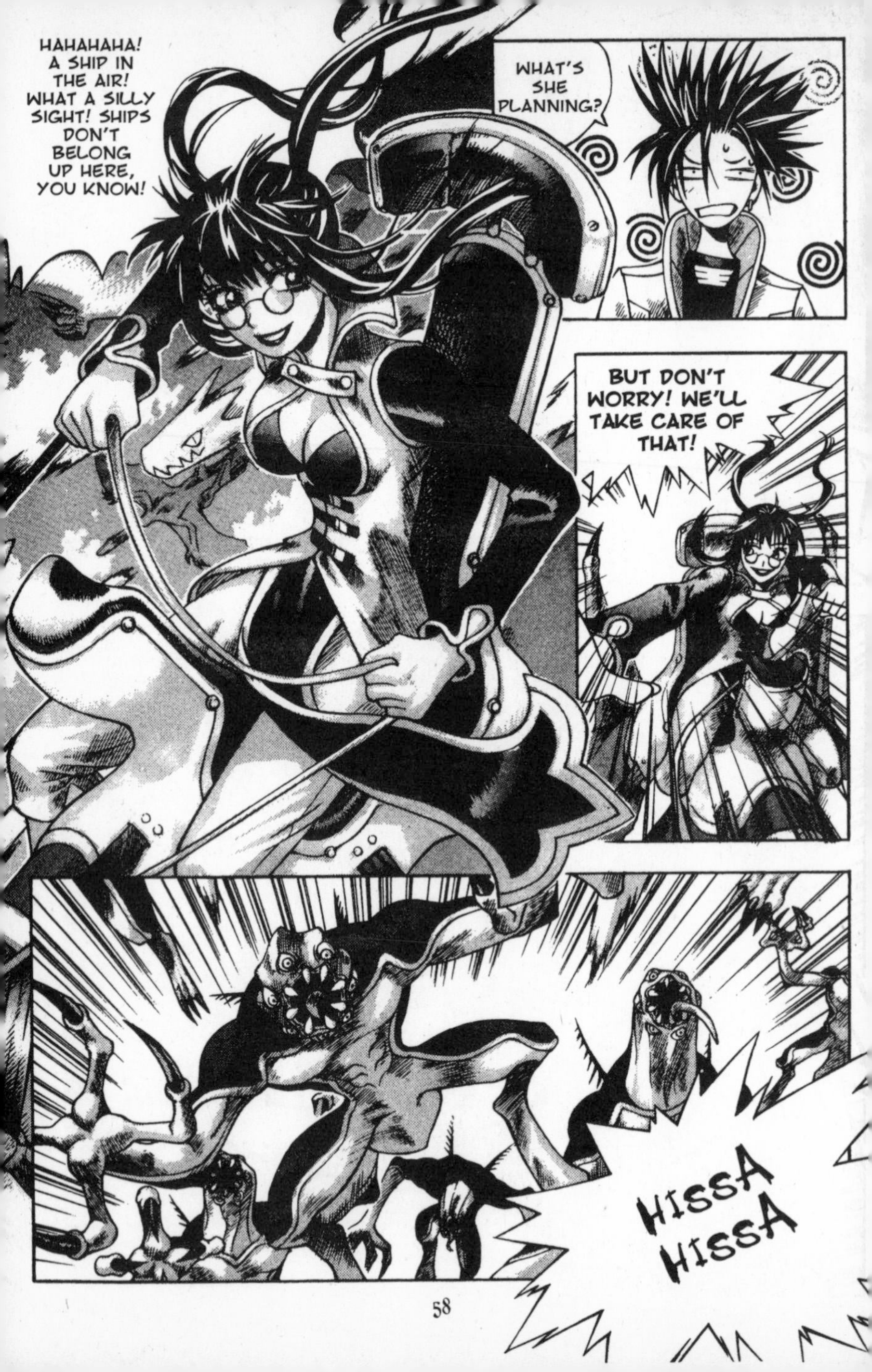
WHAT'S SHE PLANNING?
HAHAHAHA! A SHIP IN THE AIR! WHAT A SILLY SIGHT! SHIPS DON'T BELONG UP HERE, YOU KNOW!
BUT DON'T WORRY! WE'LL TAKE CARE OF THAT!
HISSA HISSA

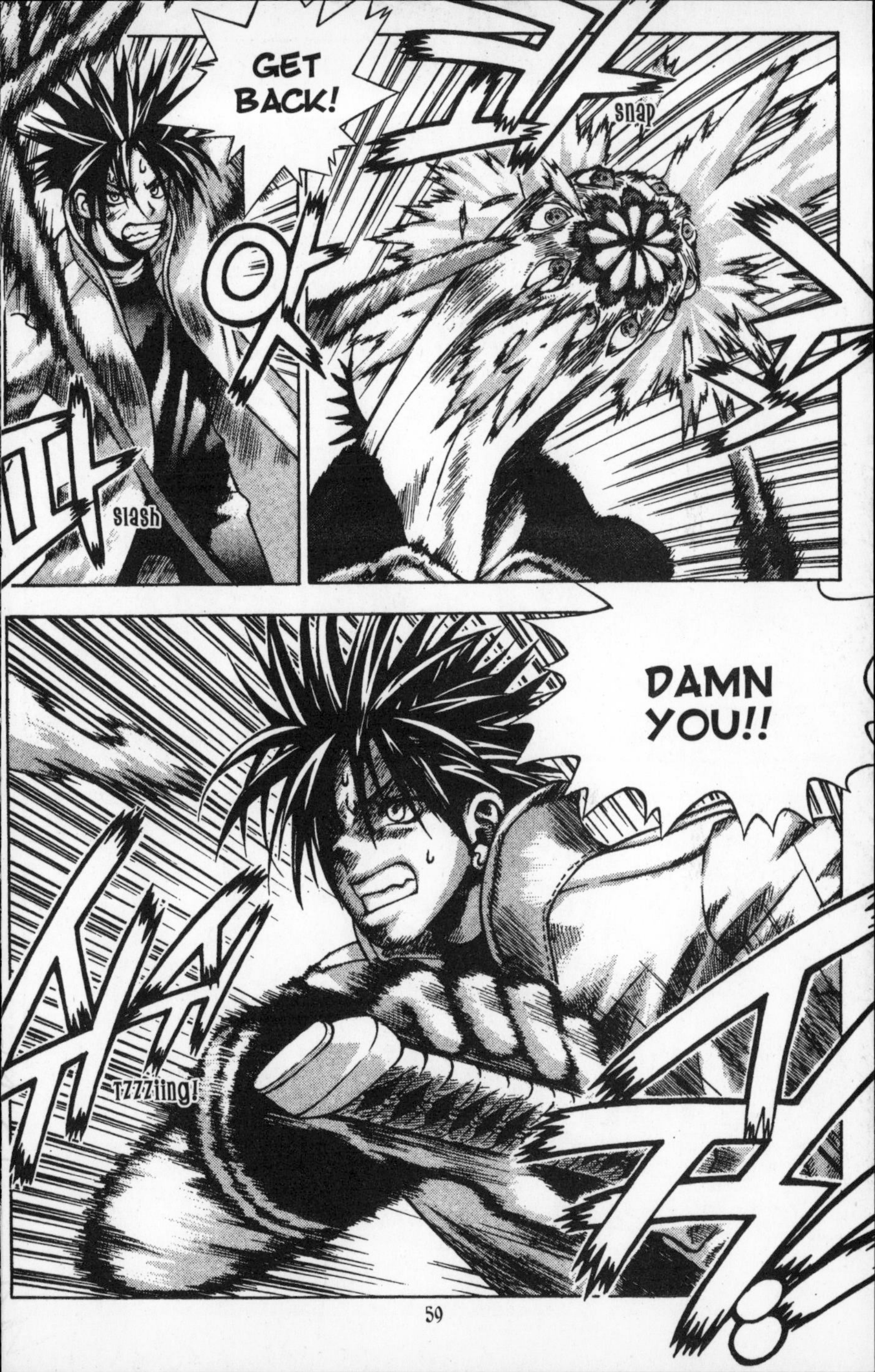
snap
GET BACK!
slash
DAMN YOU!!
tzzziing!

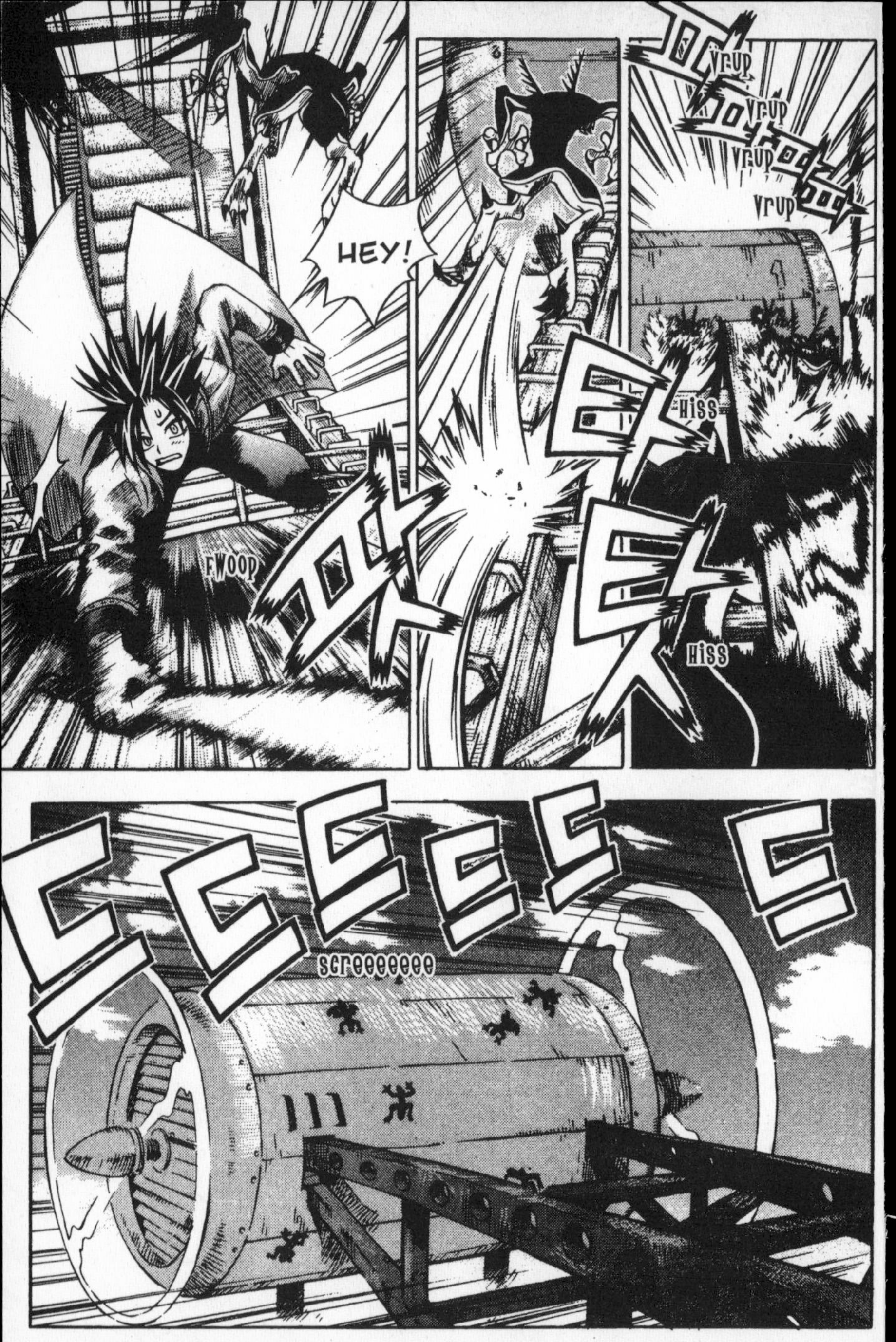
vrup
vrup
vrup
vrup
Hiss
Hiss
HEY!
fWoop
screeeeeeee

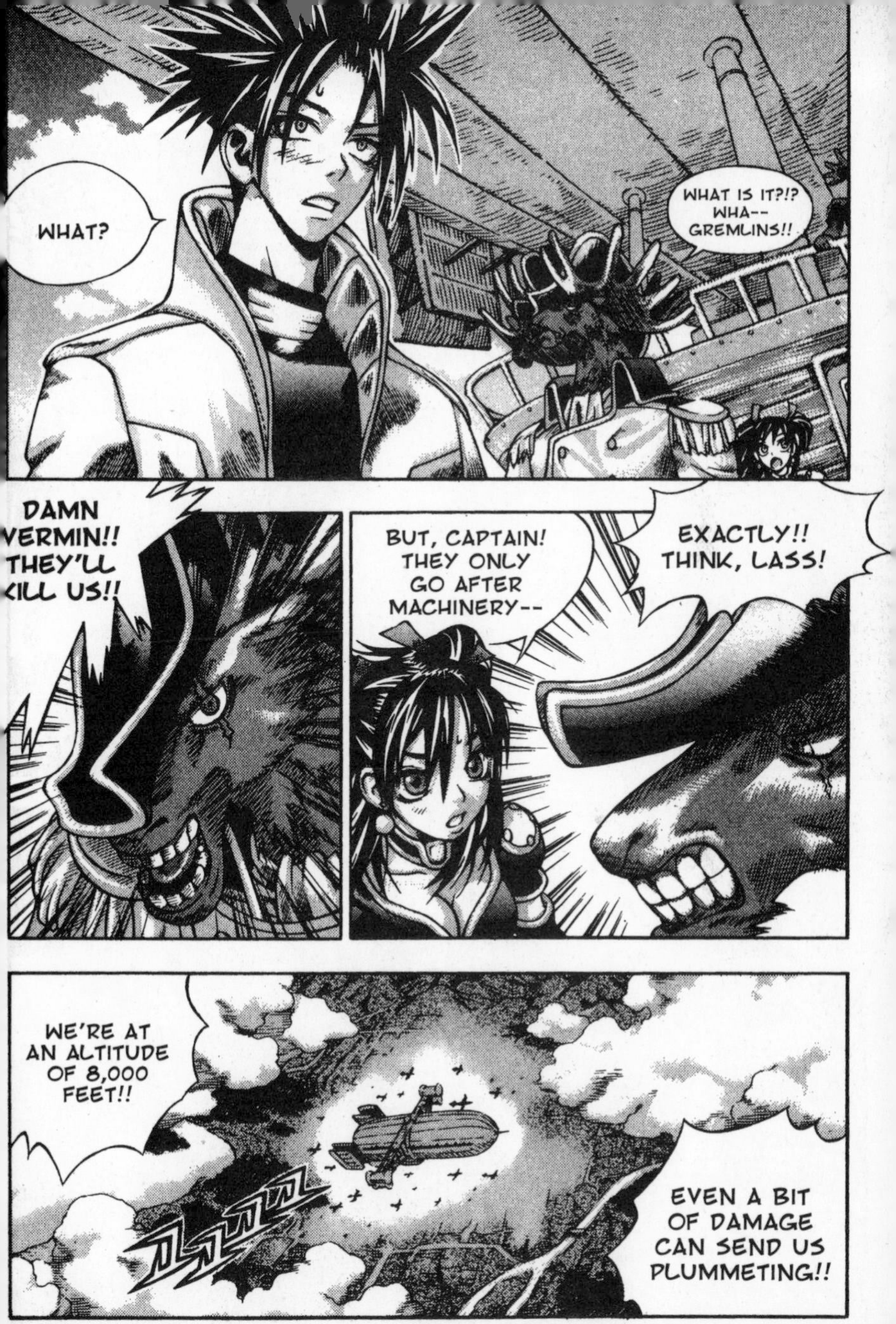
WHAT?
WHAT IS IT?!? WHA-- GREMLINS!!
DAMN VERMIN!! THEY'LL KILL US!!
BUT, CAPTAIN! THEY ONLY GO AFTER MACHINERY--
EXACTLY!! THINK, LASS!
WE'RE AT AN ALTITUDE OF 8,000 FEET!!
EVEN A BIT OF DAMAGE CAN SEND US PLUMMETING!!

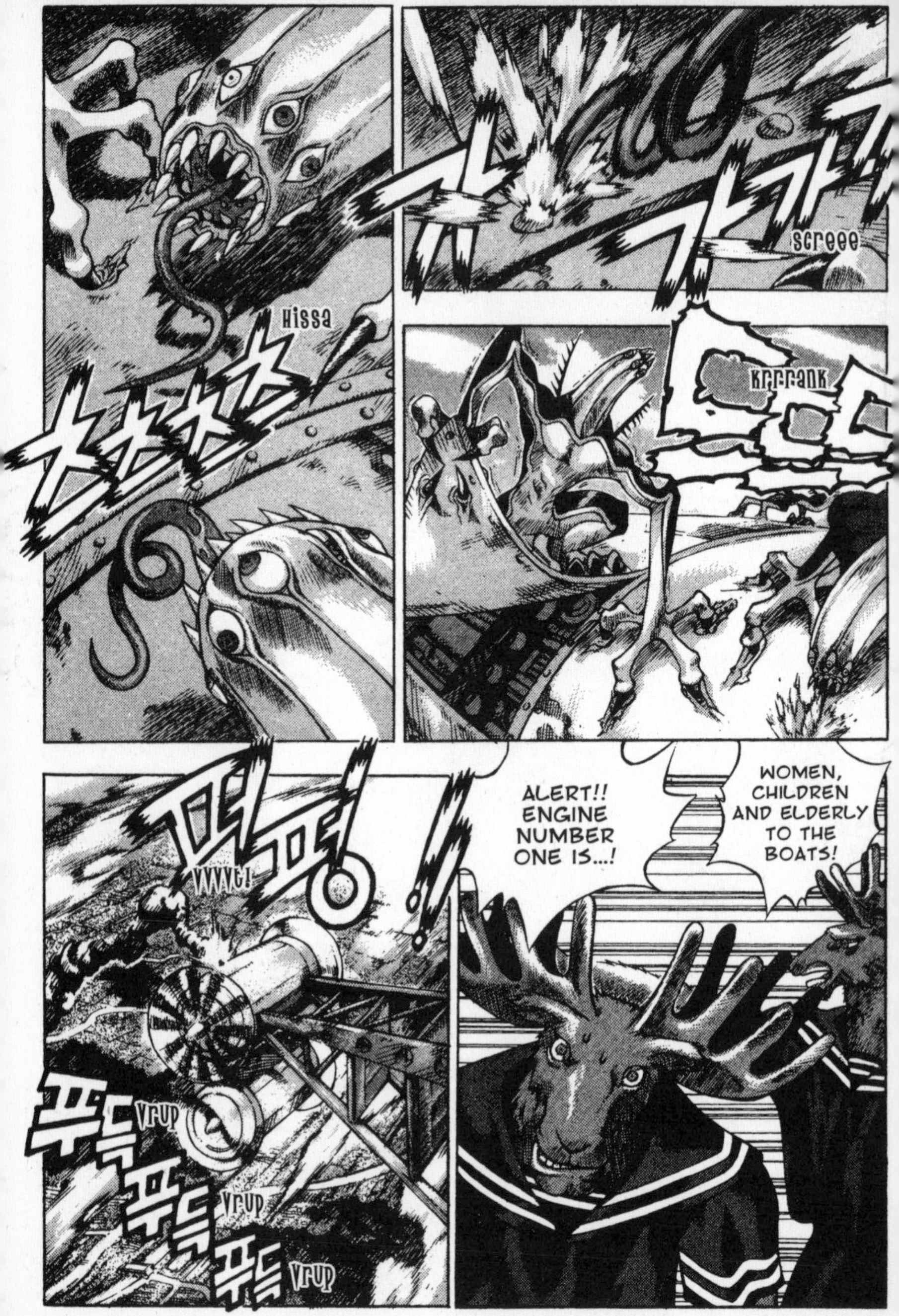
HISSA
SCREEE
KRRRANK
VVVVG!
VRUP
VRUP
VRUP
ALERT!! ENGINE NUMBER ONE IS...!
WOMEN, CHILDREN AND ELDERLY TO THE BOATS!

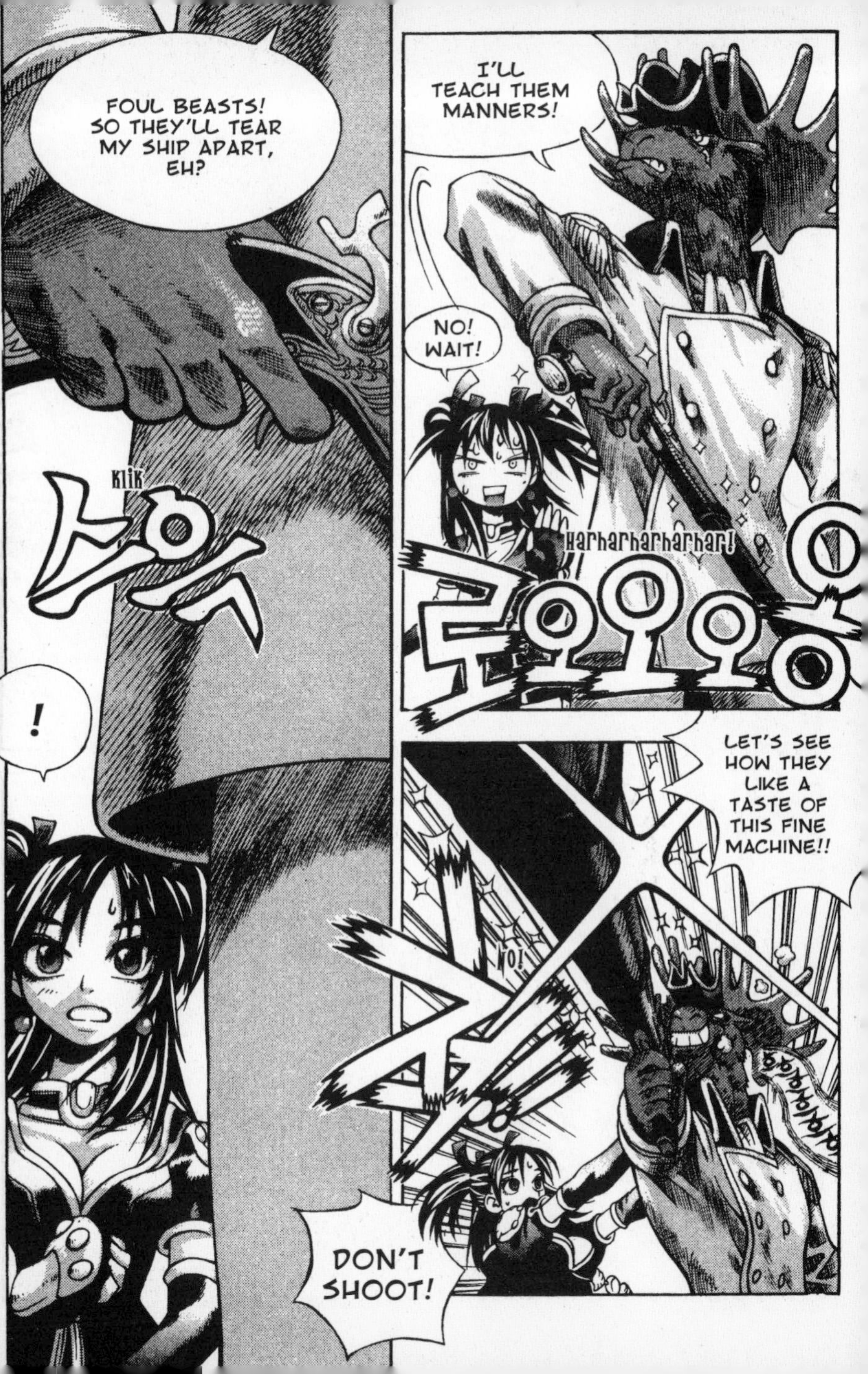
FOUL BEASTS! SO THEY'LL TEAR MY SHIP APART, EH?
Klik
!
I'LL TEACH THEM MANNERS!
NO! WAIT!
Harharharharharhar!
LET'S SEE HOW THEY LIKE A TASTE OF THIS FINE MACHINE!!
NO!
DON'T SHOOT!

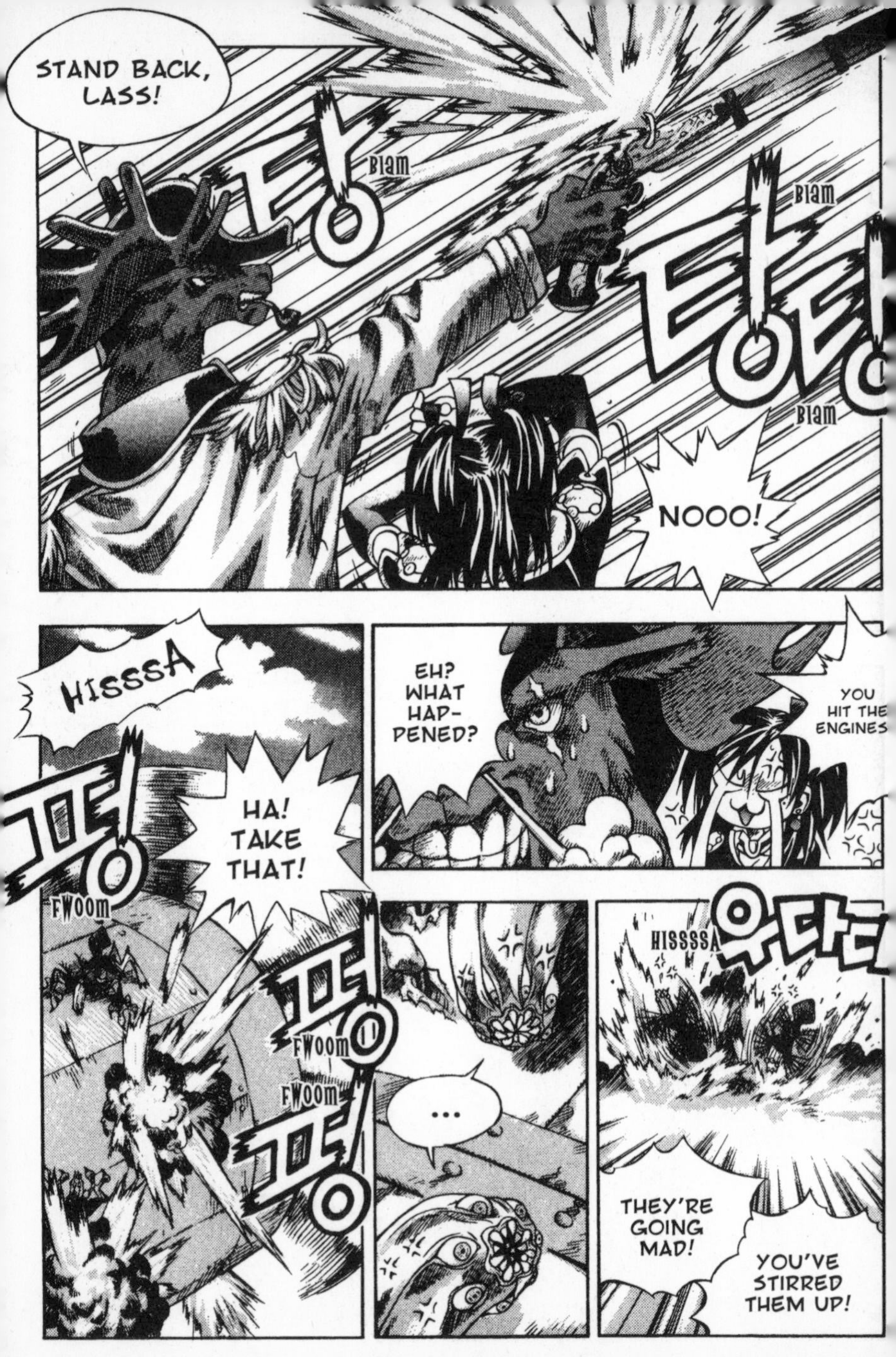
STAND BACK, LASS!
BLAM
BLAM
BLAM
NOOO!
HISSSA
HA! TAKE THAT!
FWOOM
FWOOM
FWOOM
EH? WHAT HAP-PENED?
YOU HIT THE ENGINES
...
HISSSSA
THEY'RE GOING MAD!
YOU'VE STIRRED THEM UP!

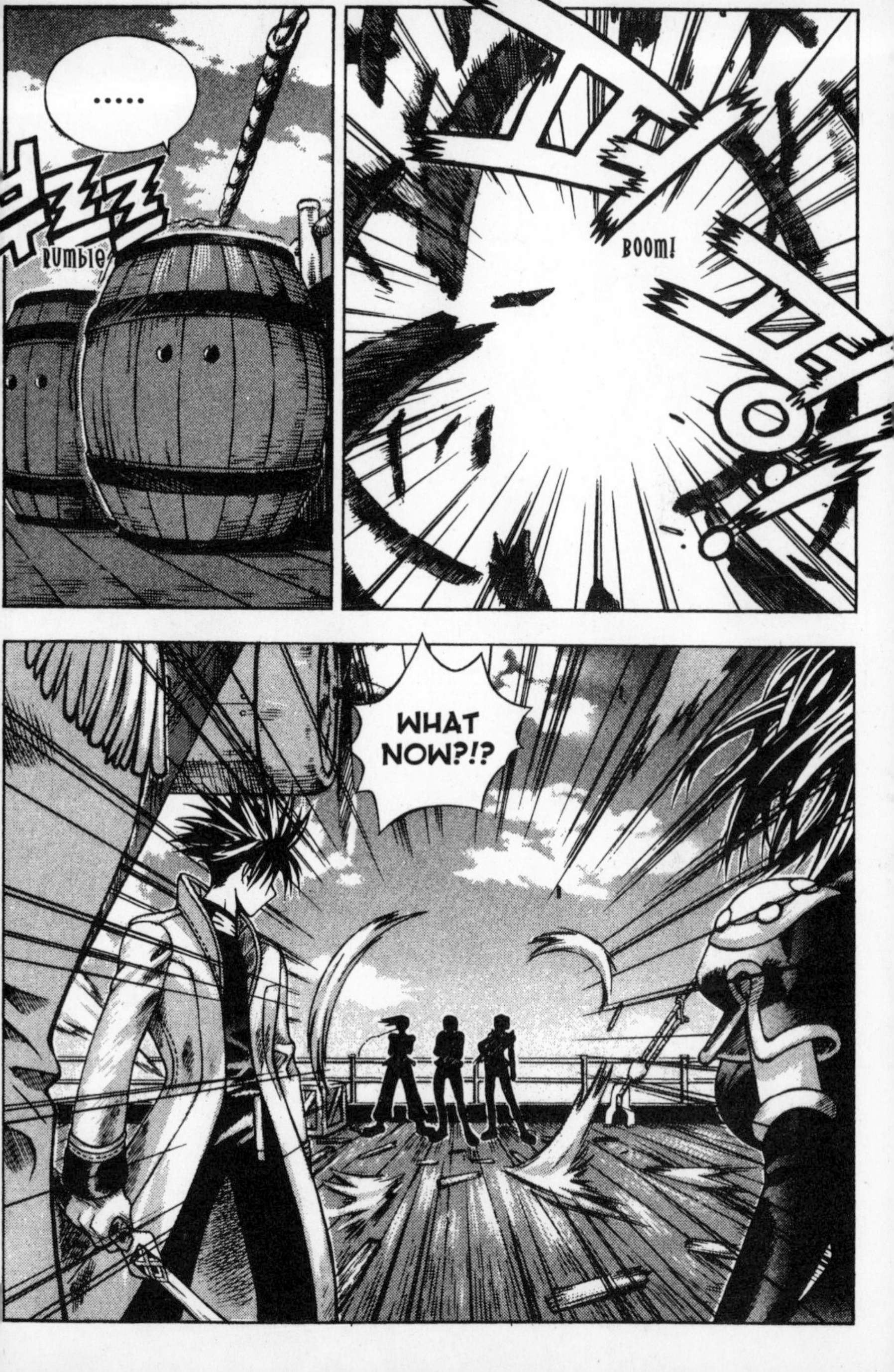
BOOM!
......
RUMBLE
WHAT NOW?!?

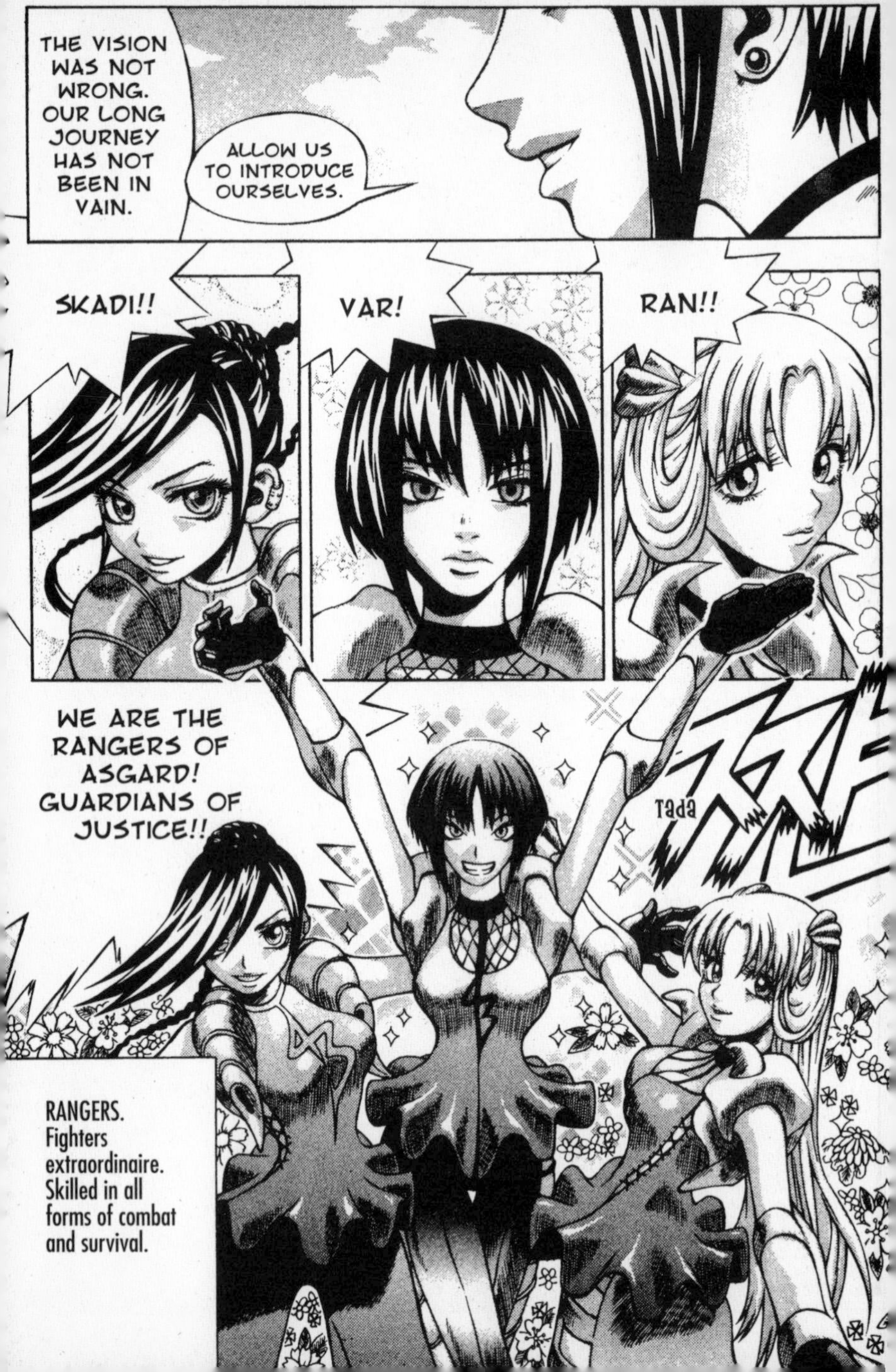
THE VISION WAS NOT WRONG. OUR LONG JOURNEY HAS NOT BEEN IN VAIN.
ALLOW US TO INTRODUCE OURSELVES.
SKADI!!
VAR!
RAN!!
WE ARE THE RANGERS OF ASGARD! GUARDIANS OF JUSTICE!!
TADA
RANGERS. Fighters extraordinaire. Skilled in all forms of combat and survival.

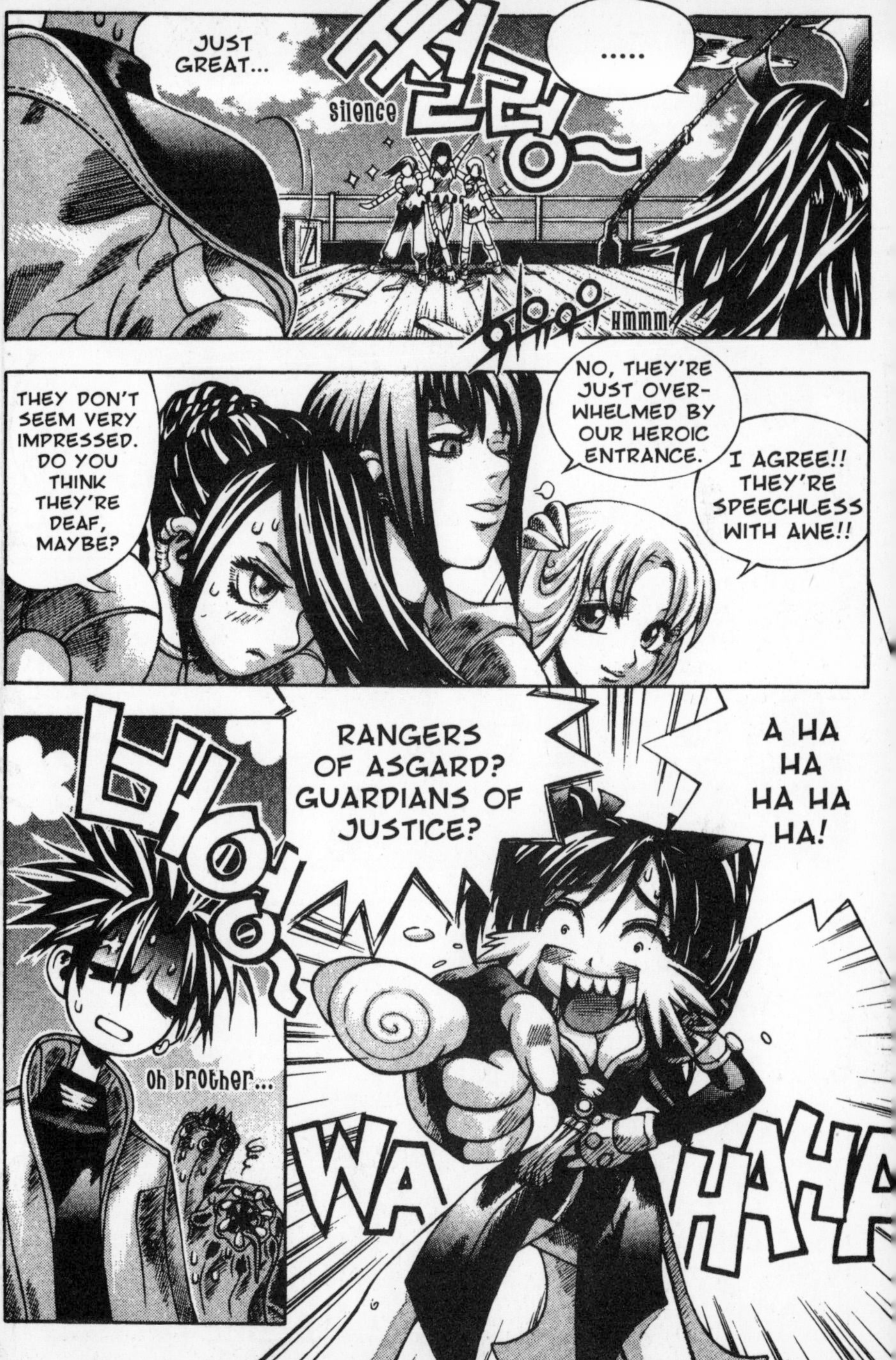
JUST GREAT...
Silence
.....
HMMM
THEY DON'T SEEM VERY IMPRESSED. DO YOU THINK THEY'RE DEAF, MAYBE?
NO, THEY'RE JUST OVER-WHELMED BY OUR HEROIC ENTRANCE.
I AGREE!! THEY'RE SPEECHLESS WITH AWE!!
RANGERS OF ASGARD? GUARDIANS OF JUSTICE?
A HA HA HA HA HA!
Oh brother...
WA HAHA

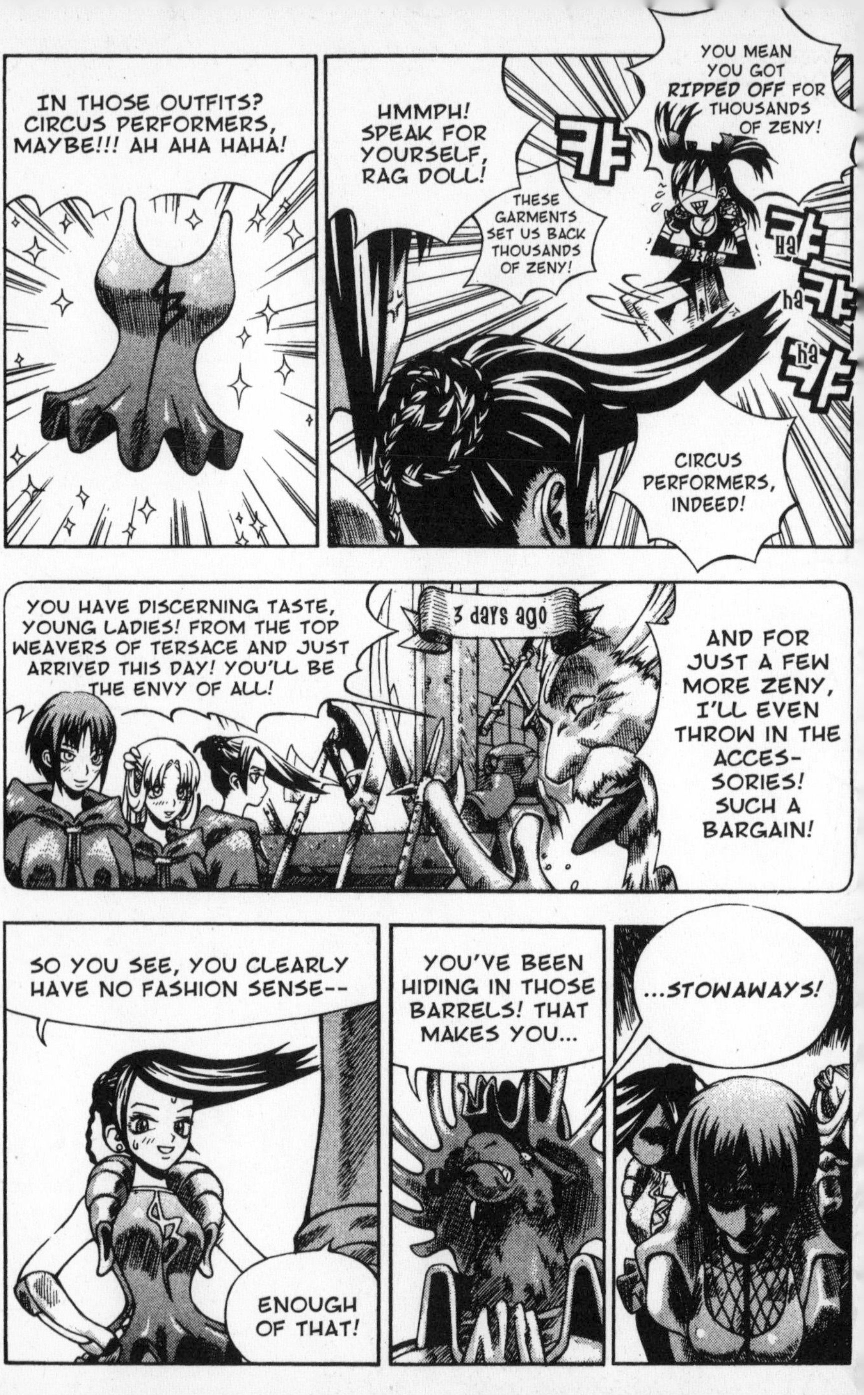
IN THOSE OUTFITS? CIRCUS PERFORMERS, MAYBE!!! AH AHA HAHA!
HMMPH! SPEAK FOR YOURSELF, RAG DOLL!
THESE GARMENTS SET US BACK THOUSANDS OF ZENY!
YOU MEAN YOU GOT RIPPED OFF FOR THOUSANDS OF ZENY!
카
카 HA
카 ha
카 ha
CIRCUS PERFORMERS, INDEED!
3 days ago
YOU HAVE DISCERNING TASTE, YOUNG LADIES! FROM THE TOP WEAVERS OF TERSACE AND JUST ARRIVED THIS DAY! YOU'LL BE THE ENVY OF ALL!
AND FOR JUST A FEW MORE ZENY, I'LL EVEN THROW IN THE ACCES-SORIES! SUCH A BARGAIN!
SO YOU SEE, YOU CLEARLY HAVE NO FASHION SENSE--
ENOUGH OF THAT!
YOU'VE BEEN HIDING IN THOSE BARRELS! THAT MAKES YOU...
...STOWAWAYS!

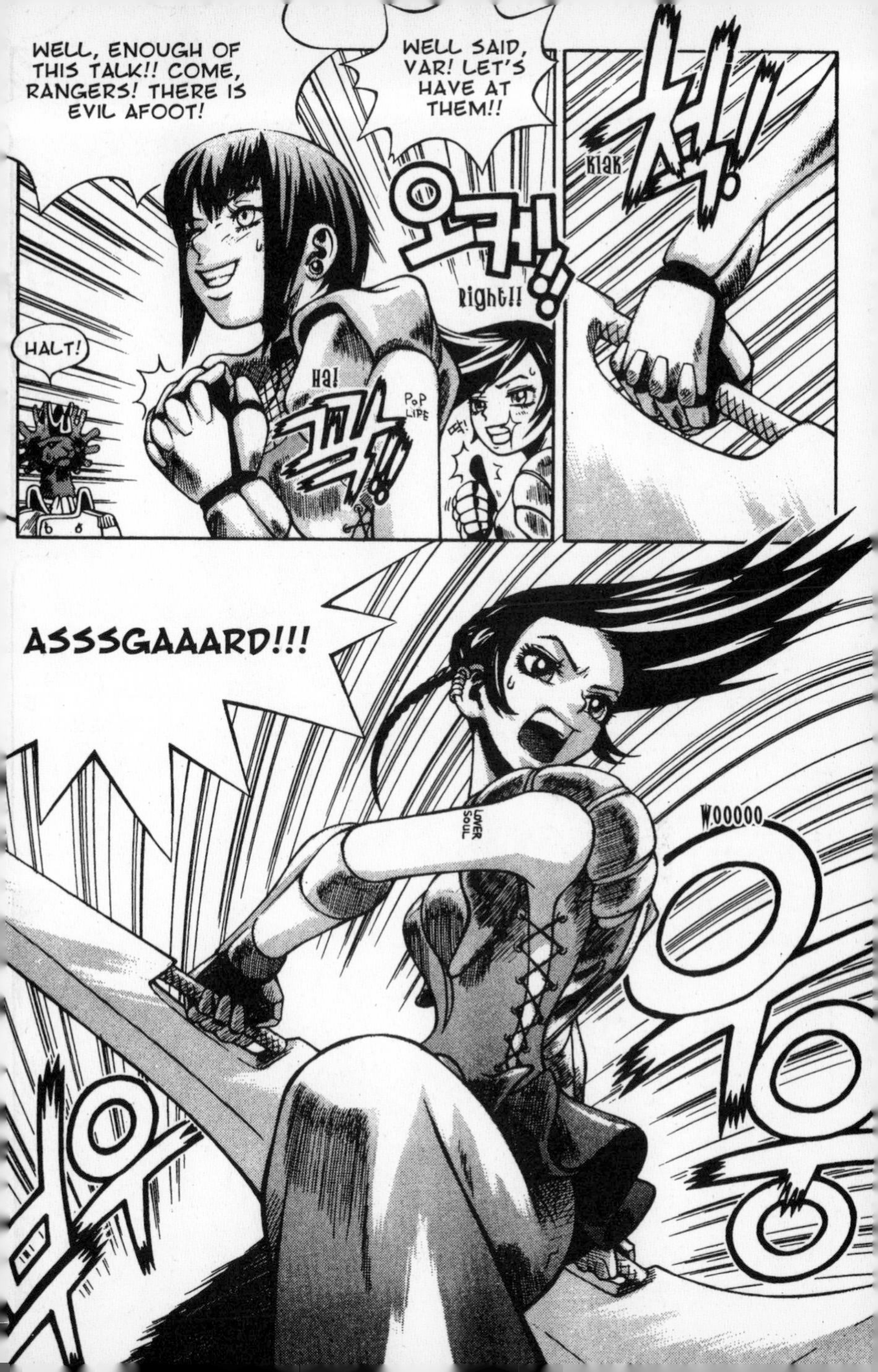

WELL, ENOUGH OF THIS TALK!! COME, RANGERS! THERE IS EVIL AFOOT!
WELL SAID, VAR! LET'S HAVE AT THEM!!
Right!!
HALT!
Ha!
KIAK
ASSSGAARD!!!
LOVER SOUL
W.OOOOO

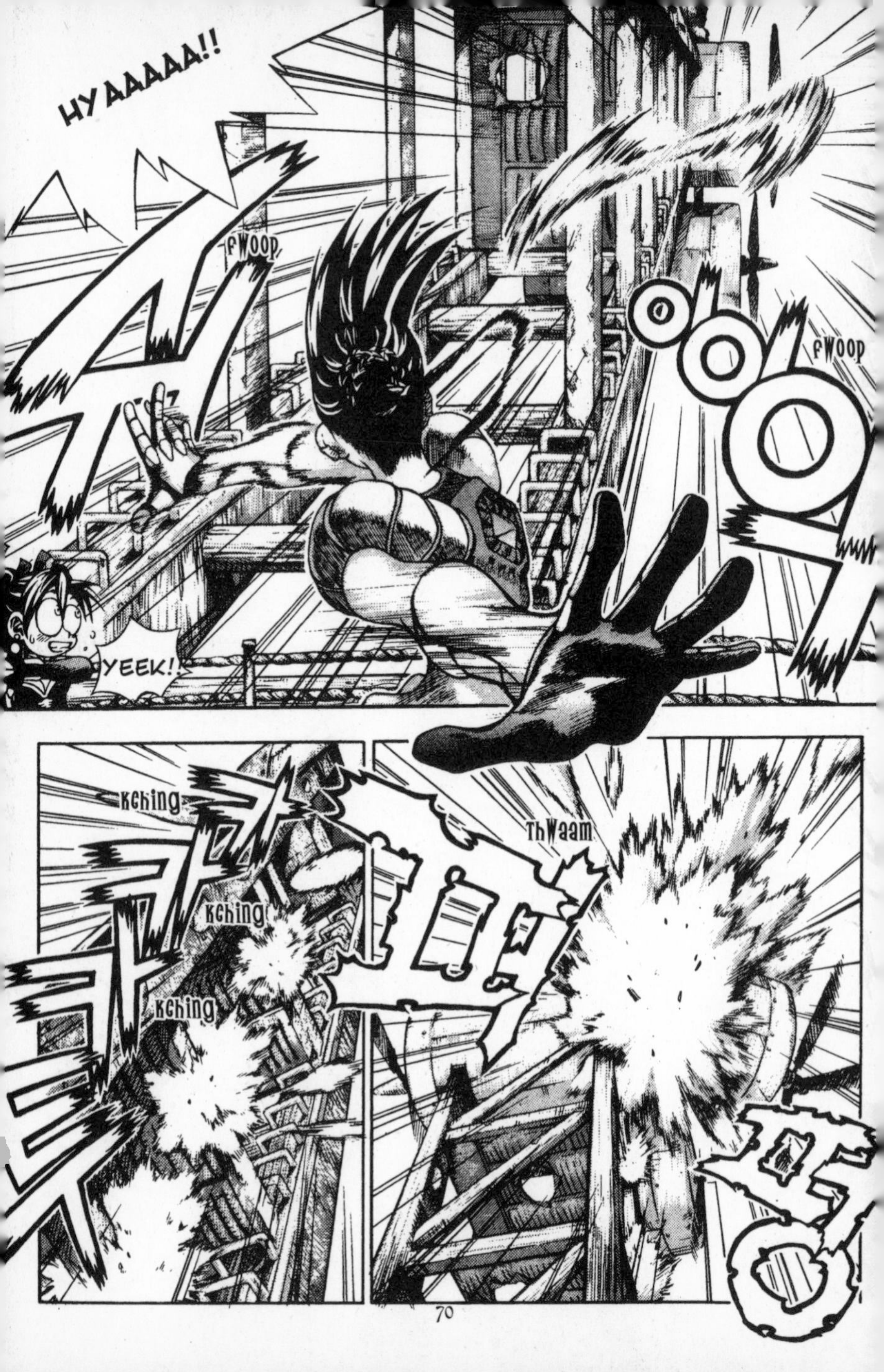
FWOOP
HYAAAAA!!
FWOOP
YEEK!!
Thwaam
Kching
Kching
Kching

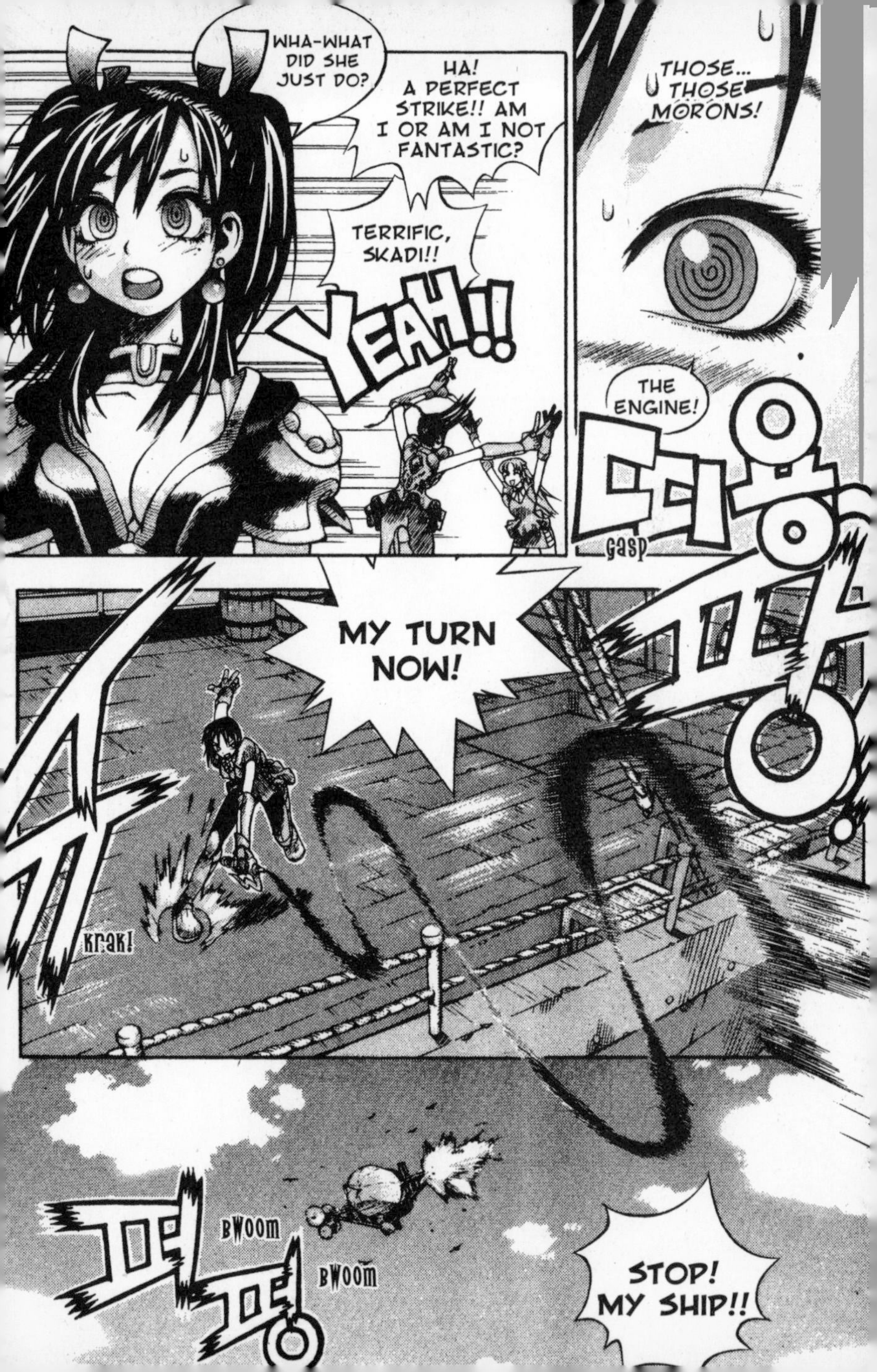
WHA-WHAT DID SHE JUST DO?
HA! A PERFECT STRIKE!! AM I OR AM I NOT FANTASTIC?
TERRIFIC, SKADI!!
YEAH!!
THOSE... THOSE MORONS!
THE ENGINE!
GASP
MY TURN NOW!
KRAK!
BWOOM
BWOOM
STOP! MY SHIP!!

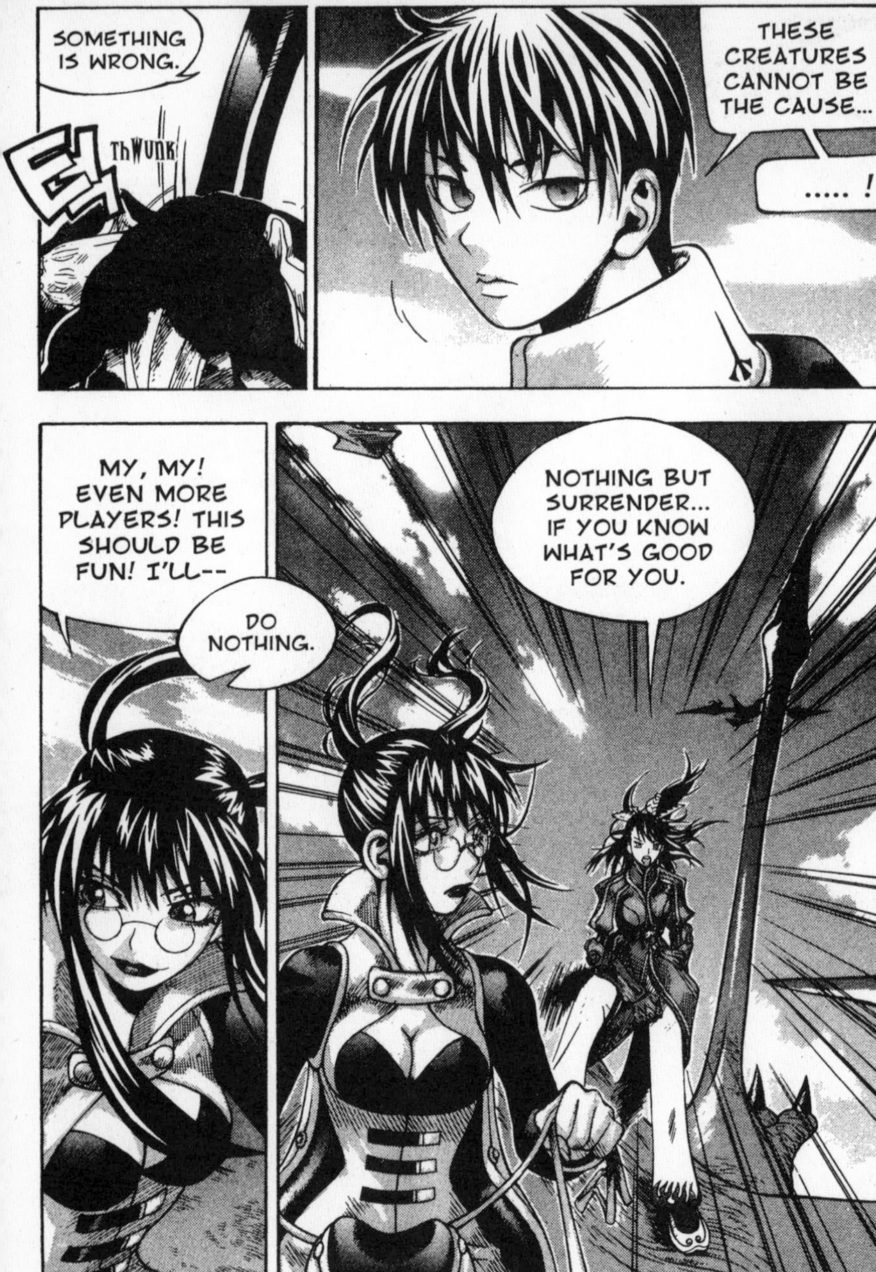
SOMETHING IS WRONG.
ThWUNK
THESE CREATURES CANNOT BE THE CAUSE...
..... !
MY, MY! EVEN MORE PLAYERS! THIS SHOULD BE FUN! I'LL--
DO NOTHING.
NOTHING BUT SURRENDER... IF YOU KNOW WHAT'S GOOD FOR YOU.

RAGNAROK
라그나로크
IN TO THE ABYSS

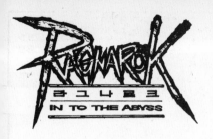

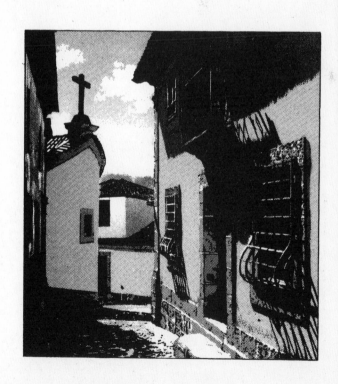

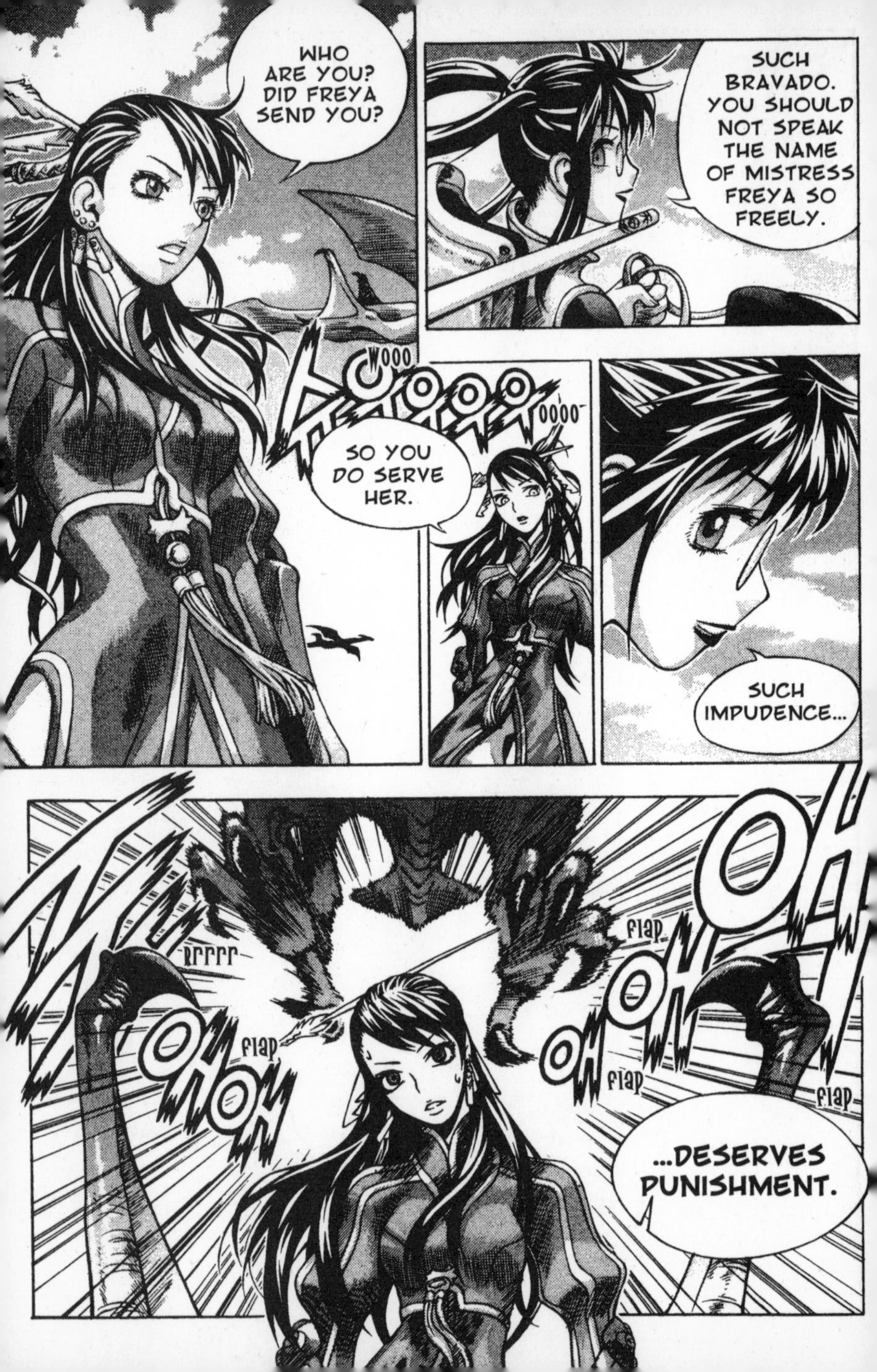
WHO ARE YOU? DID FREYA SEND YOU?
SUCH BRAVADO. YOU SHOULD NOT SPEAK THE NAME OF MISTRESS FREYA SO FREELY.
WOOO
OOOO
SO YOU DO SERVE HER.
SUCH IMPUDENCE...
rrrr
flap
flap
flap
flap
...DESERVES PUNISHMENT.

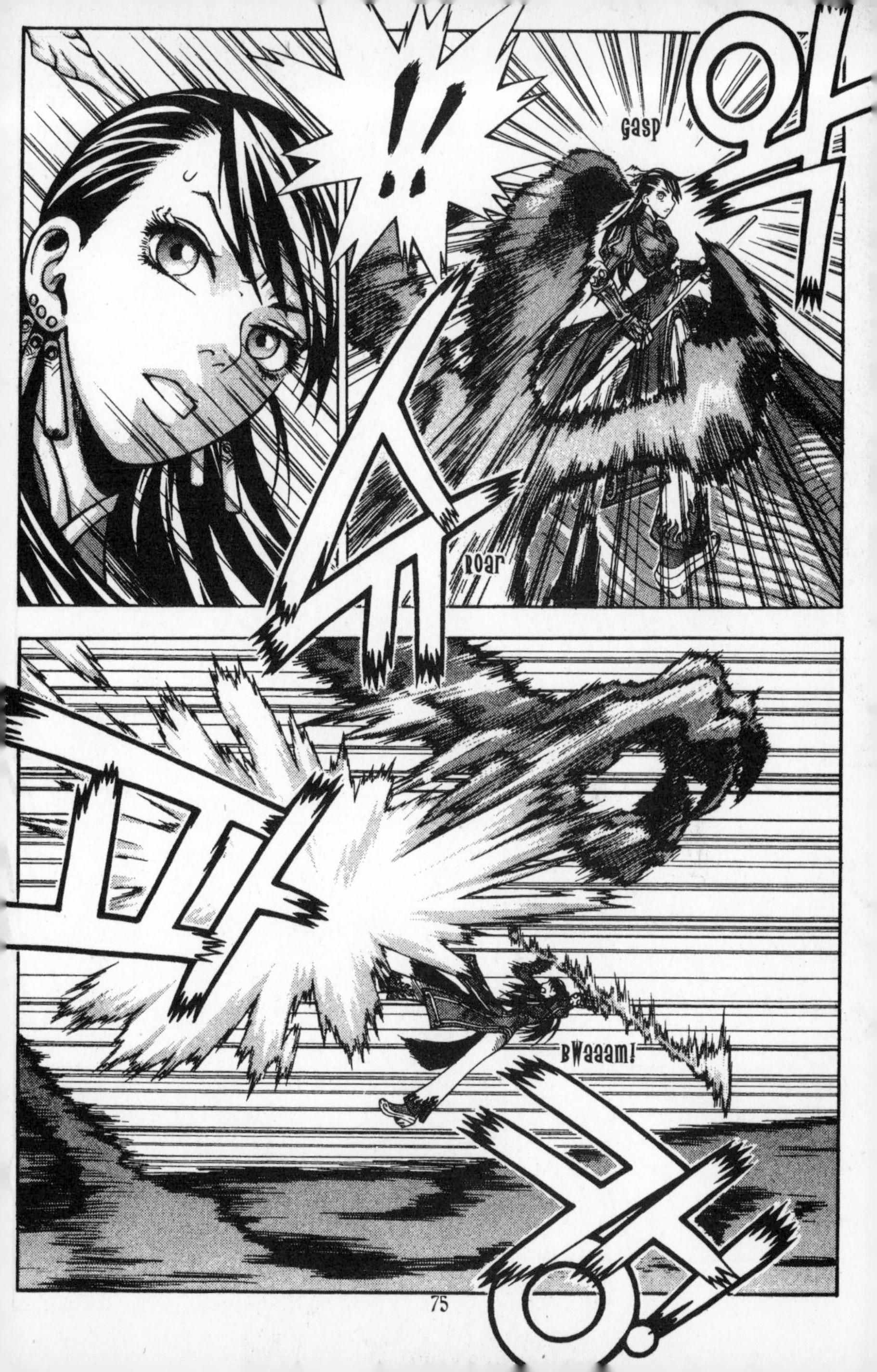
Gasp
!!
Roar
BWaaam!

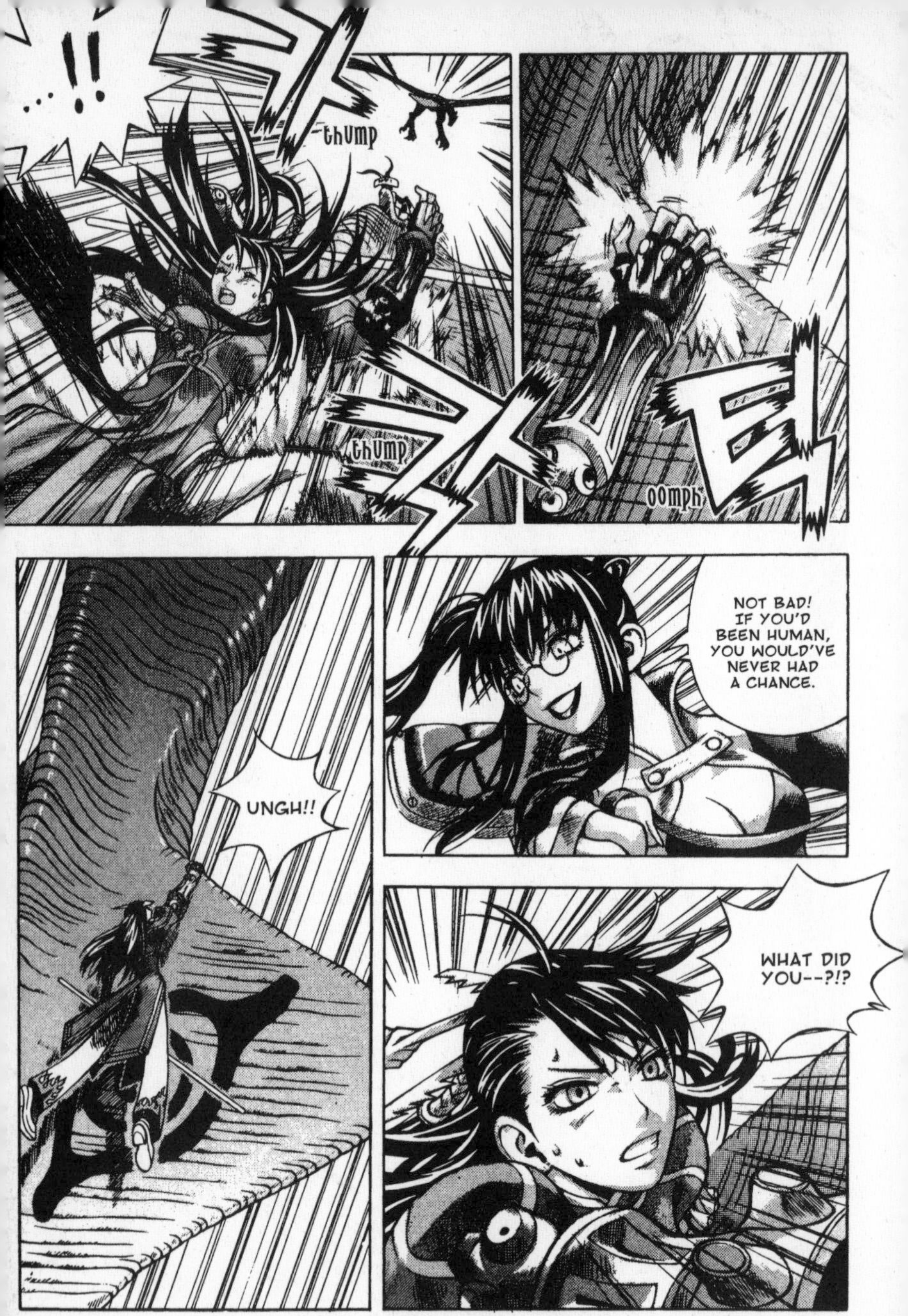
...!!
thump
thump
oomph
UNGH!!
NOT BAD! IF YOU'D BEEN HUMAN, YOU WOULD'VE NEVER HAD A CHANCE.
WHAT DID YOU--?!?

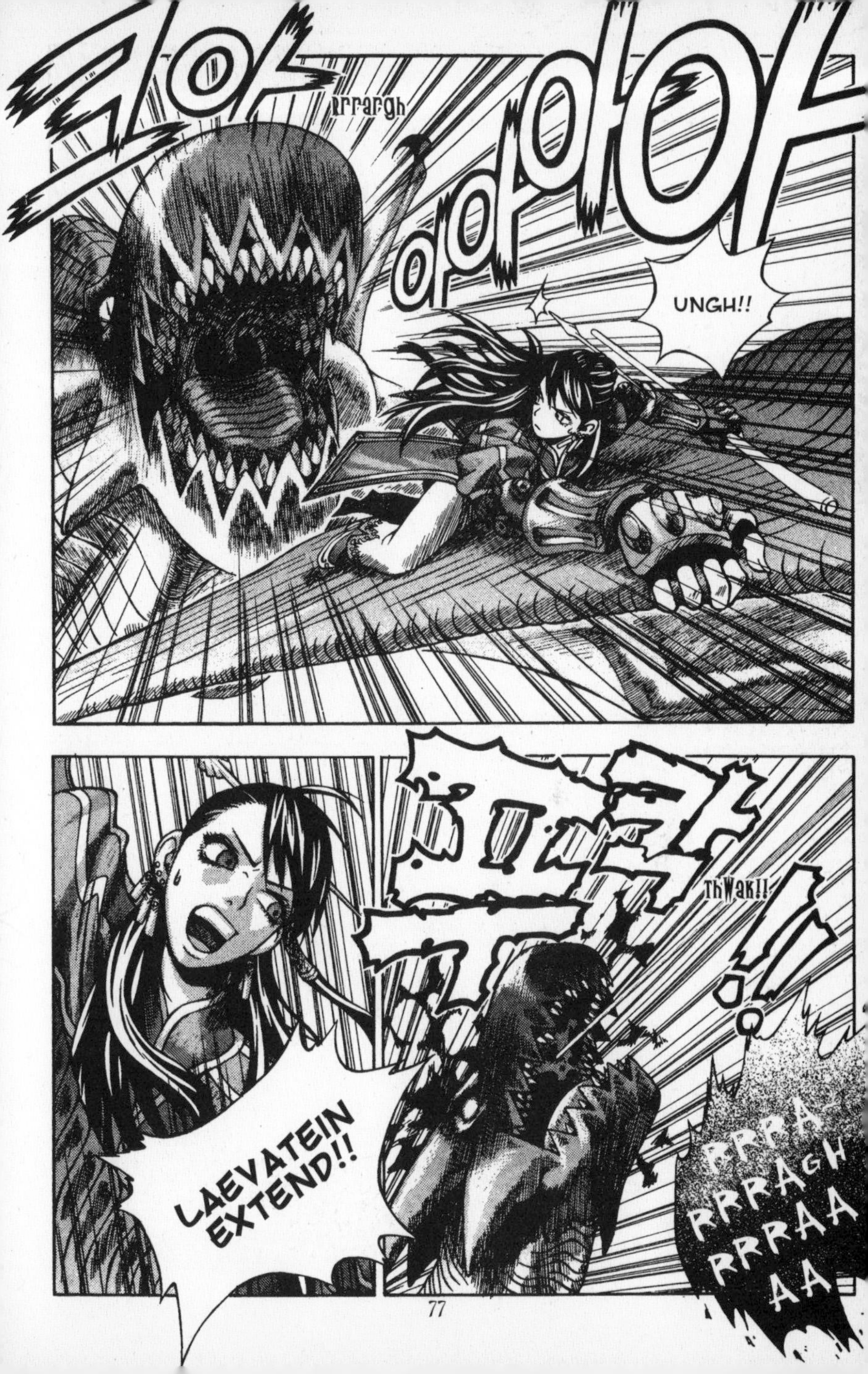
rrrargh
UNGH!!
LAEVATEIN EXTEND!!
ThWak!!
RRRA
RRRAGH
RRRAA
RRRAA
AA

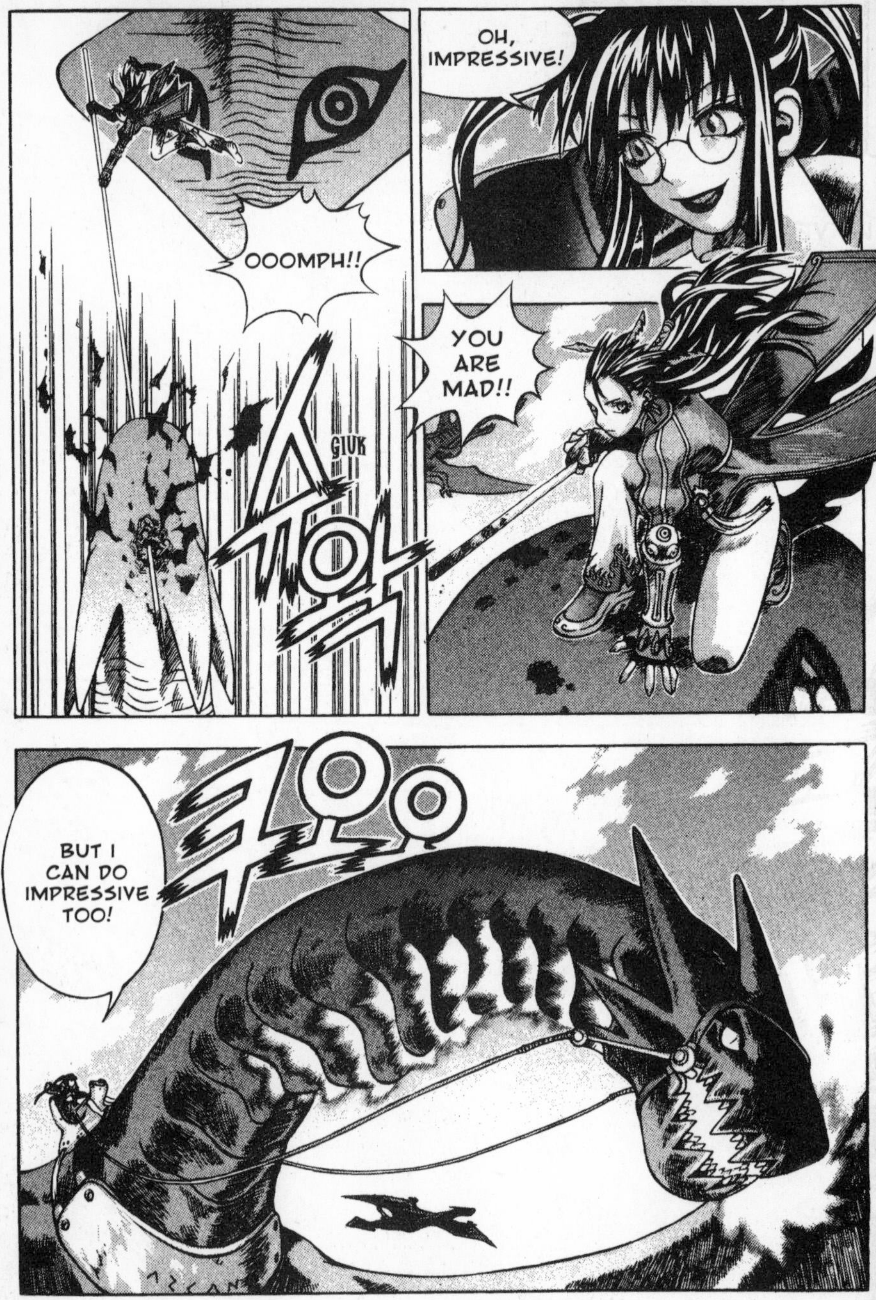
OOOMPH!!
GIUK
OH, IMPRESSIVE!
YOU ARE MAD!!
BUT I CAN DO IMPRESSIVE TOO!

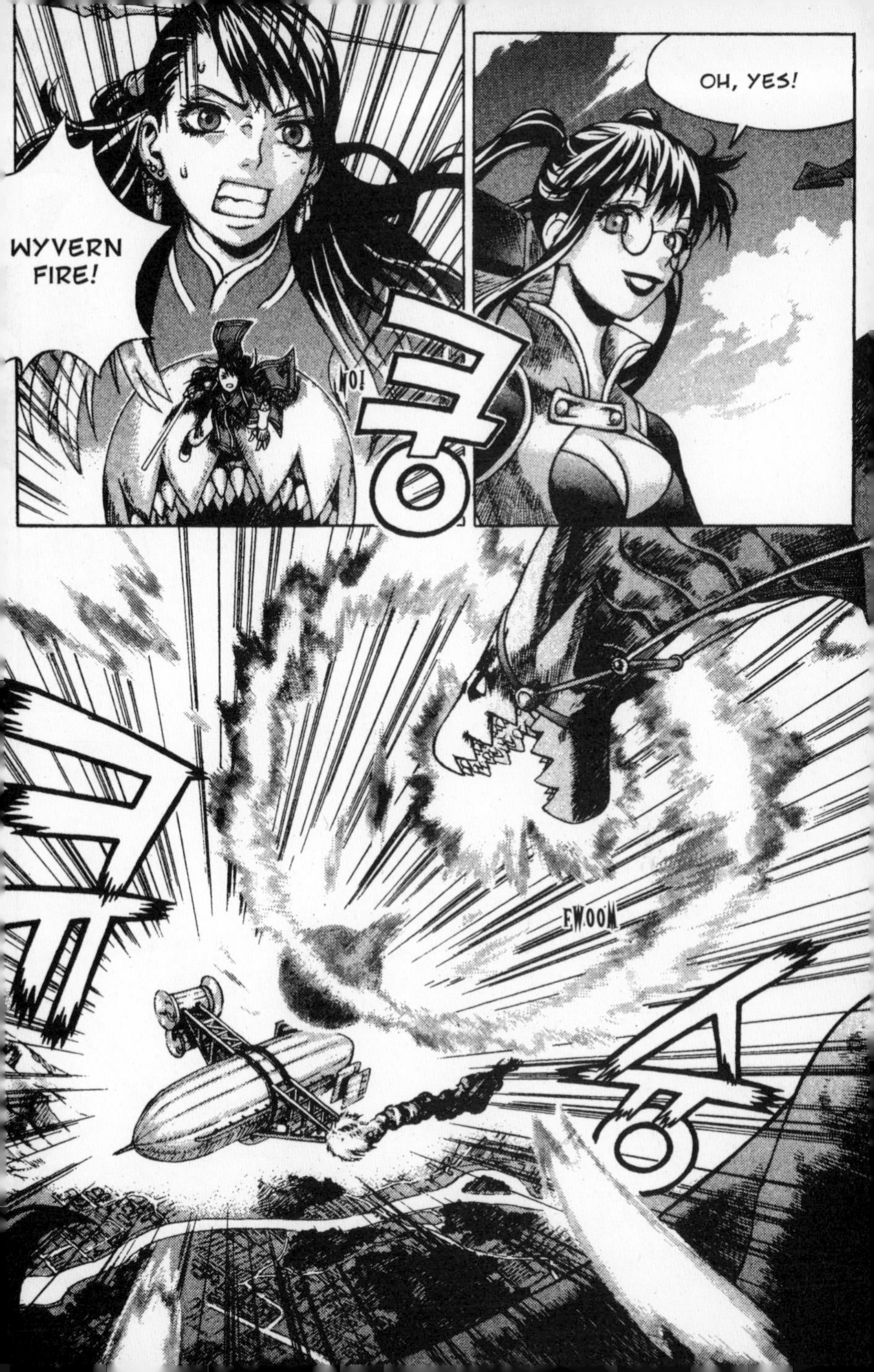
OH, YES!
WYVERN FIRE!
NO!
FWOOM

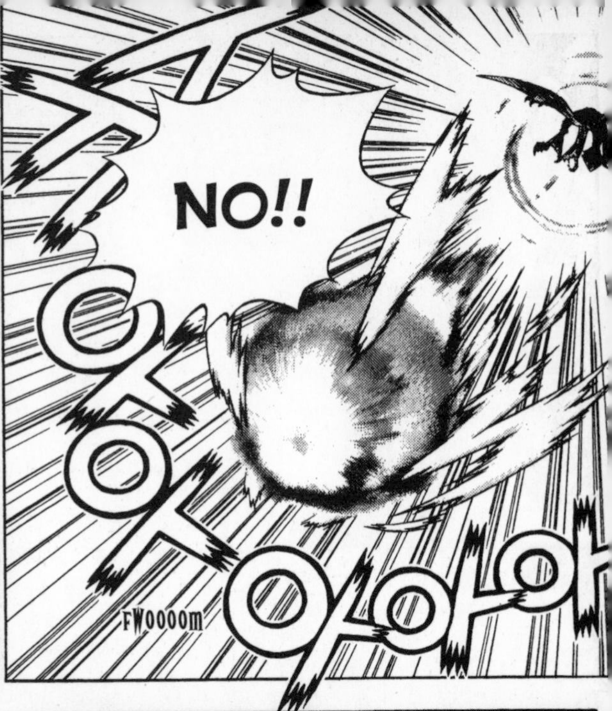
NO!!
FWOOOOM
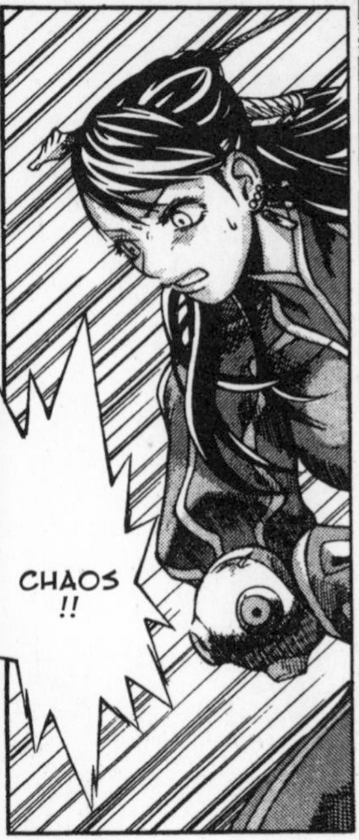
CHAOS
!!
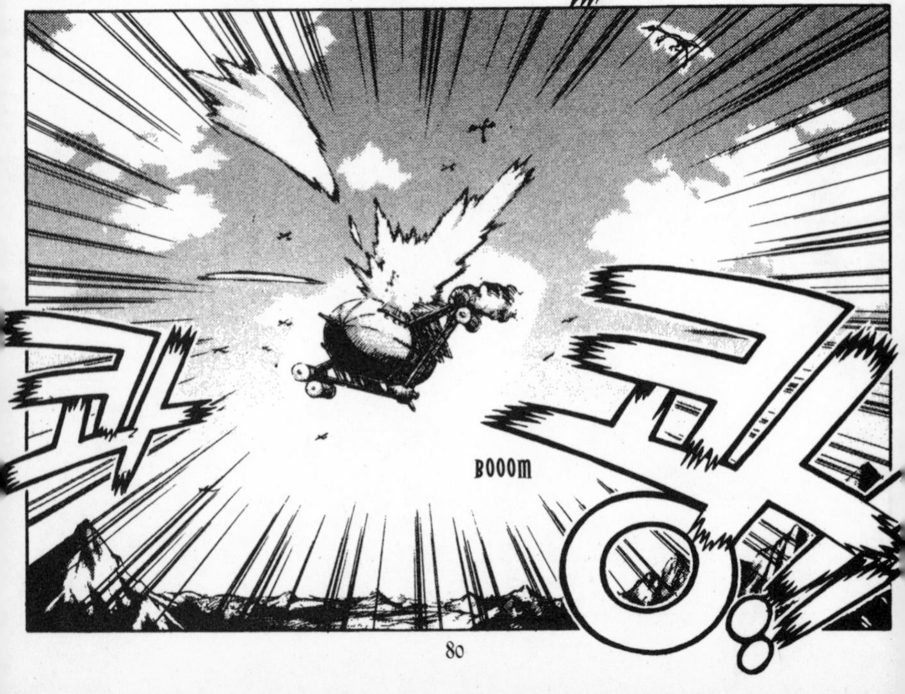
BOOOM

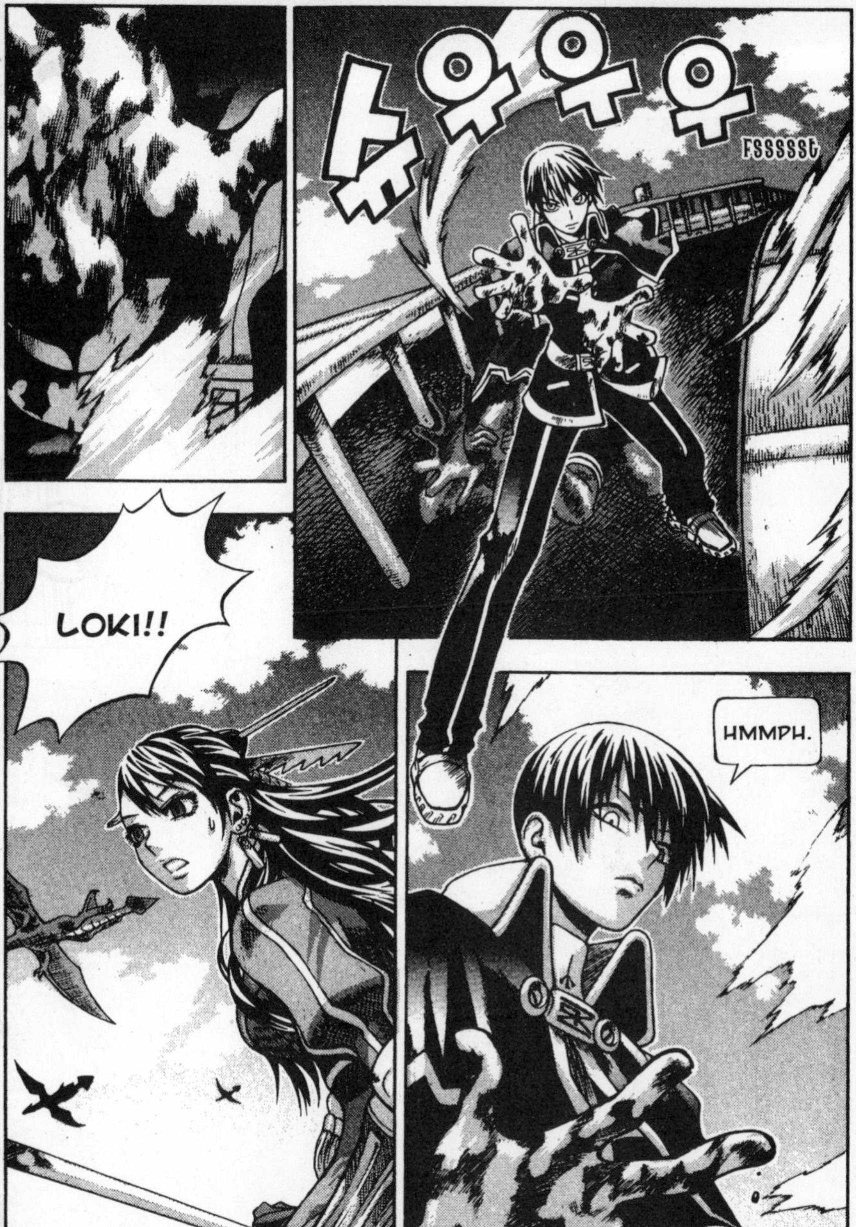
FSSSSSt
LOKI!!
HMMPH.

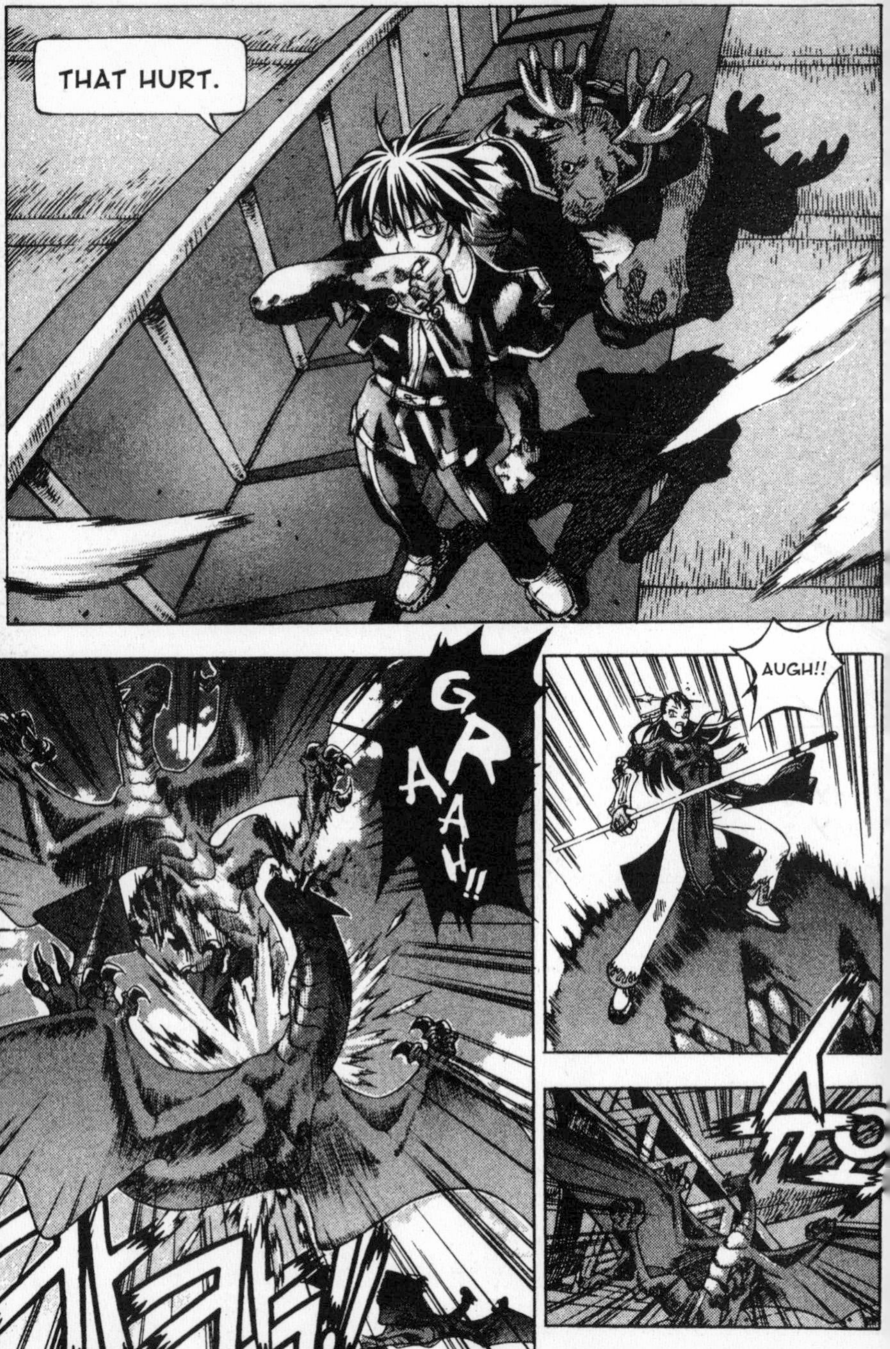
THAT HURT.
AUGH!!
GRAAH!!

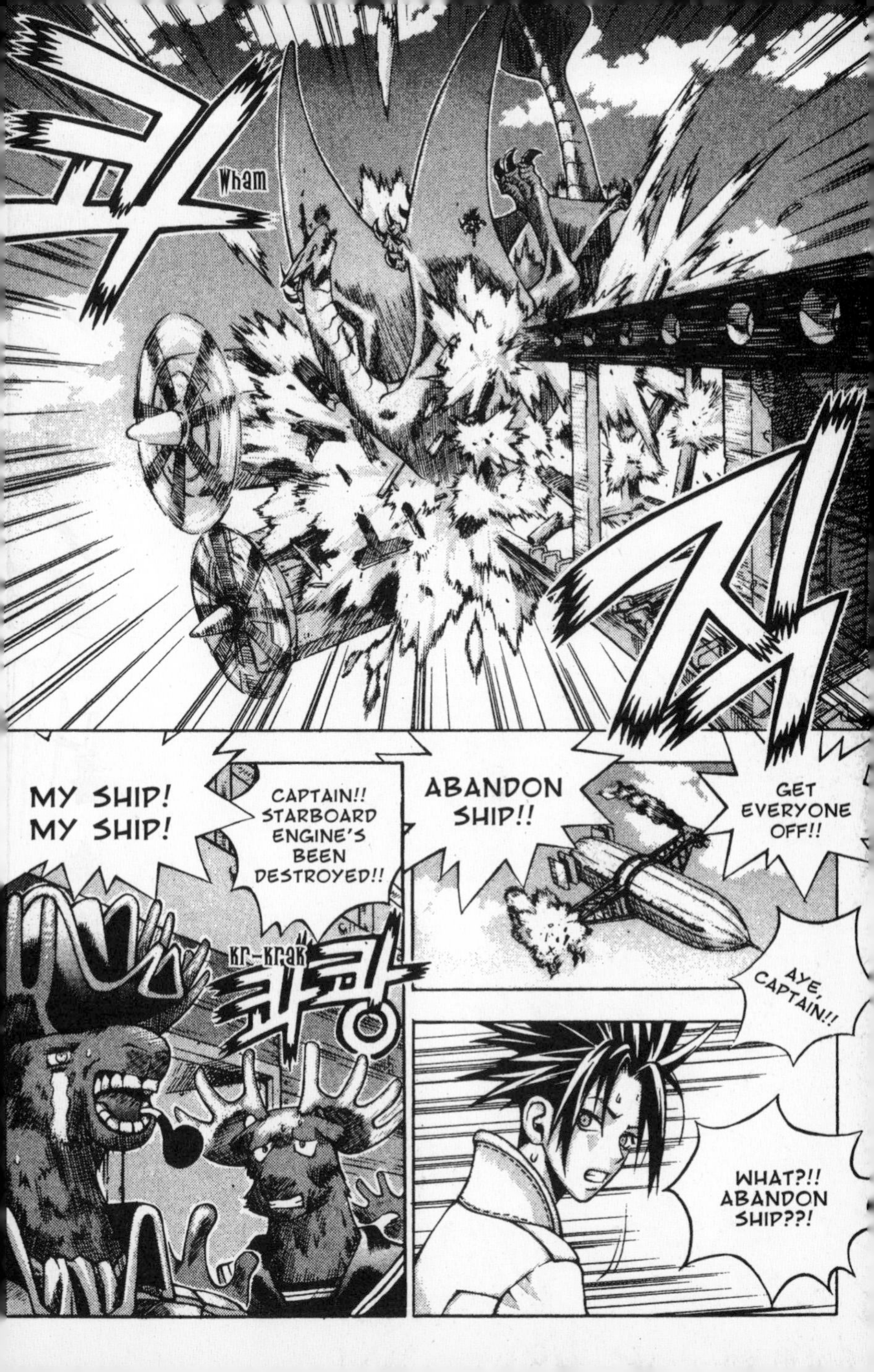
Wham
MY SHIP! MY SHIP!
CAPTAIN!! STARBOARD ENGINE'S BEEN DESTROYED!!
Kr-krak
ABANDON SHIP!!
GET EVERYONE OFF!!
AYE, CAPTAIN!!
WHAT?!! ABANDON SHIP??!

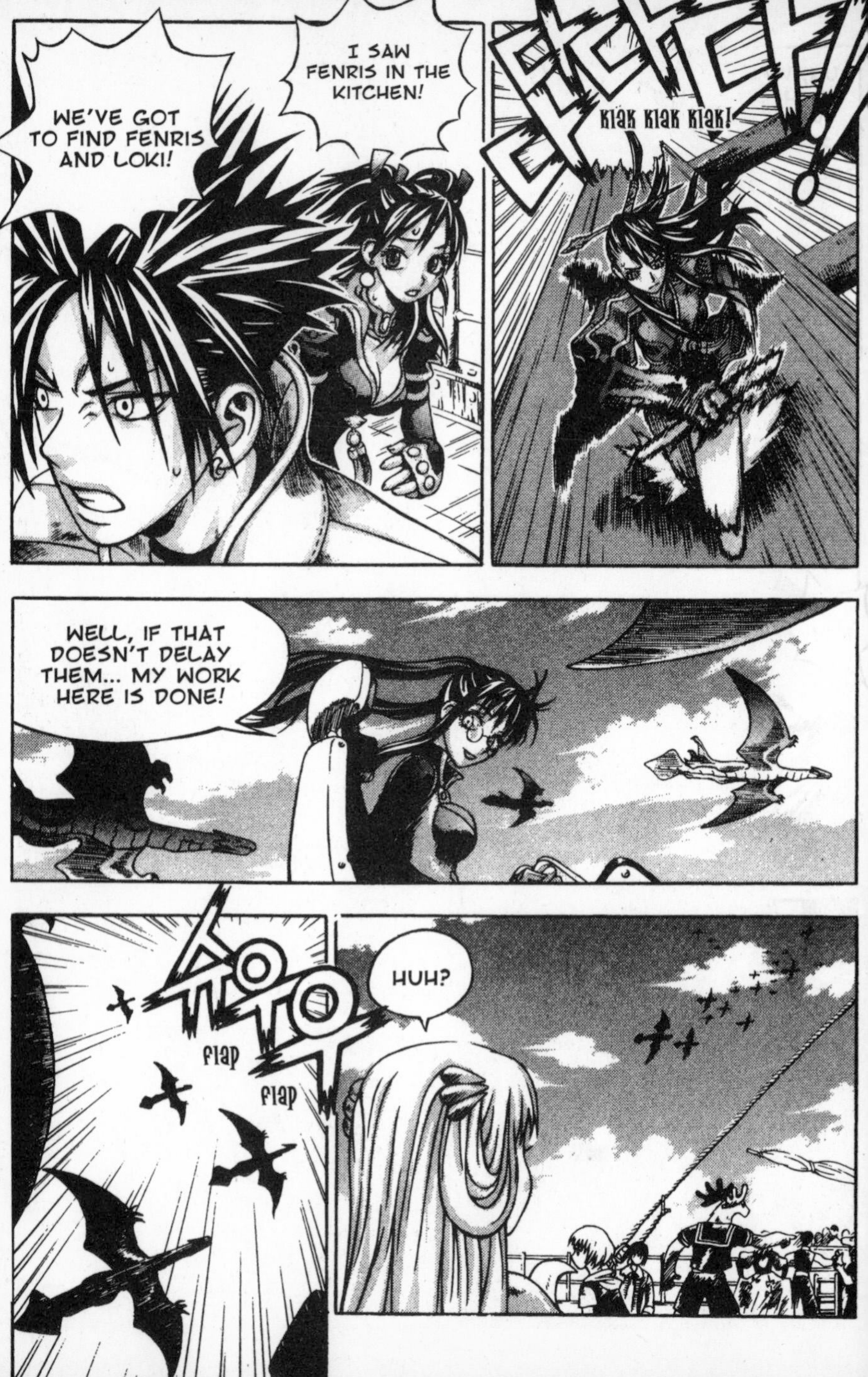
WE'VE GOT TO FIND FENRIS AND LOKI!
I SAW FENRIS IN THE KITCHEN!
Klak klak klak!
WELL, IF THAT DOESN'T DELAY THEM... MY WORK HERE IS DONE!
flap
flap
HUH?

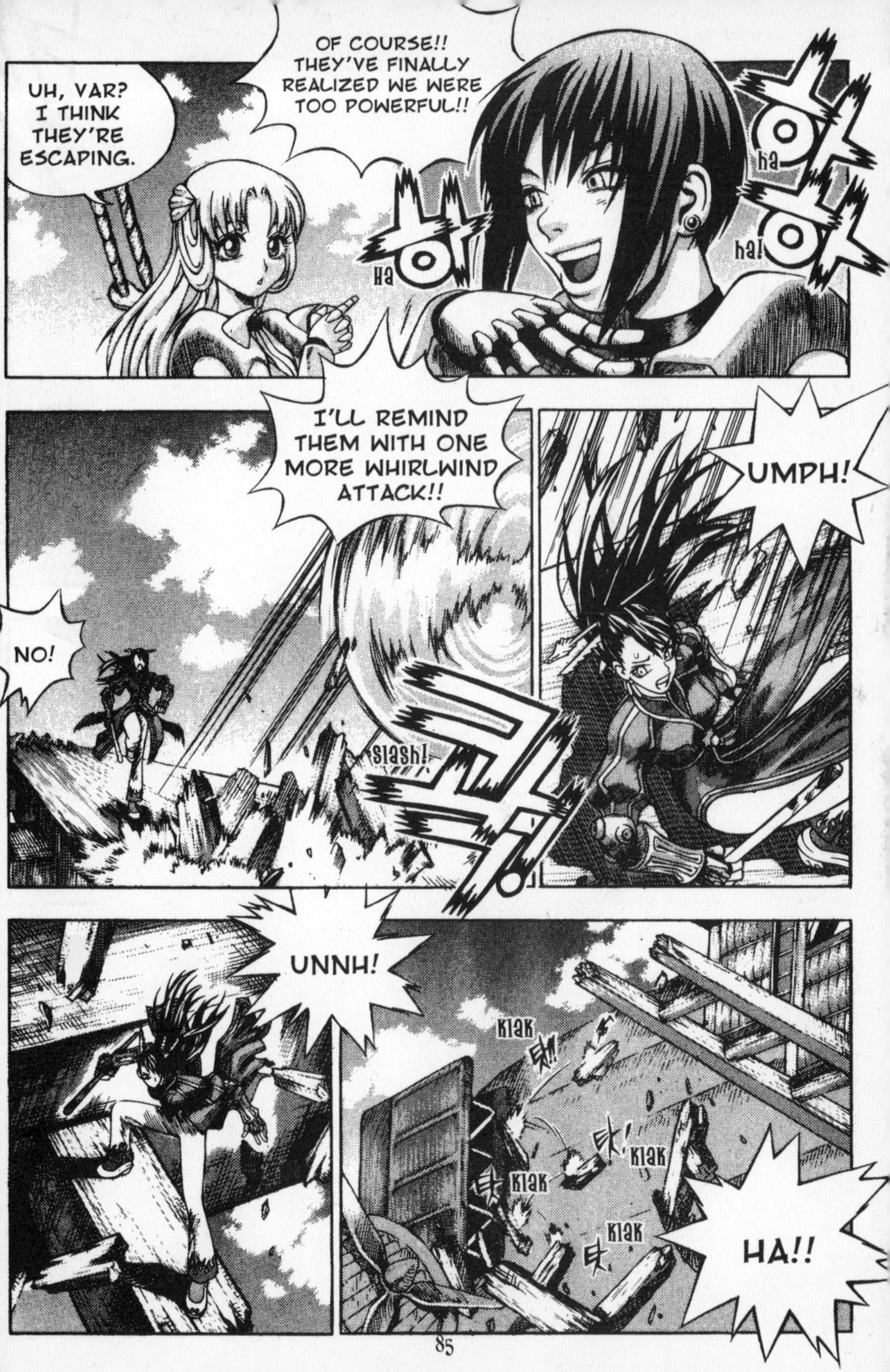
UH, VAR? I THINK THEY'RE ESCAPING.
OF COURSE!! THEY'VE FINALLY REALIZED WE WERE TOO POWERFUL!!
HA
ha
ha!
I'LL REMIND THEM WITH ONE MORE WHIRLWIND ATTACK!!
NO!
slash!
UMPH!
UNNH!
klak
klak
klak
klak
HA!!

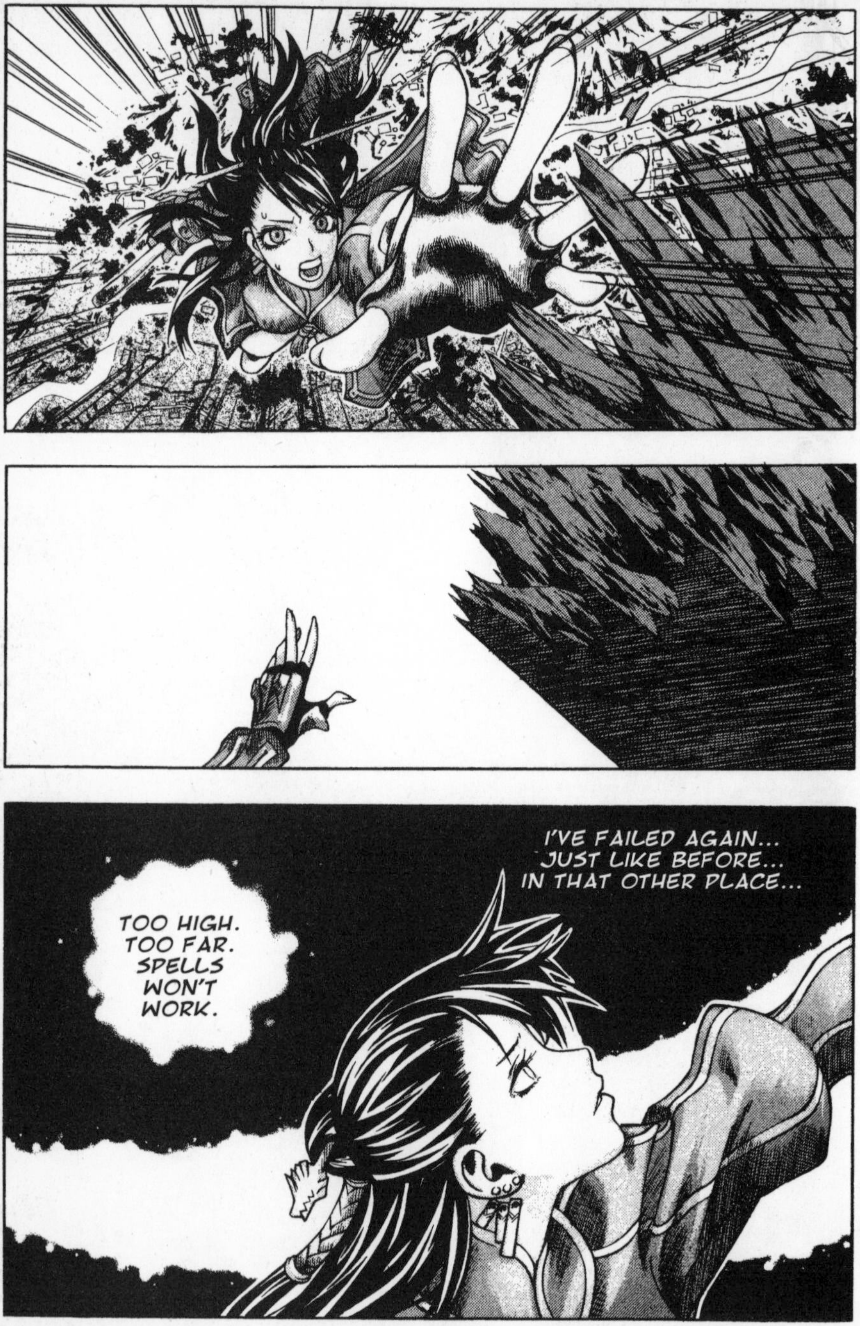
I'VE FAILED AGAIN...
JUST LIKE BEFORE...
IN THAT OTHER PLACE...
TOO HIGH. TOO FAR. SPELLS WON'T WORK.

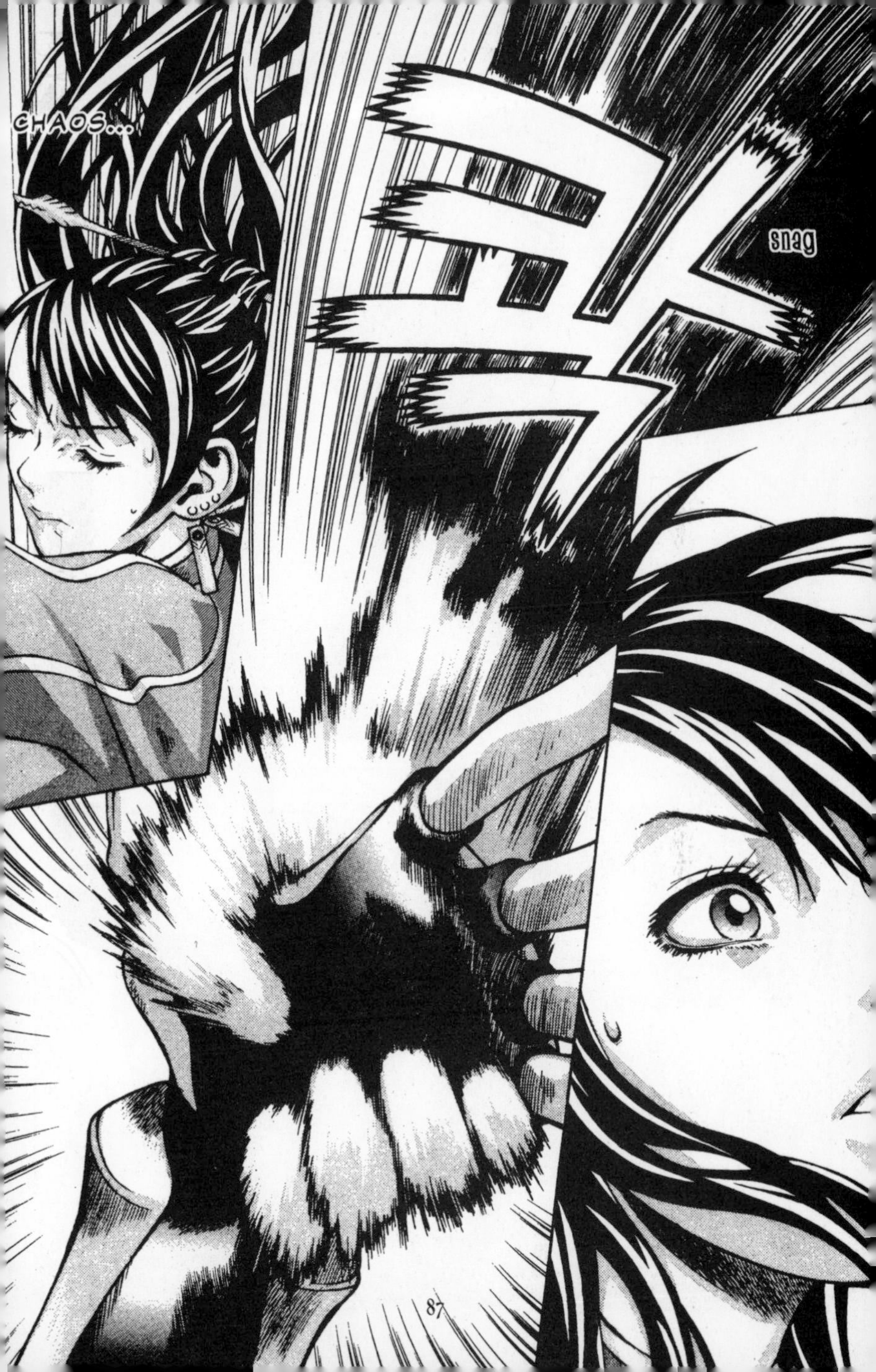
snag
CHAOS...

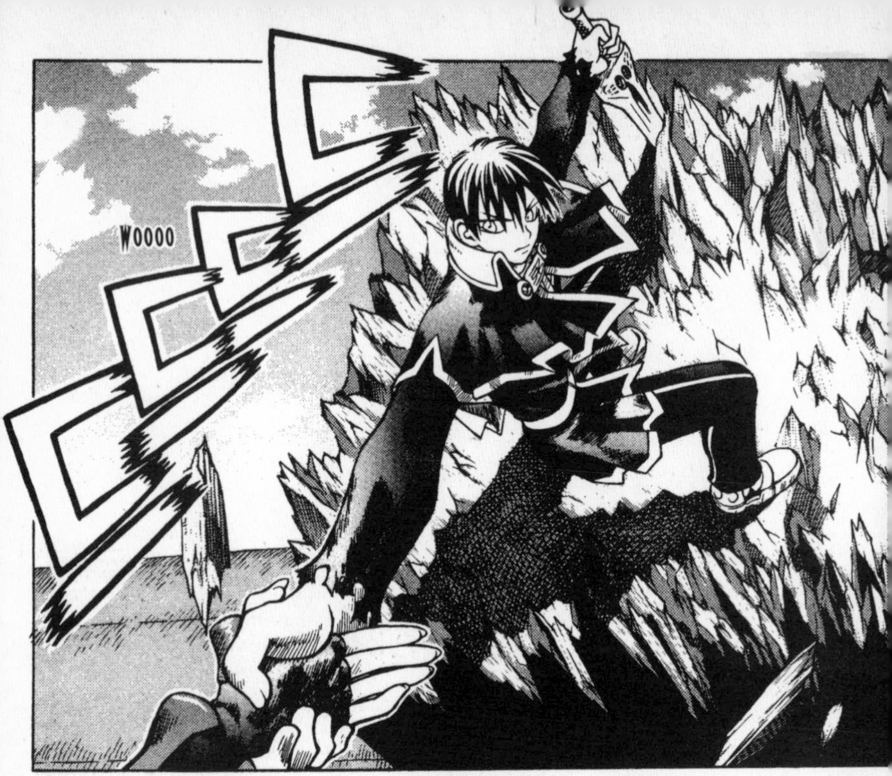
WOOOO

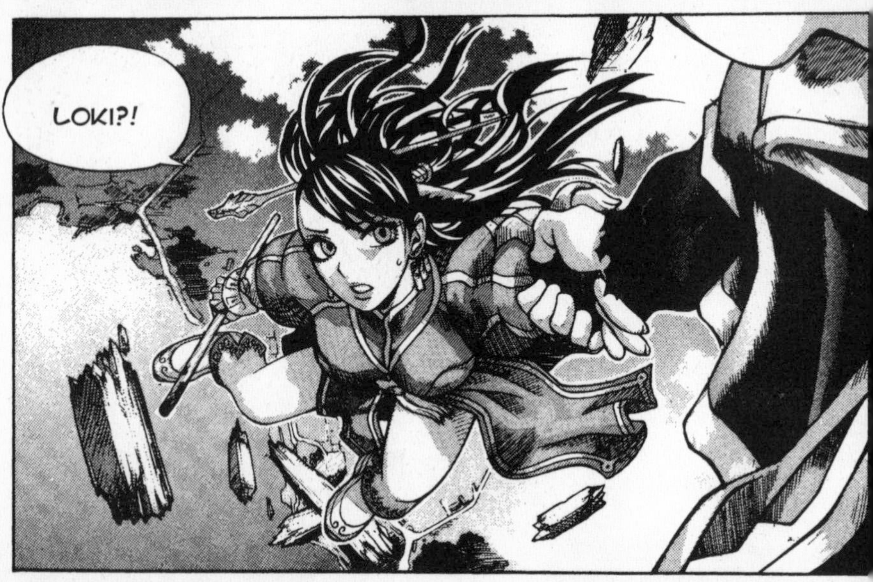
LOKI?!

RAGNAROK
라그나로크
IN TO THE ABYSS

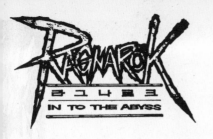

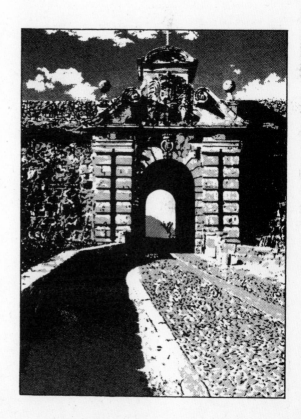

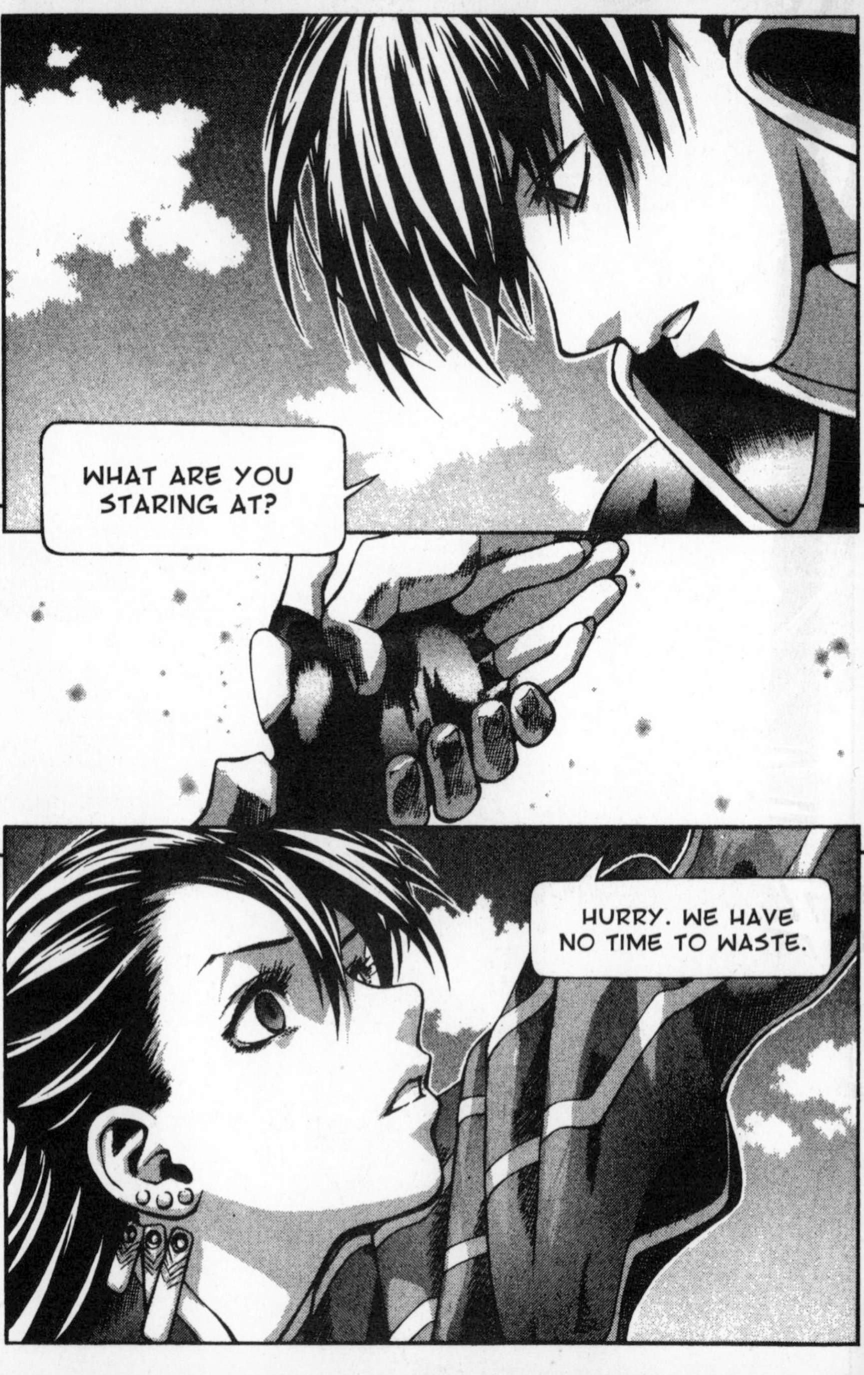
WHAT ARE YOU STARING AT?
HURRY. WE HAVE NO TIME TO WASTE.

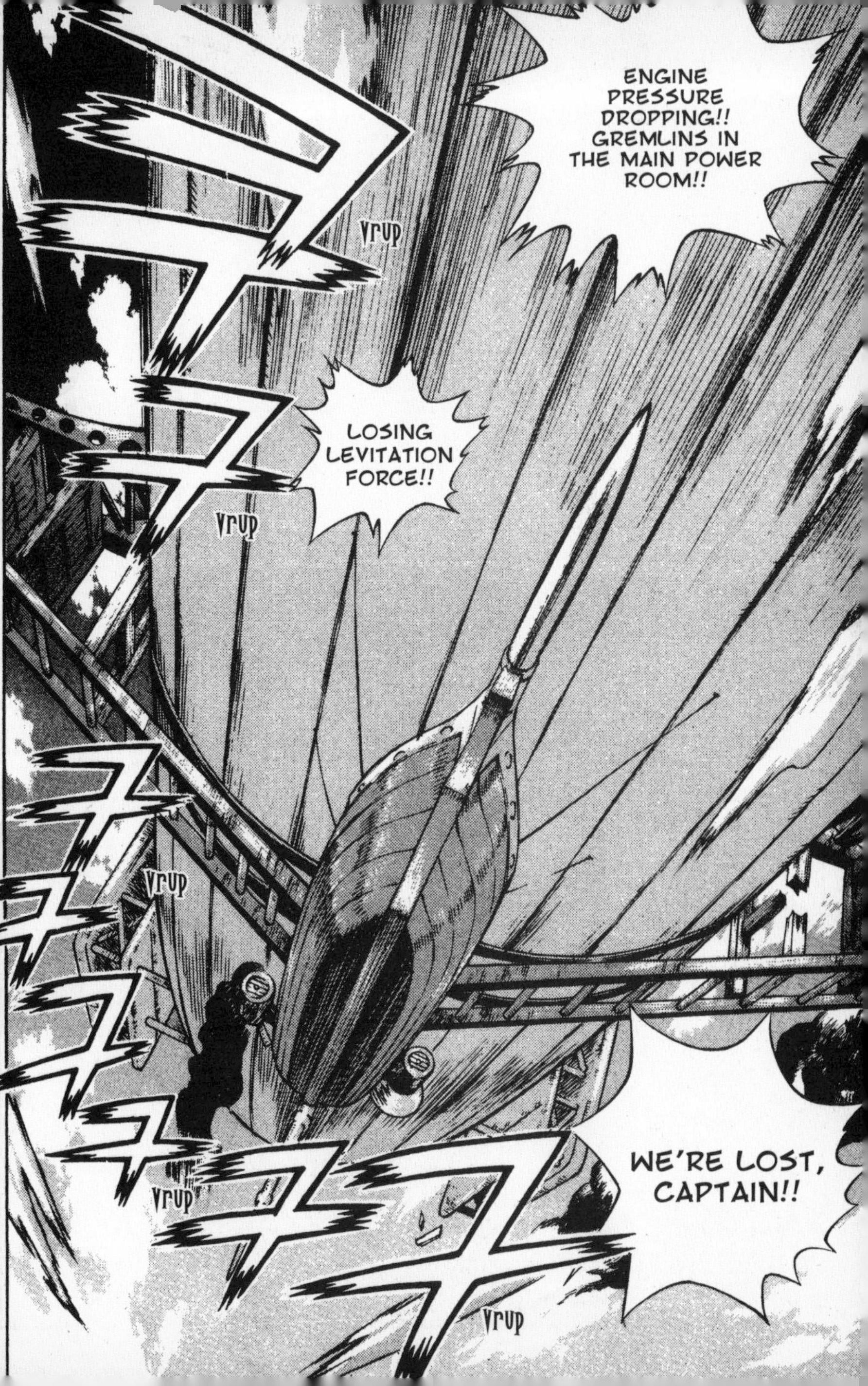
ENGINE PRESSURE DROPPING!! GREMLINS IN THE MAIN POWER ROOM!!
VRUP
LOSING LEVITATION FORCE!!
VRUP
VRUP
WE'RE LOST, CAPTAIN!!
VRUP
VRUP

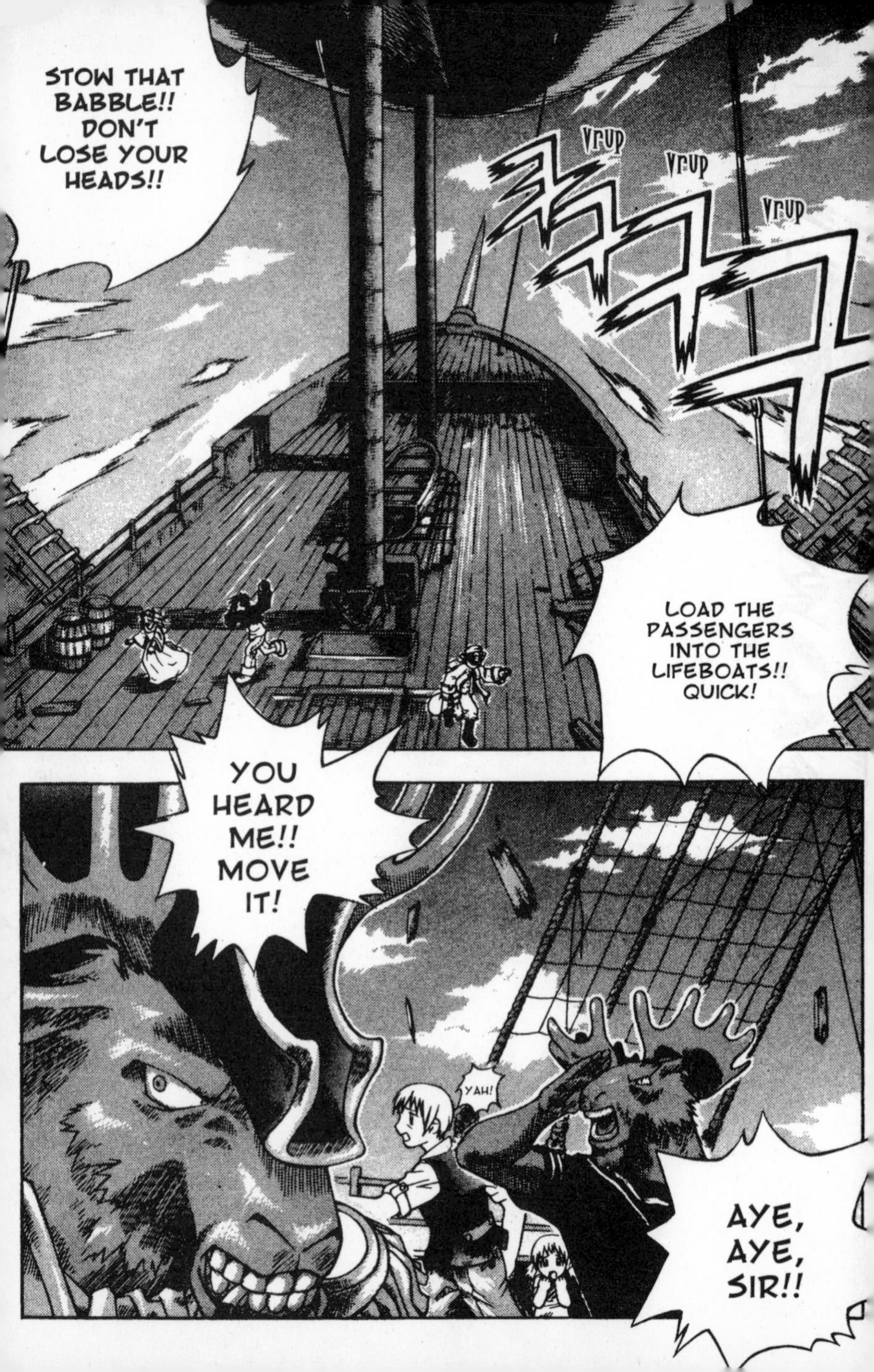
VRUP
VRUP
VRUP
STOW THAT BABBLE!! DON'T LOSE YOUR HEADS!!
LOAD THE PASSENGERS INTO THE LIFEBOATS!! QUICK!
YOU HEARD ME!! MOVE IT!
YAH!
AYE, AYE, SIR!!

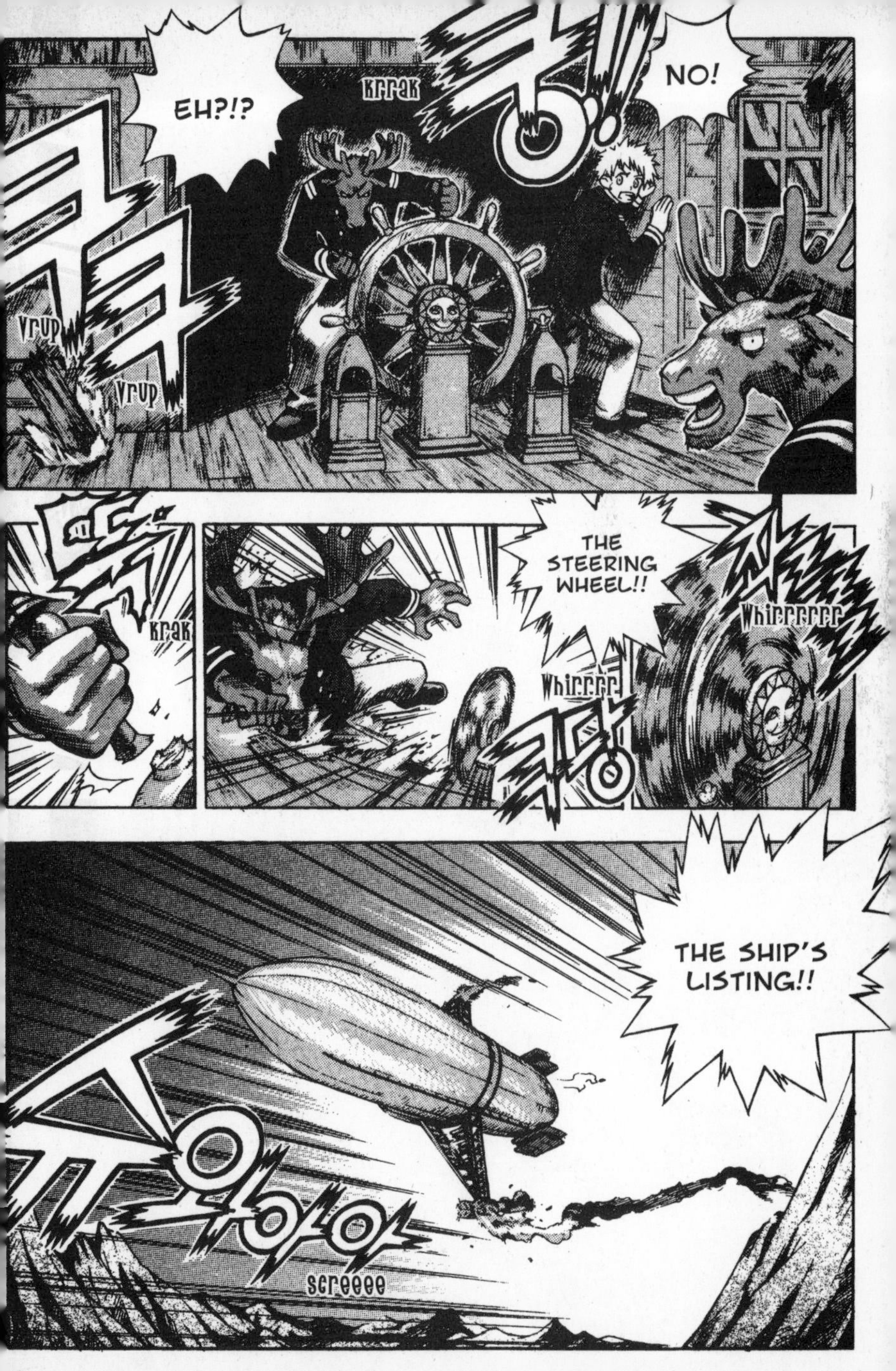
NO!
krrak
EH?!?
Vrup
Vrup
Whirrrrrr
THE STEERING WHEEL!!
Whirrrr
krak
THE SHIP'S LISTING!!
screeee

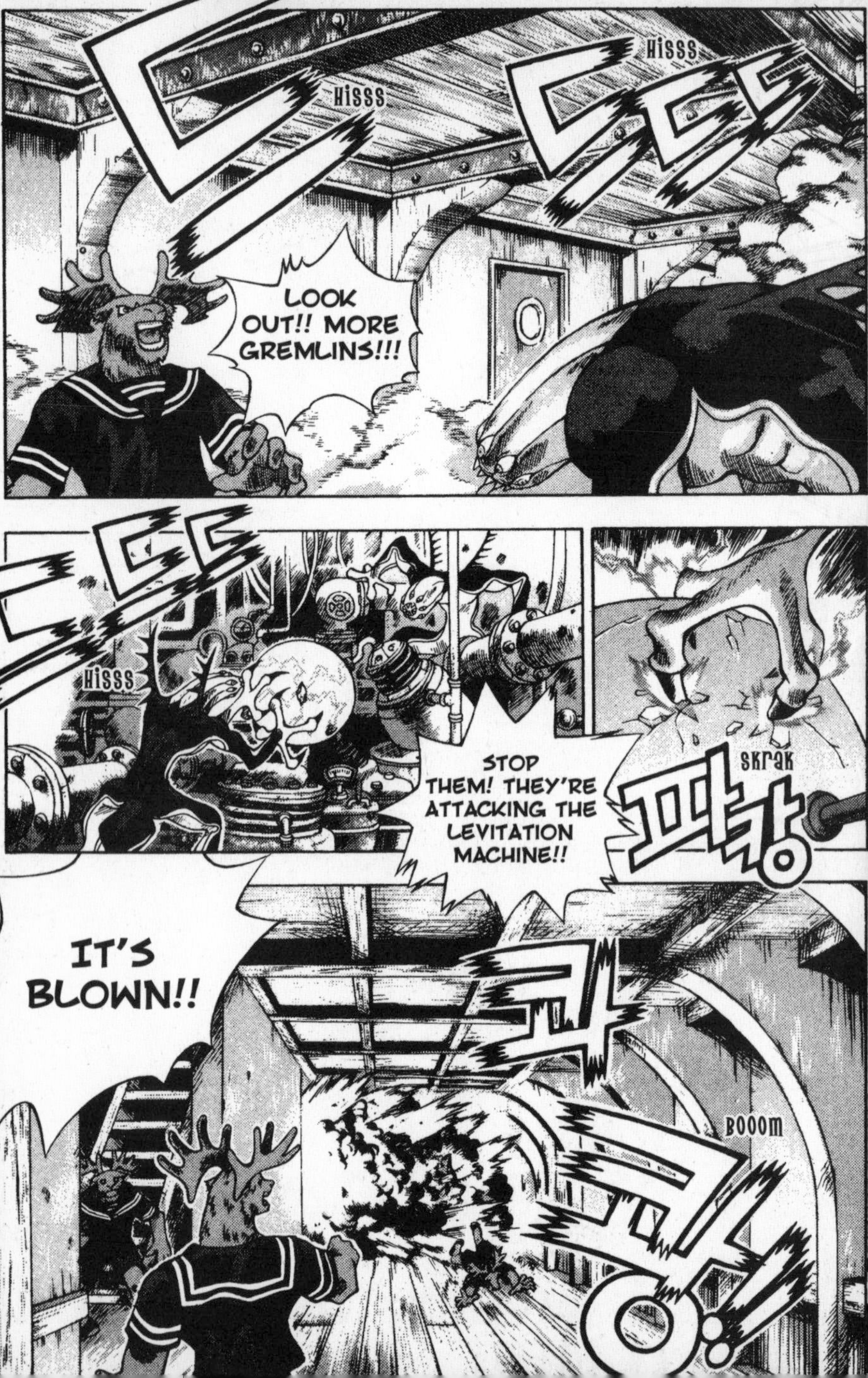
HISSS
HISSS
LOOK OUT!! MORE GREMLINS!!!
HISSS
STOP THEM! THEY'RE ATTACKING THE LEVITATION MACHINE!!
SKRAK
IT'S BLOWN!!
BOOOM

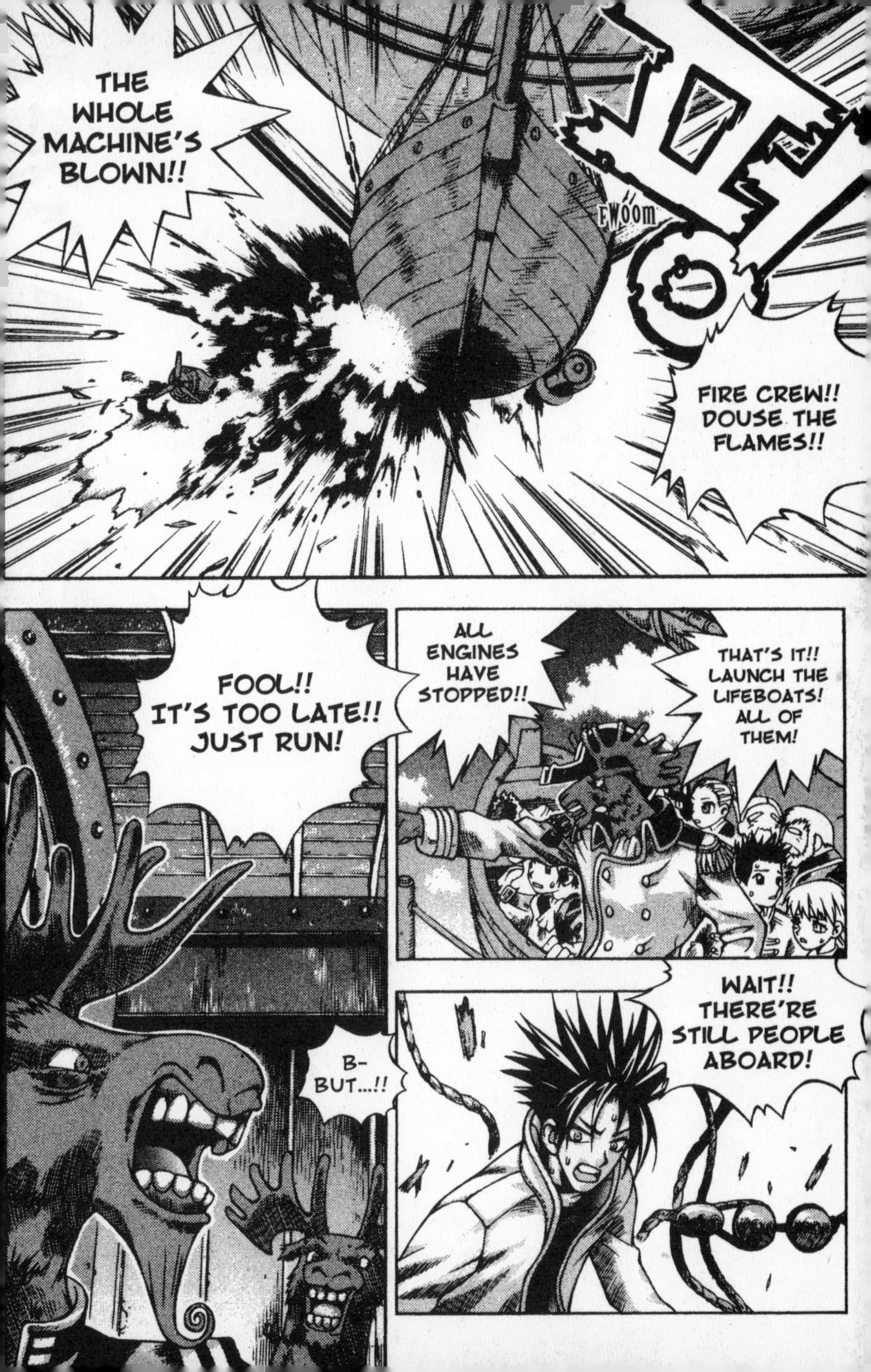
FWOOM
THE WHOLE MACHINE'S BLOWN!!
FIRE CREW!! DOUSE THE FLAMES!!
ALL ENGINES HAVE STOPPED!!
THAT'S IT!! LAUNCH THE LIFEBOATS! ALL OF THEM!
WAIT!! THERE'RE STILL PEOPLE ABOARD!
FOOL!! IT'S TOO LATE!! JUST RUN!
B- BUT...!!

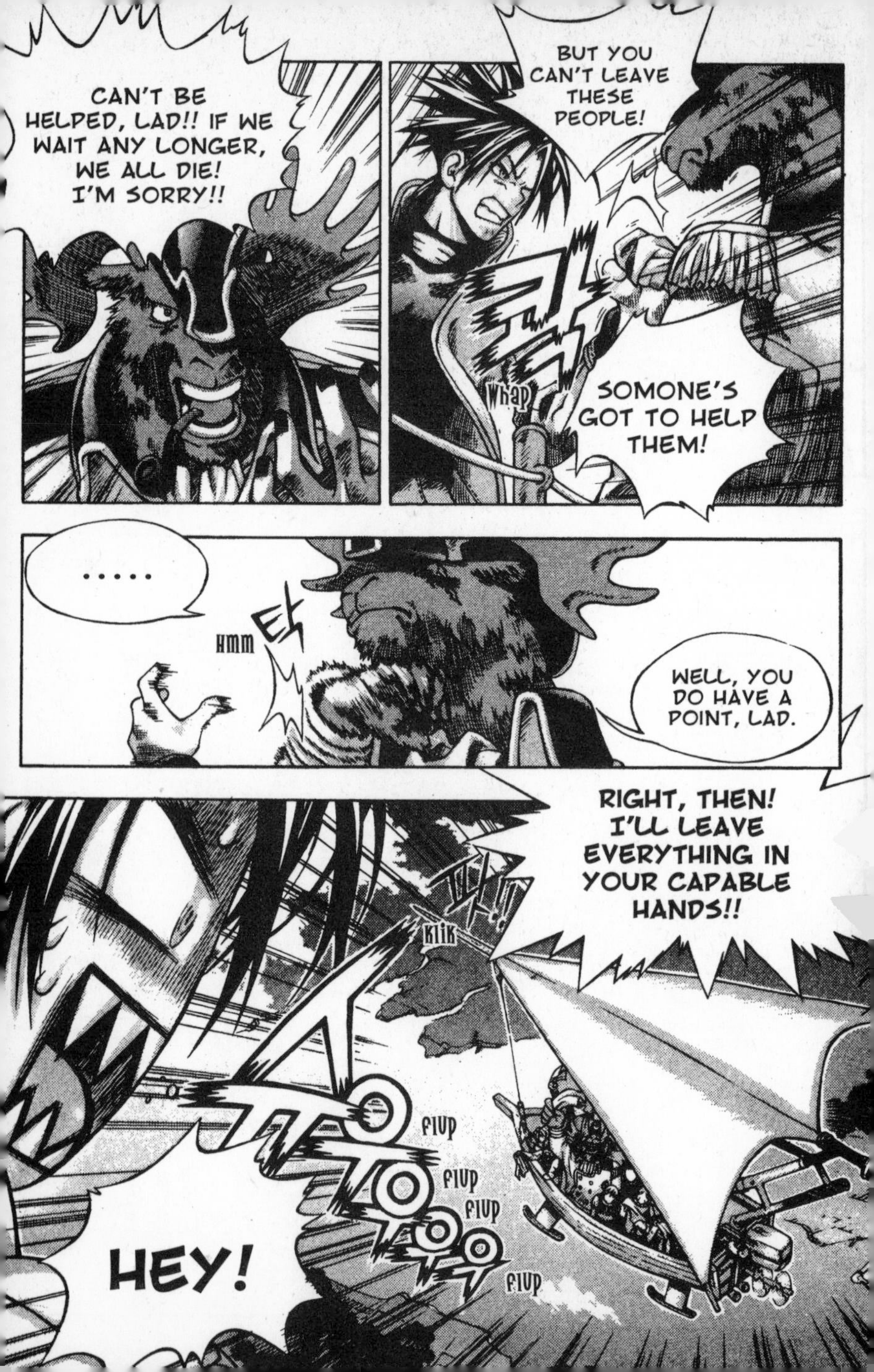
CAN'T BE HELPED, LAD!! IF WE WAIT ANY LONGER, WE ALL DIE! I'M SORRY!!
BUT YOU CAN'T LEAVE THESE PEOPLE!
WHAP
SOMONE'S GOT TO HELP THEM!
......
HMM
WELL, YOU DO HAVE A POINT, LAD.
RIGHT, THEN! I'LL LEAVE EVERYTHING IN YOUR CAPABLE HANDS!!
KLIK
FLUP
FLUP
FLUP
FLUP
HEY!

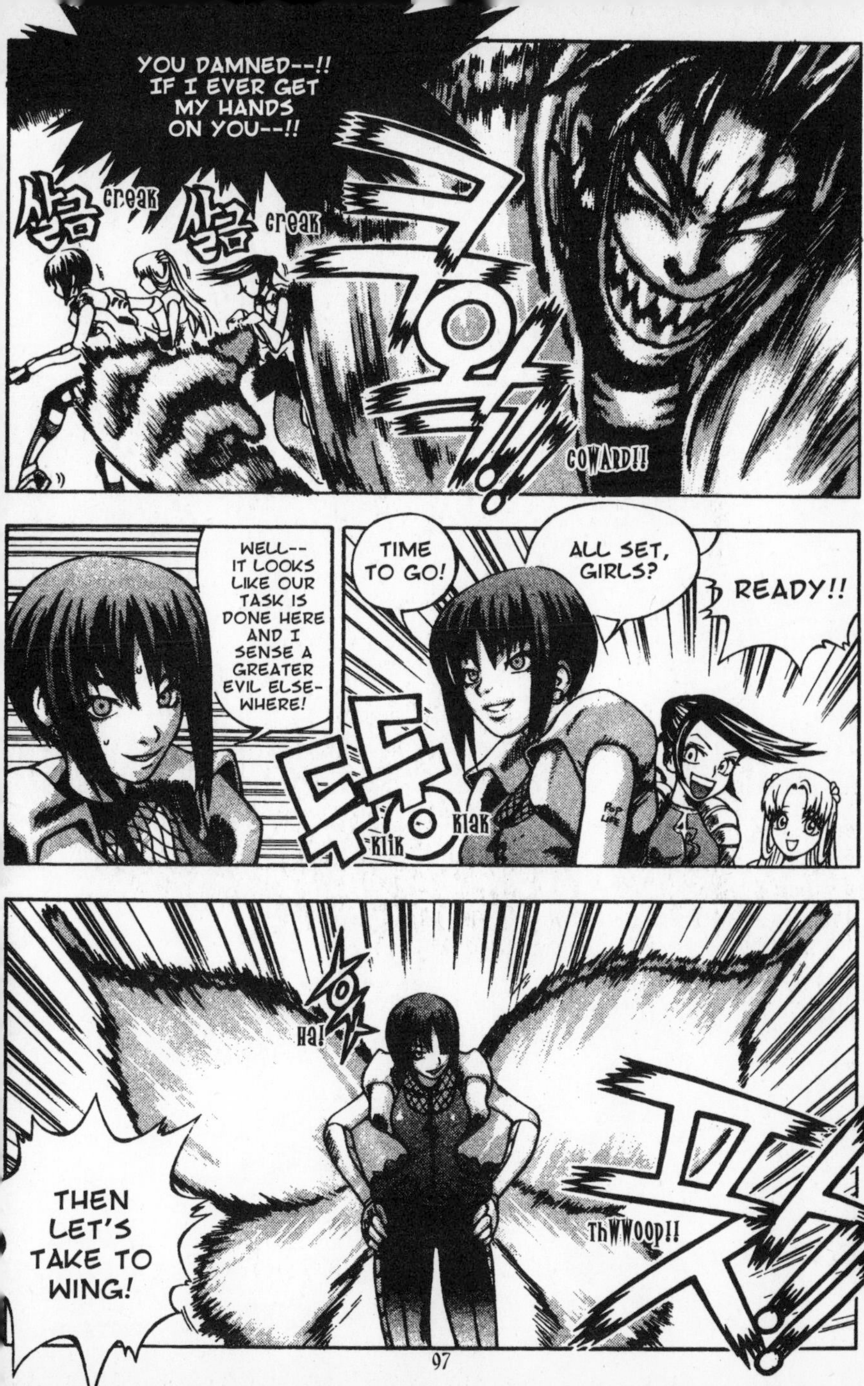
YOU DAMNED--!! IF I EVER GET MY HANDS ON YOU--!!
creak
creak
COWARD!!
WELL-- IT LOOKS LIKE OUR TASK IS DONE HERE AND I SENSE A GREATER EVIL ELSE-WHERE!
TIME TO GO!
ALL SET, GIRLS?
READY!!
Klik
Klak
HA!
THEN LET'S TAKE TO WING!
ThWWoop!!

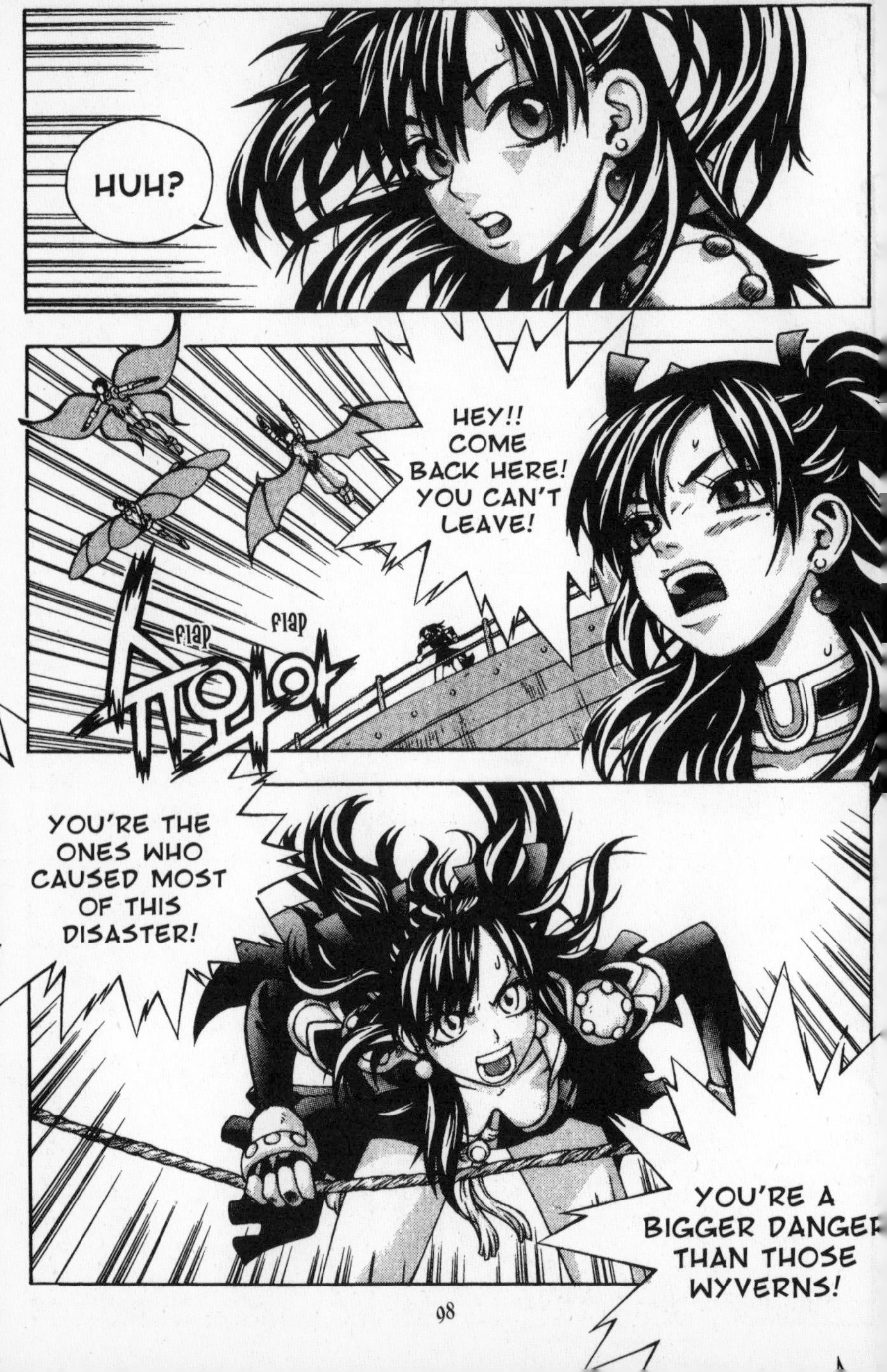
HUH?
HEY!! COME BACK HERE! YOU CAN'T LEAVE!
FLAP
FLAP
YOU'RE THE ONES WHO CAUSED MOST OF THIS DISASTER!
YOU'RE A BIGGER DANGER THAN THOSE WYVERNS!

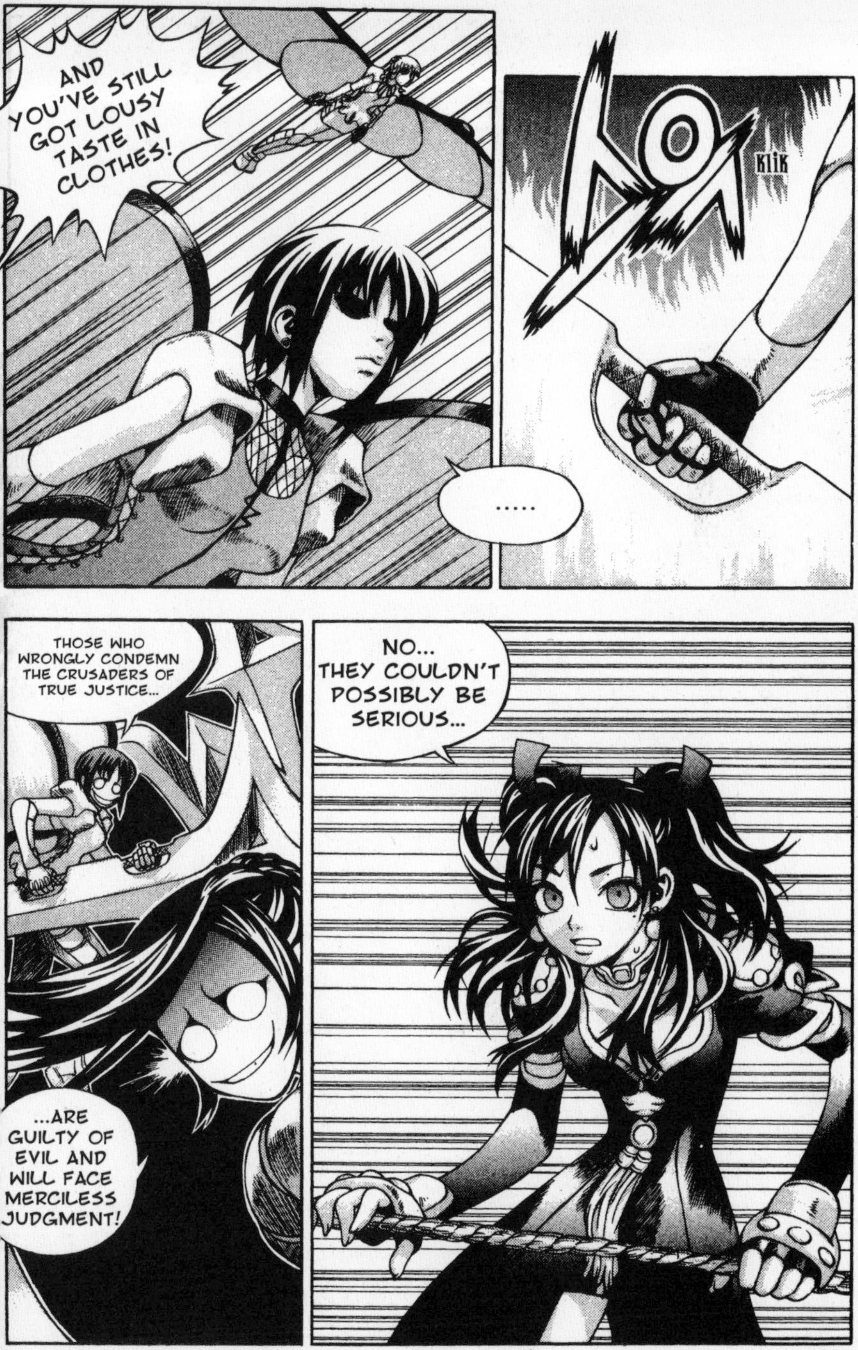
AND YOU'VE STILL GOT LOUSY TASTE IN CLOTHES!
.....
KLIK
THOSE WHO WRONGLY CONDEMN THE CRUSADERS OF TRUE JUSTICE...
...ARE GUILTY OF EVIL AND WILL FACE MERCILESS JUDGMENT!
NO... THEY COULDN'T POSSIBLY BE SERIOUS...

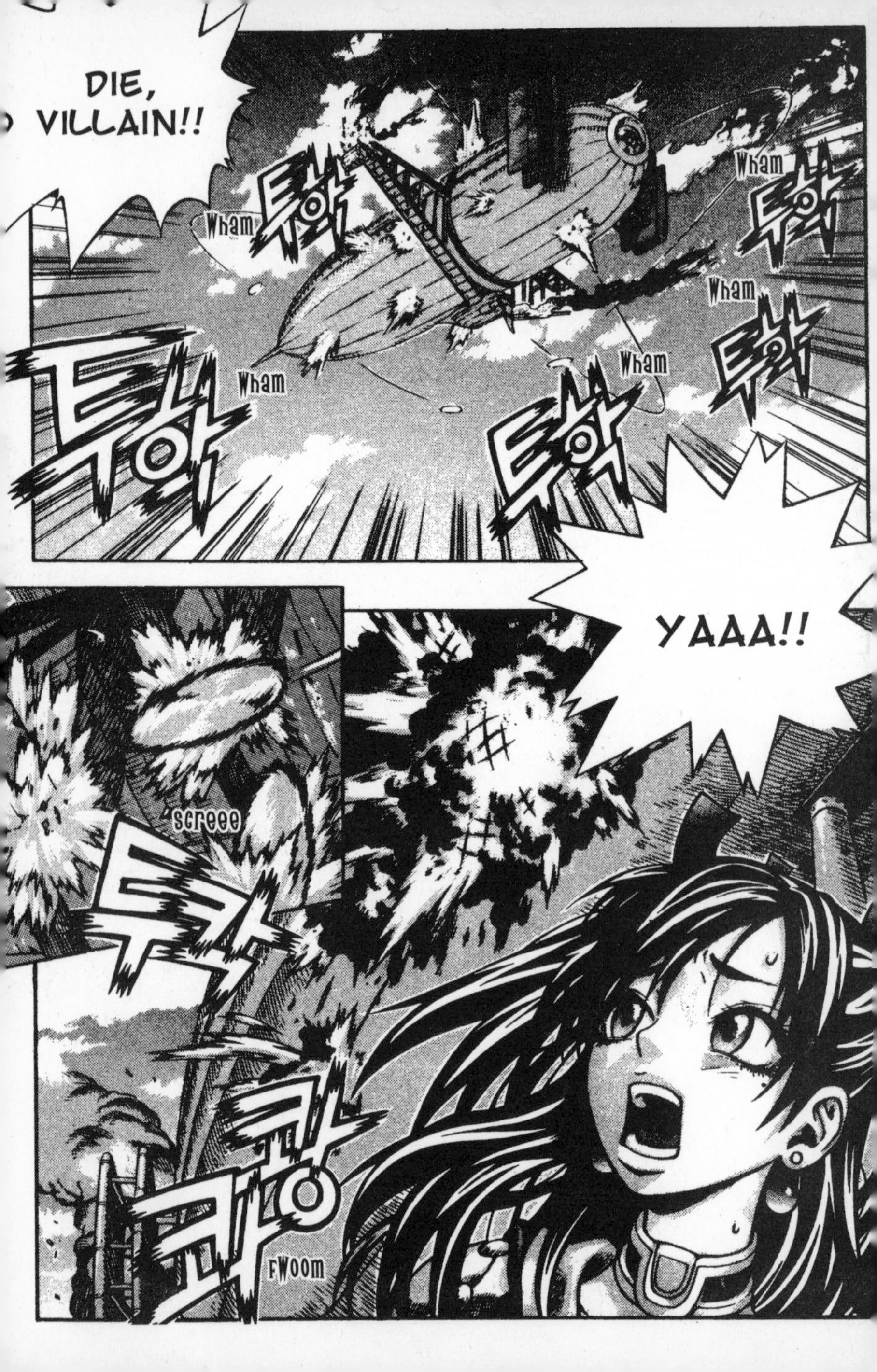
DIE, VILLAIN!!
Wham
Wham
Wham
Wham
Wham
YAAA!!
screee
FWoom

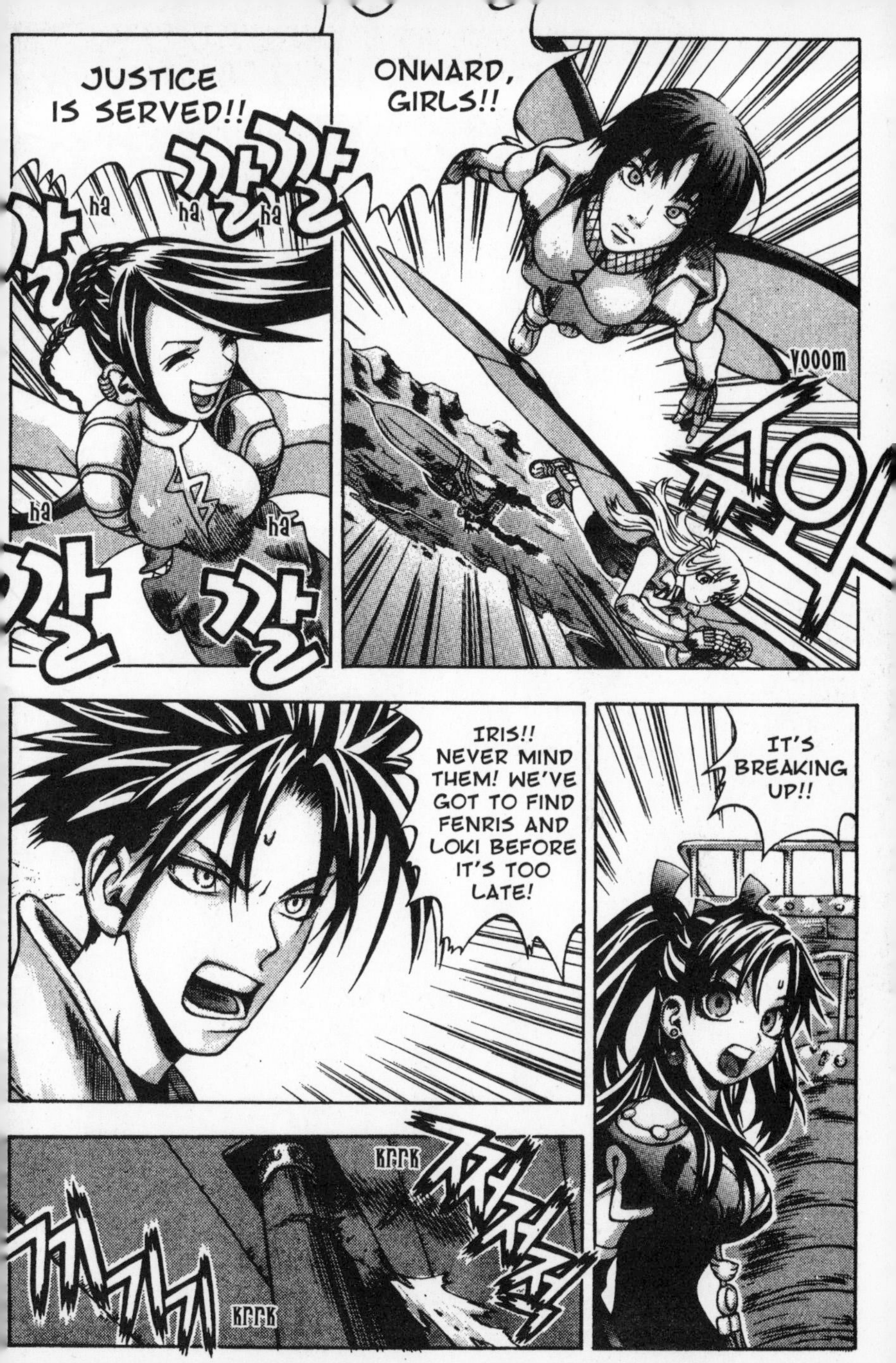

JUSTICE IS SERVED!!
ha ha ha
ha ha
ONWARD, GIRLS!!
yooom
IRIS!! NEVER MIND THEM! WE'VE GOT TO FIND FENRIS AND LOKI BEFORE IT'S TOO LATE!
IT'S BREAKING UP!!
KRRK
KRRK

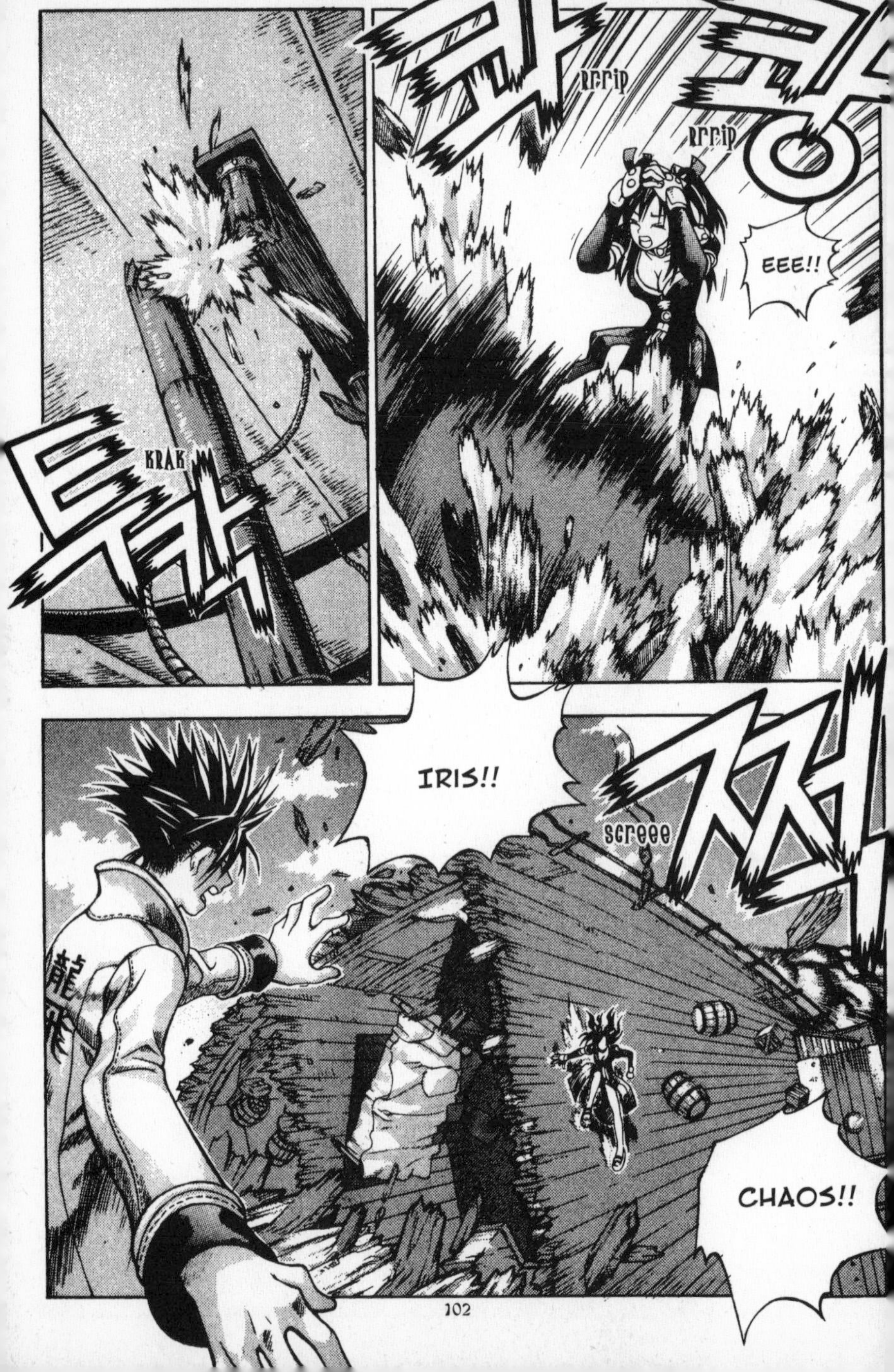
KRAK
RRRIP
RRRIP
EEE!!
IRIS!!
SCREEE
CHAOS!!

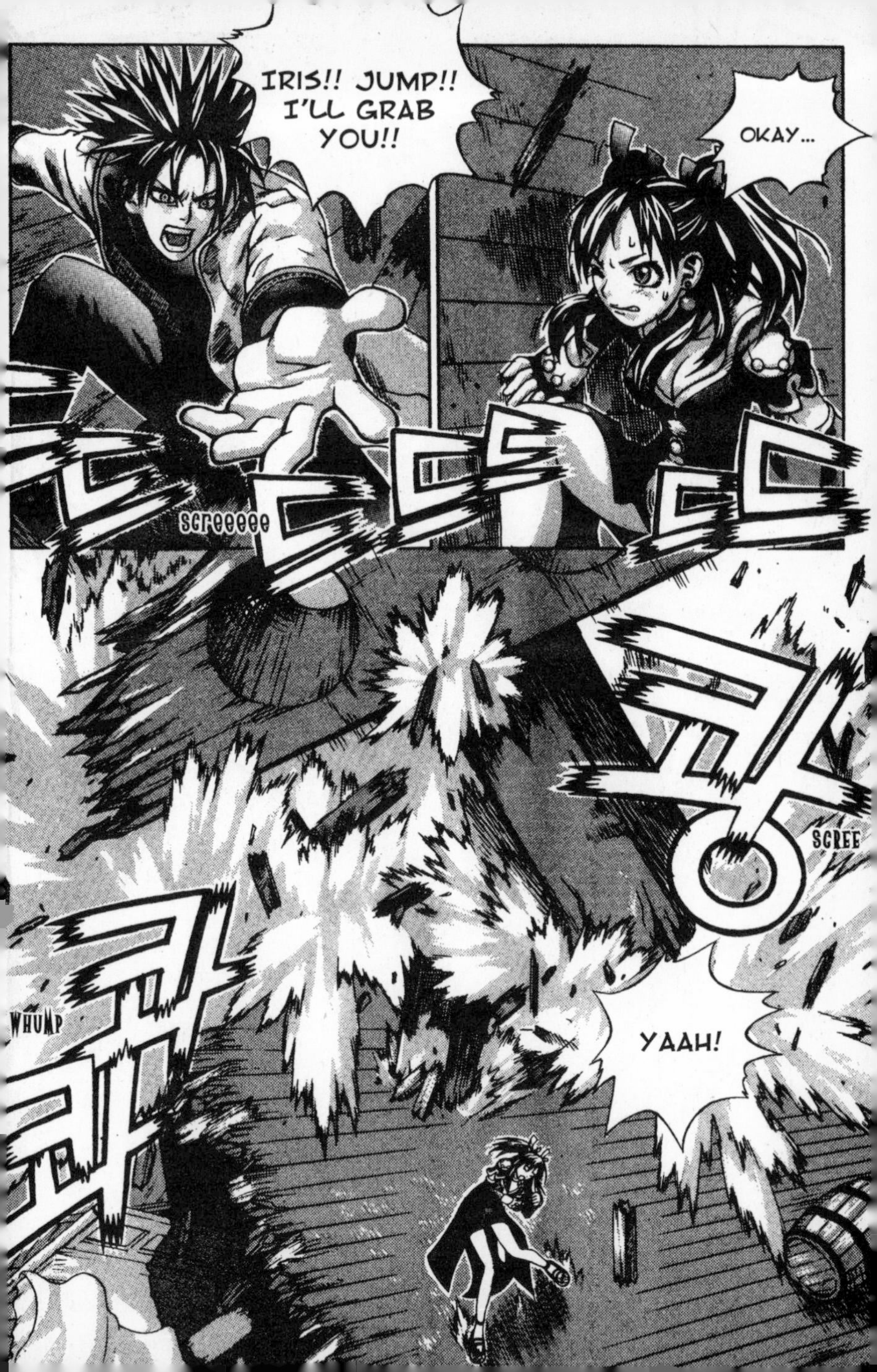
IRIS!! JUMP!! I'LL GRAB YOU!!
OKAY...
SCREEEEEE
SCREE
WHUMP
YAAH!

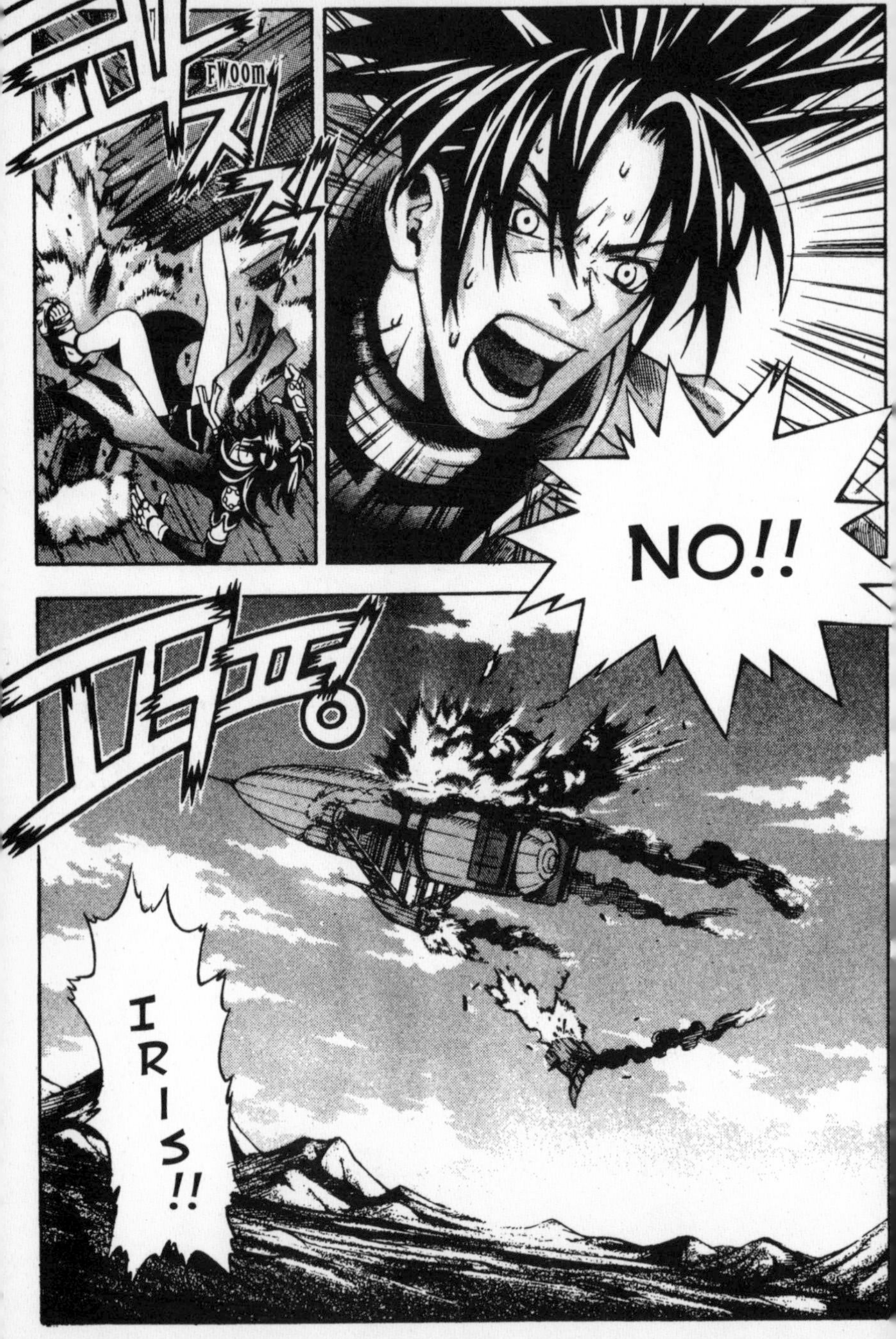
FWOOM
NO!!
IRIS!!

RAGNARÖK

라그나로크

IN TO THE ABYSS

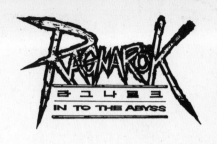

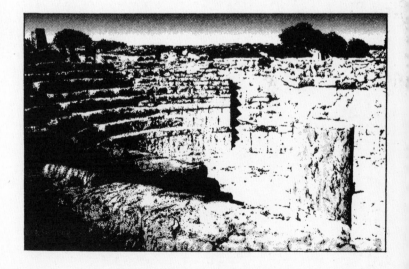

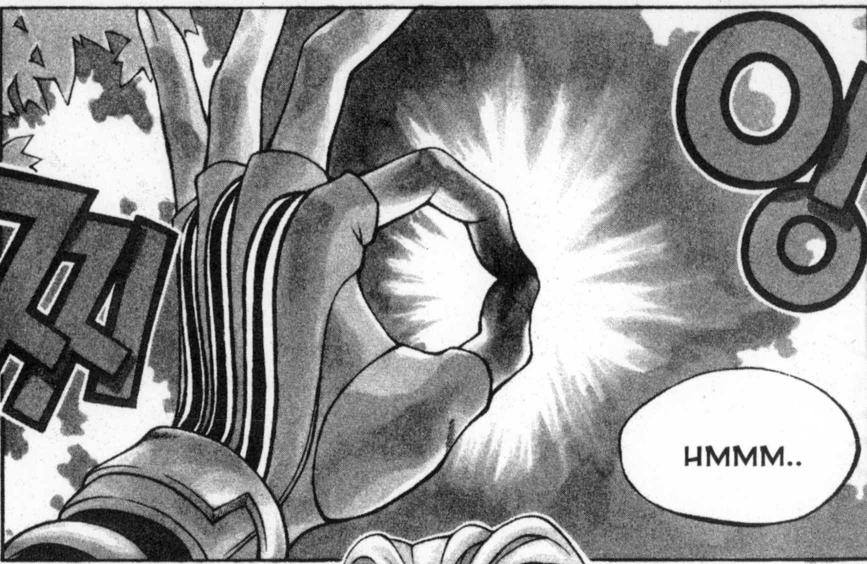
HMMM..

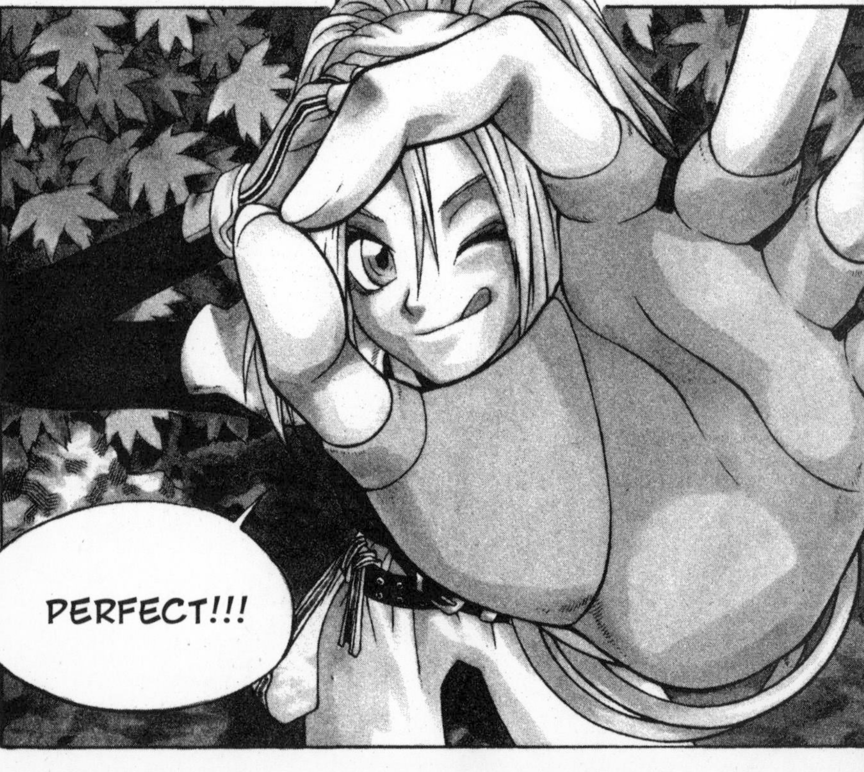
PERFECT!!!

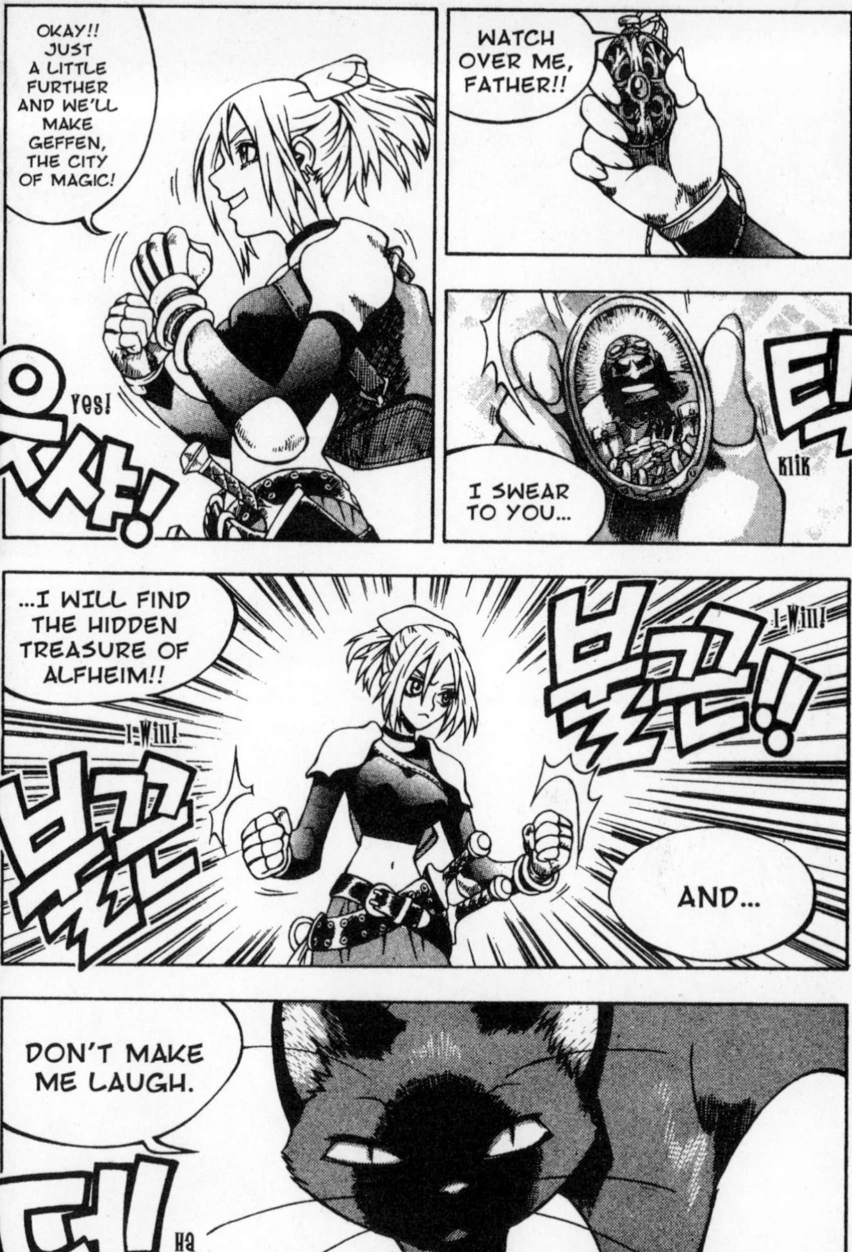
OKAY!! JUST A LITTLE FURTHER AND WE'LL MAKE GEFFEN, THE CITY OF MAGIC!
Yes!
WATCH OVER ME, FATHER!!
I SWEAR TO YOU...
틱
Klik
...I WILL FIND THE HIDDEN TREASURE OF ALFHEIM!!
불끈!!
I Will!
불끈
I Will!
AND...
DON'T MAKE ME LAUGH.
Ha

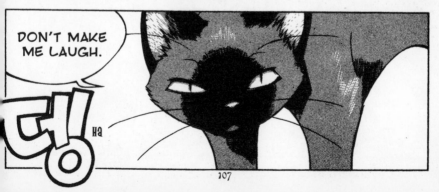

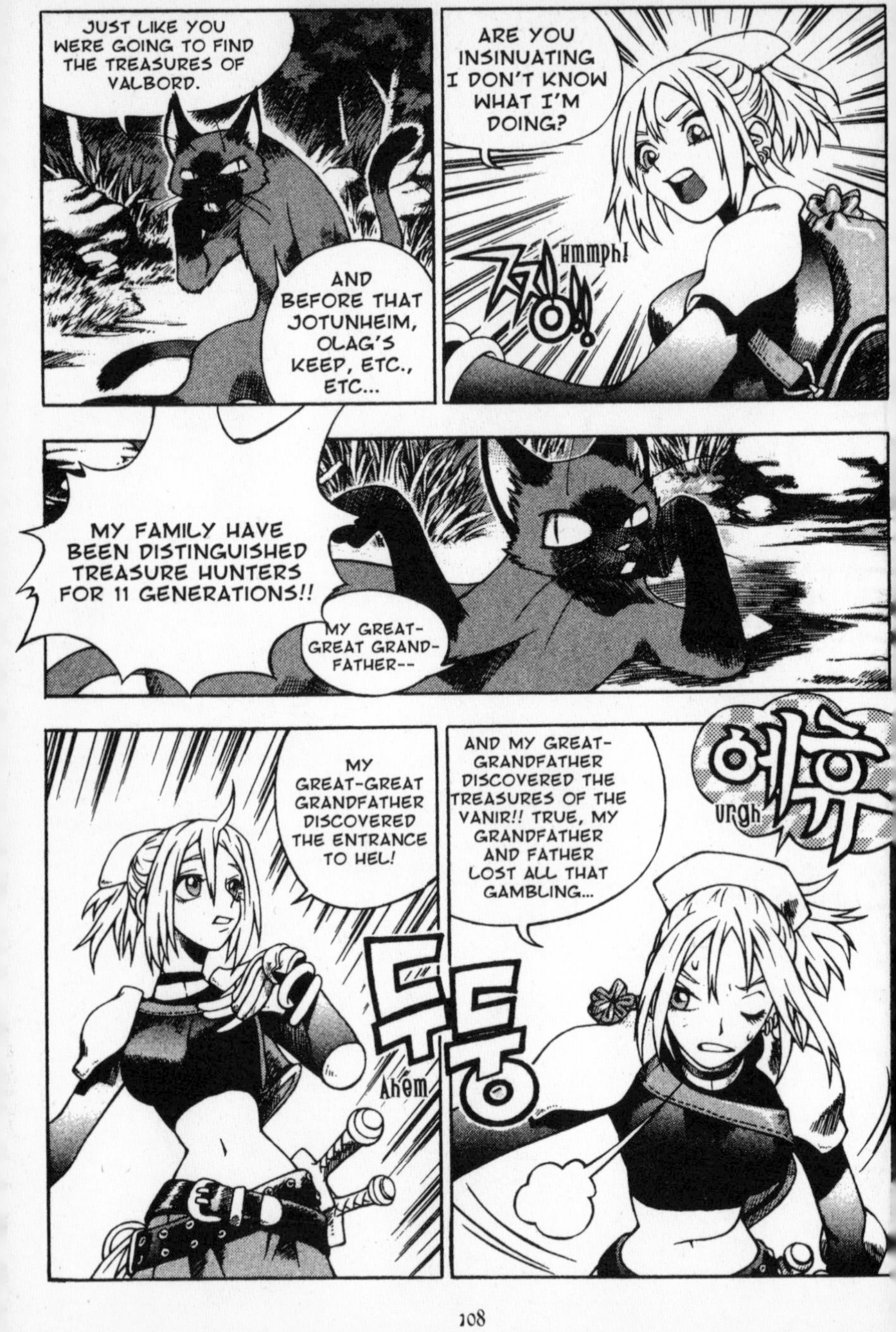
JUST LIKE YOU WERE GOING TO FIND THE TREASURES OF VALBORD.
AND BEFORE THAT JOTUNHEIM, OLAG'S KEEP, ETC., ETC...
ARE YOU INSINUATING I DON'T KNOW WHAT I'M DOING?
Hmmph!
MY FAMILY HAVE BEEN DISTINGUISHED TREASURE HUNTERS FOR 11 GENERATIONS!!
MY GREAT-GREAT GRANDFATHER--
MY GREAT-GREAT GRANDFATHER DISCOVERED THE ENTRANCE TO HEL!
두둥
Ahem
AND MY GREAT-GRANDFATHER DISCOVERED THE TREASURES OF THE VANIR!! TRUE, MY GRANDFATHER AND FATHER LOST ALL THAT GAMBLING...
에휴
Urgh

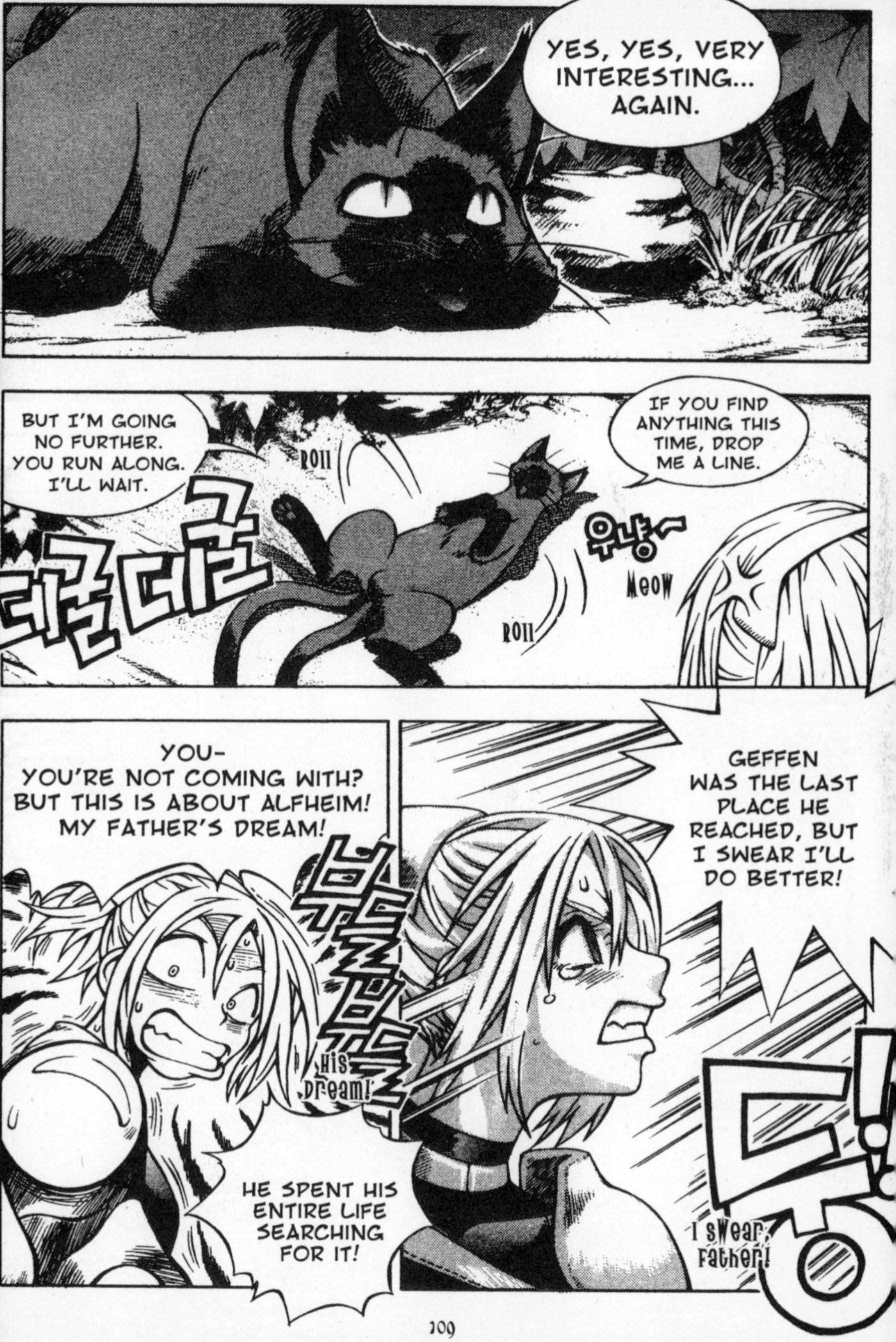

YES, YES, VERY INTERESTING... AGAIN.
BUT I'M GOING NO FURTHER. YOU RUN ALONG. I'LL WAIT.
데굴데굴
ROll
ROll
IF YOU FIND ANYTHING THIS TIME, DROP ME A LINE.
우냥~
MEOW
YOU- YOU'RE NOT COMING WITH? BUT THIS IS ABOUT ALFHEIM! MY FATHER'S DREAM!
His Dream!
HE SPENT HIS ENTIRE LIFE SEARCHING FOR IT!
GEFFEN WAS THE LAST PLACE HE REACHED, BUT I SWEAR I'LL DO BETTER!
I sWear, Father!

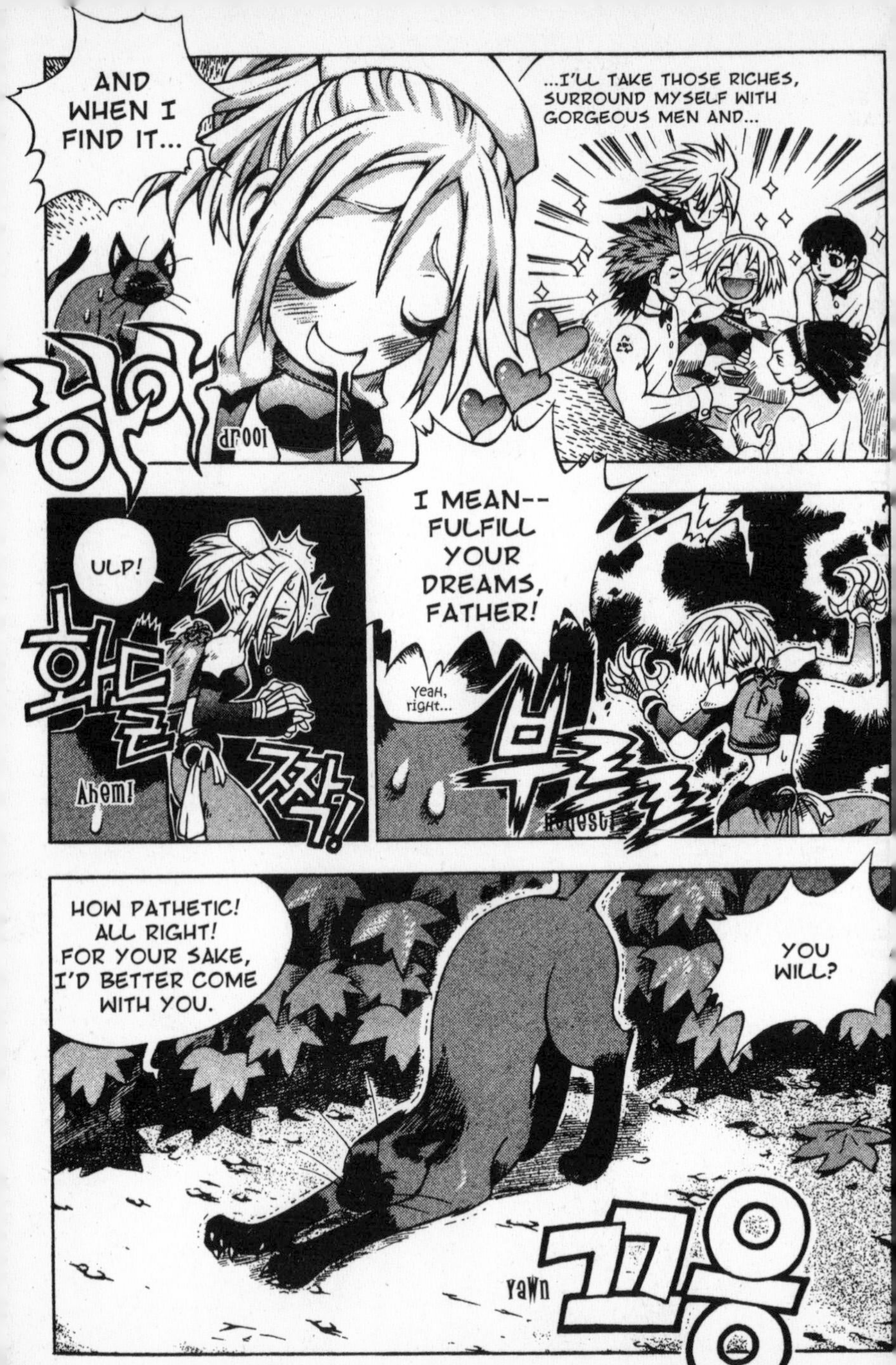
AND WHEN I FIND IT...
...I'LL TAKE THOSE RICHES, SURROUND MYSELF WITH GORGEOUS MEN AND...
drool
ULP!
Ahem!
I MEAN-- FULFILL YOUR DREAMS, FATHER!
Yeah, right...
HOW PATHETIC! ALL RIGHT! FOR YOUR SAKE, I'D BETTER COME WITH YOU.
YOU WILL?
yawn

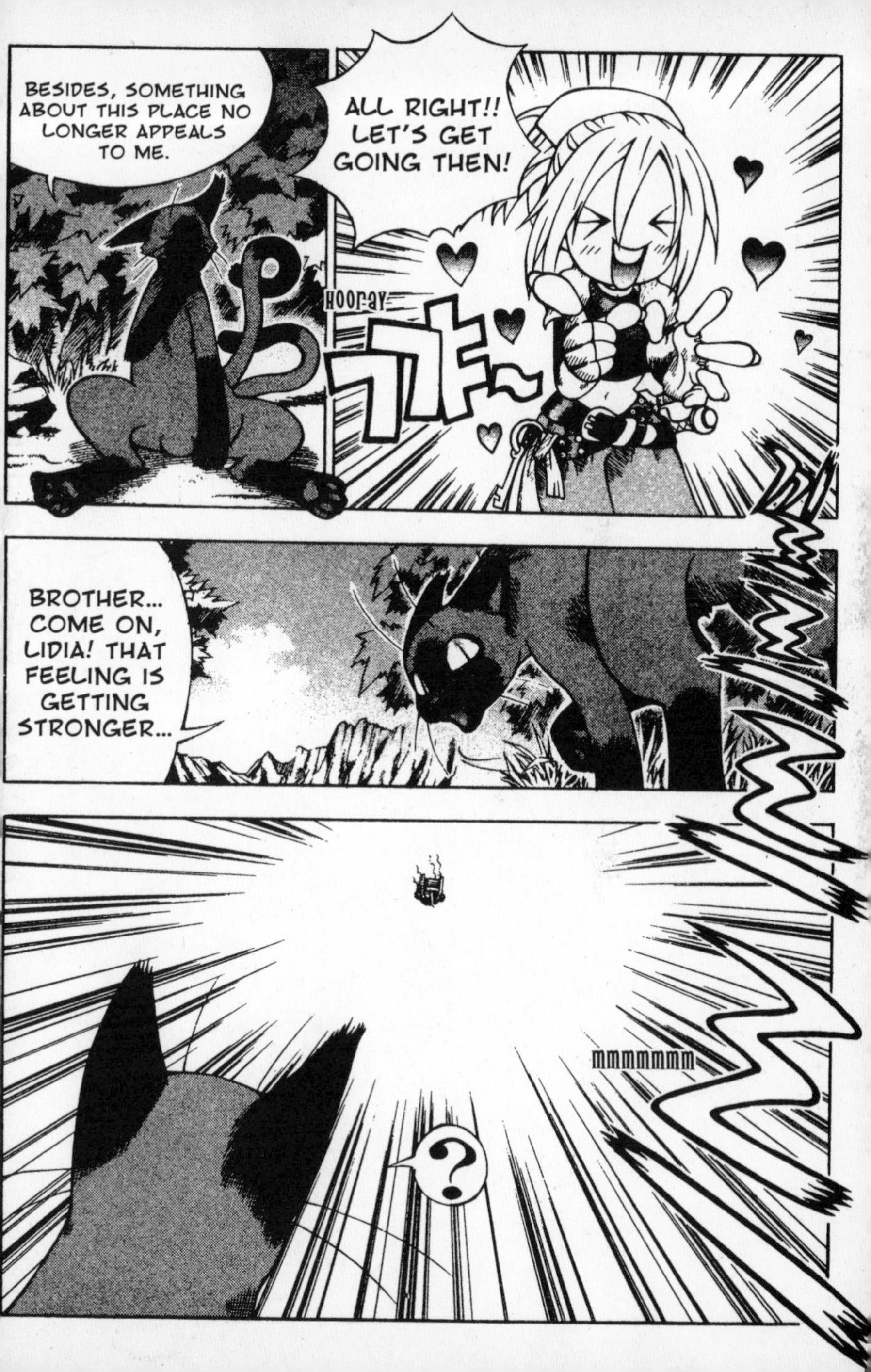
ALL RIGHT!! LET'S GET GOING THEN!
HOORAY
ウキ～
BESIDES, SOMETHING ABOUT THIS PLACE NO LONGER APPEALS TO ME.
BROTHER... COME ON, LIDIA! THAT FEELING IS GETTING STRONGER...
mmmmmmm
?

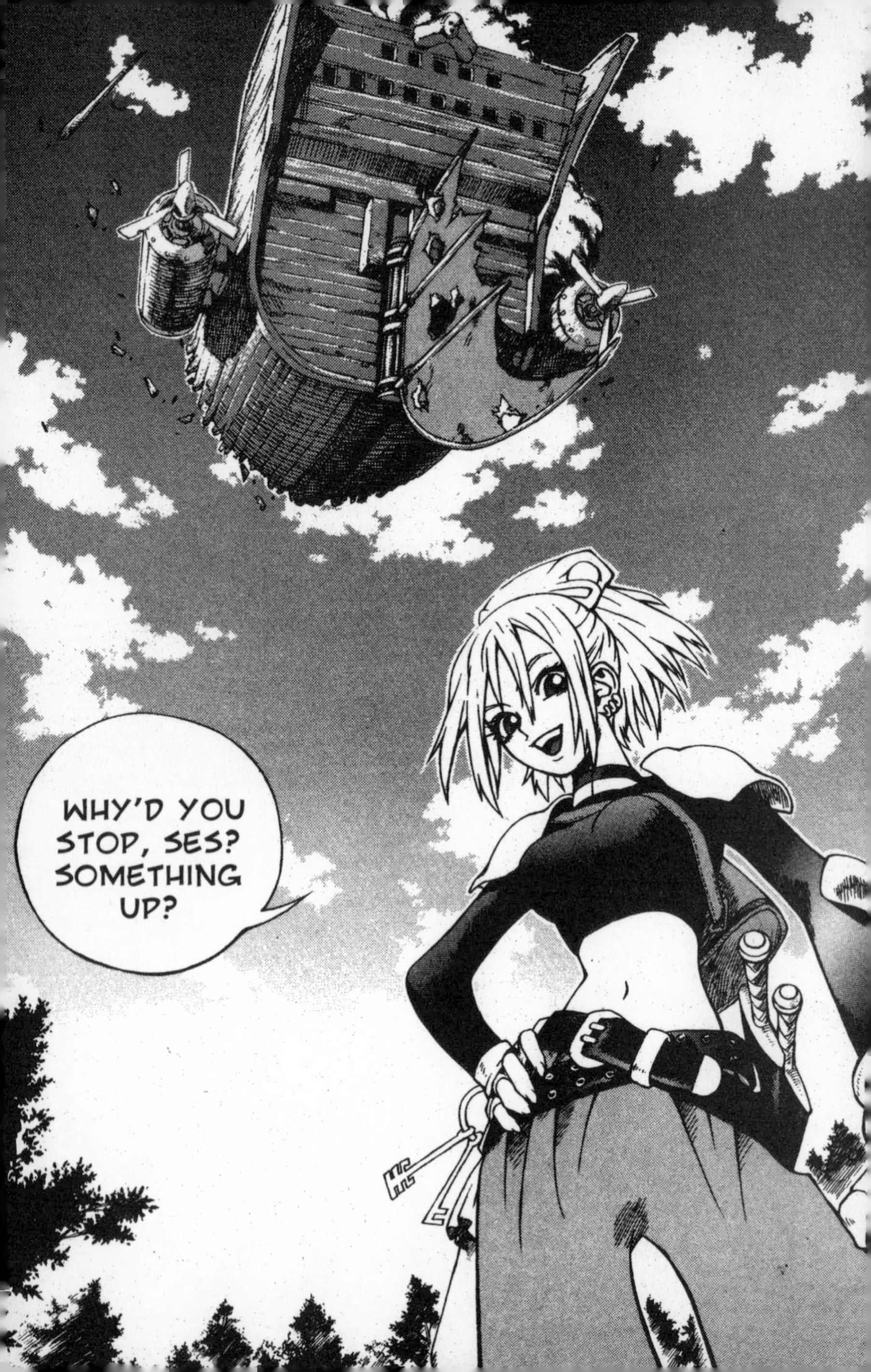
WHY'D YOU STOP, SES? SOMETHING UP?

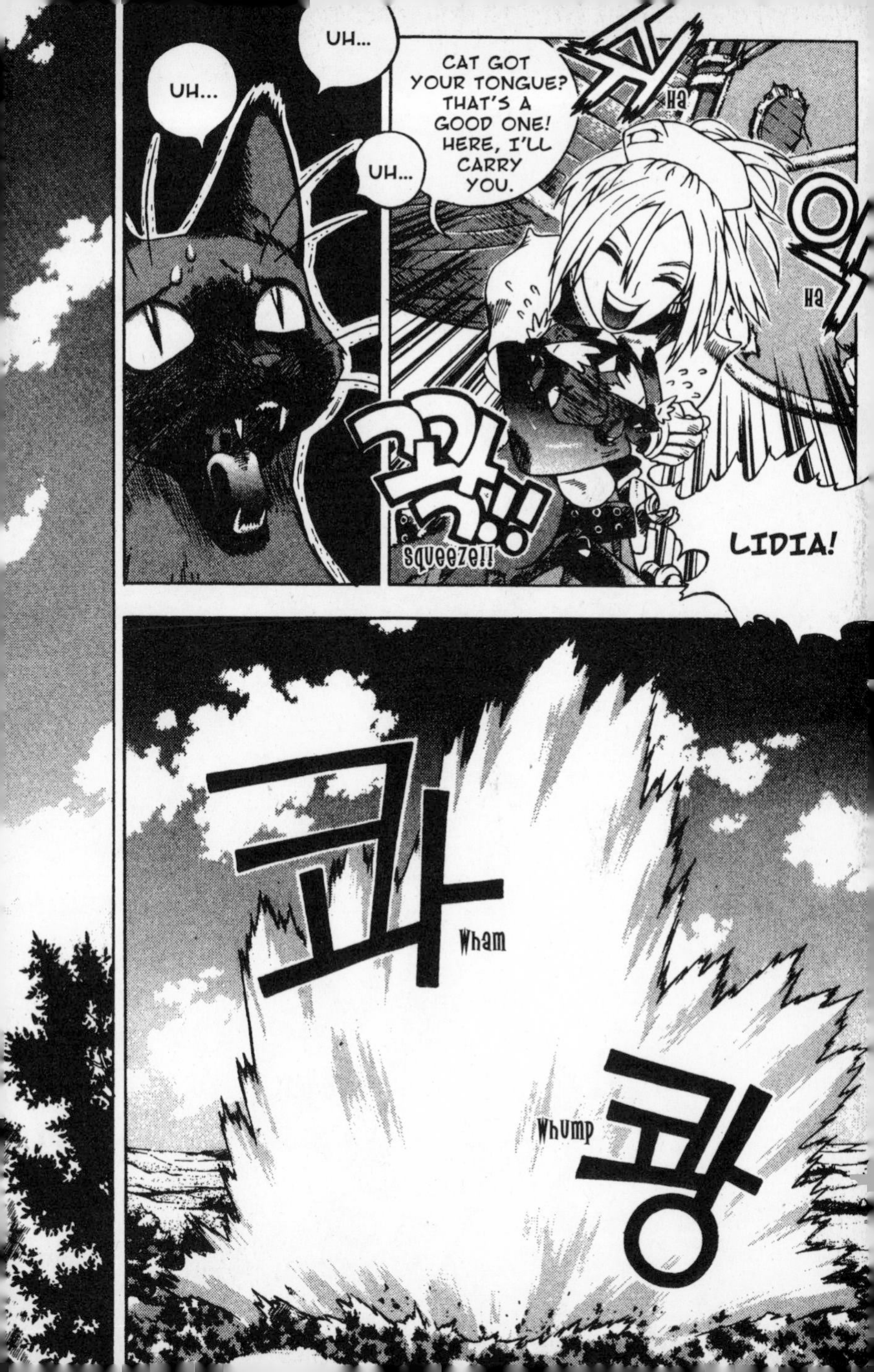
UH...
UH...
UH...
CAT GOT YOUR TONGUE? THAT'S A GOOD ONE! HERE, I'LL CARRY YOU.
HA
HA
squeeze!!
LIDIA!
Wham
Whump

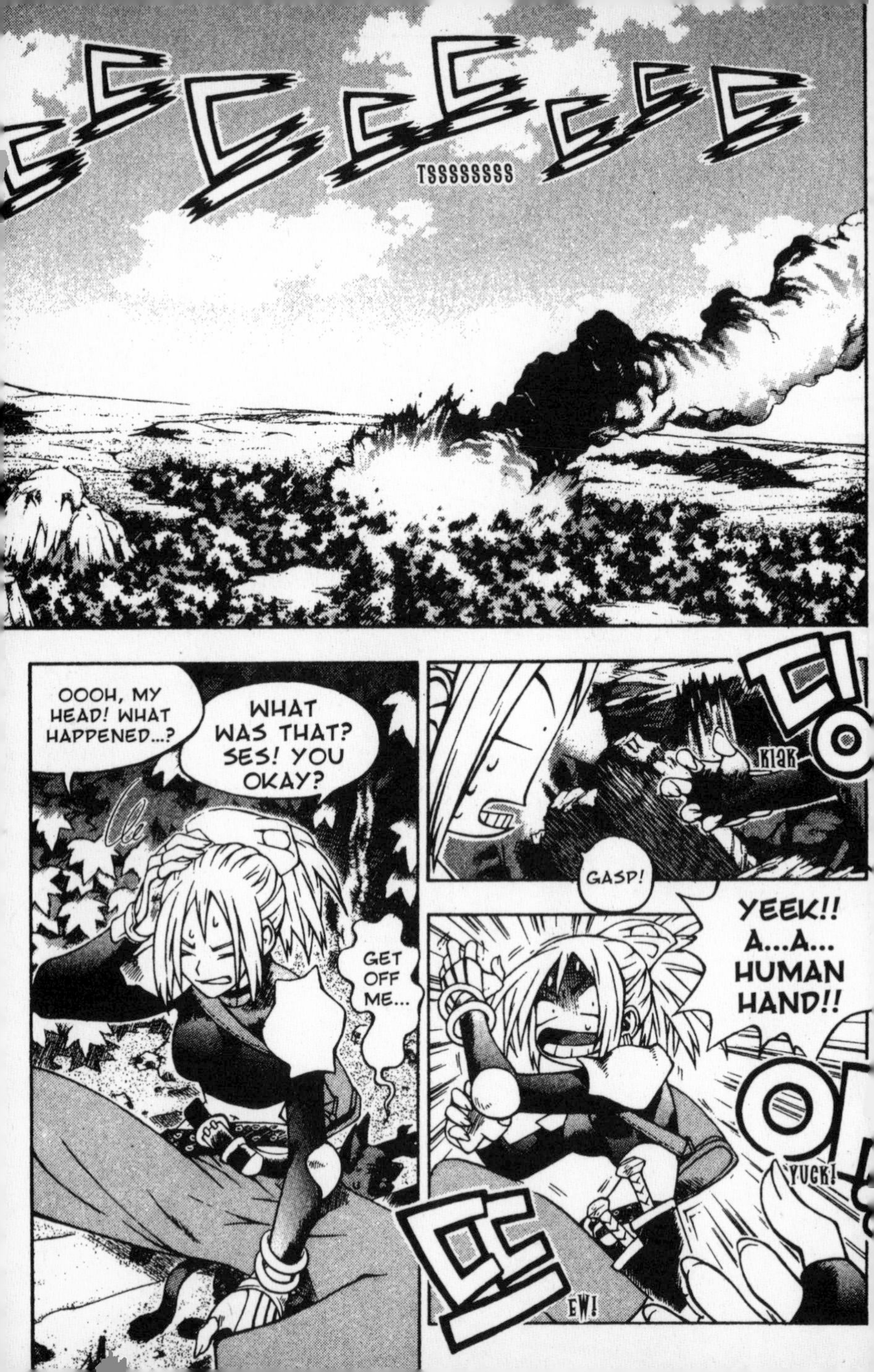
TSSSSSSSS
OOOH, MY HEAD! WHAT HAPPENED...?
WHAT WAS THAT? SES! YOU OKAY?
GET OFF ME...
KIAK
GASP!
YEEK!! A...A... HUMAN HAND!!
YUCK!
EW!

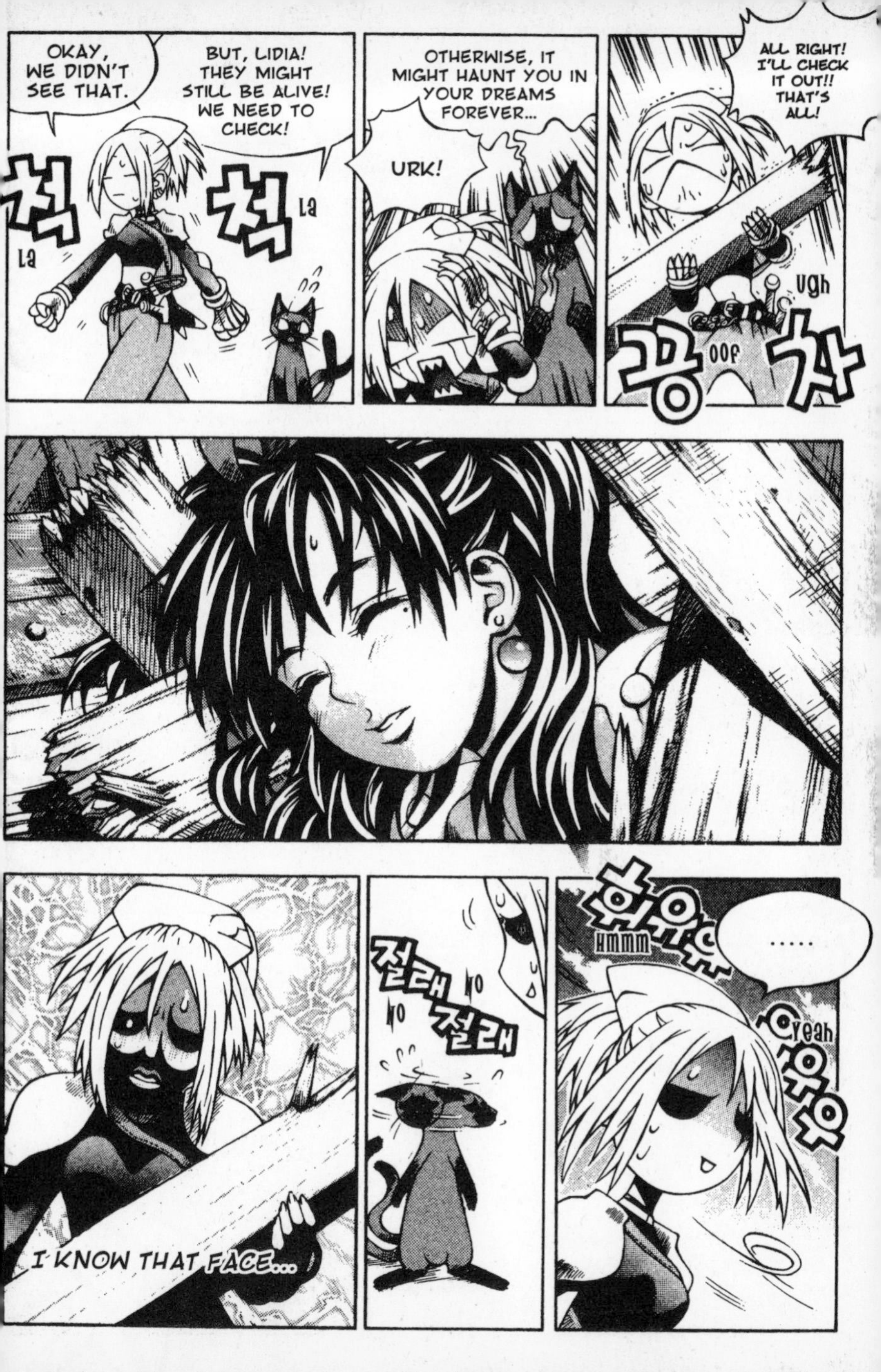
OKAY, WE DIDN'T SEE THAT.
BUT, LIDIA! THEY MIGHT STILL BE ALIVE! WE NEED TO CHECK!
척
LA
척
LA
OTHERWISE, IT MIGHT HAUNT YOU IN YOUR DREAMS FOREVER...
URK!
ALL RIGHT! I'LL CHECK IT OUT!! THAT'S ALL!
UGH
끙
OOF
차
I KNOW THAT FACE...
절레
NO
NO
절레
.....
HMMM
YEAH

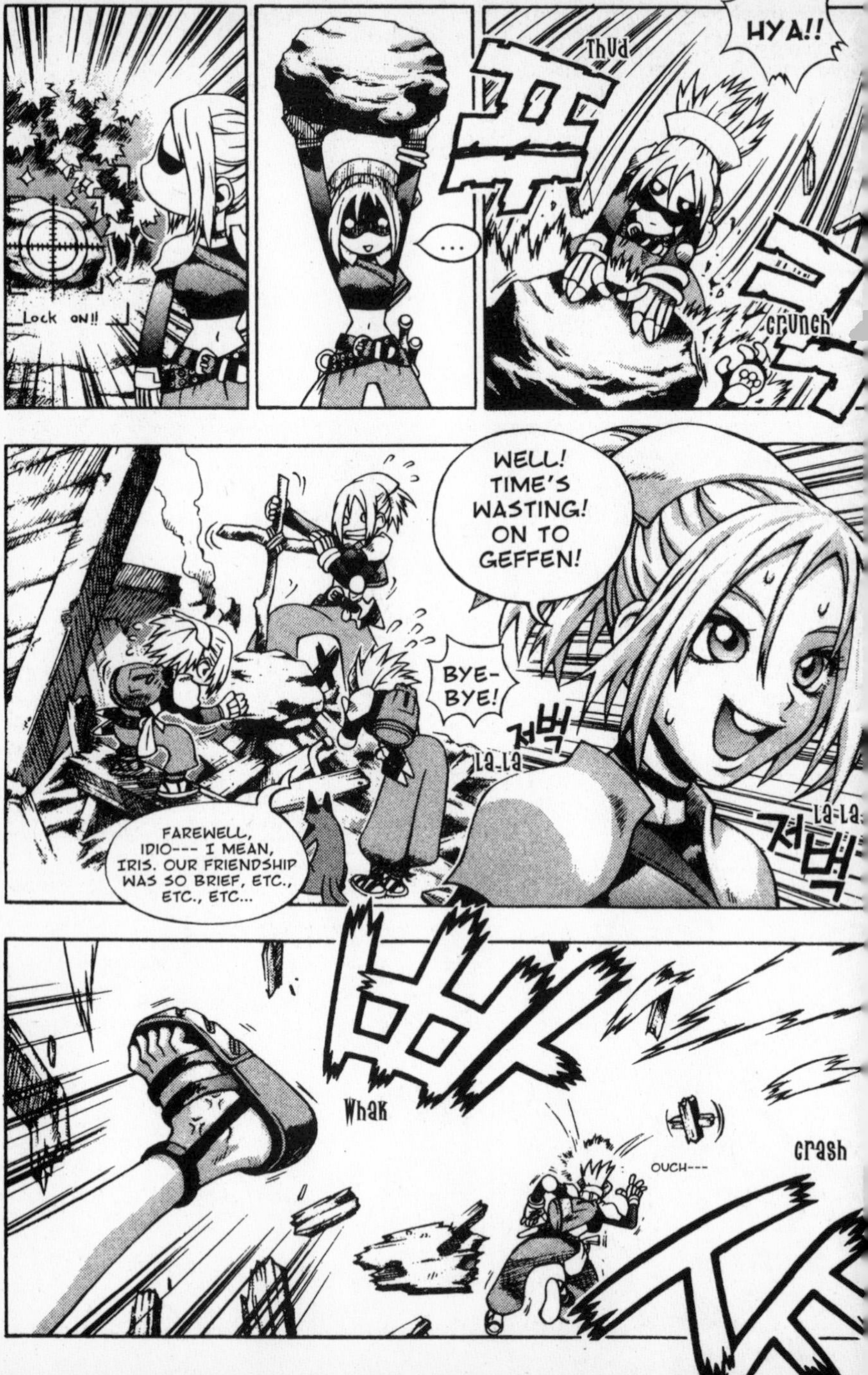
Lock ON!!
...
Thud
HYA!!
crunch
WELL! TIME'S WASTING! ON TO GEFFEN!
BYE-BYE!
저벅
La-la
La-la
저벅
FAREWELL, IDIO--- I MEAN, IRIS. OUR FRIENDSHIP WAS SO BRIEF, ETC., ETC., ETC...
Whak
OUCH---
crash

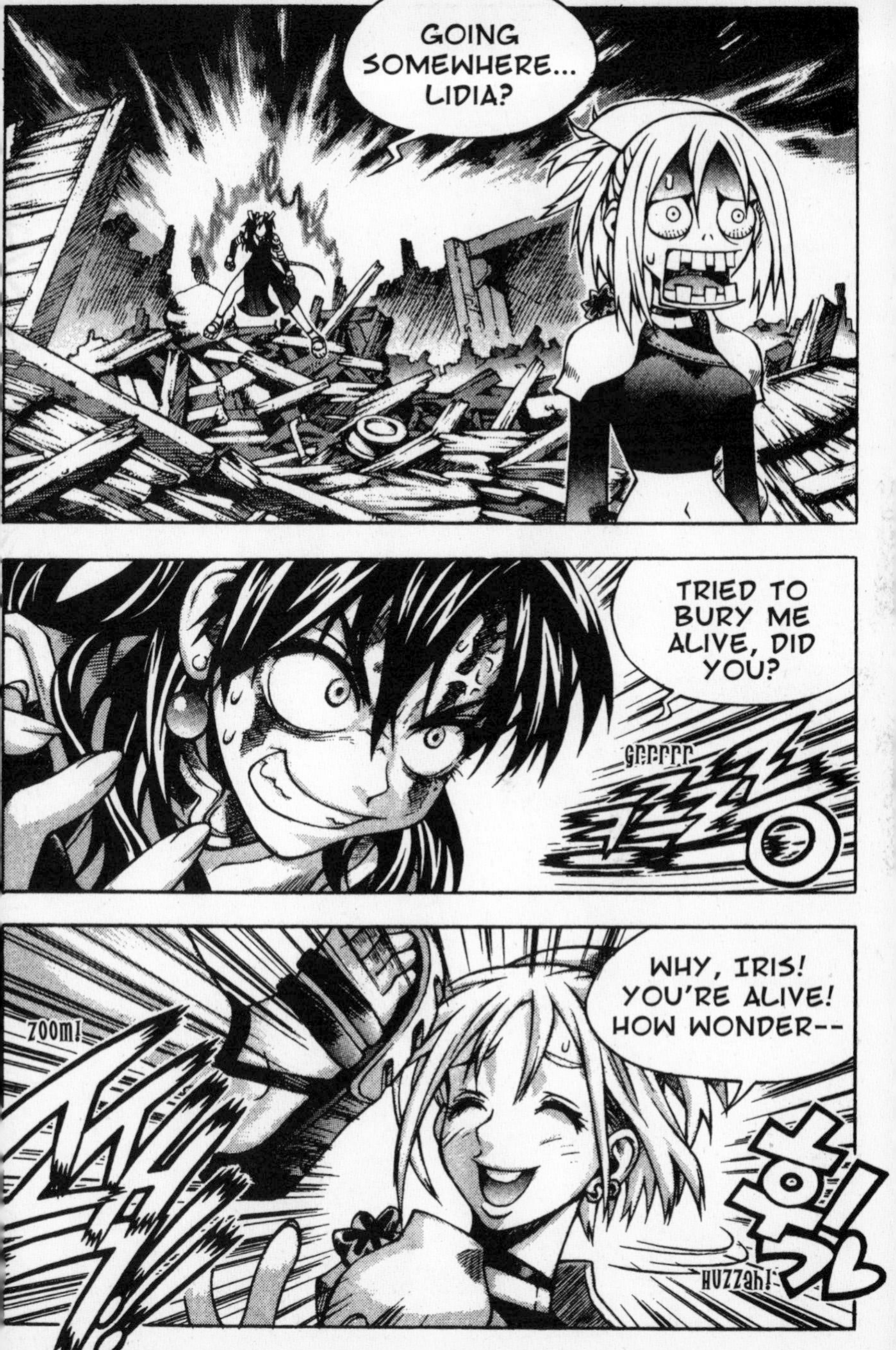
GOING SOMEWHERE... LIDIA?
TRIED TO BURY ME ALIVE, DID YOU?
GRRRRR
WHY, IRIS! YOU'RE ALIVE! HOW WONDER--
HUZZAH!
ZOOM!

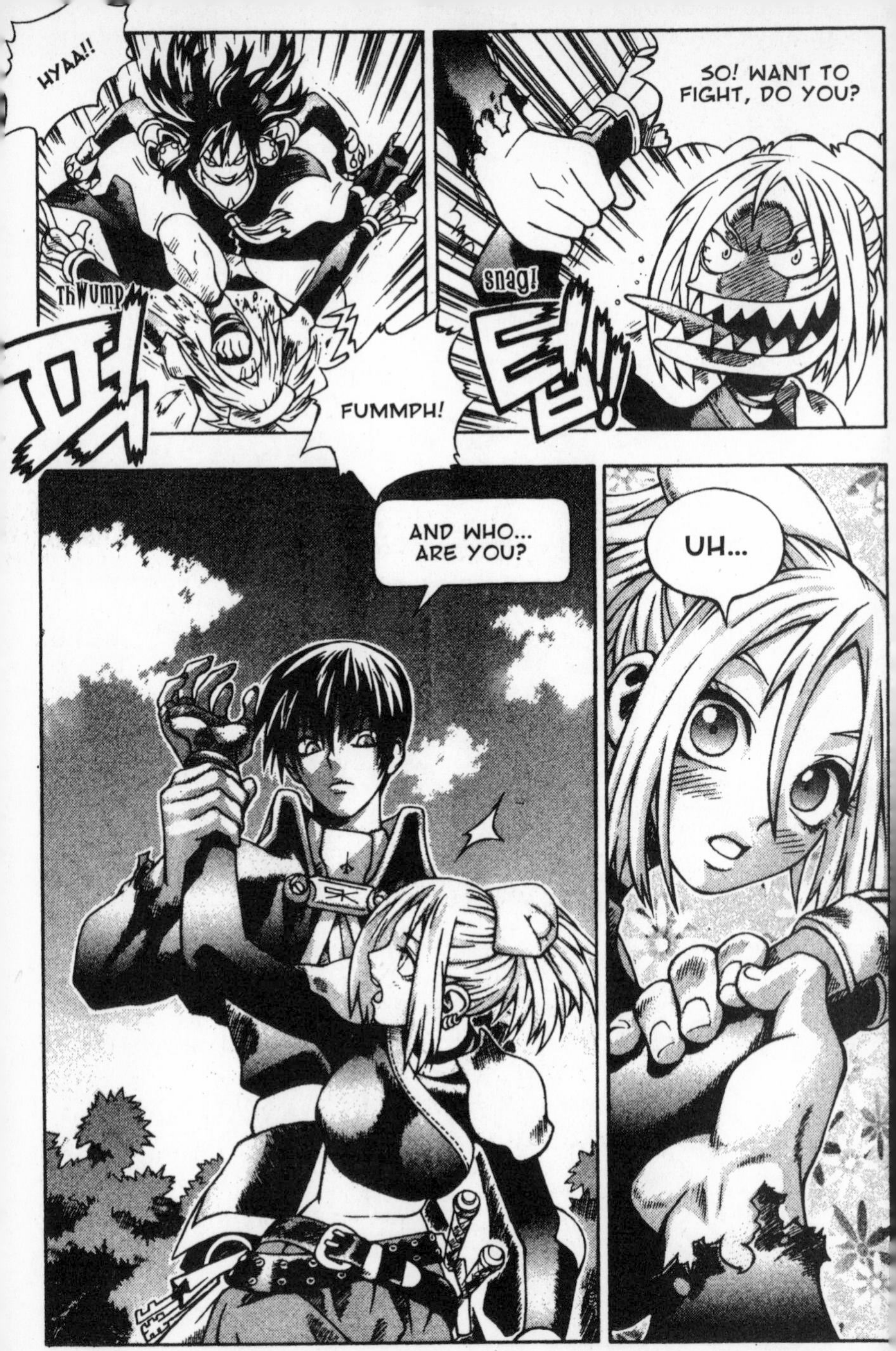
HYAA!!
ThWump
snag!
SO! WANT TO FIGHT, DO YOU?
FUMMPH!
AND WHO... ARE YOU?
UH...

RAGNAROK
라그나로크
IN TO THE ABYSS

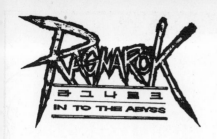

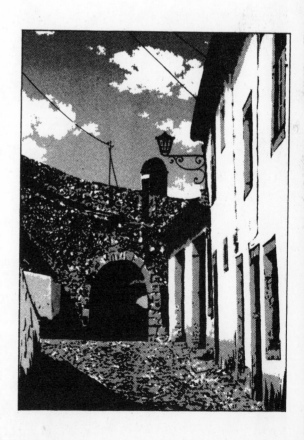

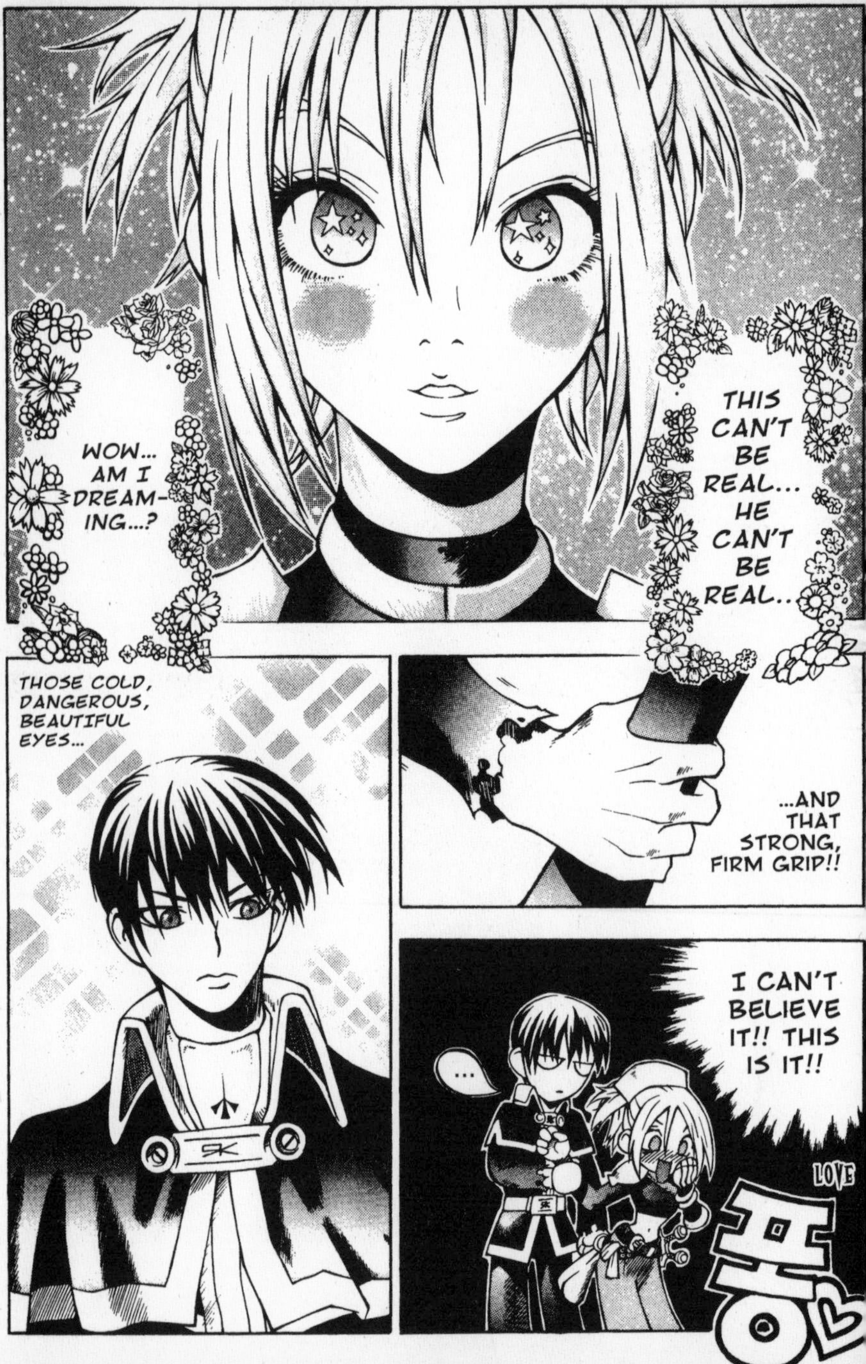
WOW... AM I DREAMING...?
THIS CAN'T BE REAL... HE CAN'T BE REAL..
THOSE COLD, DANGEROUS, BEAUTIFUL EYES...
...AND THAT STRONG, FIRM GRIP!!
...
I CAN'T BELIEVE IT!! THIS IS IT!!
LOVE

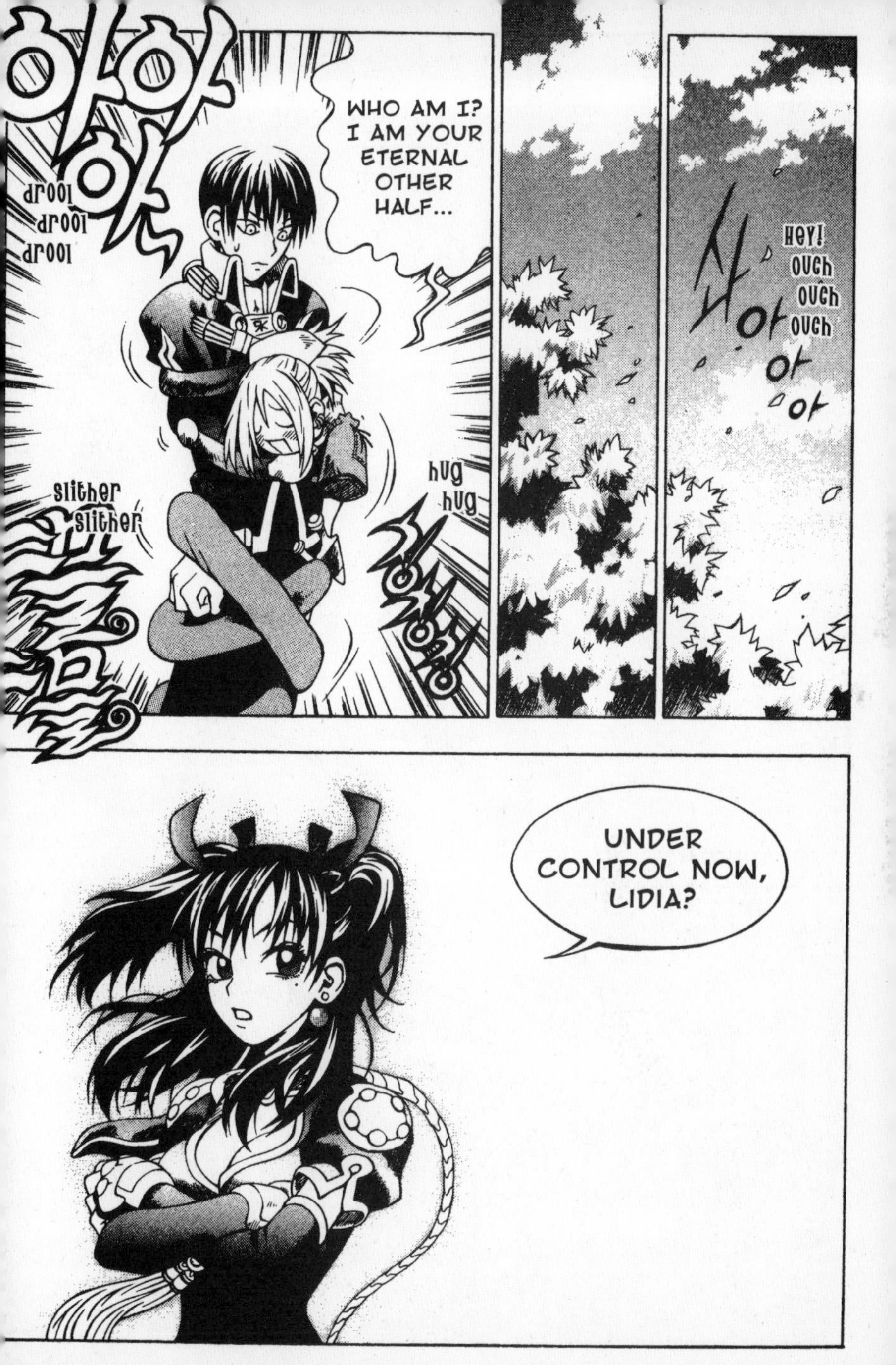
WHO AM I? I AM YOUR ETERNAL OTHER HALF...
drool drool drool
hug hug
slither slither
HEY! OUCH OUCH OUCH
UNDER CONTROL NOW, LIDIA?

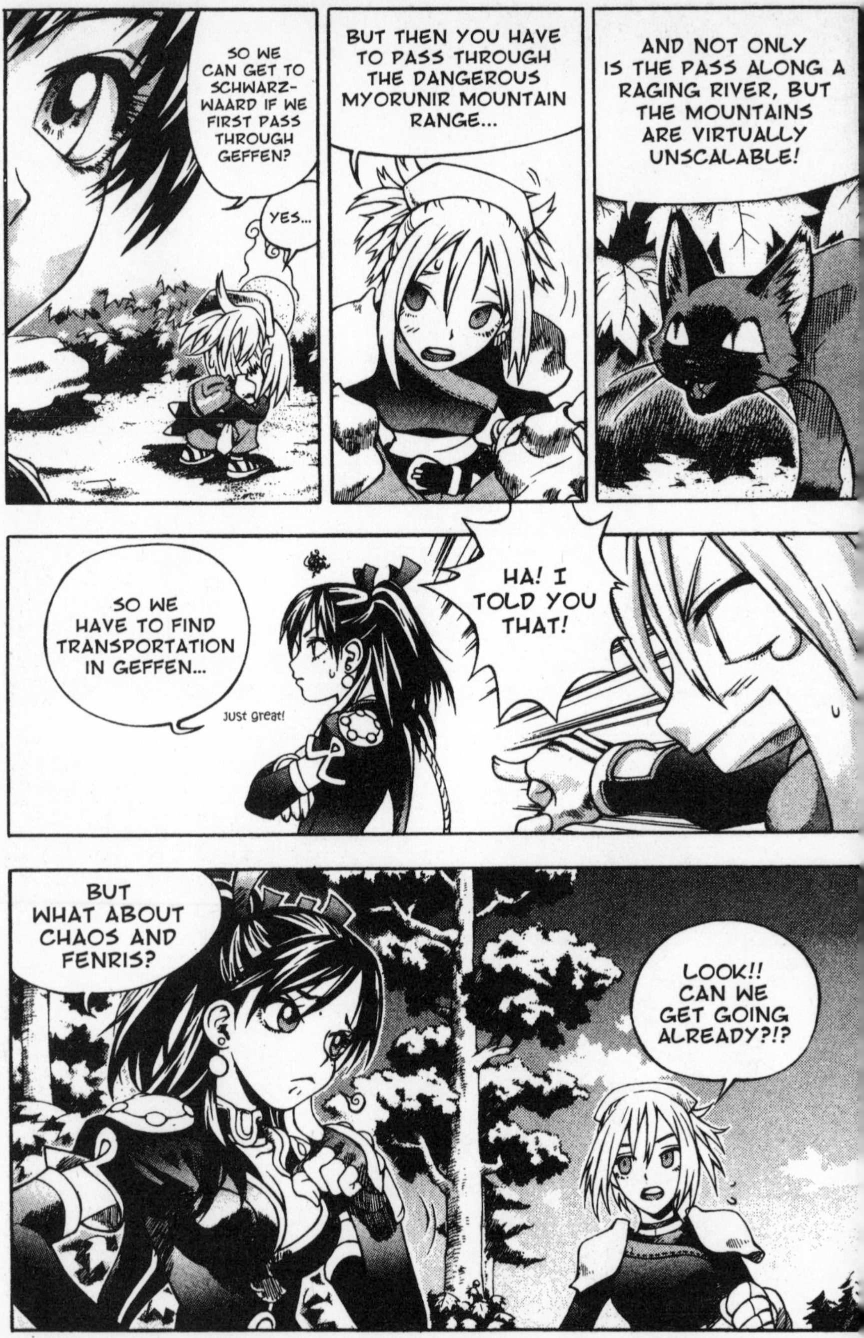
SO WE CAN GET TO SCHWARZ-WAARD IF WE FIRST PASS THROUGH GEFFEN?
YES...
BUT THEN YOU HAVE TO PASS THROUGH THE DANGEROUS MYORUNIR MOUNTAIN RANGE...
AND NOT ONLY IS THE PASS ALONG A RAGING RIVER, BUT THE MOUNTAINS ARE VIRTUALLY UNSCALABLE!
SO WE HAVE TO FIND TRANSPORTATION IN GEFFEN...
Just great!
HA! I TOLD YOU THAT!
BUT WHAT ABOUT CHAOS AND FENRIS?
LOOK!! CAN WE GET GOING ALREADY?!?

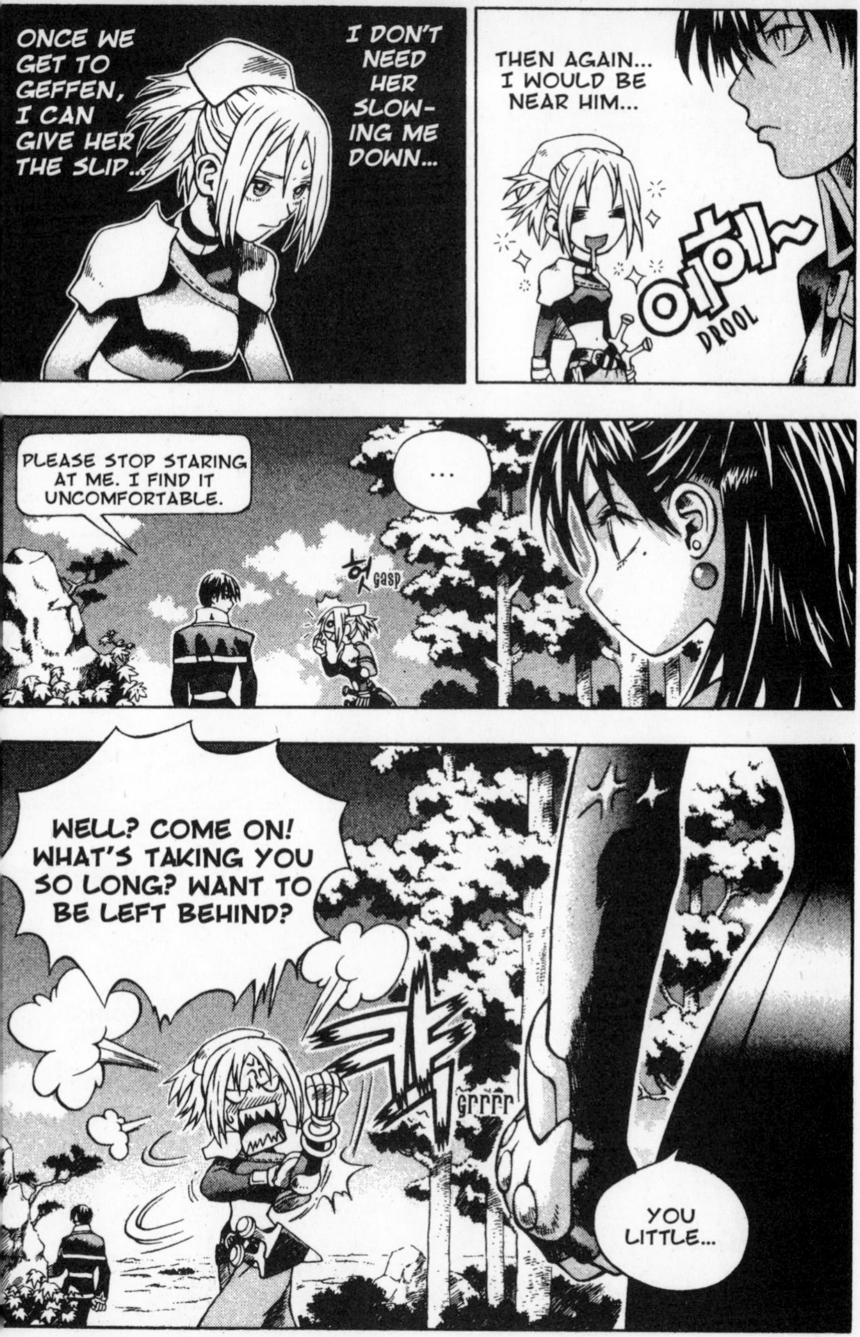
ONCE WE GET TO GEFFEN, I CAN GIVE HER THE SLIP...
I DON'T NEED HER SLOWING ME DOWN...
THEN AGAIN... I WOULD BE NEAR HIM...
에헤~
DROOL
PLEASE STOP STARING AT ME. I FIND IT UNCOMFORTABLE.
...
헉
GASP
WELL? COME ON! WHAT'S TAKING YOU SO LONG? WANT TO BE LEFT BEHIND?
GRRRR
YOU LITTLE...

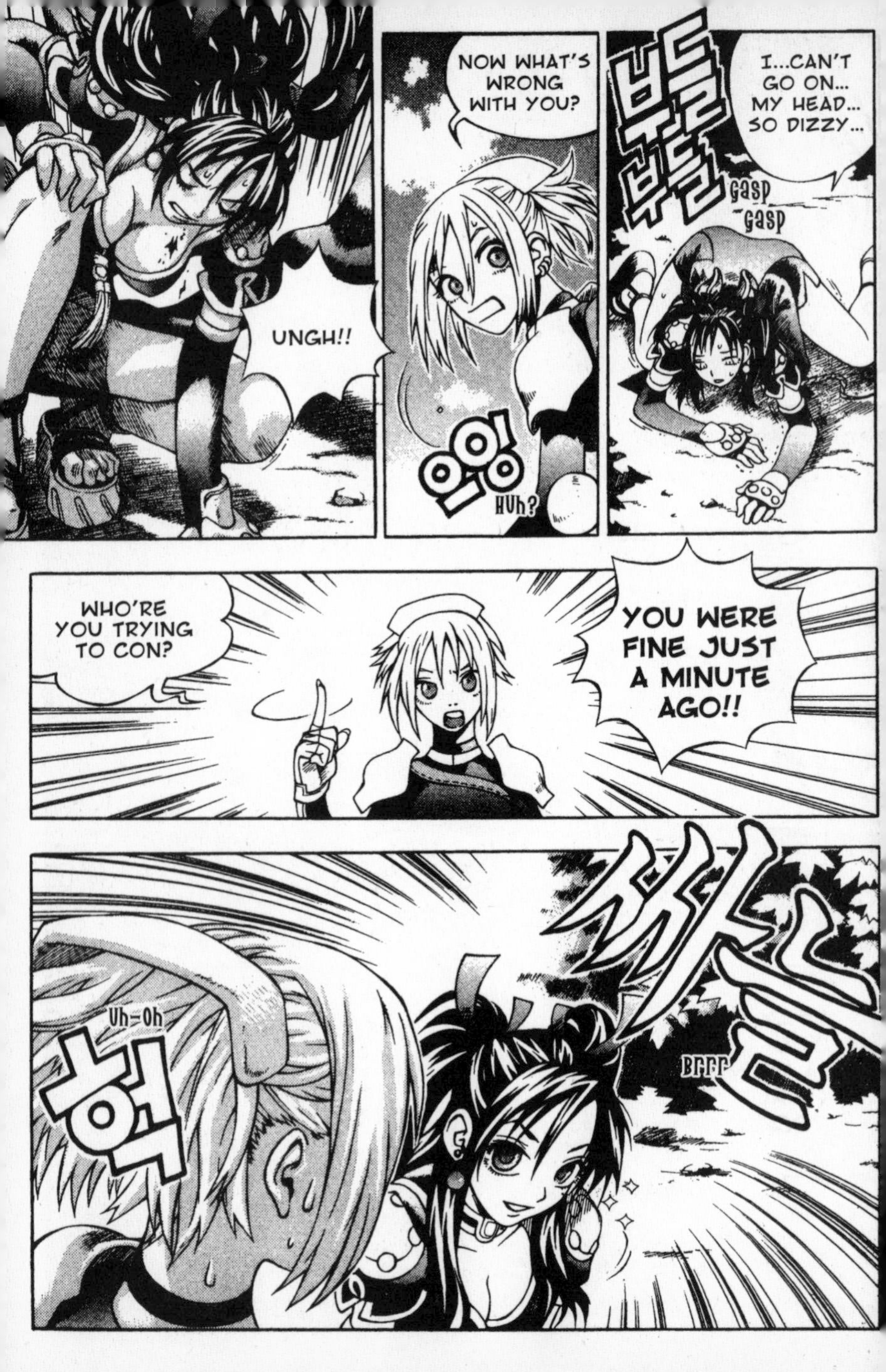
UNGH!!
NOW WHAT'S WRONG WITH YOU?
HUh?
I...CAN'T GO ON... MY HEAD... SO DIZZY...
GASP GASP
WHO'RE YOU TRYING TO CON?
YOU WERE FINE JUST A MINUTE AGO!!
헉
Uh-Oh
Brrr

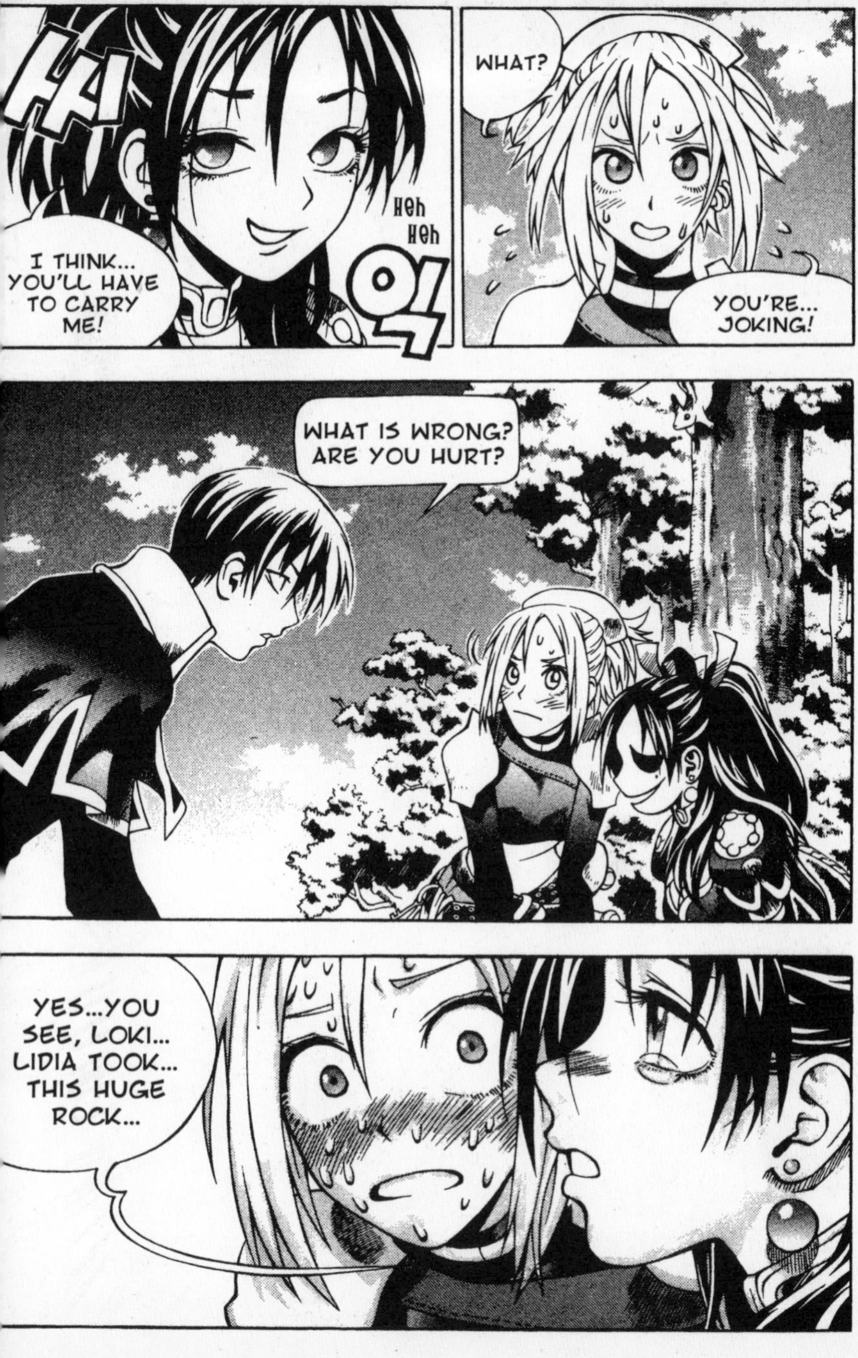
I THINK... YOU'LL HAVE TO CARRY ME!
Heh Heh
WHAT?
YOU'RE... JOKING!
WHAT IS WRONG? ARE YOU HURT?
YES...YOU SEE, LOKI... LIDIA TOOK... THIS HUGE ROCK...

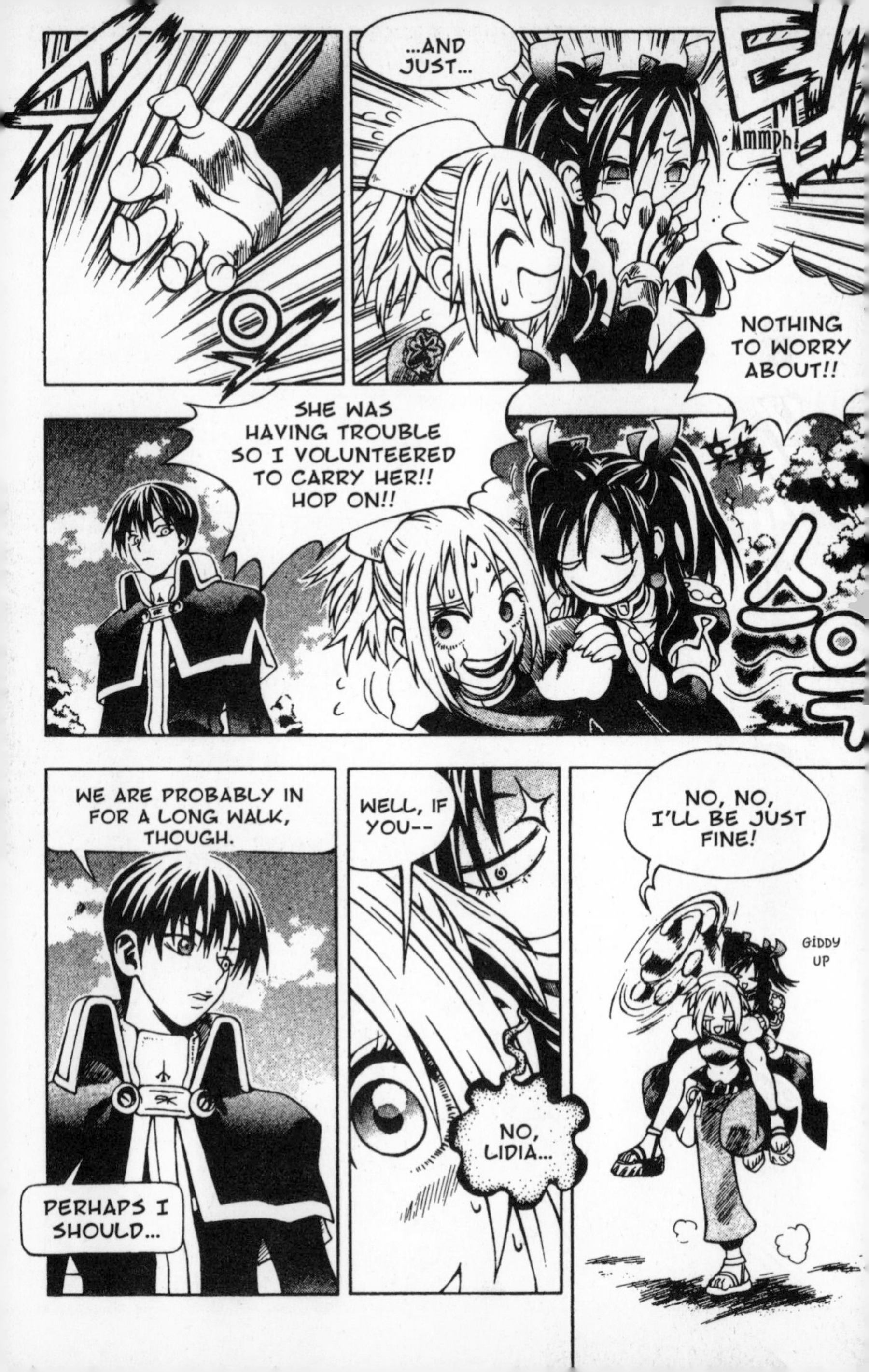
...AND JUST...
Mmmph!
NOTHING TO WORRY ABOUT!!
SHE WAS HAVING TROUBLE SO I VOLUNTEERED TO CARRY HER!! HOP ON!!
WE ARE PROBABLY IN FOR A LONG WALK, THOUGH.
PERHAPS I SHOULD...
WELL, IF YOU--
NO, LIDIA...
NO, NO, I'LL BE JUST FINE!
GIDDY UP

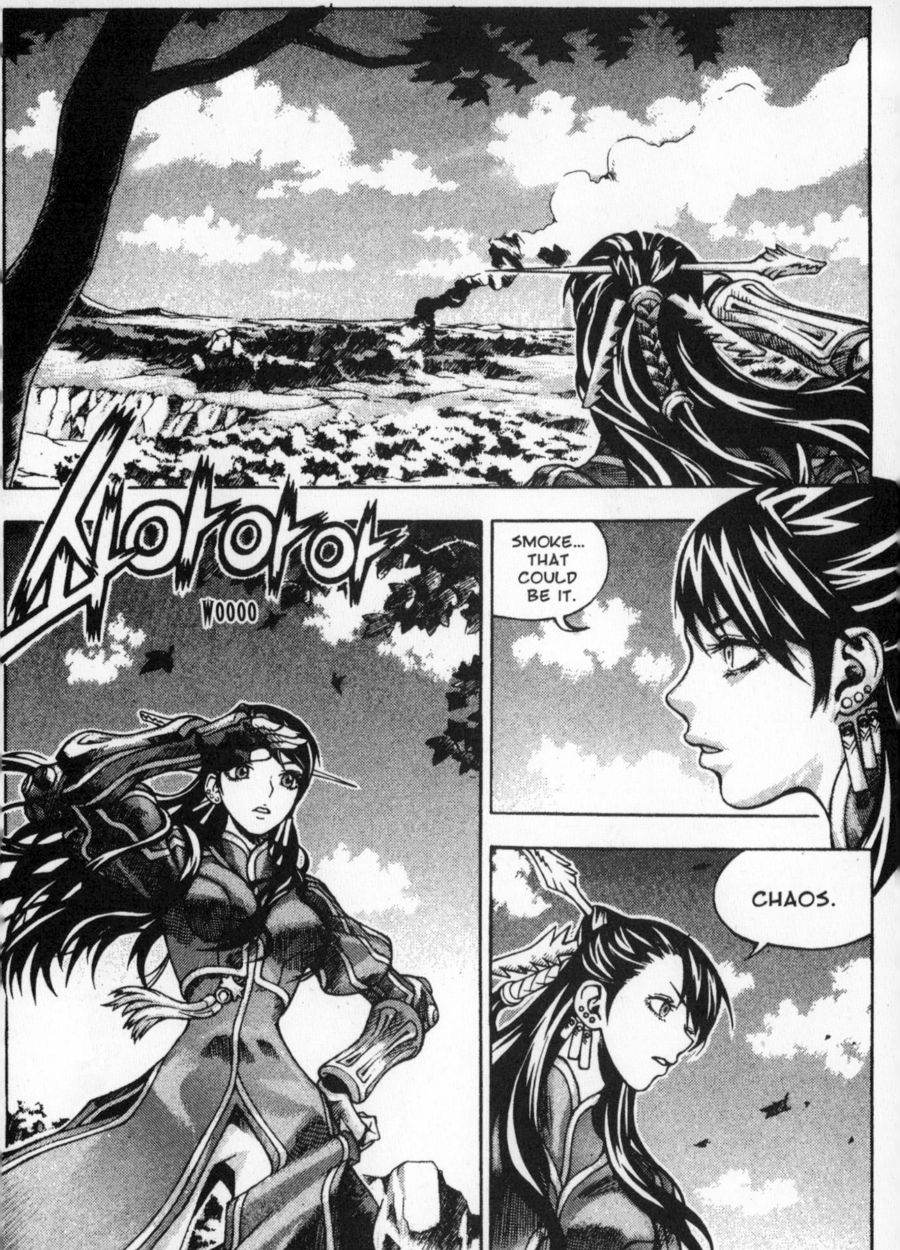
SMOKE... THAT COULD BE IT.
CHAOS.
WOOOO

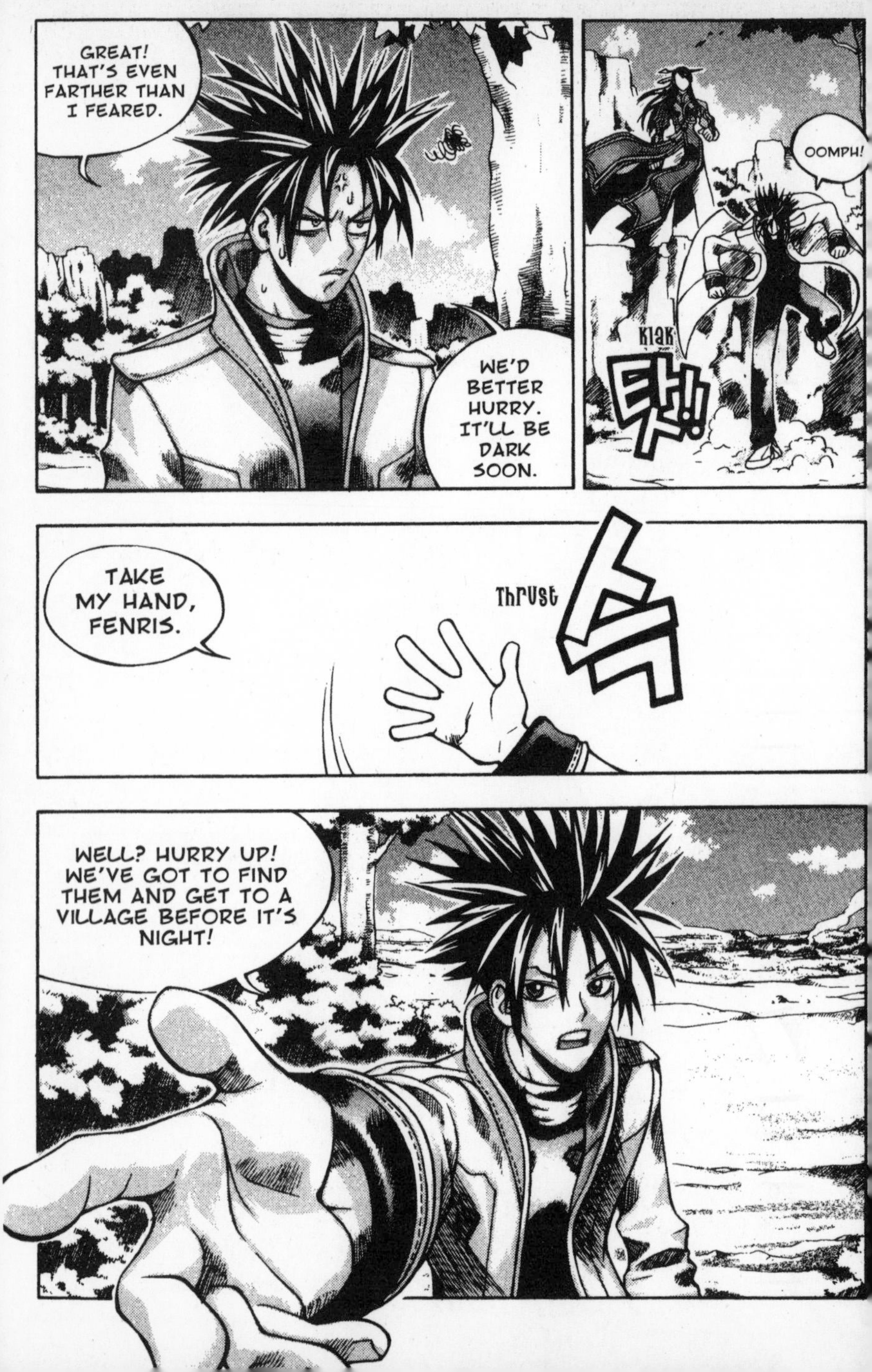
GREAT! THAT'S EVEN FARTHER THAN I FEARED.
WE'D BETTER HURRY. IT'LL BE DARK SOON.
OOMPH!
KLAK
탁!!
TAKE MY HAND, FENRIS.
Thrust
WELL? HURRY UP! WE'VE GOT TO FIND THEM AND GET TO A VILLAGE BEFORE IT'S NIGHT!

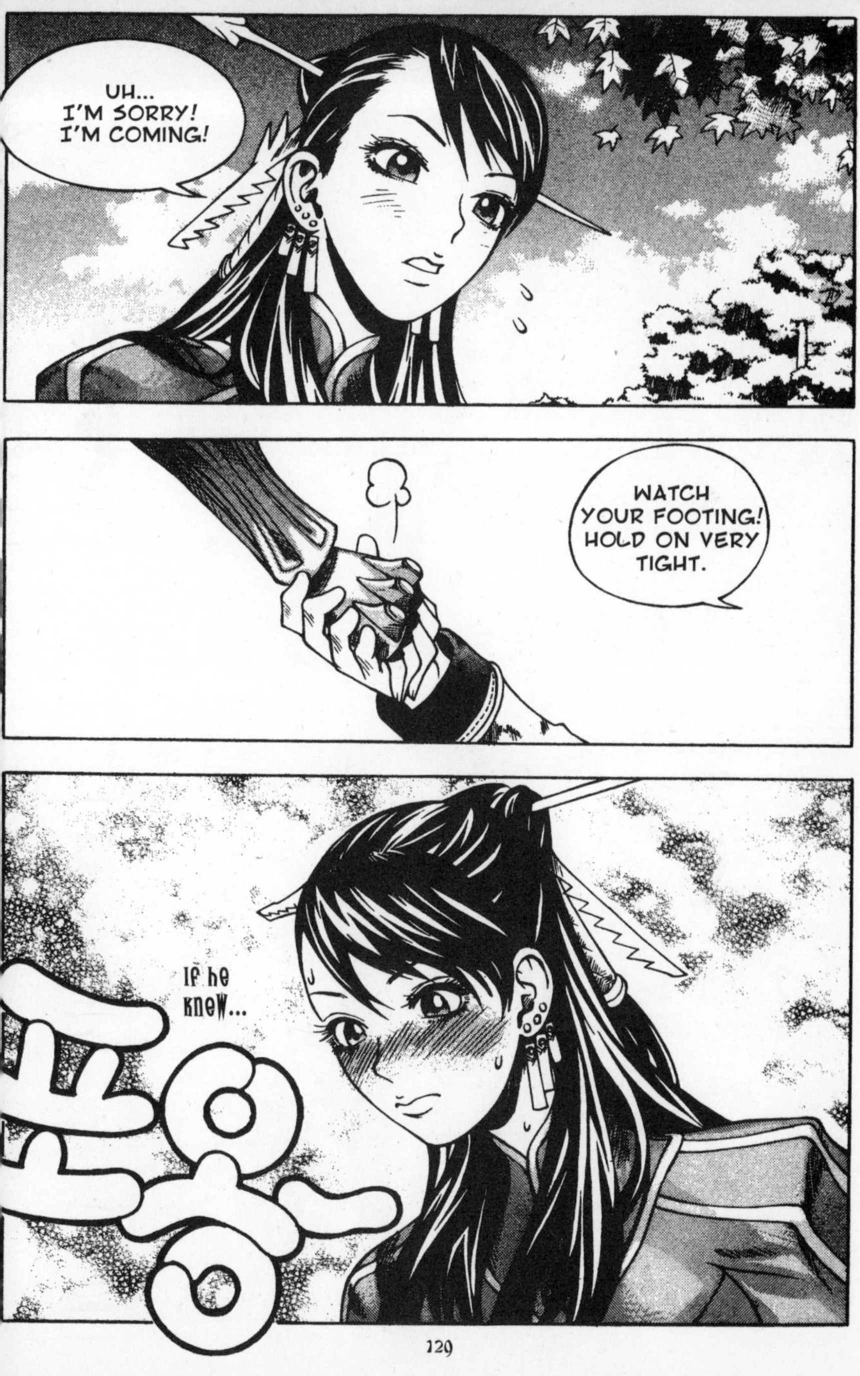
UH... I'M SORRY! I'M COMING!
WATCH YOUR FOOTING! HOLD ON VERY TIGHT.
If he knew...

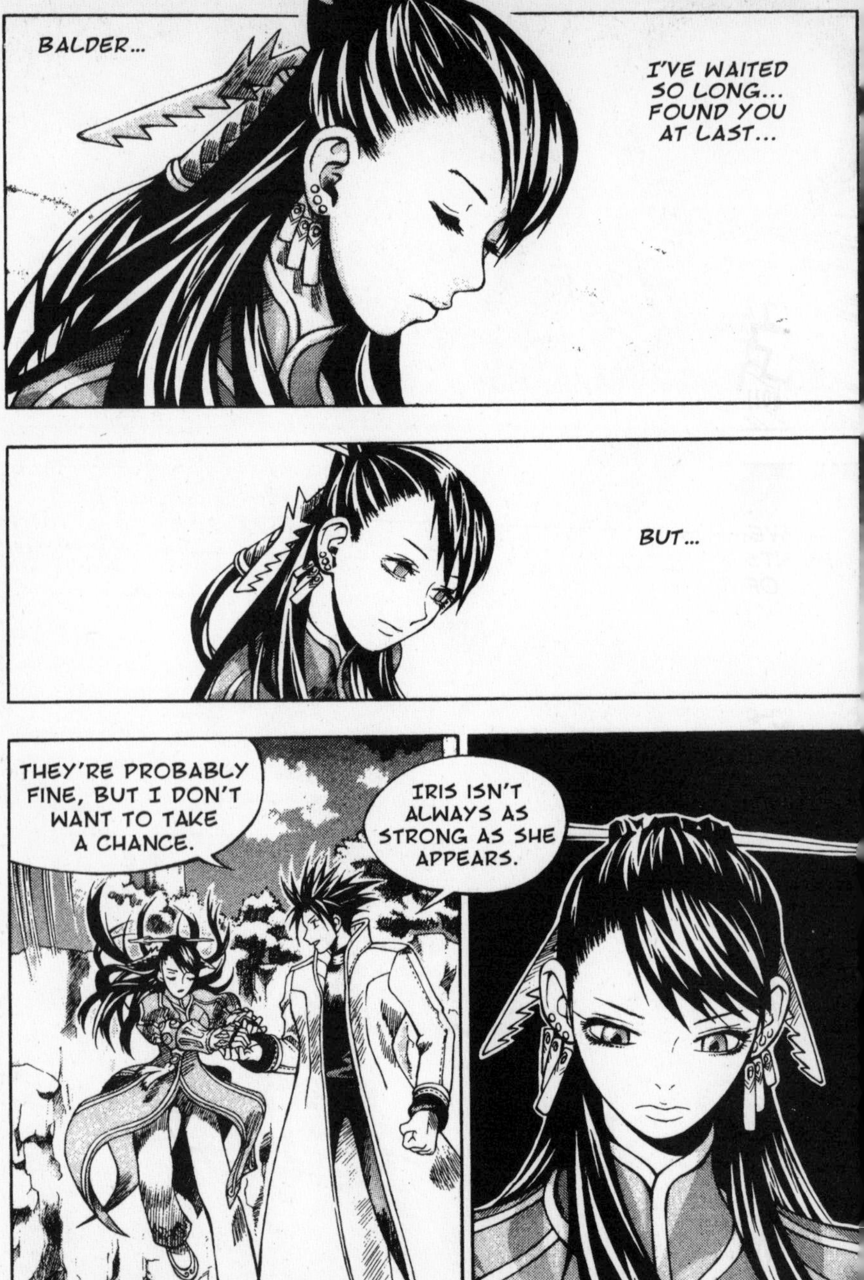
BALDER...
I'VE WAITED SO LONG... FOUND YOU AT LAST...
BUT...
THEY'RE PROBABLY FINE, BUT I DON'T WANT TO TAKE A CHANCE.
IRIS ISN'T ALWAYS AS STRONG AS SHE APPEARS.

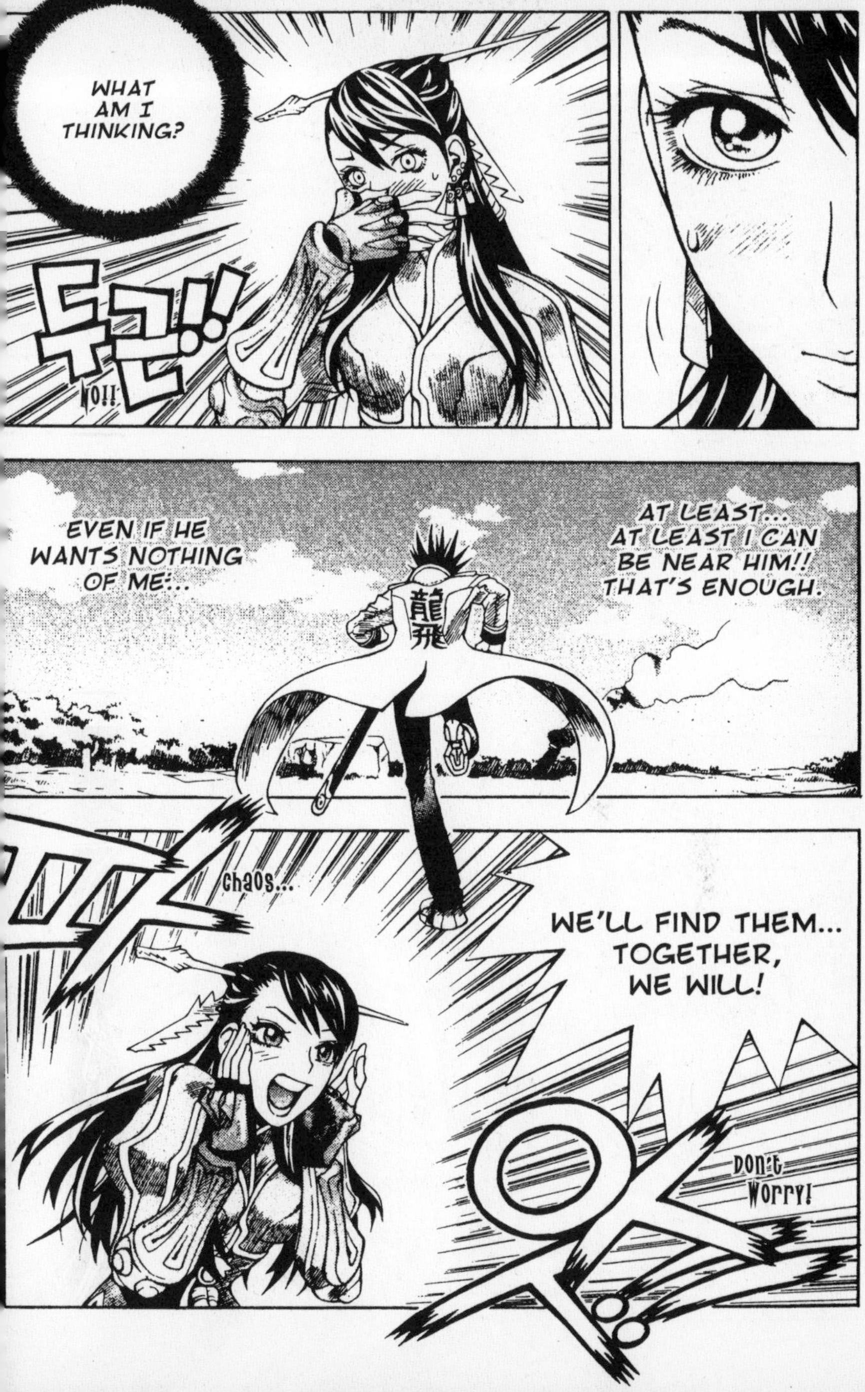
WHAT AM I THINKING?
NO!!
EVEN IF HE WANTS NOTHING OF ME...
AT LEAST... AT LEAST I CAN BE NEAR HIM!! THAT'S ENOUGH.
chaos...
WE'LL FIND THEM... TOGETHER, WE WILL!
Don't Worry!

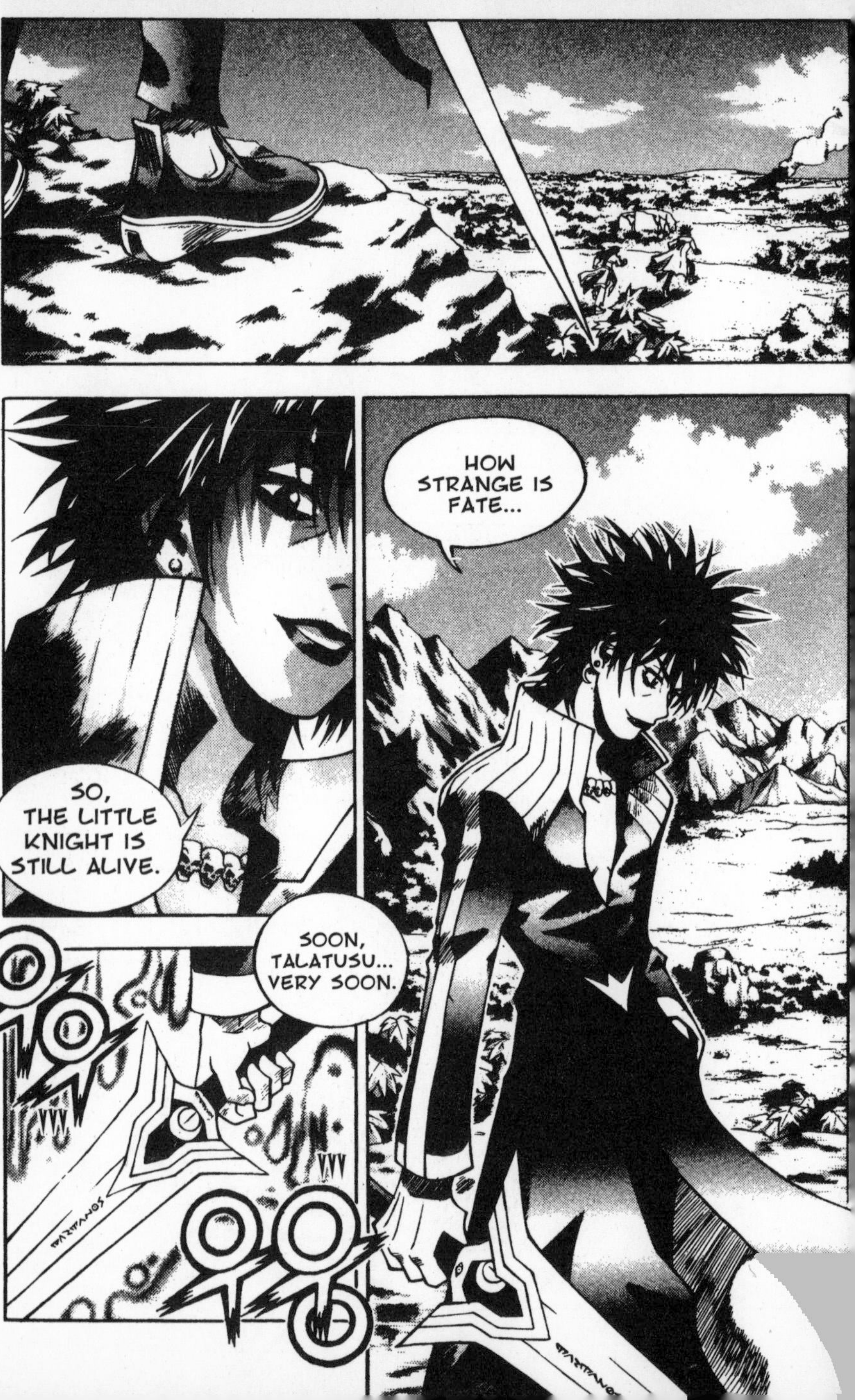
HOW STRANGE IS FATE...
SO, THE LITTLE KNIGHT IS STILL ALIVE.
SOON, TALATUSU... VERY SOON.

RAGNAROK
라그나로크
IN TO THE ABYSS

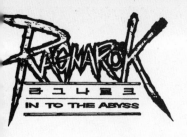

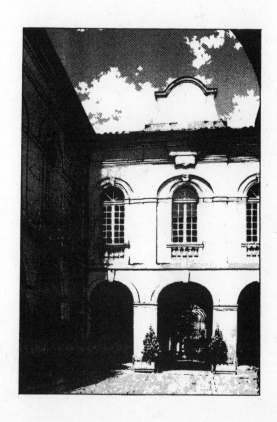

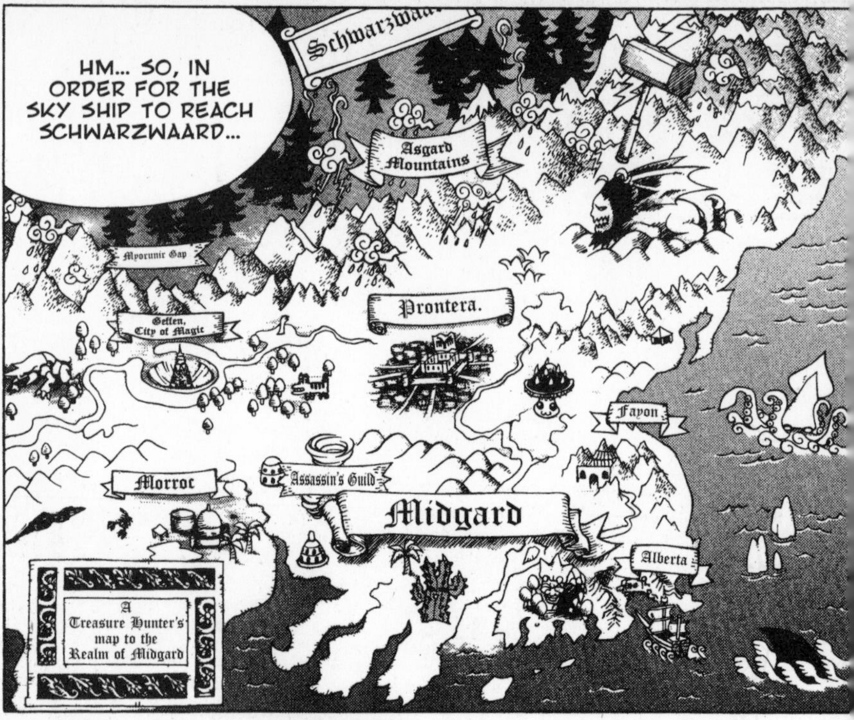
HM... SO, IN ORDER FOR THE SKY SHIP TO REACH SCHWARZWAARD...
Asgard Mountains
Myorunir Gap
Prontera.
Geffen, City of Magic
Fayon
Assassin's Guild
Morroc
Midgard
Alberta
A Treasure Hunter's map to the Realm of Midgard
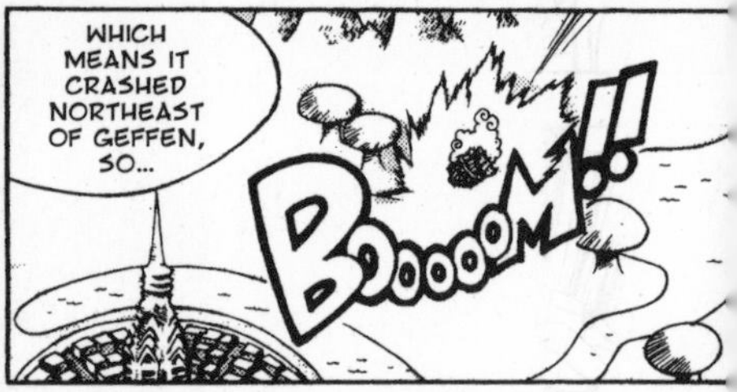
WHICH MEANS IT CRASHED NORTHEAST OF GEFFEN, SO...
BOOOOOM!!
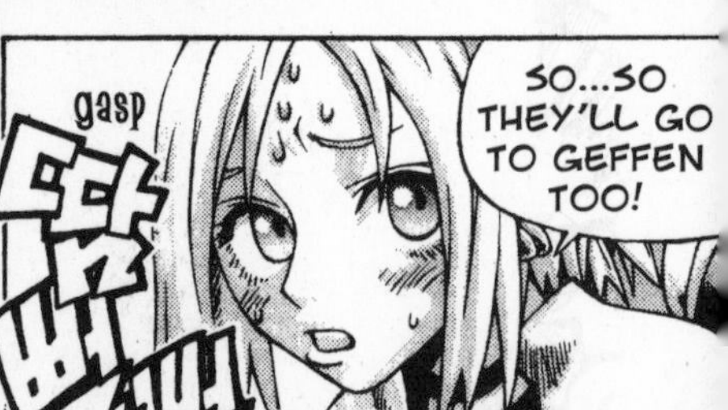
SO...SO THEY'LL GO TO GEFFEN TOO!
gasp
Wheeze
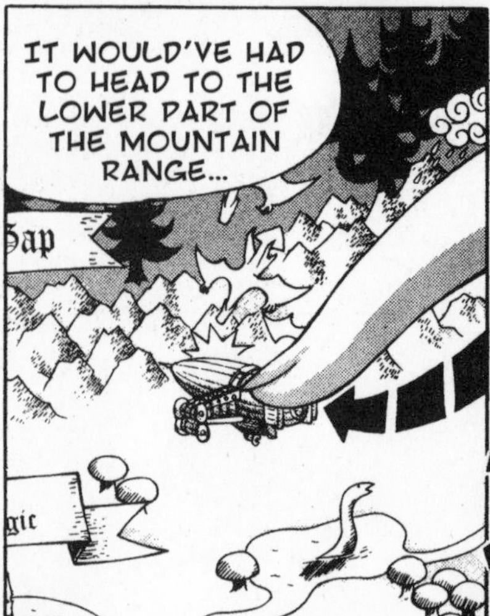
IT WOULD'VE HAD TO HEAD TO THE LOWER PART OF THE MOUNTAIN RANGE...

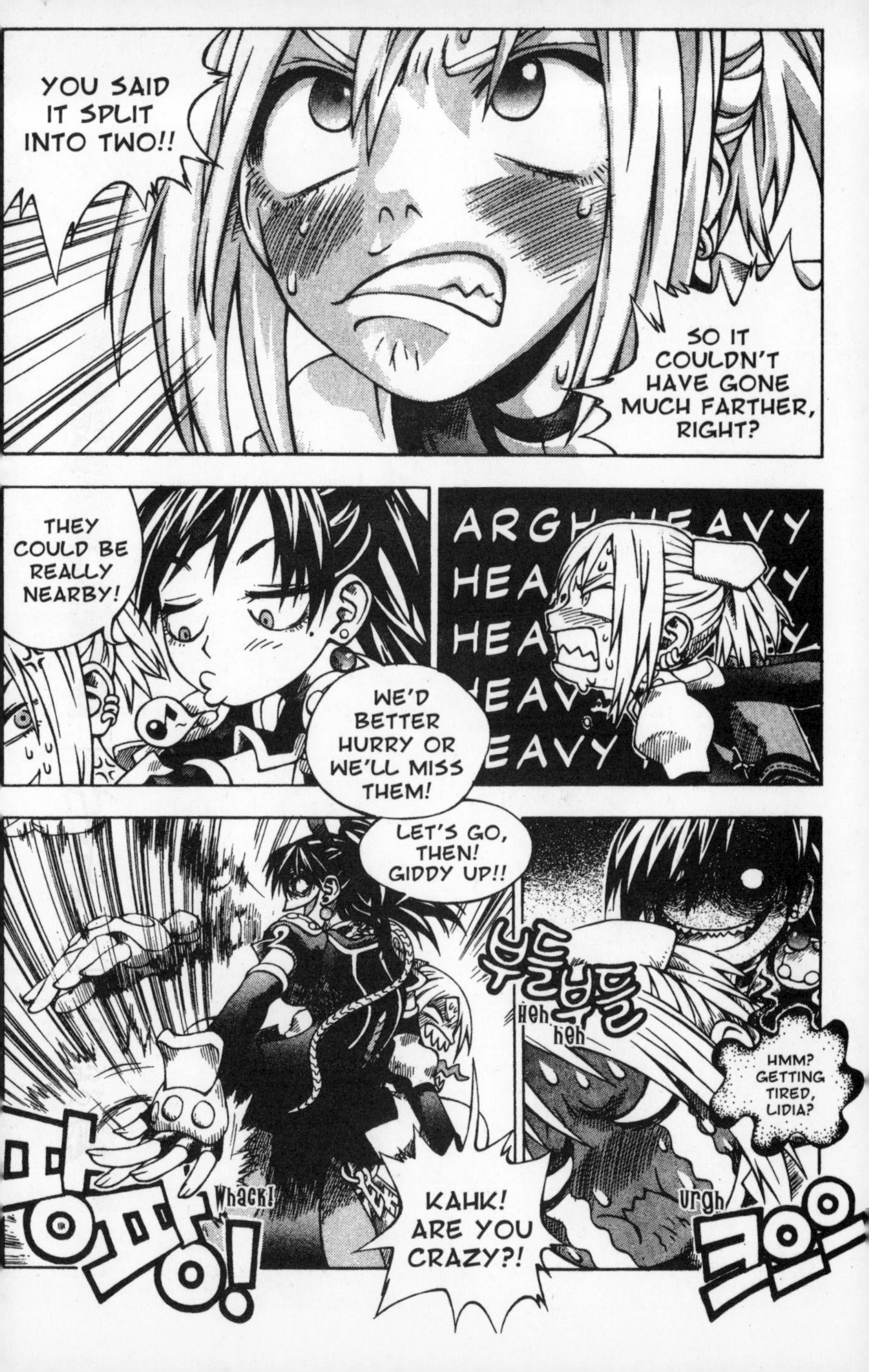
YOU SAID IT SPLIT INTO TWO!!
SO IT COULDN'T HAVE GONE MUCH FARTHER, RIGHT?
THEY COULD BE REALLY NEARBY!
WE'D BETTER HURRY OR WE'LL MISS THEM!
ARGH HEAVY HEAVY HEAVY HEAVY HEAVY
LET'S GO, THEN! GIDDY UP!!
Whack!
KAHK! ARE YOU CRAZY?!
부들부들
heh heh
HMM? GETTING TIRED, LIDIA?
urgh

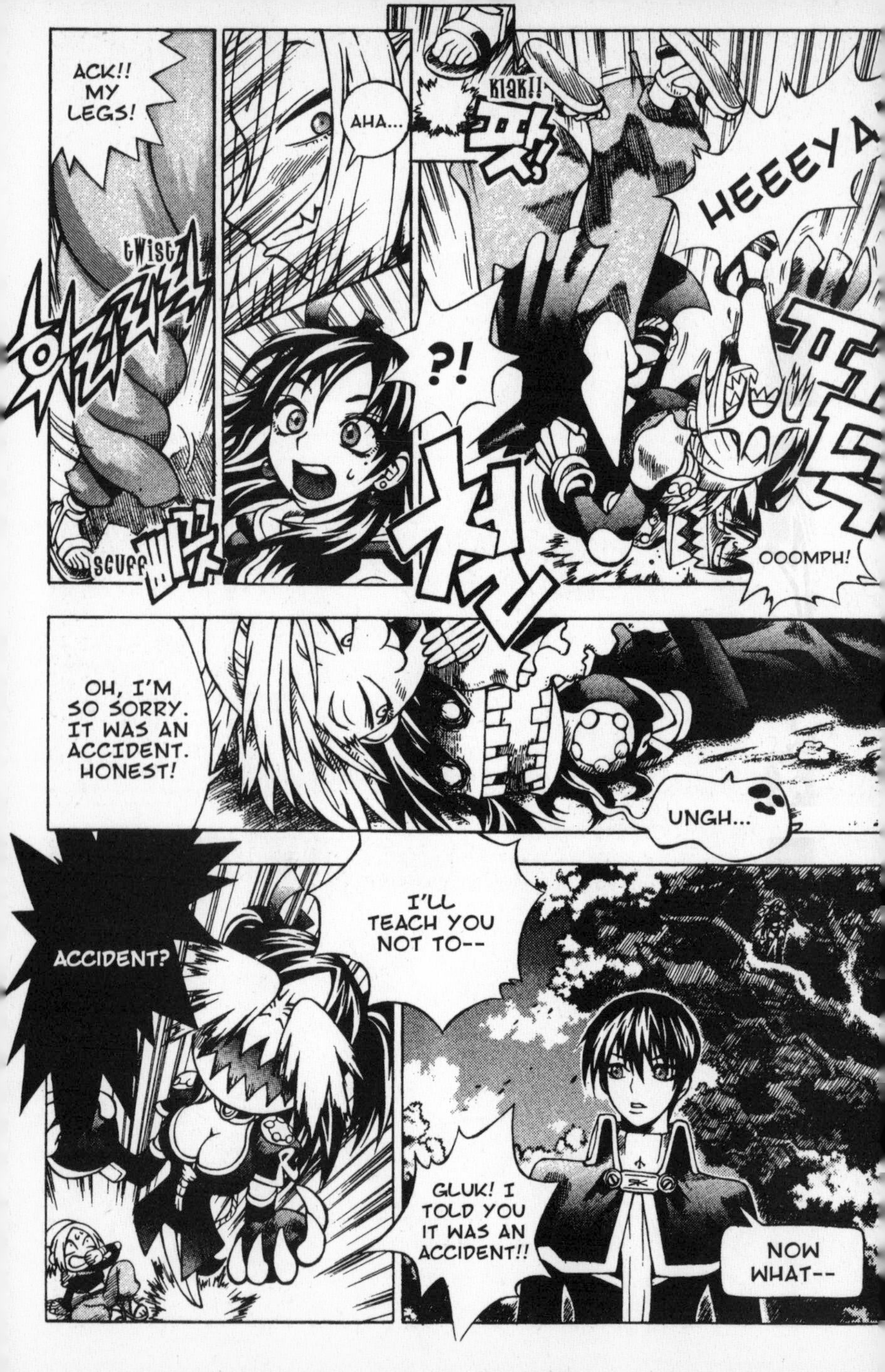
ACK!! MY LEGS!
TWIST
SCUFF
AHA...
KIAK!!
HEEEYA
?!
OOOMPH!
OH, I'M SO SORRY. IT WAS AN ACCIDENT. HONEST!
UNGH...
ACCIDENT?
I'LL TEACH YOU NOT TO--
GLUK! I TOLD YOU IT WAS AN ACCIDENT!!
NOW WHAT--

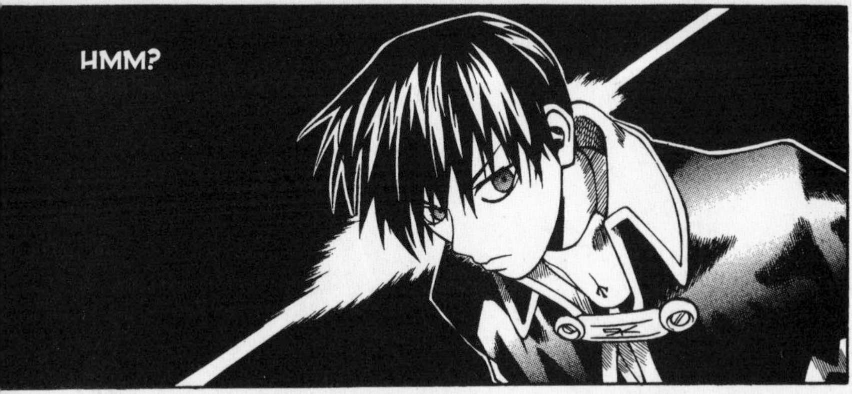
HMM?
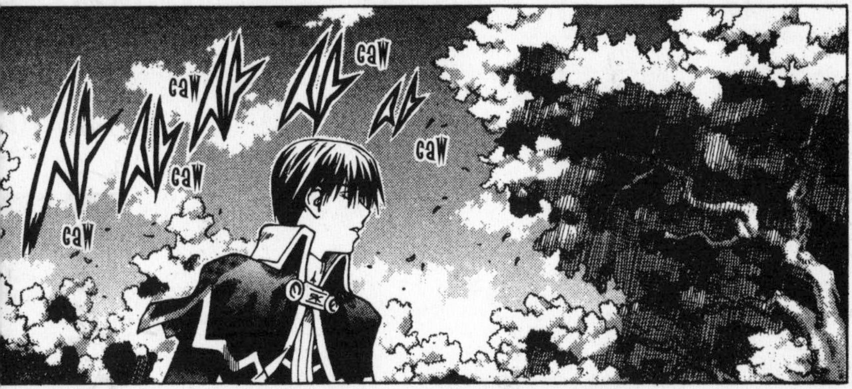
caw
caw
caw
caw
caw
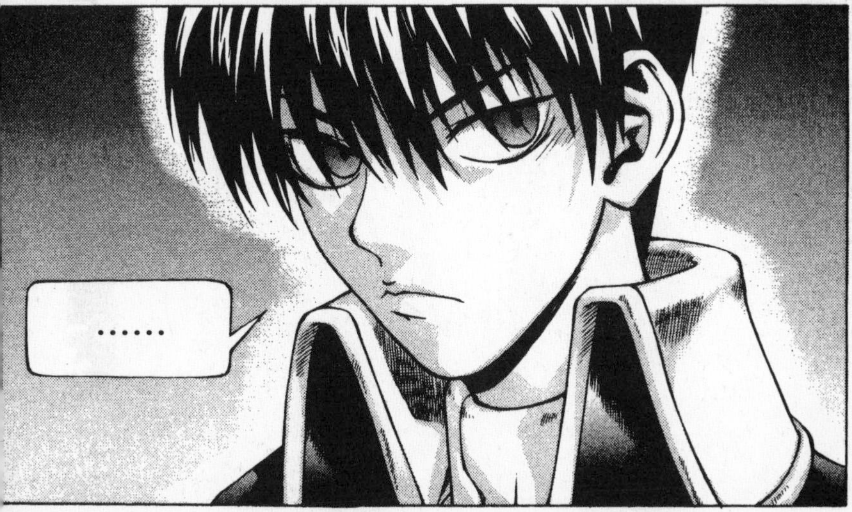
......

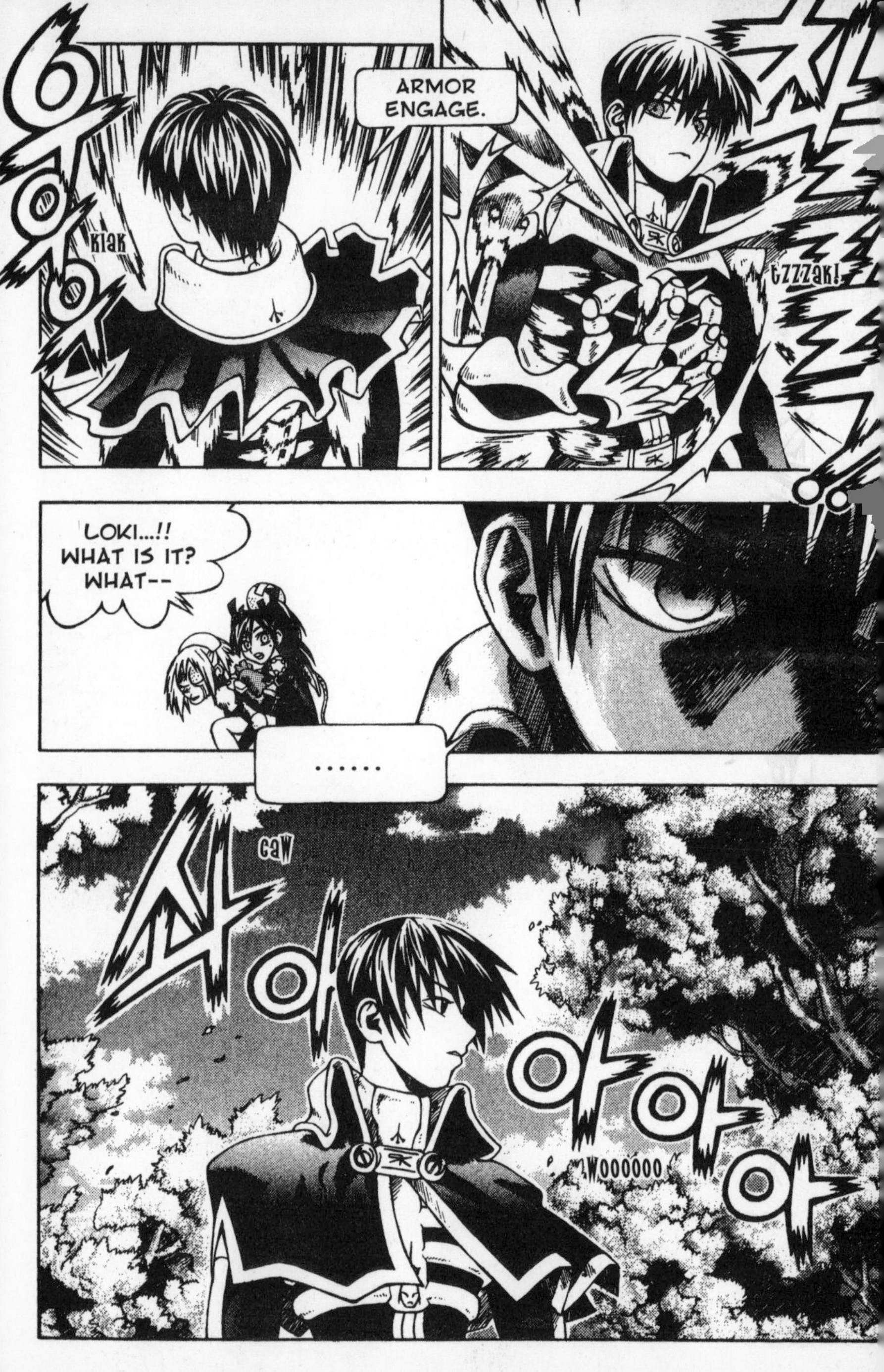
TZZZAK!
ARMOR ENGAGE.
KIAK
LOKI...!! WHAT IS IT? WHAT--
......
CAW
WOOOOOO

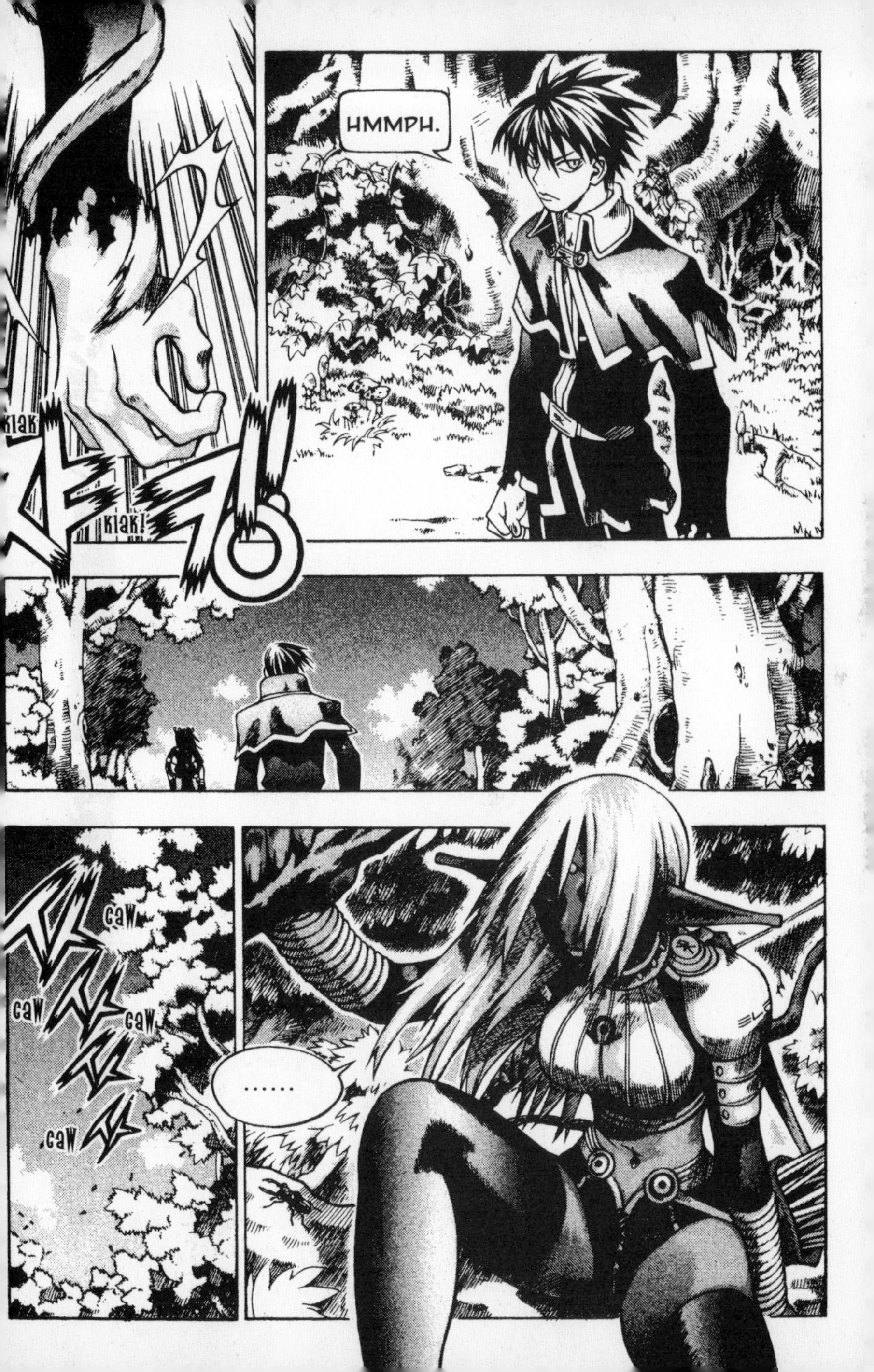
HMMPH.
KIAK
KIAK!
CAW
CAW
CAW
CAW
....

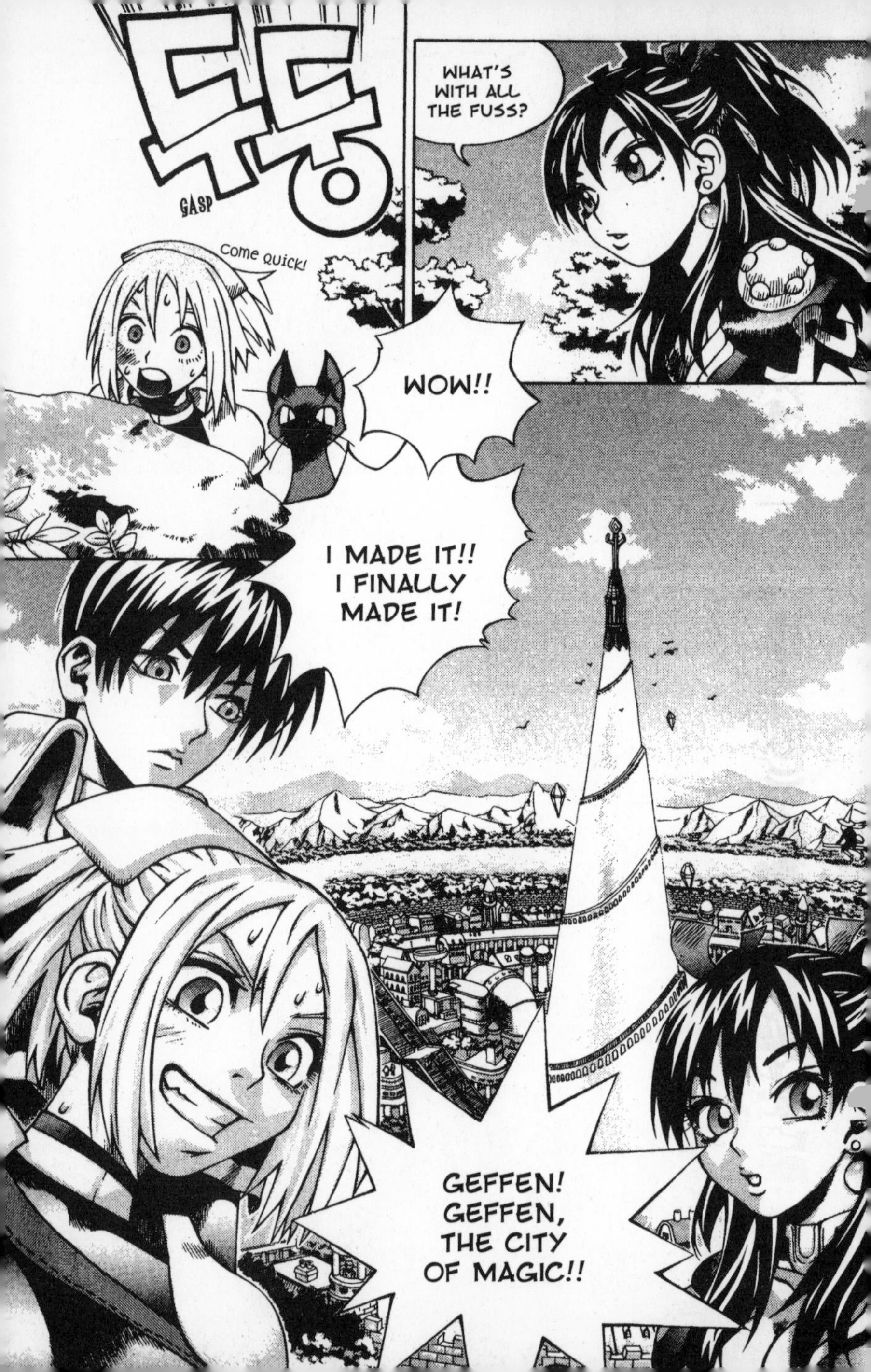
두둥
GASP
WHAT'S WITH ALL THE FUSS?
Come quick!
WOW!!
I MADE IT!! I FINALLY MADE IT!
GEFFEN! GEFFEN, THE CITY OF MAGIC!!

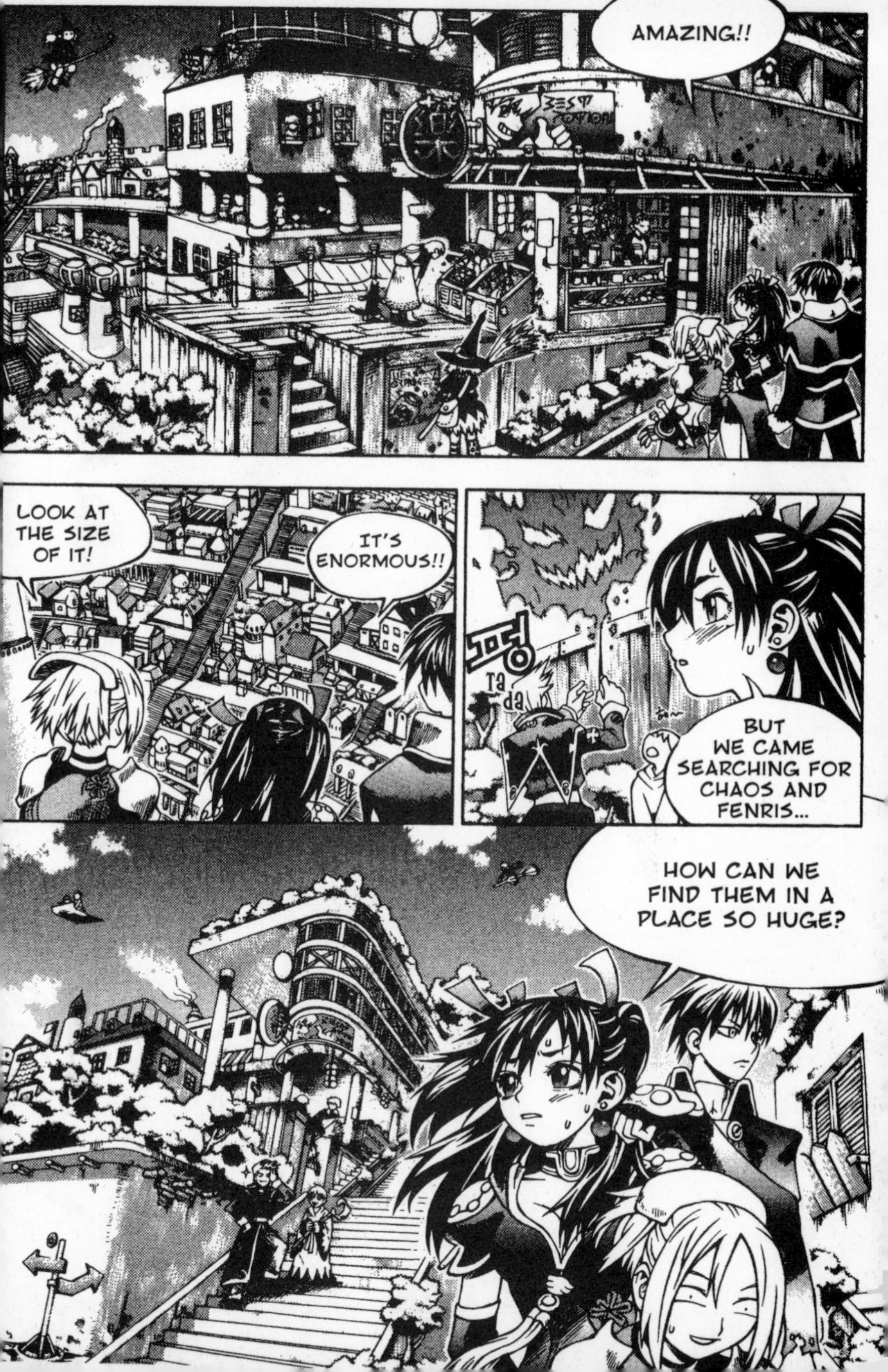
AMAZING!!
LOOK AT THE SIZE OF IT!
IT'S ENORMOUS!!
TA DA
BUT WE CAME SEARCHING FOR CHAOS AND FENRIS...
HOW CAN WE FIND THEM IN A PLACE SO HUGE?

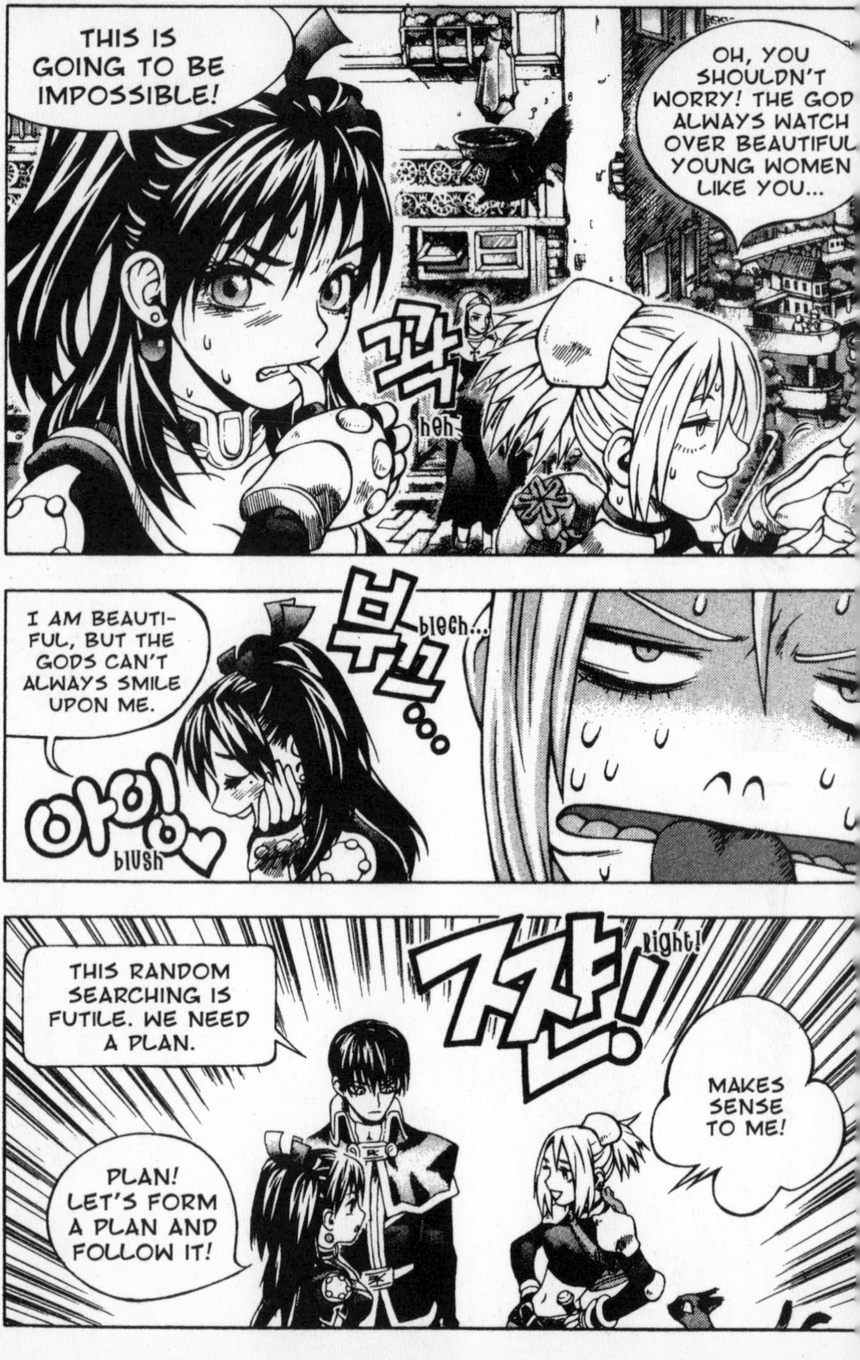
THIS IS GOING TO BE IMPOSSIBLE!
heh
OH, YOU SHOULDN'T WORRY! THE GOD ALWAYS WATCH OVER BEAUTIFUL YOUNG WOMEN LIKE YOU...
I AM BEAUTI-FUL, BUT THE GODS CAN'T ALWAYS SMILE UPON ME.
blush
blech...
THIS RANDOM SEARCHING IS FUTILE. WE NEED A PLAN.
PLAN! LET'S FORM A PLAN AND FOLLOW IT!
Right!
MAKES SENSE TO ME!

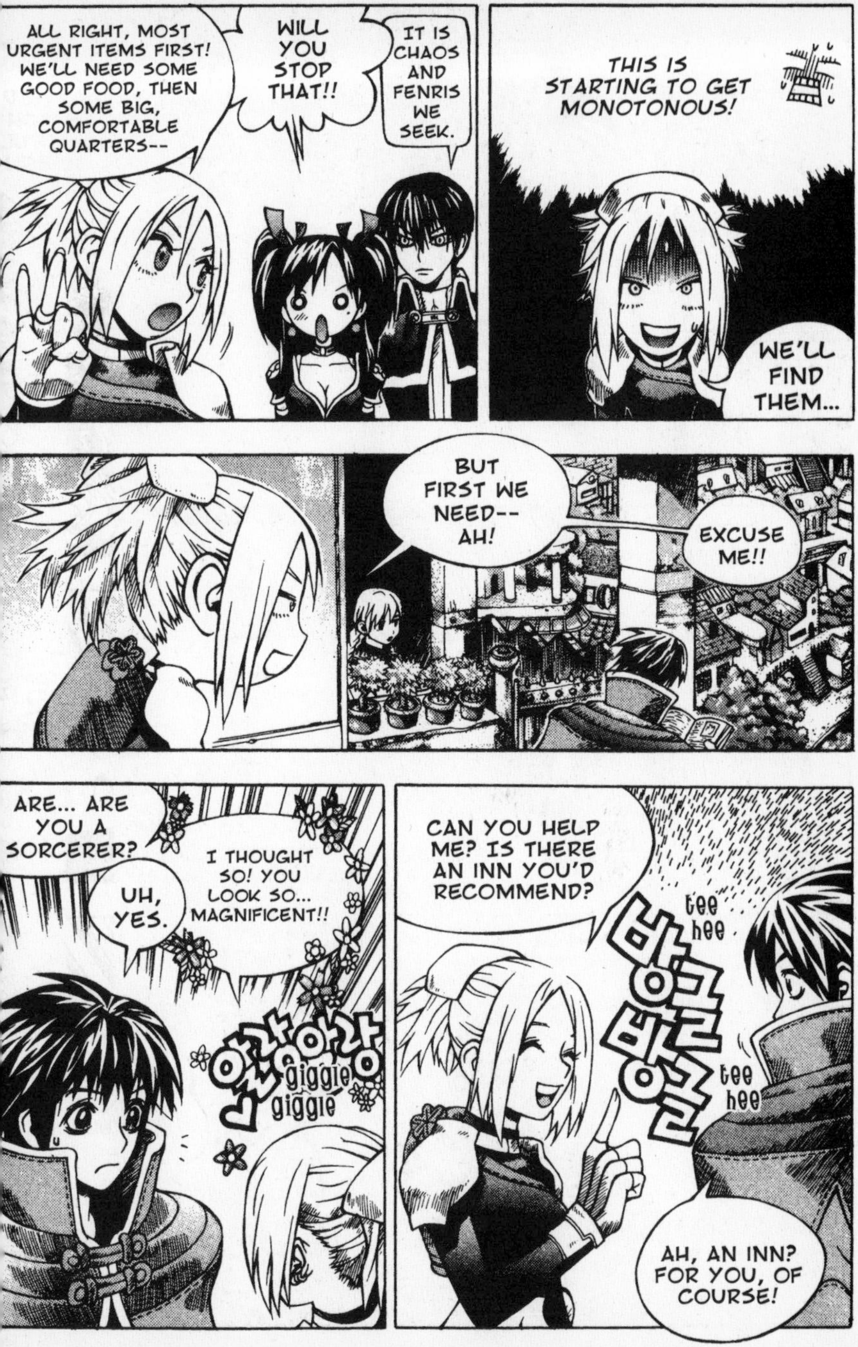
ALL RIGHT, MOST URGENT ITEMS FIRST! WE'LL NEED SOME GOOD FOOD, THEN SOME BIG, COMFORTABLE QUARTERS--
WILL YOU STOP THAT!!
IT IS CHAOS AND FENRIS WE SEEK.
THIS IS STARTING TO GET MONOTONOUS!
WE'LL FIND THEM...
BUT FIRST WE NEED-- AH!
EXCUSE ME!!
ARE... ARE YOU A SORCERER?
UH, YES.
I THOUGHT SO! YOU LOOK SO... MAGNIFICENT!!
giggle giggle
CAN YOU HELP ME? IS THERE AN INN YOU'D RECOMMEND?
tee hee
tee hee
AH, AN INN? FOR YOU, OF COURSE!

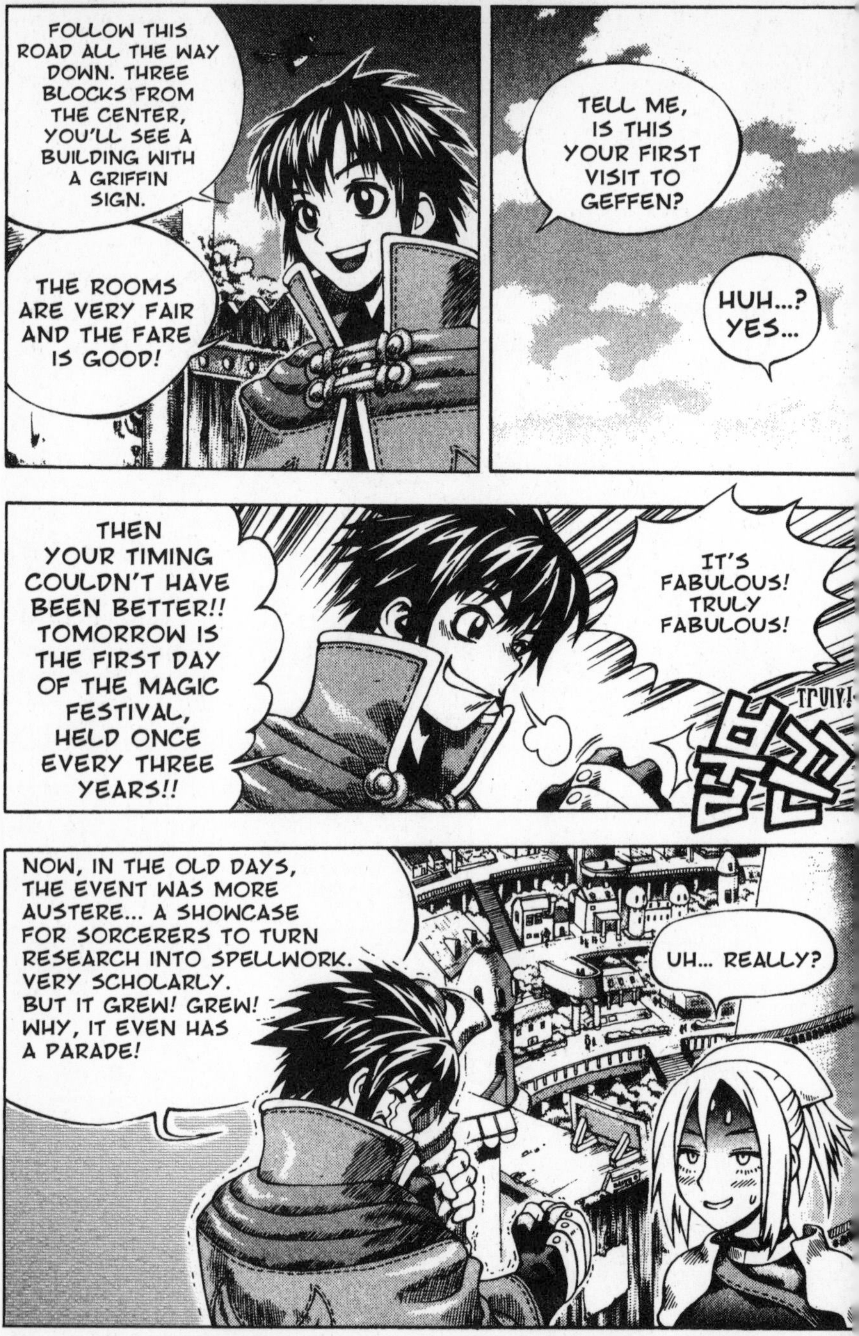
FOLLOW THIS ROAD ALL THE WAY DOWN. THREE BLOCKS FROM THE CENTER, YOU'LL SEE A BUILDING WITH A GRIFFIN SIGN.
THE ROOMS ARE VERY FAIR AND THE FARE IS GOOD!
TELL ME, IS THIS YOUR FIRST VISIT TO GEFFEN?
HUH...? YES...
THEN YOUR TIMING COULDN'T HAVE BEEN BETTER!! TOMORROW IS THE FIRST DAY OF THE MAGIC FESTIVAL, HELD ONCE EVERY THREE YEARS!!
IT'S FABULOUS! TRULY FABULOUS!
TRULY!
NOW, IN THE OLD DAYS, THE EVENT WAS MORE AUSTERE... A SHOWCASE FOR SORCERERS TO TURN RESEARCH INTO SPELLWORK. VERY SCHOLARLY. BUT IT GREW! GREW! WHY, IT EVEN HAS A PARADE!
UH... REALLY?

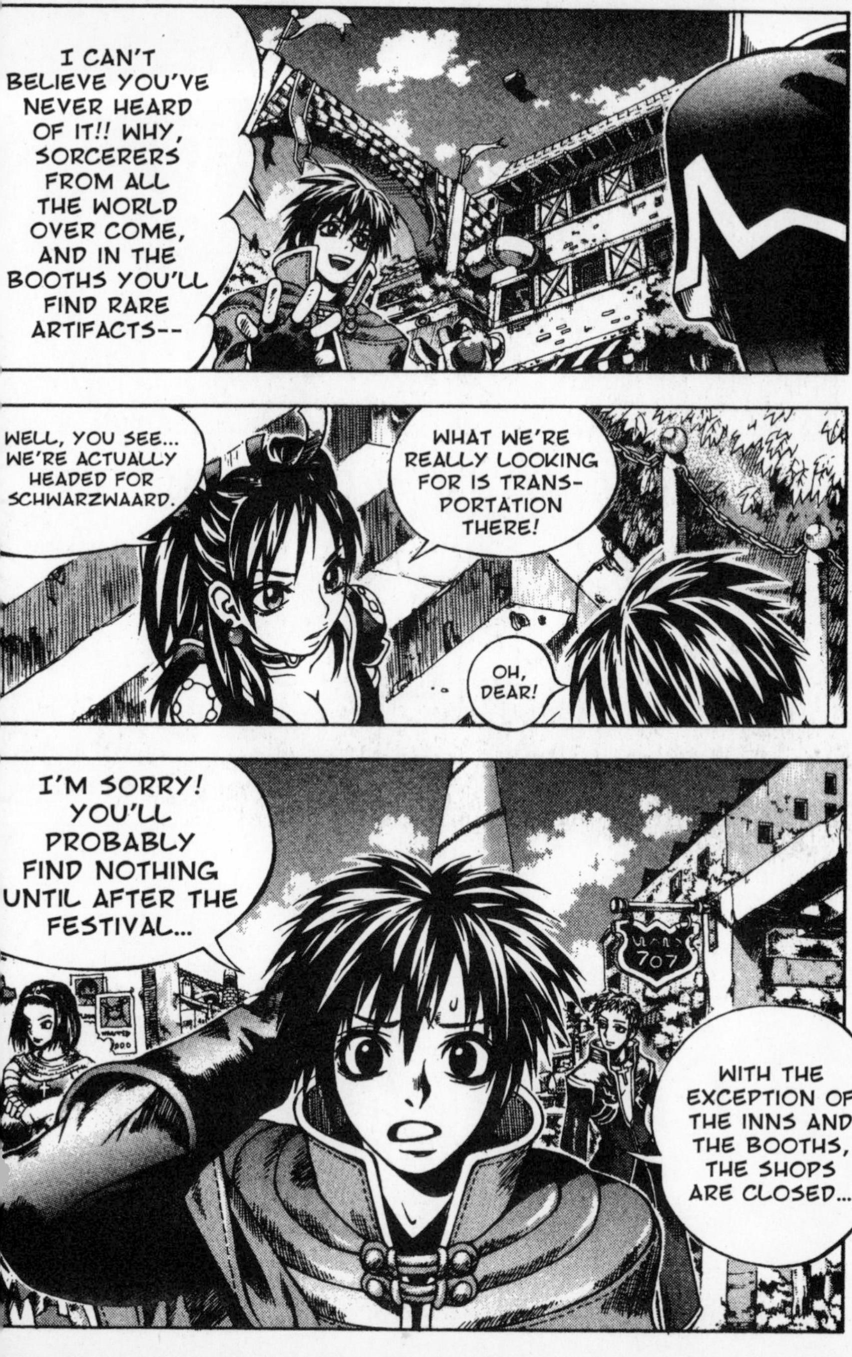
I CAN'T BELIEVE YOU'VE NEVER HEARD OF IT!! WHY, SORCERERS FROM ALL THE WORLD OVER COME, AND IN THE BOOTHS YOU'LL FIND RARE ARTIFACTS--
WELL, YOU SEE... WE'RE ACTUALLY HEADED FOR SCHWARZWAARD.
WHAT WE'RE REALLY LOOKING FOR IS TRANS-PORTATION THERE!
OH, DEAR!
I'M SORRY! YOU'LL PROBABLY FIND NOTHING UNTIL AFTER THE FESTIVAL...
WITH THE EXCEPTION OF THE INNS AND THE BOOTHS, THE SHOPS ARE CLOSED...

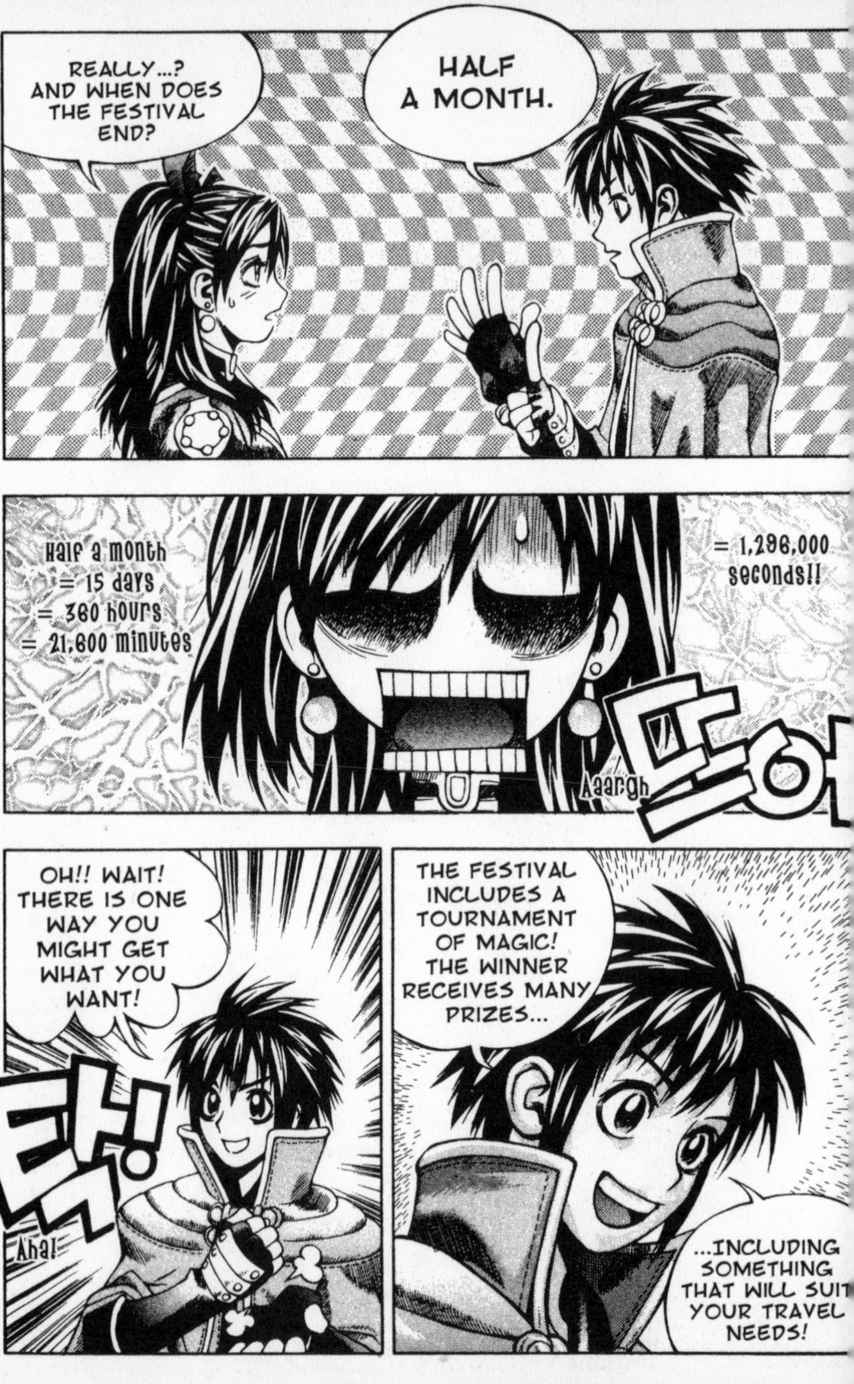
REALLY...? AND WHEN DOES THE FESTIVAL END?
HALF A MONTH.
Half a month = 15 days = 360 hours = 21,600 minutes
= 1,296,000 seconds!!
Aaargh
OH!! WAIT! THERE IS ONE WAY YOU MIGHT GET WHAT YOU WANT!
Aha!
THE FESTIVAL INCLUDES A TOURNAMENT OF MAGIC! THE WINNER RECEIVES MANY PRIZES...
...INCLUDING SOMETHING THAT WILL SUIT YOUR TRAVEL NEEDS!

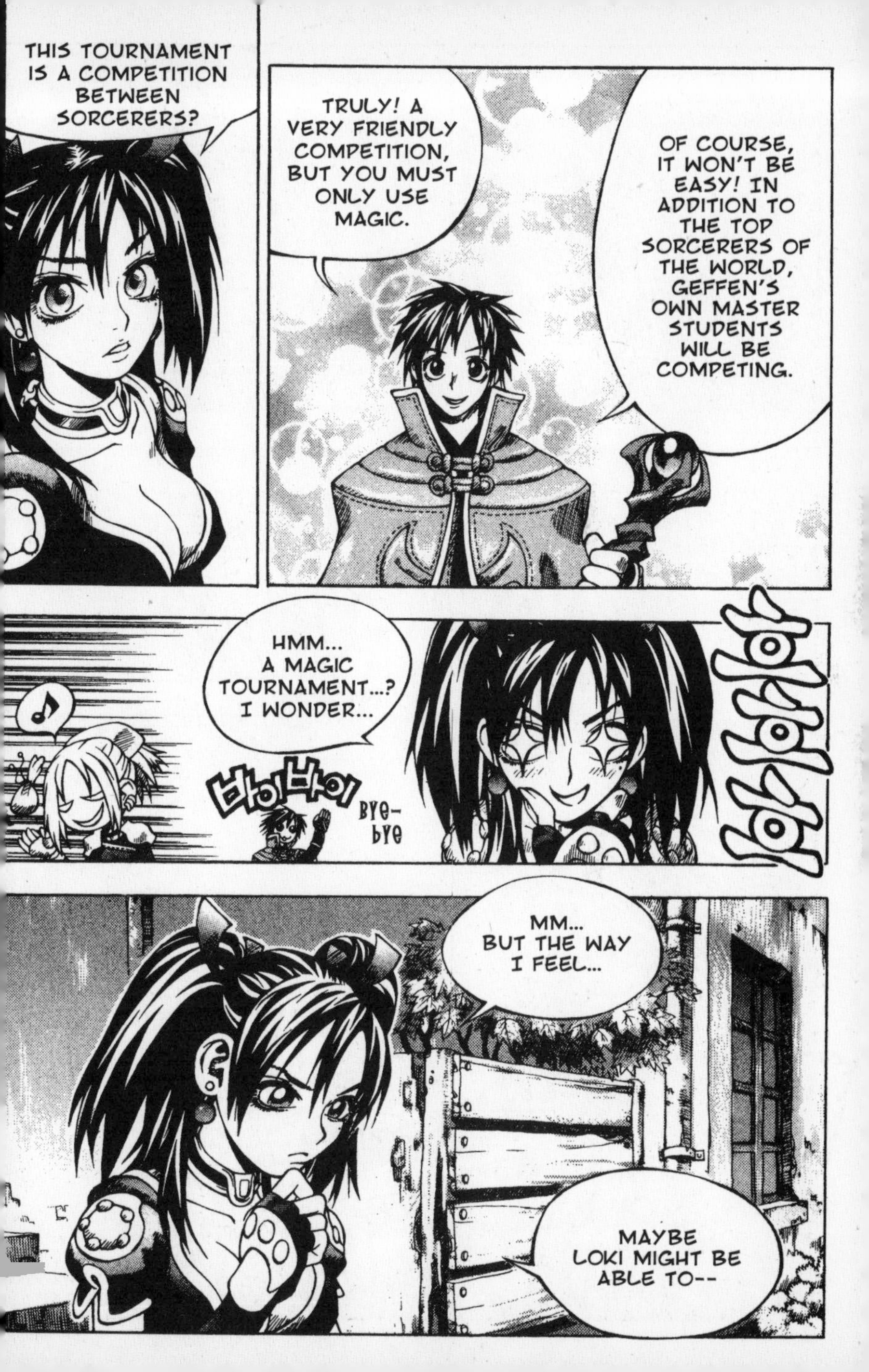
THIS TOURNAMENT IS A COMPETITION BETWEEN SORCERERS?
TRULY! A VERY FRIENDLY COMPETITION, BUT YOU MUST ONLY USE MAGIC.
OF COURSE, IT WON'T BE EASY! IN ADDITION TO THE TOP SORCERERS OF THE WORLD, GEFFEN'S OWN MASTER STUDENTS WILL BE COMPETING.
HMM... A MAGIC TOURNAMENT...? I WONDER...
바이바이
BYE-BYE
MM... BUT THE WAY I FEEL...
MAYBE LOKI MIGHT BE ABLE TO--

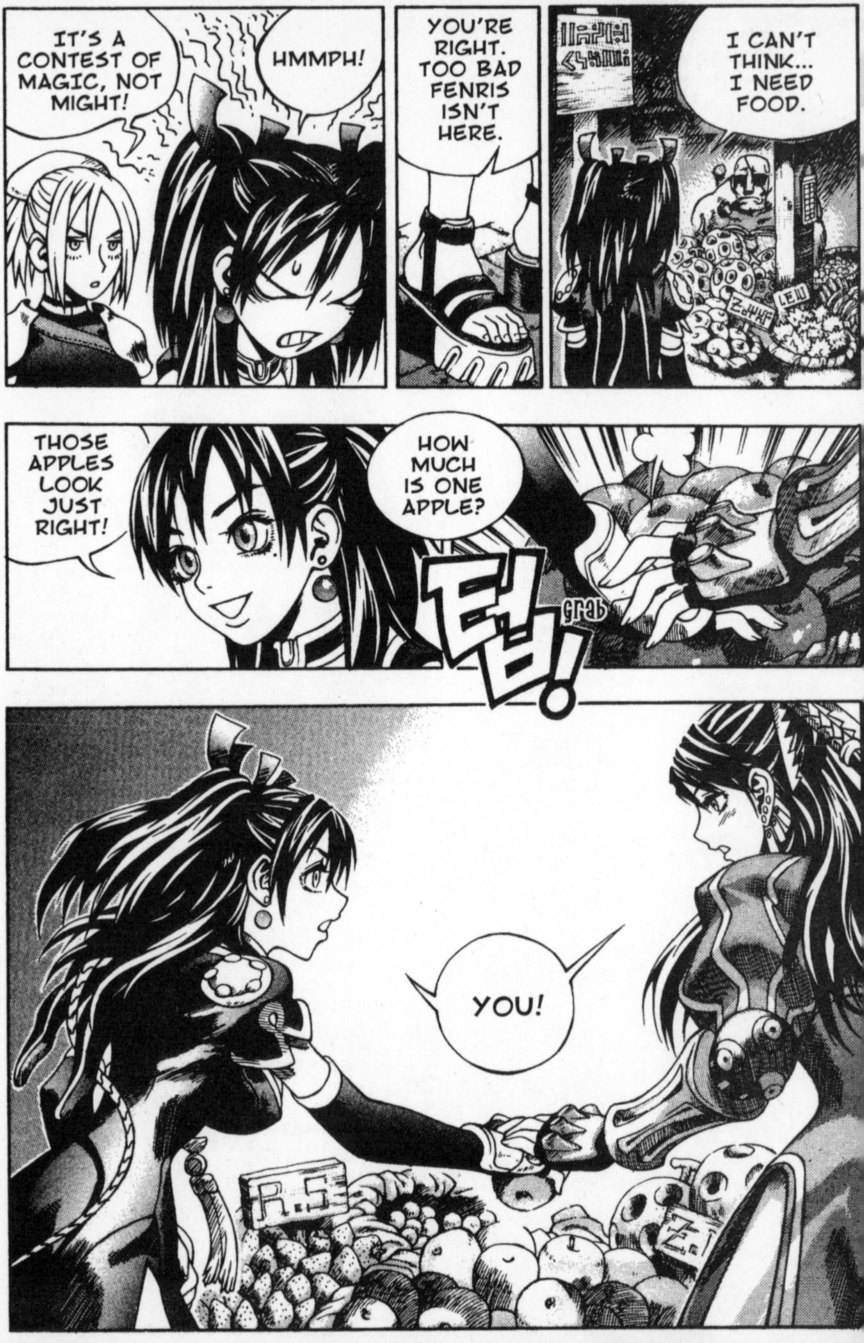
IT'S A CONTEST OF MAGIC, NOT MIGHT!
HMMPH!
YOU'RE RIGHT. TOO BAD FENRIS ISN'T HERE.
I CAN'T THINK... I NEED FOOD.
THOSE APPLES LOOK JUST RIGHT!
HOW MUCH IS ONE APPLE?
GRAB
YOU!

RAGNAROK
라그나로크
IN TO THE ABYSS

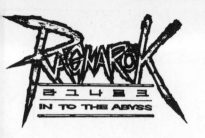

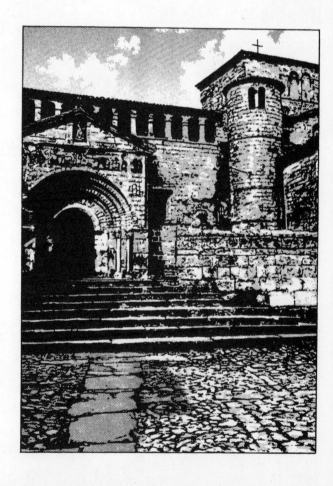

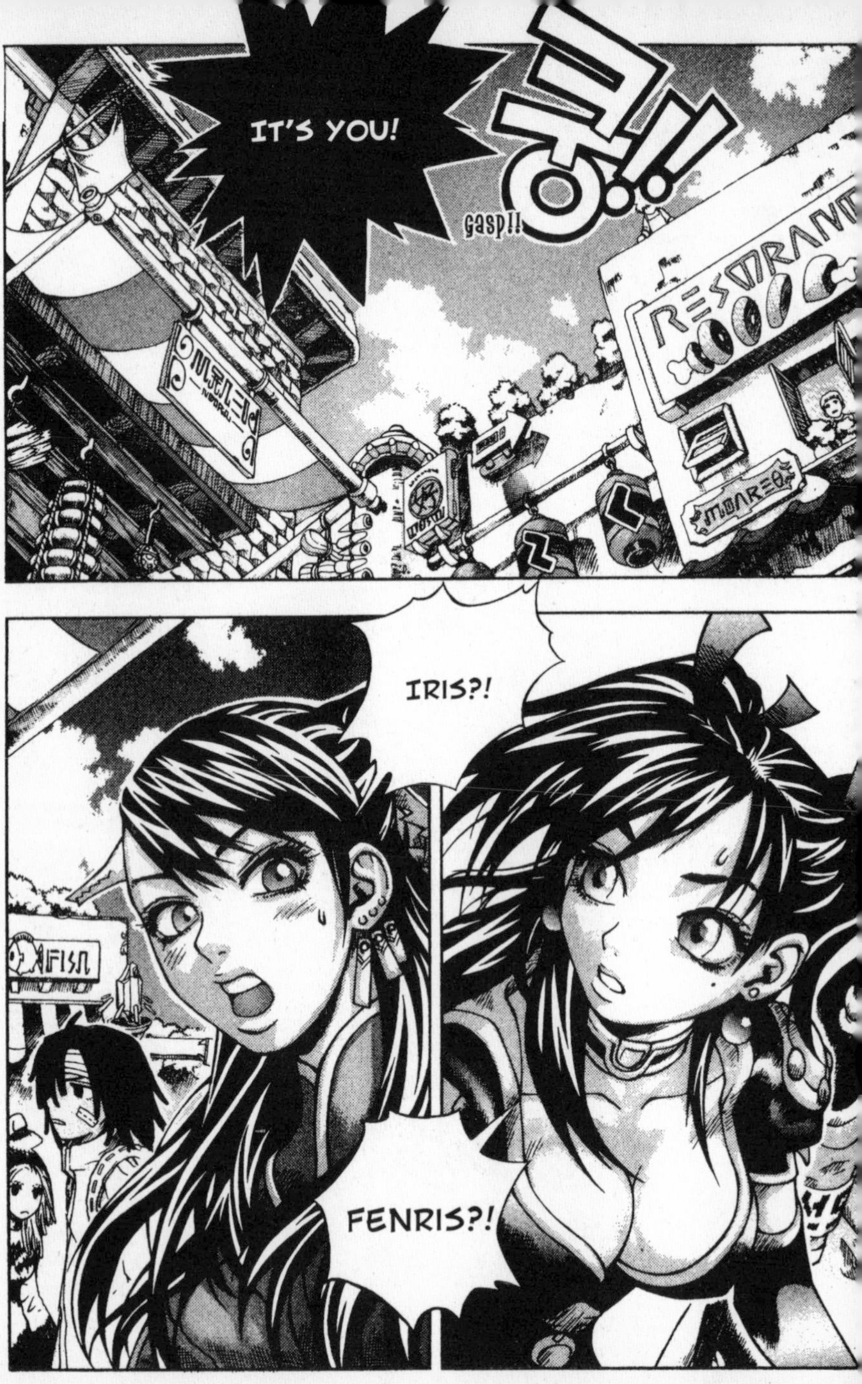
IT'S YOU!
GASP!!
IRIS?!
FENRIS?!

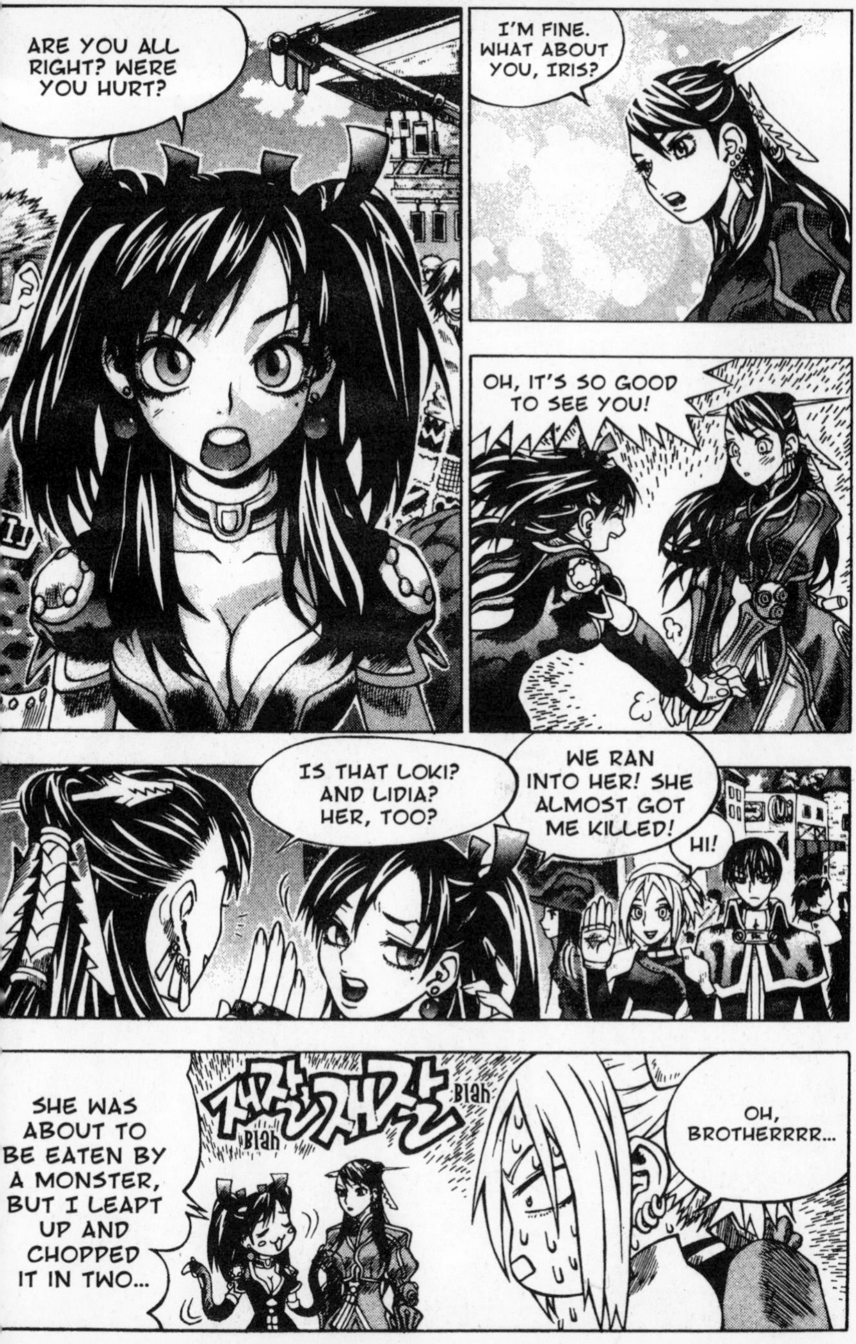
ARE YOU ALL RIGHT? WERE YOU HURT?
I'M FINE. WHAT ABOUT YOU, IRIS?
OH, IT'S SO GOOD TO SEE YOU!
IS THAT LOKI? AND LIDIA? HER, TOO?
WE RAN INTO HER! SHE ALMOST GOT ME KILLED!
HI!
SHE WAS ABOUT TO BE EATEN BY A MONSTER, BUT I LEAPT UP AND CHOPPED IT IN TWO...
Blah
Blah
OH, BROTHERRRR...

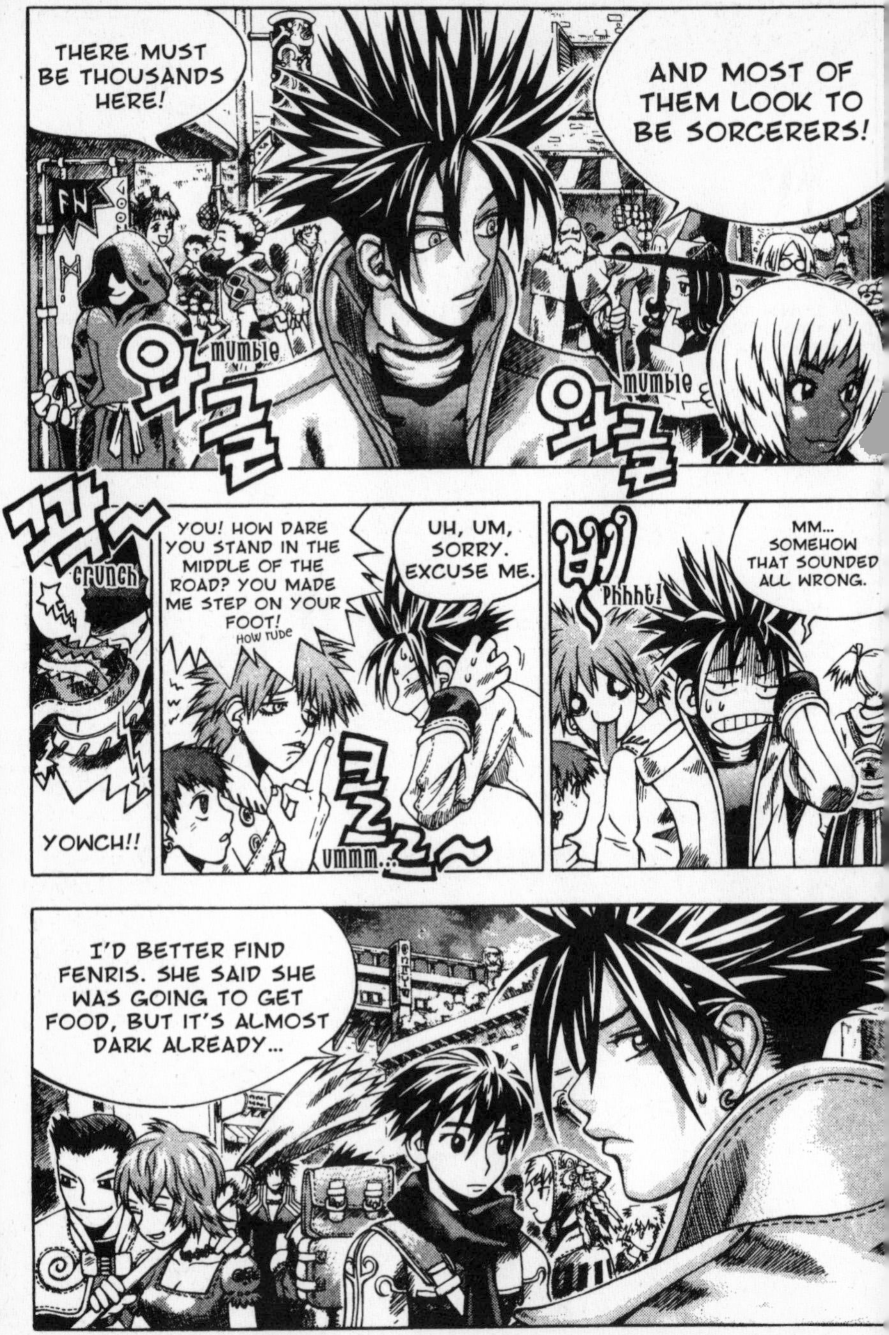
THERE MUST BE THOUSANDS HERE!
AND MOST OF THEM LOOK TO BE SORCERERS!
와글
mumble
와글
mumble
꽉~
crunch
YOWCH!!
YOU! HOW DARE YOU STAND IN THE MIDDLE OF THE ROAD? YOU MADE ME STEP ON YOUR FOOT!
HOW rude
UH, UM, SORRY. EXCUSE ME.
ummm...
Phhht!
MM... SOMEHOW THAT SOUNDED ALL WRONG.
I'D BETTER FIND FENRIS. SHE SAID SHE WAS GOING TO GET FOOD, BUT IT'S ALMOST DARK ALREADY...

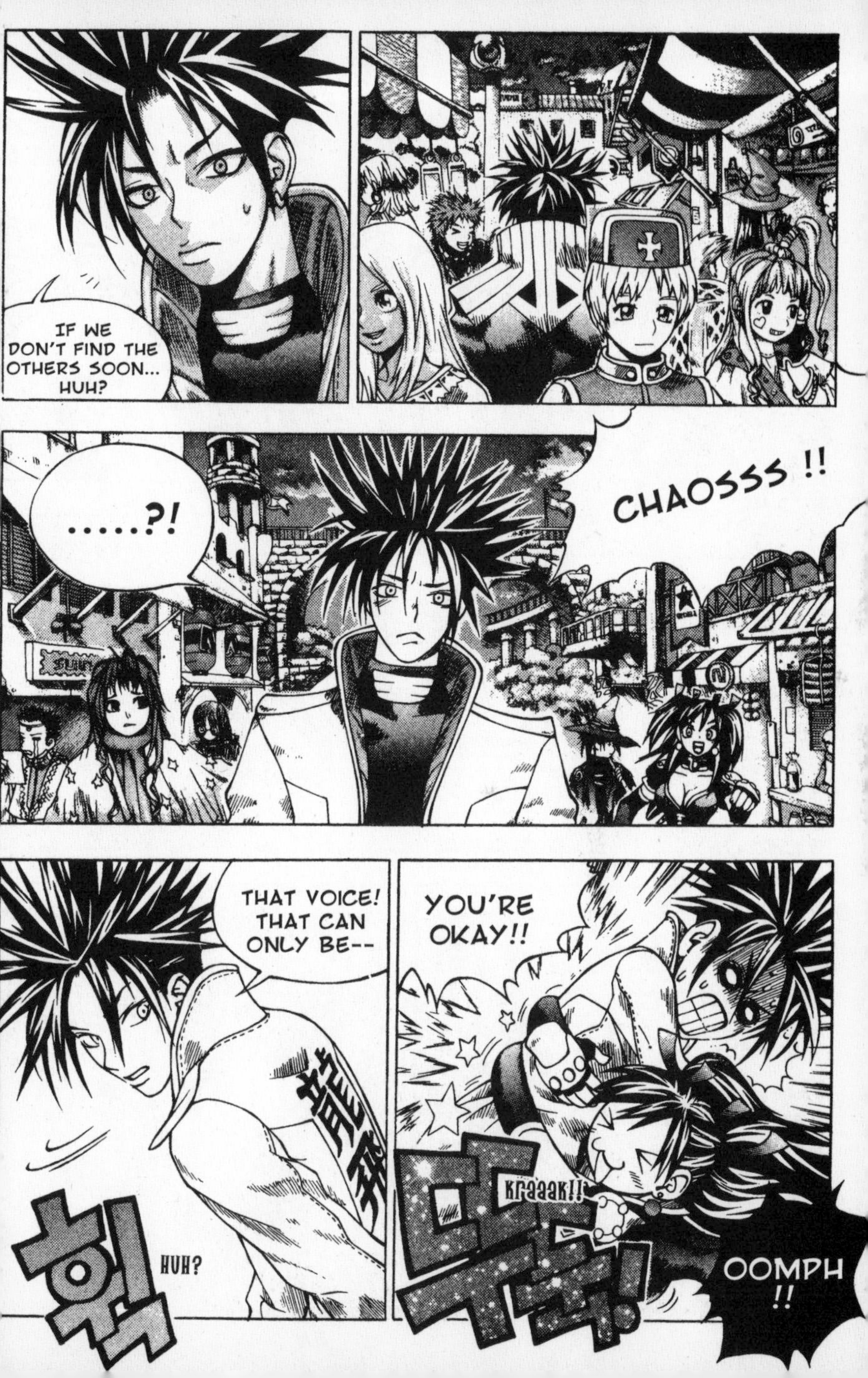
IF WE DON'T FIND THE OTHERS SOON... HUH?
CHAOSSS !!
......?!
THAT VOICE! THAT CAN ONLY BE--
HUH?
YOU'RE OKAY!!
KRAAAK!!
OOMPH !!

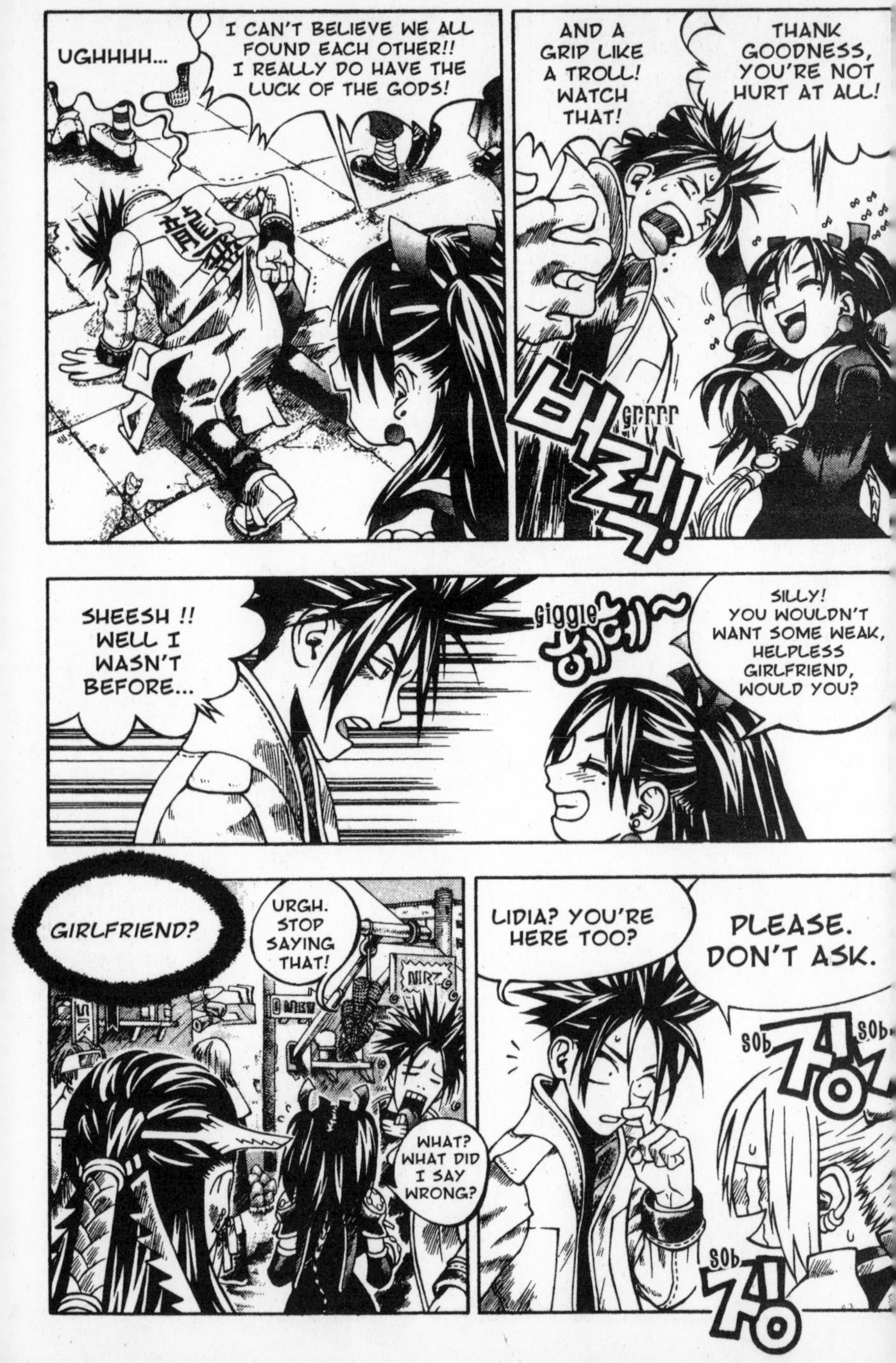
UGHHHH...
I CAN'T BELIEVE WE ALL FOUND EACH OTHER!! I REALLY DO HAVE THE LUCK OF THE GODS!
AND A GRIP LIKE A TROLL! WATCH THAT!
THANK GOODNESS, YOU'RE NOT HURT AT ALL!
GRRRR
SHEESH !! WELL I WASN'T BEFORE...
GIGGLE
SILLY! YOU WOULDN'T WANT SOME WEAK, HELPLESS GIRLFRIEND, WOULD YOU?
GIRLFRIEND?
URGH. STOP SAYING THAT!
WHAT? WHAT DID I SAY WRONG?
LIDIA? YOU'RE HERE TOO?
PLEASE. DON'T ASK.
SOB
SOB
SOB

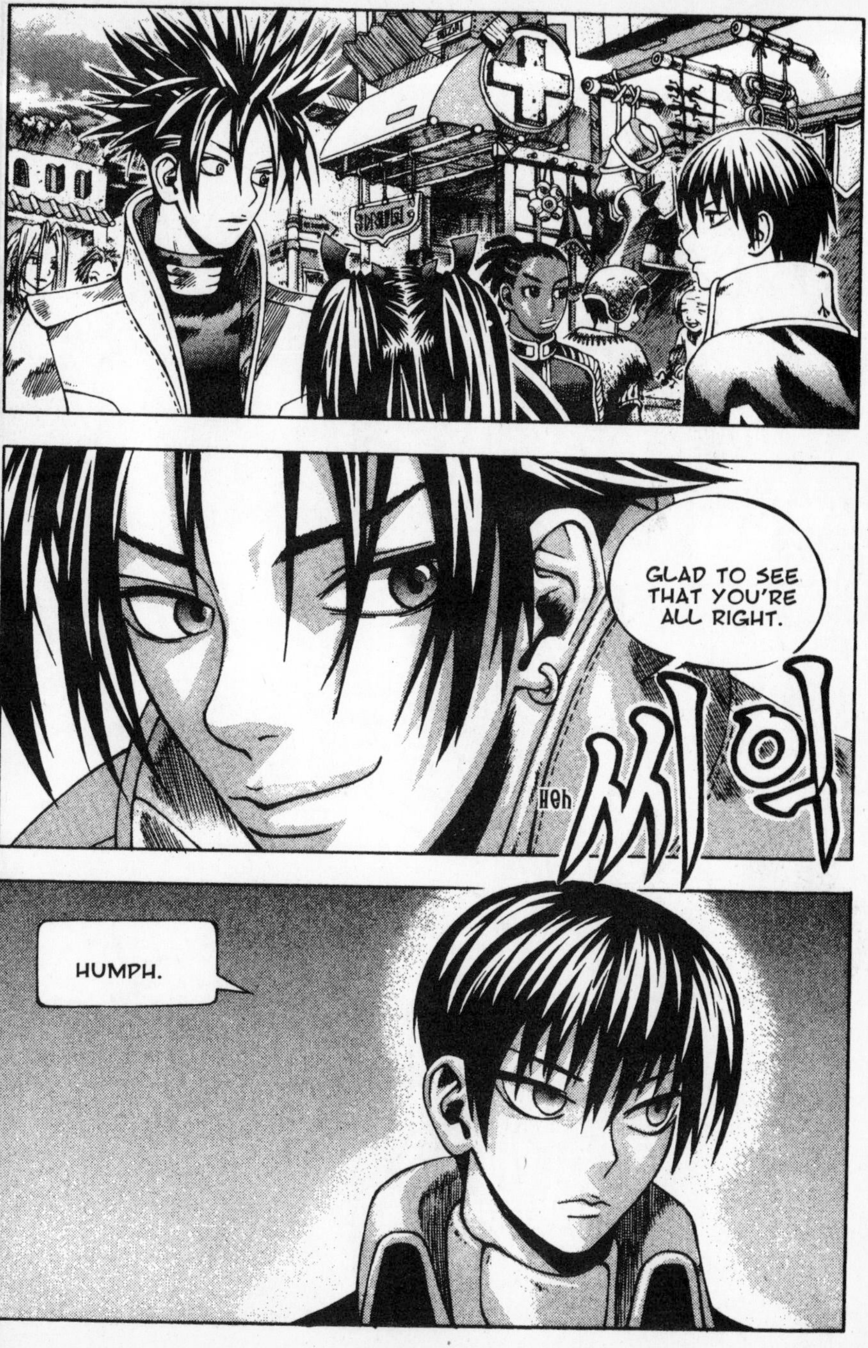
GLAD TO SEE THAT YOU'RE ALL RIGHT.
Heh
HUMPH.

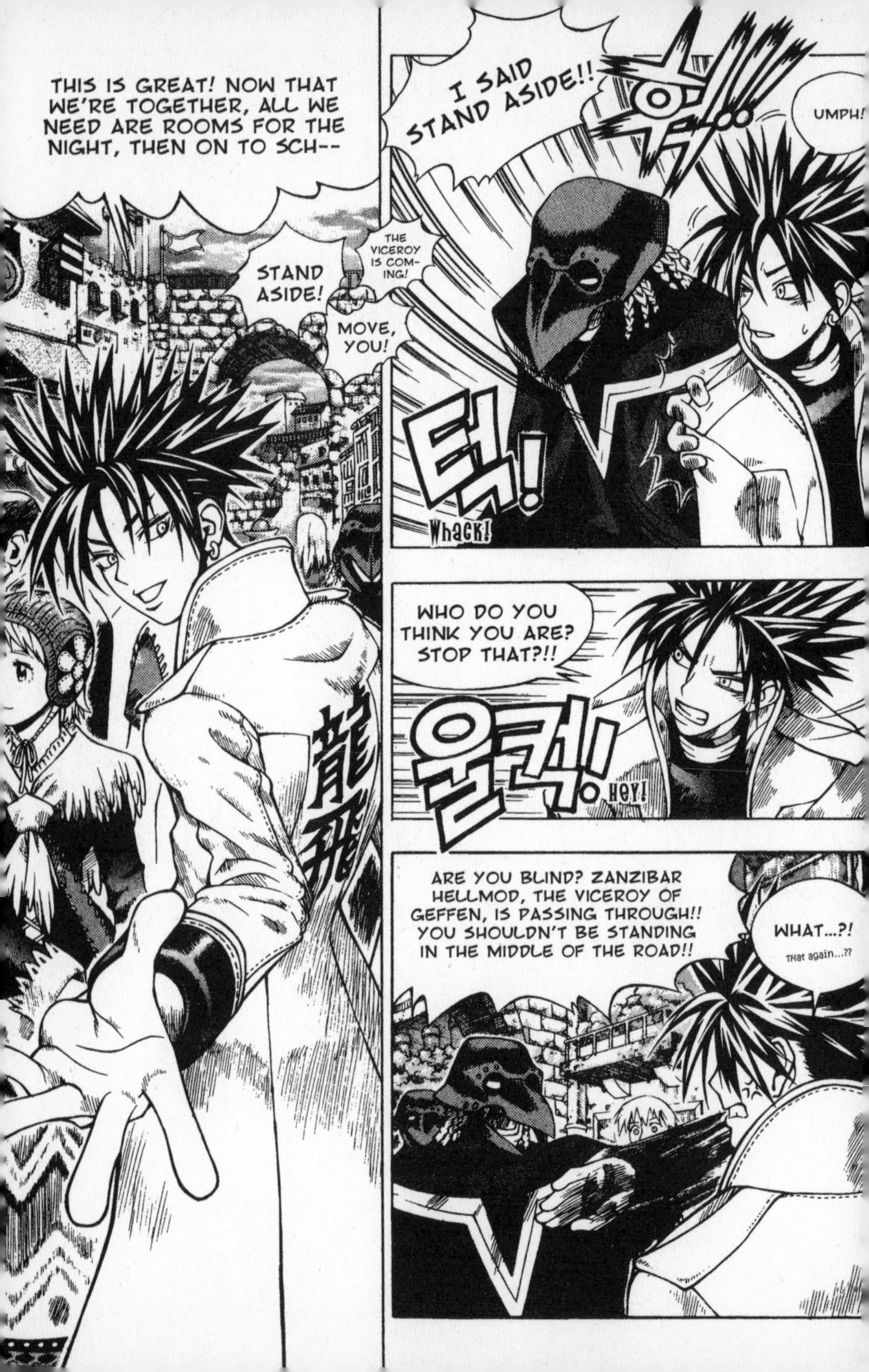

THIS IS GREAT! NOW THAT WE'RE TOGETHER, ALL WE NEED ARE ROOMS FOR THE NIGHT, THEN ON TO SCH--
STAND ASIDE!
THE VICEROY IS COMING!
MOVE, YOU!
I SAID STAND ASIDE!!
UMPH!
턱!
Whack!
WHO DO YOU THINK YOU ARE? STOP THAT?!!
울컥!
HEY!
ARE YOU BLIND? ZANZIBAR HELLMOD, THE VICEROY OF GEFFEN, IS PASSING THROUGH!! YOU SHOULDN'T BE STANDING IN THE MIDDLE OF THE ROAD!!
WHAT...?!
That again...??

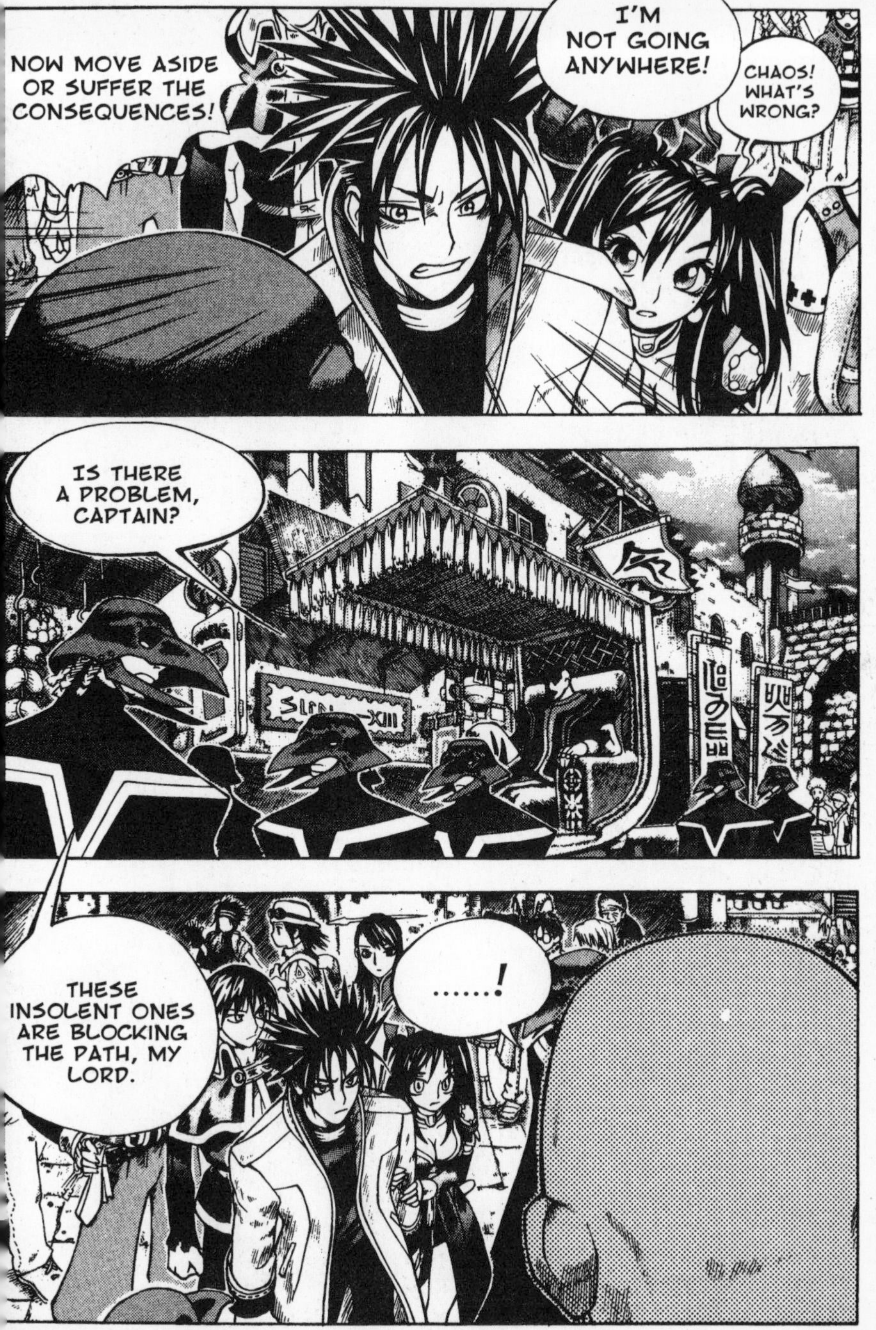
NOW MOVE ASIDE OR SUFFER THE CONSEQUENCES!
I'M NOT GOING ANYWHERE!
CHAOS! WHAT'S WRONG?
IS THERE A PROBLEM, CAPTAIN?
THESE INSOLENT ONES ARE BLOCKING THE PATH, MY LORD.
......!

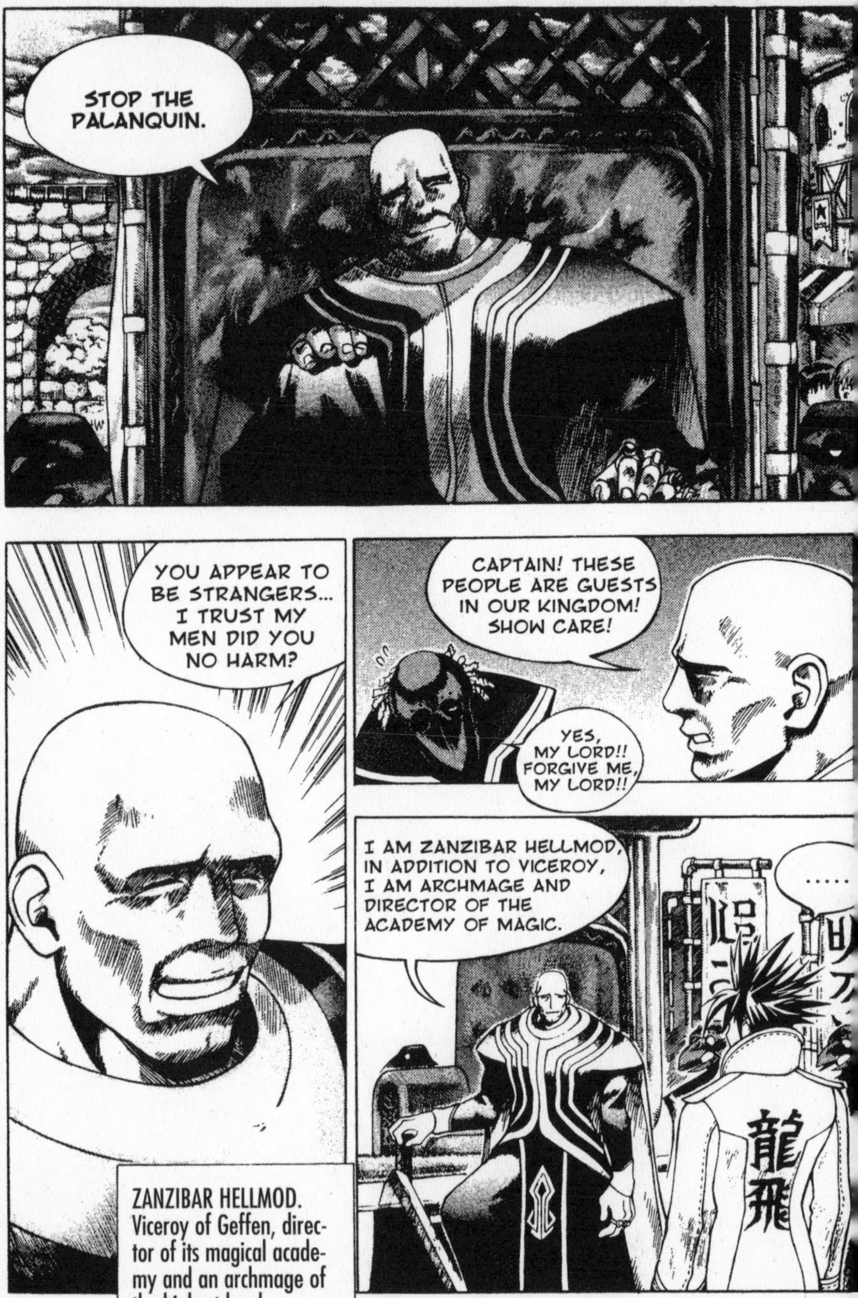
STOP THE PALANQUIN.
YOU APPEAR TO BE STRANGERS... I TRUST MY MEN DID YOU NO HARM?
CAPTAIN! THESE PEOPLE ARE GUESTS IN OUR KINGDOM! SHOW CARE!
YES, MY LORD!! FORGIVE ME, MY LORD!!
I AM ZANZIBAR HELLMOD, IN ADDITION TO VICEROY, I AM ARCHMAGE AND DIRECTOR OF THE ACADEMY OF MAGIC.
.....
ZANZIBAR HELLMOD. Viceroy of Geffen, director of its magical academy and an archmage of the highest level.

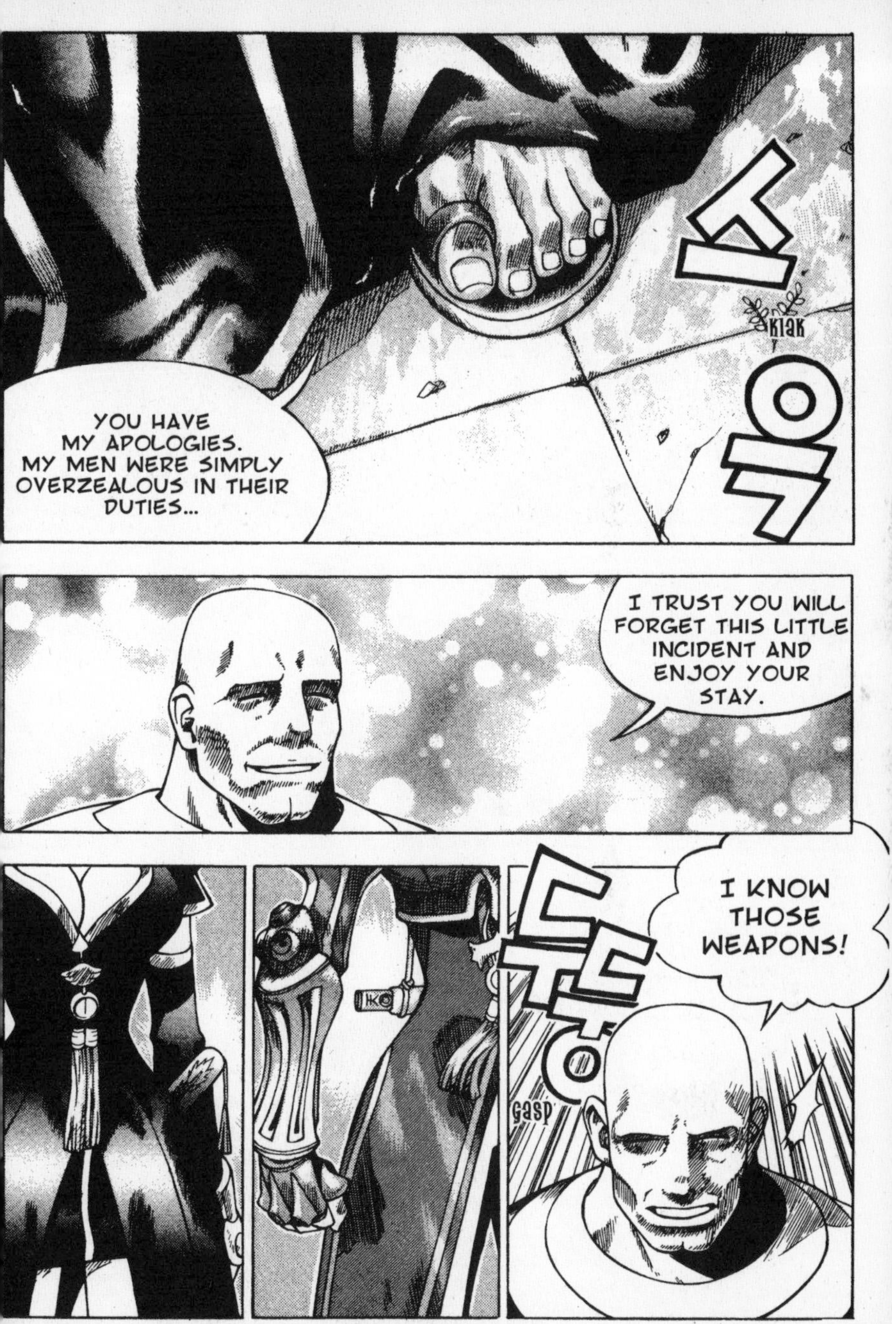
KIAK
YOU HAVE MY APOLOGIES. MY MEN WERE SIMPLY OVERZEALOUS IN THEIR DUTIES...
I TRUST YOU WILL FORGET THIS LITTLE INCIDENT AND ENJOY YOUR STAY.
GASP
I KNOW THOSE WEAPONS!

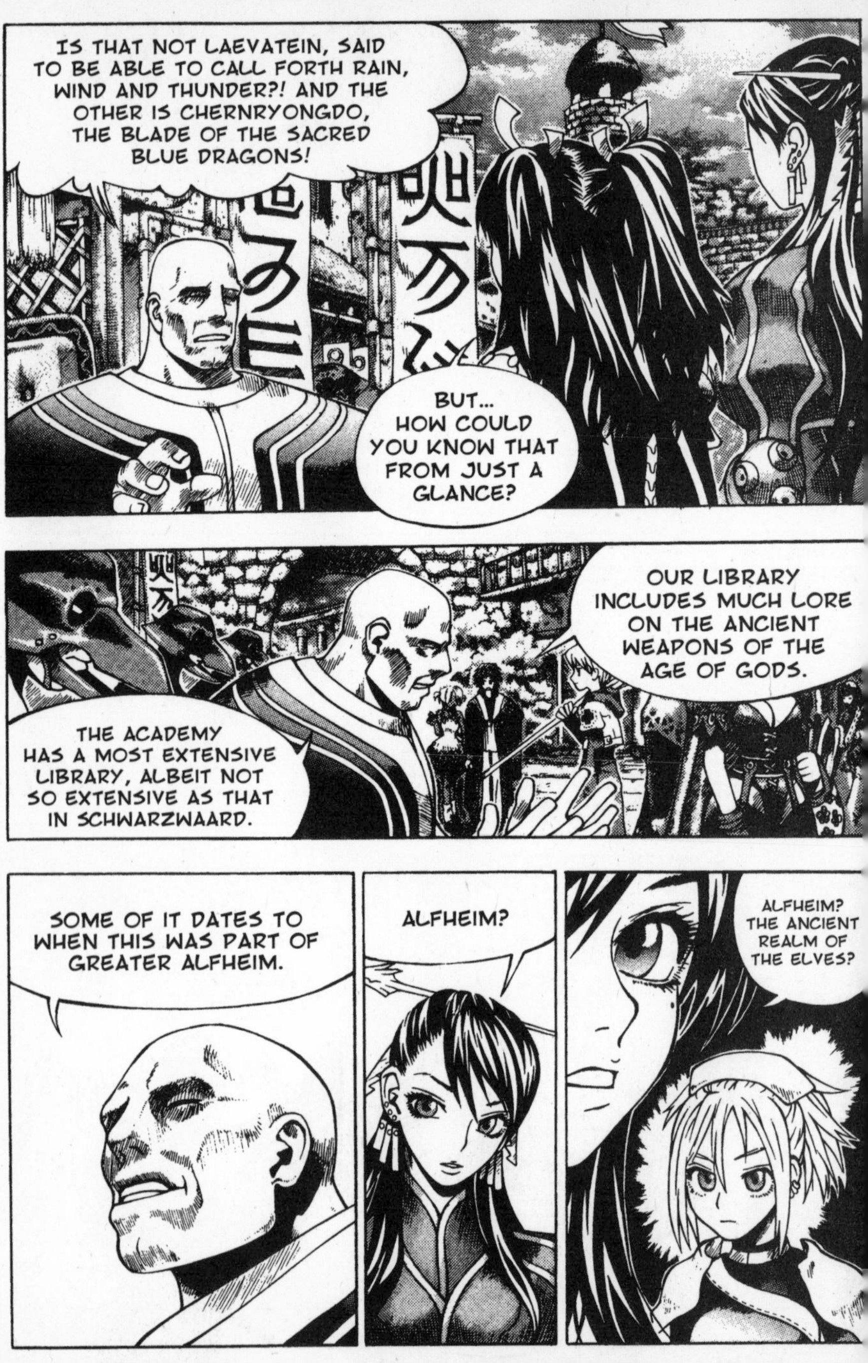
IS THAT NOT LAEVATEIN, SAID TO BE ABLE TO CALL FORTH RAIN, WIND AND THUNDER?! AND THE OTHER IS CHERNRYONGDO, THE BLADE OF THE SACRED BLUE DRAGONS!
BUT... HOW COULD YOU KNOW THAT FROM JUST A GLANCE?
THE ACADEMY HAS A MOST EXTENSIVE LIBRARY, ALBEIT NOT SO EXTENSIVE AS THAT IN SCHWARZWAARD.
OUR LIBRARY INCLUDES MUCH LORE ON THE ANCIENT WEAPONS OF THE AGE OF GODS.
SOME OF IT DATES TO WHEN THIS WAS PART OF GREATER ALFHEIM.
ALFHEIM?
ALFHEIM? THE ANCIENT REALM OF THE ELVES?

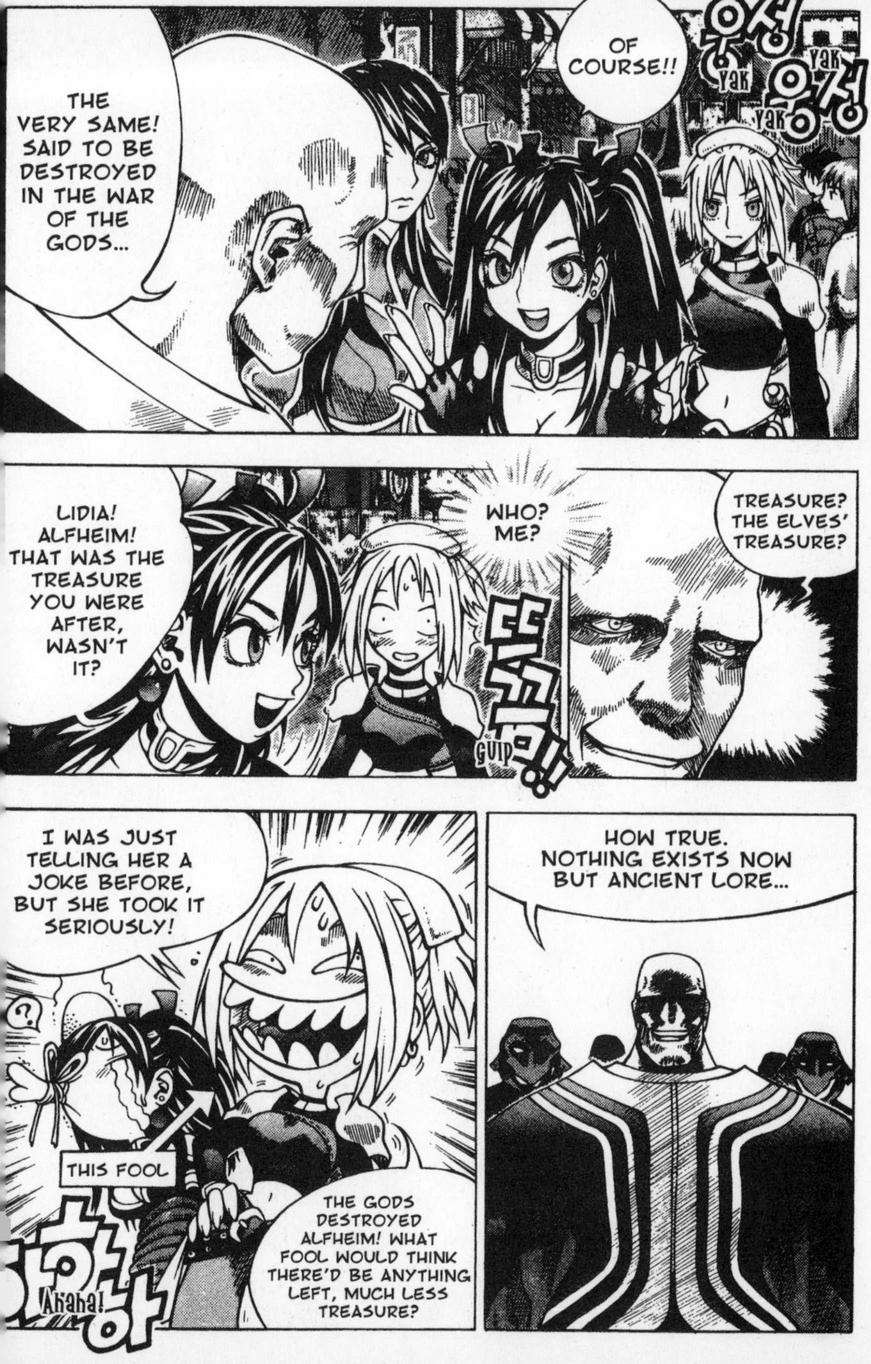
THE VERY SAME! SAID TO BE DESTROYED IN THE WAR OF THE GODS...
OF COURSE!!
YAK YAK YAK
LIDIA! ALFHEIM! THAT WAS THE TREASURE YOU WERE AFTER, WASN'T IT?
WHO? ME?
GUIP
TREASURE? THE ELVES' TREASURE?
I WAS JUST TELLING HER A JOKE BEFORE, BUT SHE TOOK IT SERIOUSLY!
?
THIS FOOL
Ahaha!
THE GODS DESTROYED ALFHEIM! WHAT FOOL WOULD THINK THERE'D BE ANYTHING LEFT, MUCH LESS TREASURE?
HOW TRUE. NOTHING EXISTS NOW BUT ANCIENT LORE...

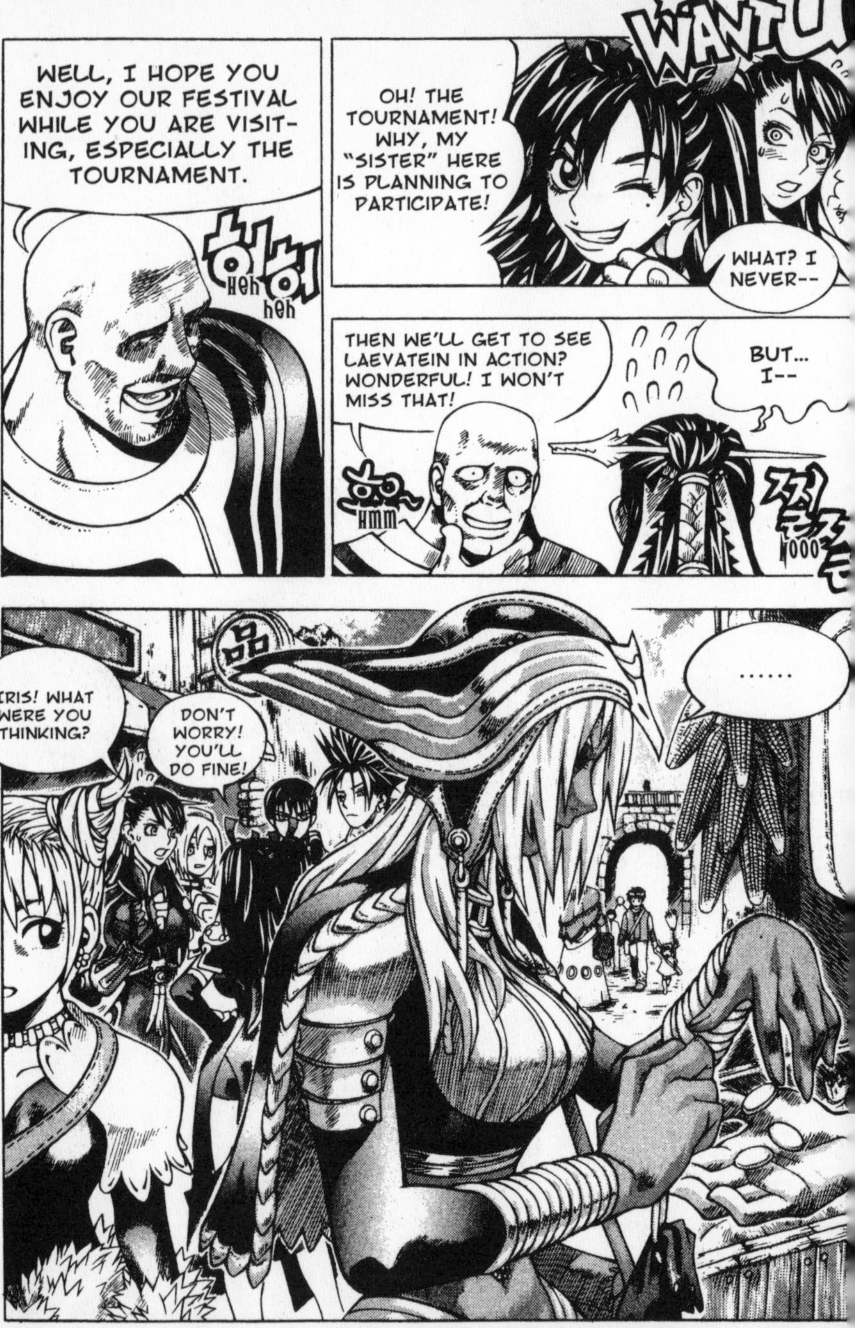
WELL, I HOPE YOU ENJOY OUR FESTIVAL WHILE YOU ARE VISIT-ING, ESPECIALLY THE TOURNAMENT.
HEH HEH
OH! THE TOURNAMENT! WHY, MY "SISTER" HERE IS PLANNING TO PARTICIPATE!
WHAT? I NEVER--
THEN WE'LL GET TO SEE LAEVATEIN IN ACTION? WONDERFUL! I WON'T MISS THAT!
HMM
BUT... I--
IRIS! WHAT WERE YOU THINKING?
DON'T WORRY! YOU'LL DO FINE!
......

RAGNAROK
라그나로크
IN TO THE ABYSS

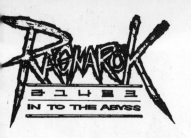

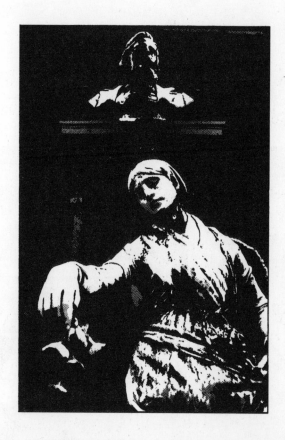

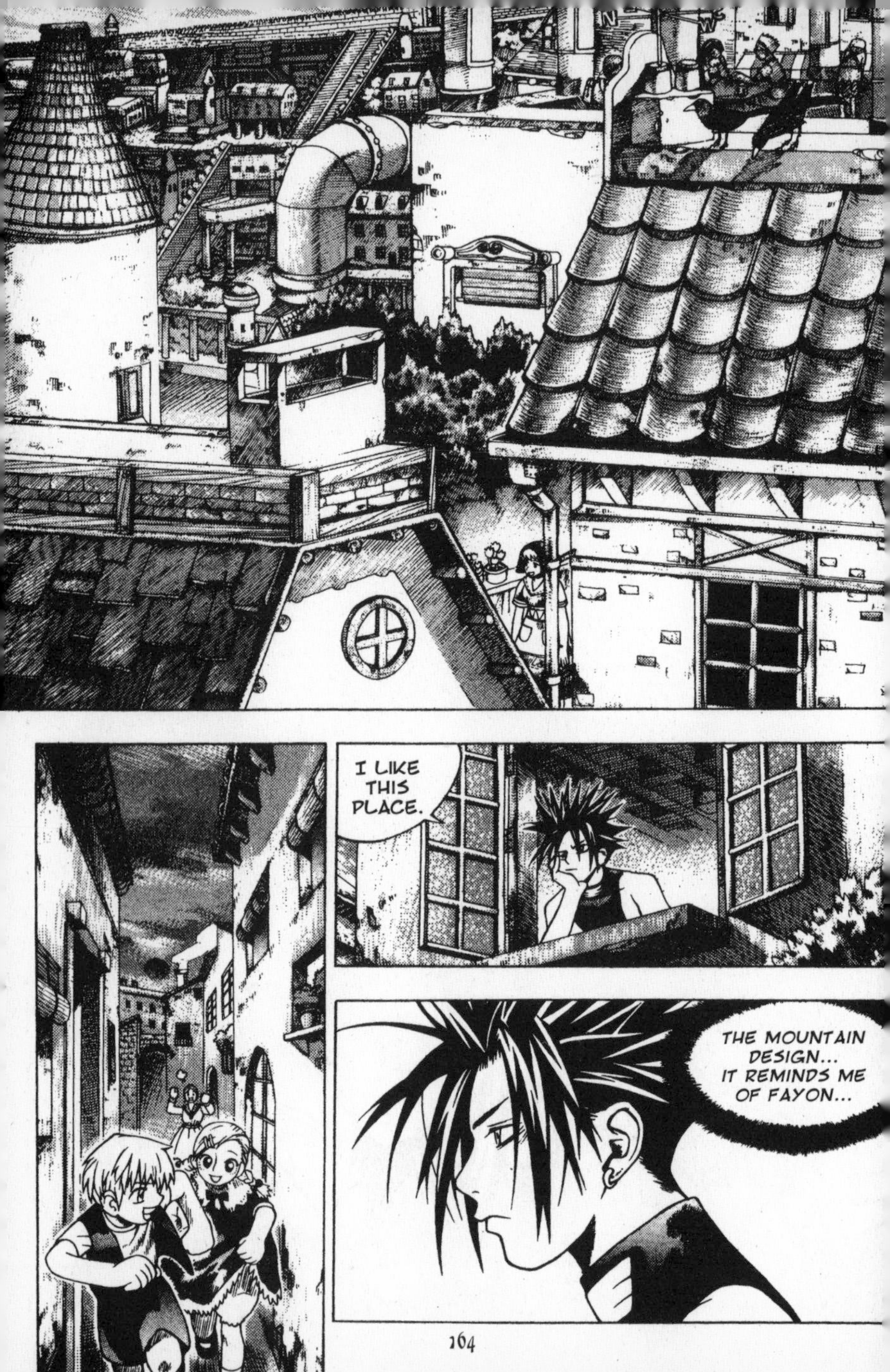
I LIKE THIS PLACE.
THE MOUNTAIN DESIGN... IT REMINDS ME OF FAYON...

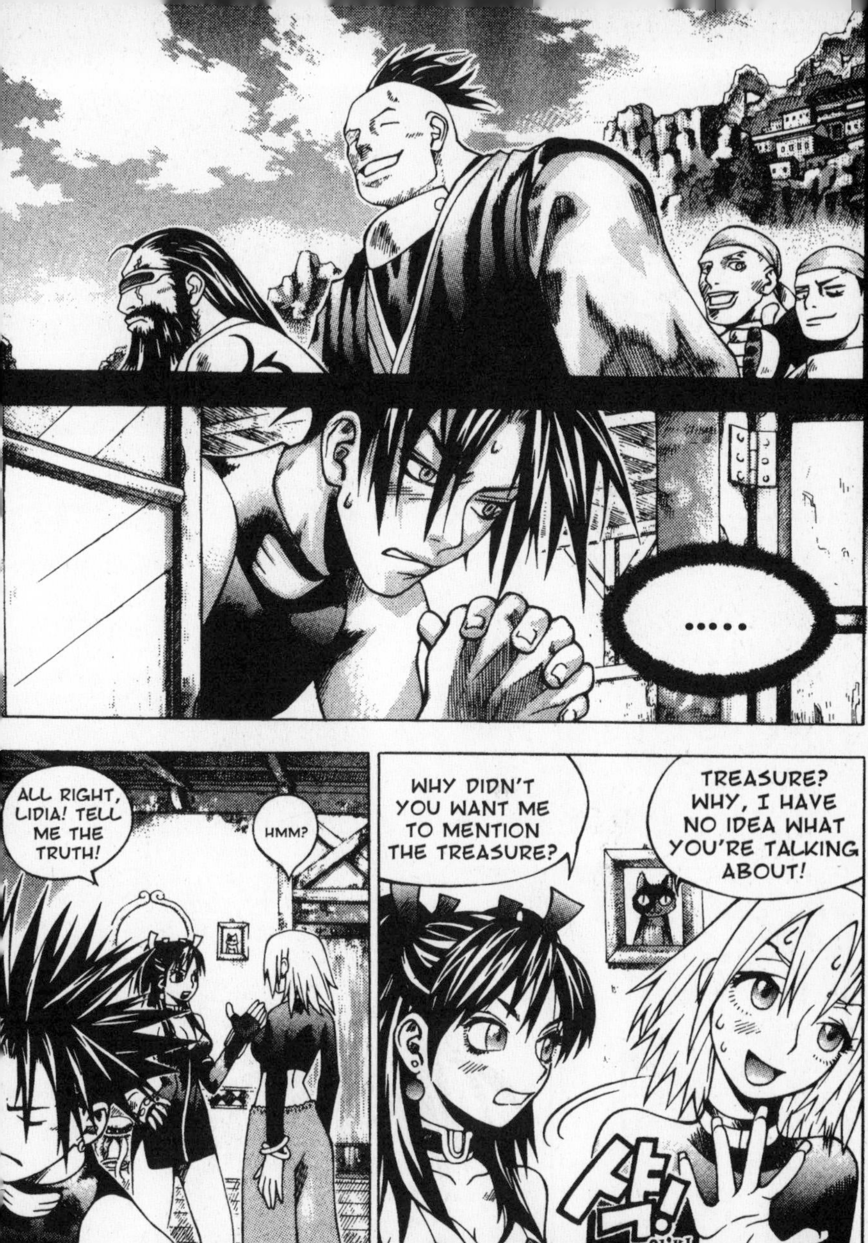
.....
ALL RIGHT, LIDIA! TELL ME THE TRUTH!
HMM?
WHY DIDN'T YOU WANT ME TO MENTION THE TREASURE?
TREASURE? WHY, I HAVE NO IDEA WHAT YOU'RE TALKING ABOUT!
flik!

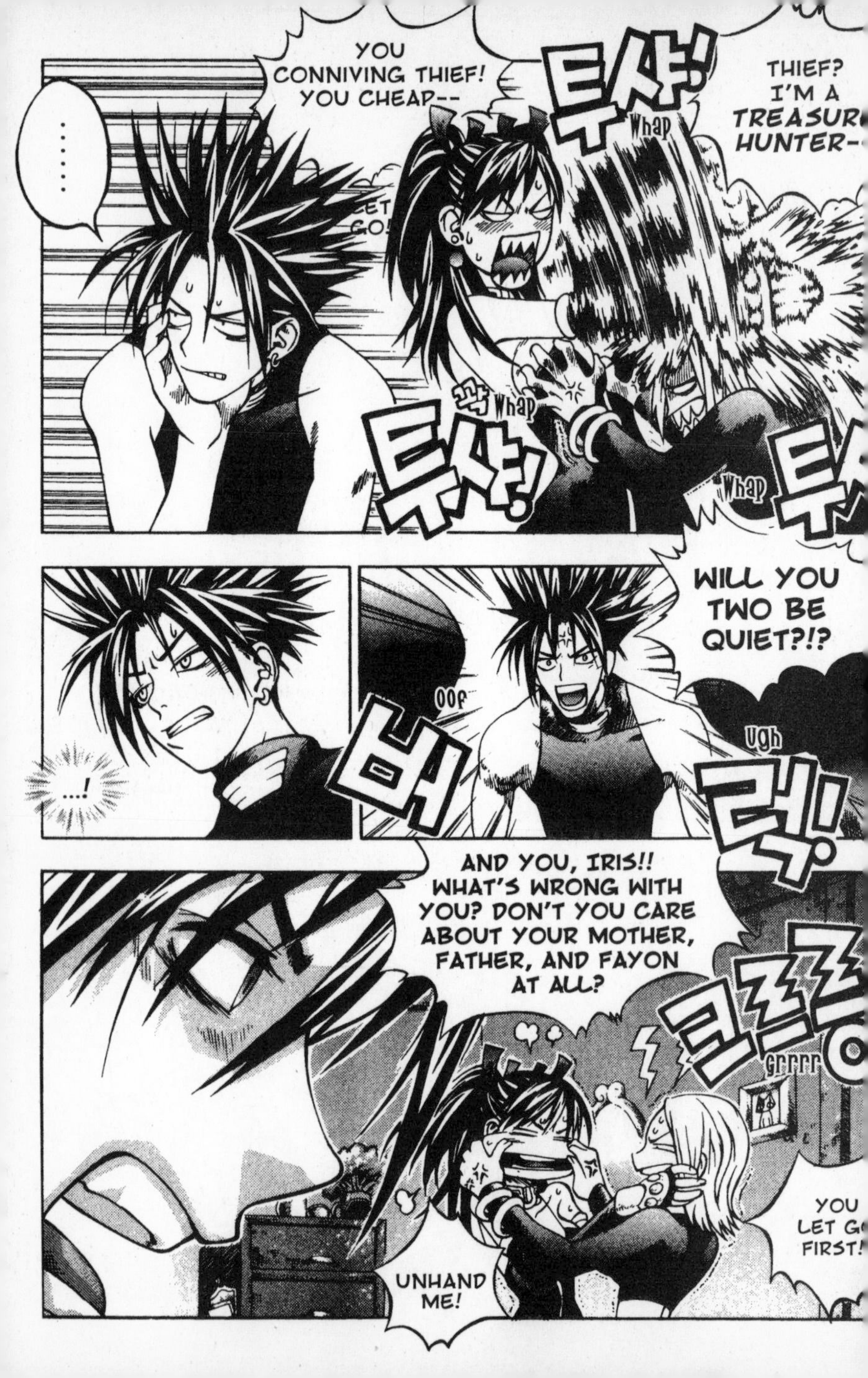
......
YOU CONNIVING THIEF! YOU CHEAP--
LET GO!
Whap
THIEF? I'M A TREASUR HUNTER-
Whap
Whap
....!
oof
WILL YOU TWO BE QUIET?!?
ugh
AND YOU, IRIS!! WHAT'S WRONG WITH YOU? DON'T YOU CARE ABOUT YOUR MOTHER, FATHER, AND FAYON AT ALL?
grrrr
UNHAND ME!
YOU LET G FIRST!

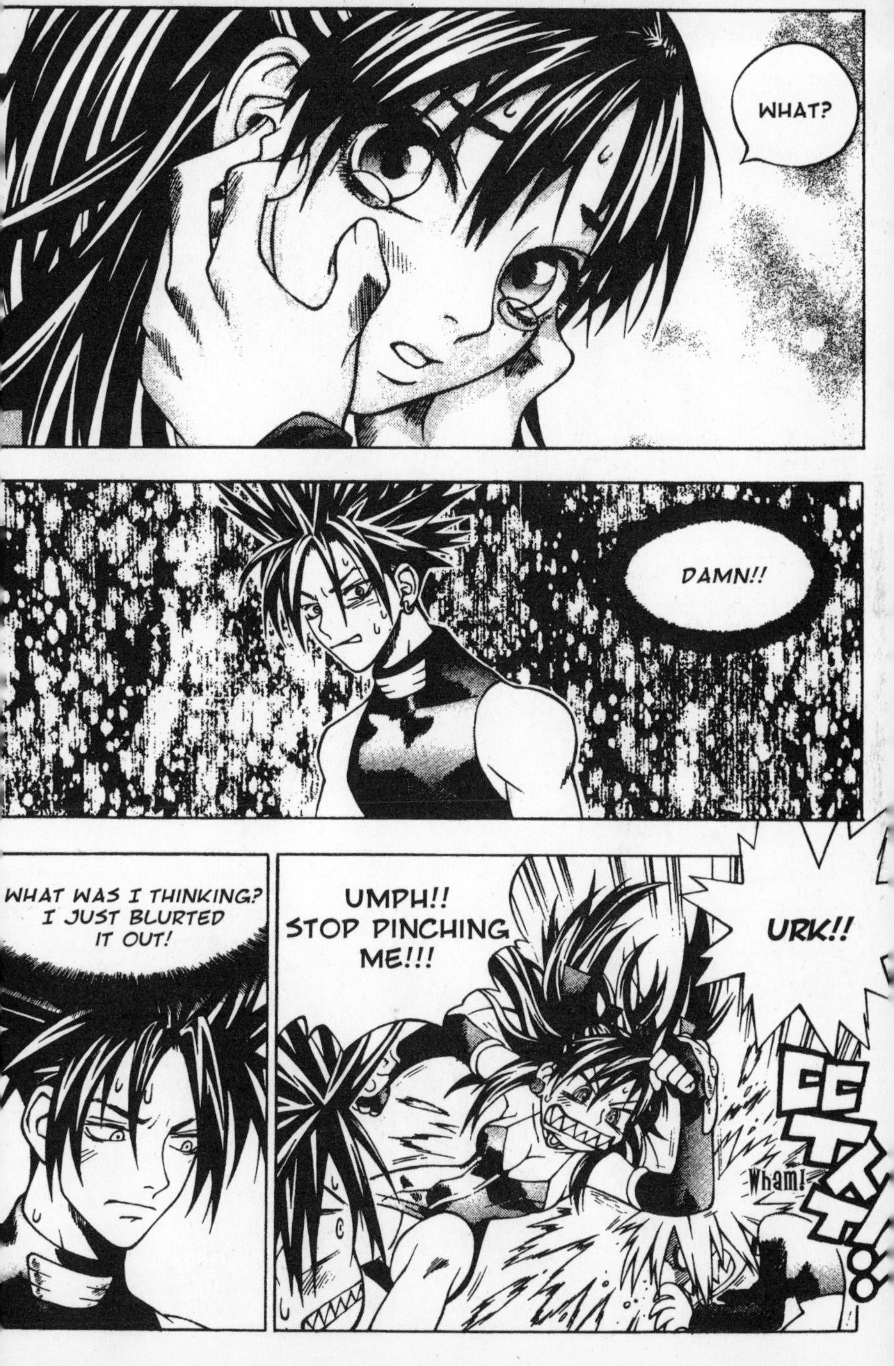
WHAT?
DAMN!!
URK!!
UMPH!! STOP PINCHING ME!!!
Wham!
WHAT WAS I THINKING? I JUST BLURTED IT OUT!

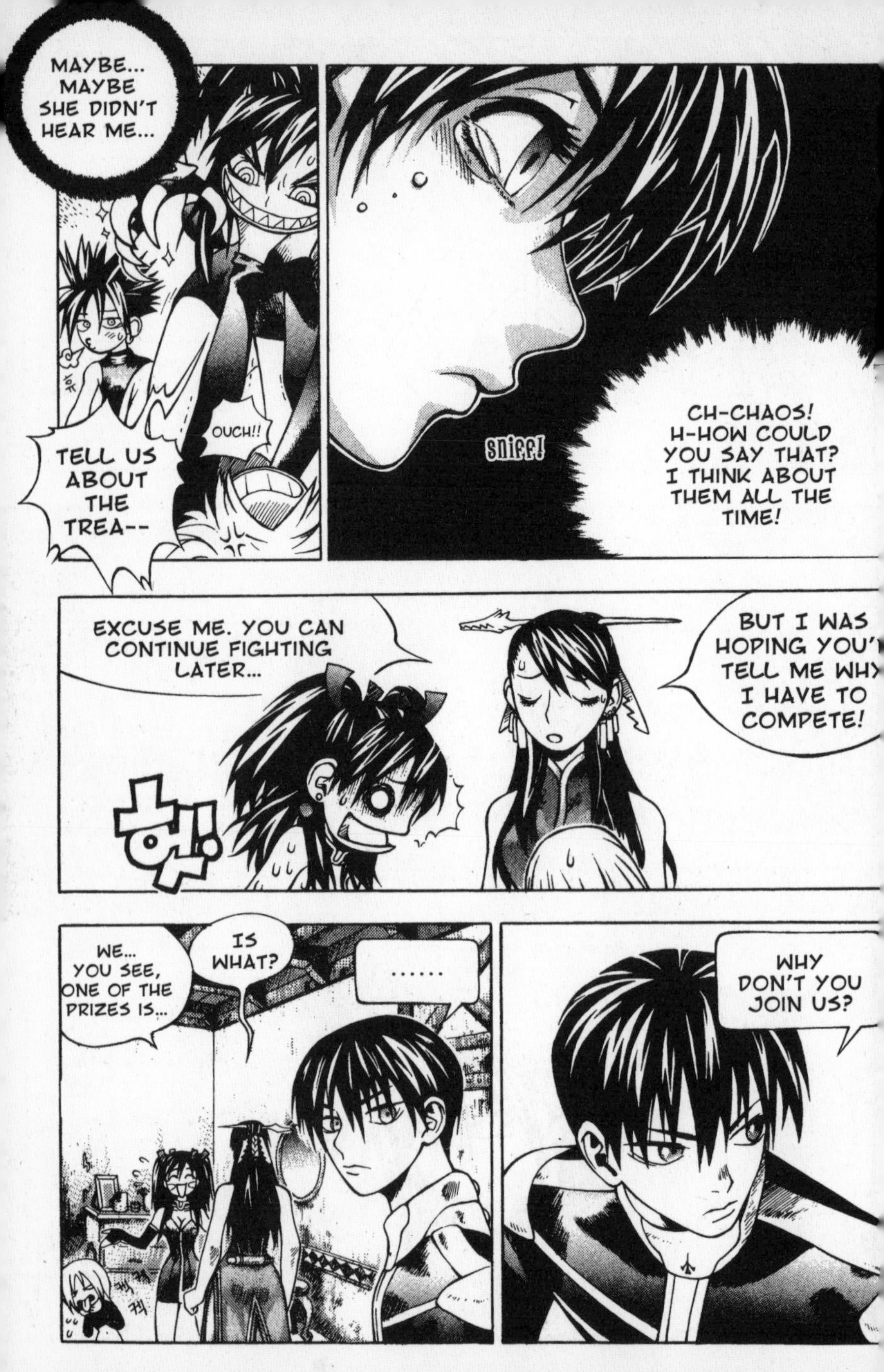
MAYBE... MAYBE SHE DIDN'T HEAR ME...
OUCH!!
TELL US ABOUT THE TREA--
SNIFF!
CH-CHAOS! H-HOW COULD YOU SAY THAT? I THINK ABOUT THEM ALL THE TIME!
EXCUSE ME. YOU CAN CONTINUE FIGHTING LATER...
BUT I WAS HOPING YOU' TELL ME WH I HAVE TO COMPETE!
WE... YOU SEE, ONE OF THE PRIZES IS...
IS WHAT?
......
WHY DON'T YOU JOIN US?

HUH?

AFTER ALL, YOU HAVE BEEN FOLLOWING US ALL AFTERNOON.

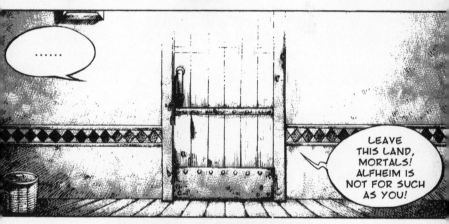

.....

LEAVE THIS LAND, MORTALS! ALFHEIM IS NOT FOR SUCH AS YOU!

WHAT'S THAT? WHAT DID YOU SAY?

I THINK YOU'D BETTER COME IN AND EXPLAIN!

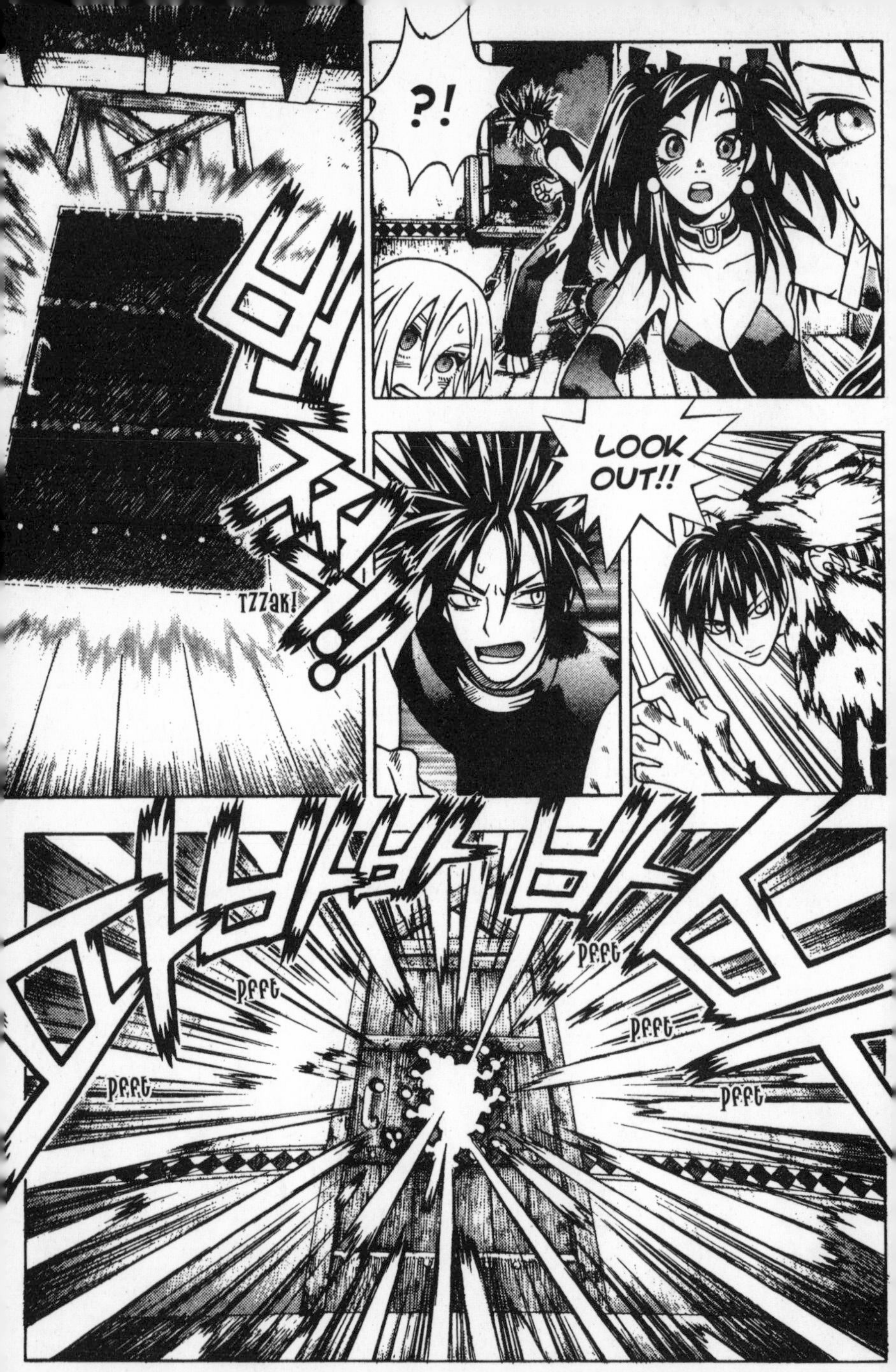
?!
TZZAK!
LOOK OUT!!
PFFT
PFFT
PFFT
PFFT
PFFT

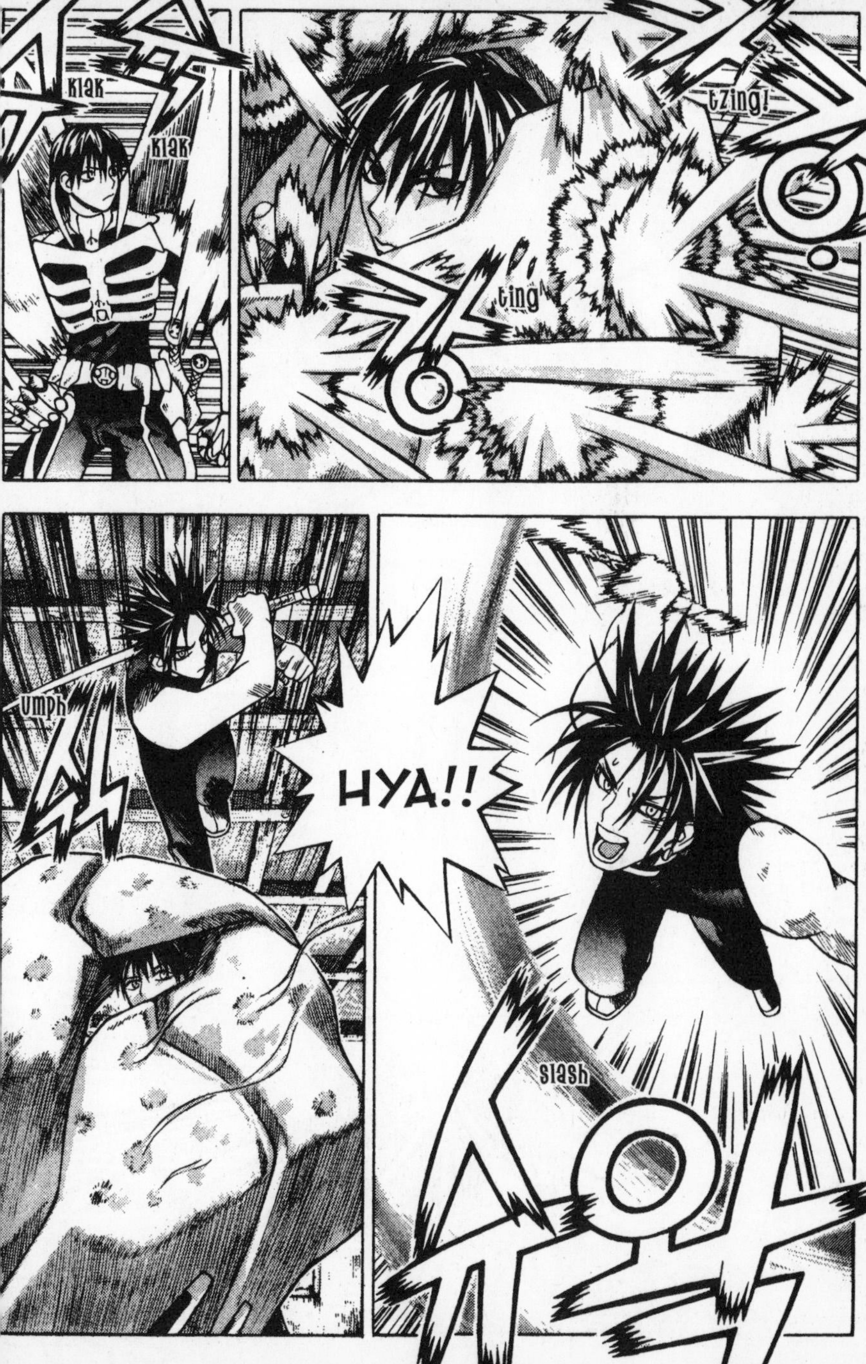
tzing!
ting
klak
klak
HYA!!
slash
umph

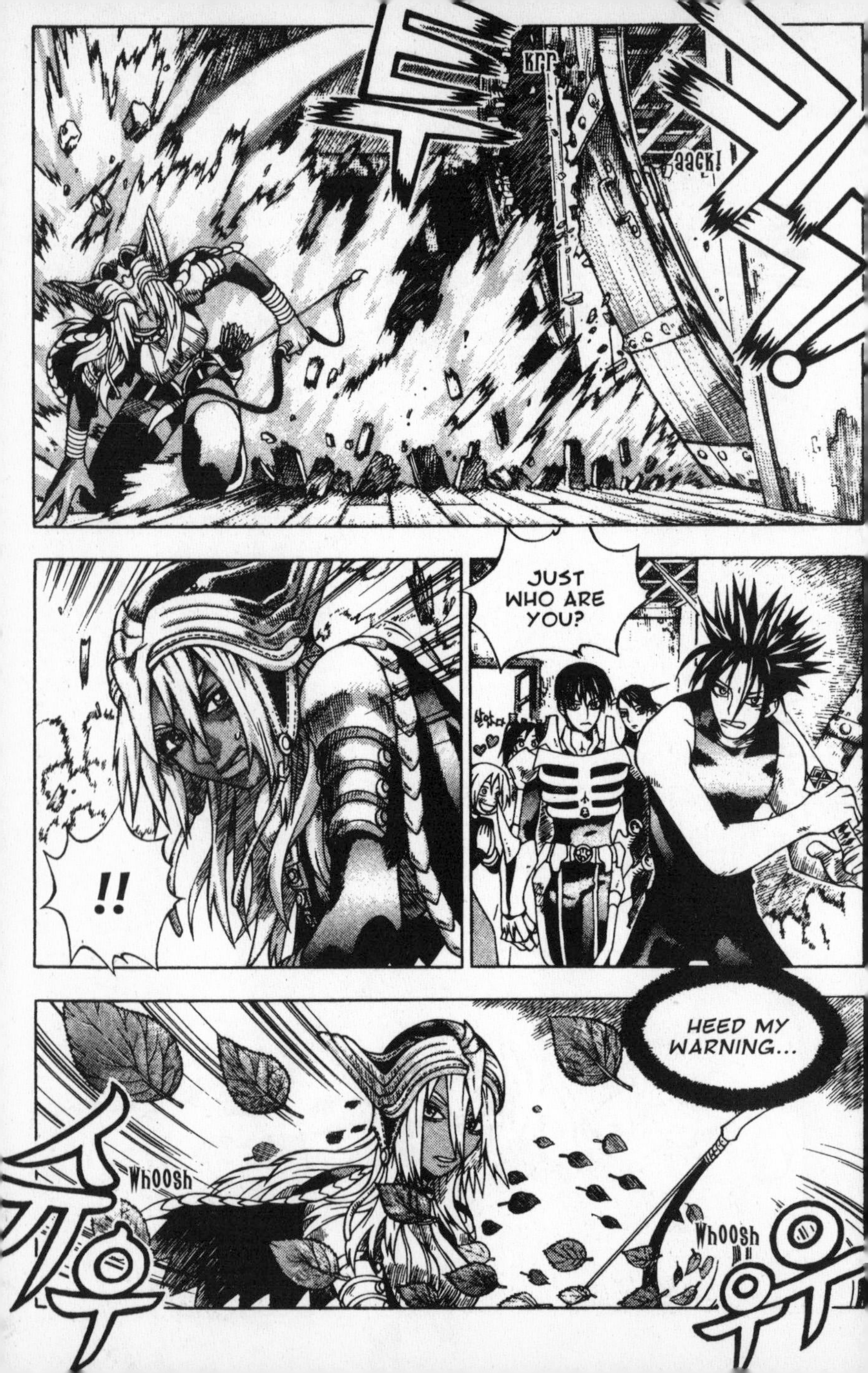
KRR
AACK!
!!
JUST WHO ARE YOU?
WHOOSH
HEED MY WARNING...
WHOOSH

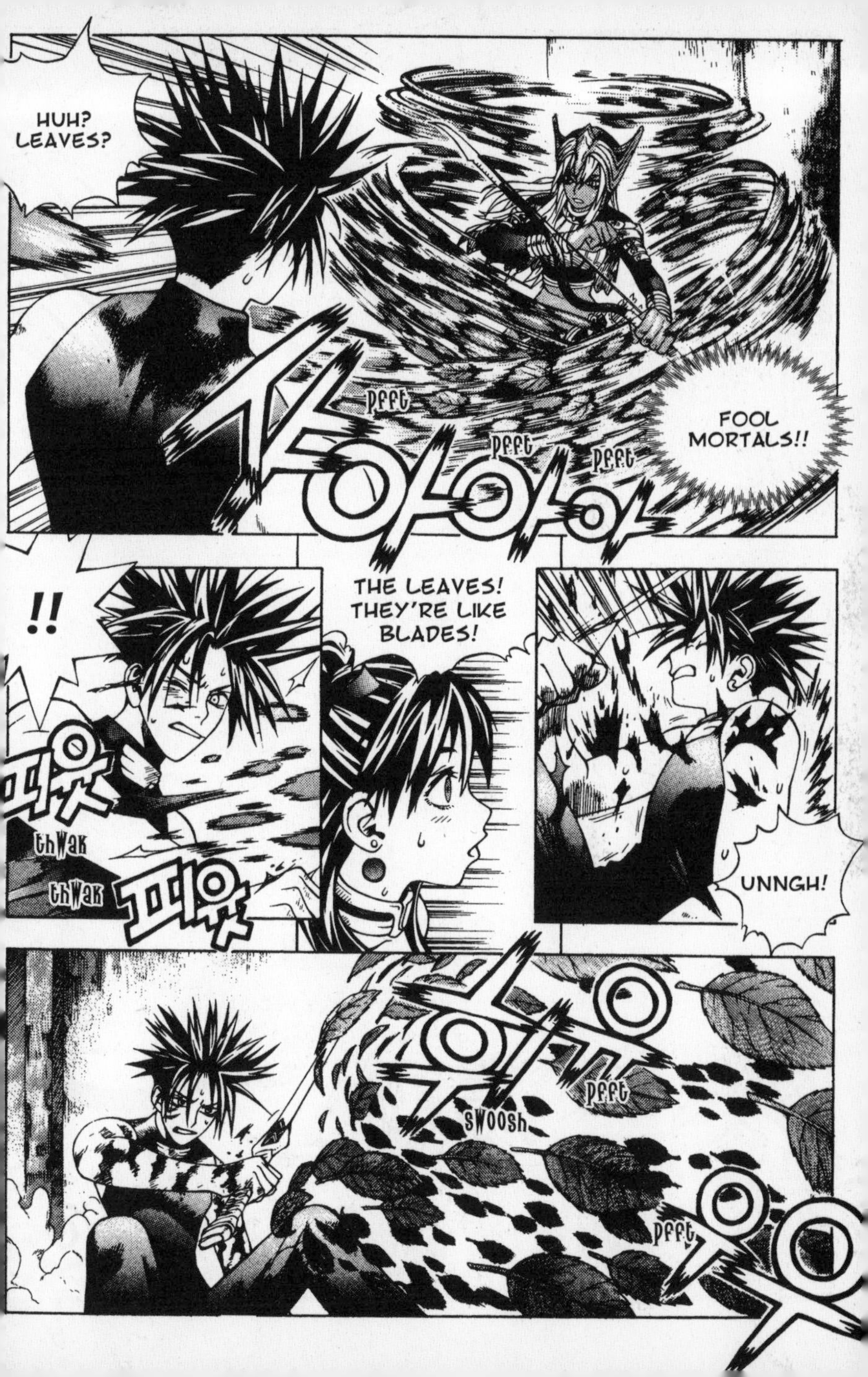
HUH? LEAVES?
pfft
pfft
pfft
FOOL MORTALS!!
!!
thwak
thwak
THE LEAVES! THEY'RE LIKE BLADES!
UNNGH!
pfft
swoosh
pfft

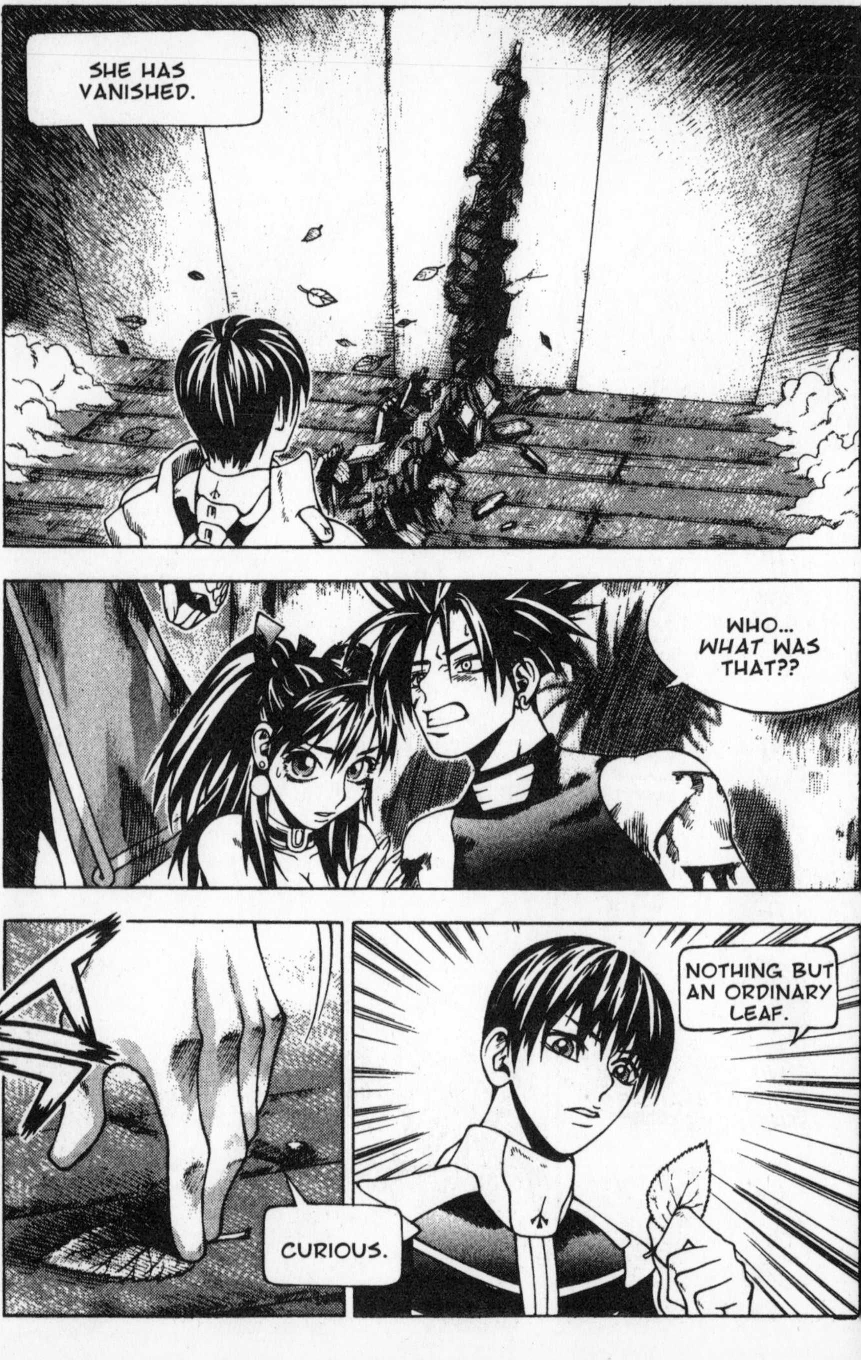
SHE HAS VANISHED.
WHO... WHAT WAS THAT??
NOTHING BUT AN ORDINARY LEAF.
CURIOUS.

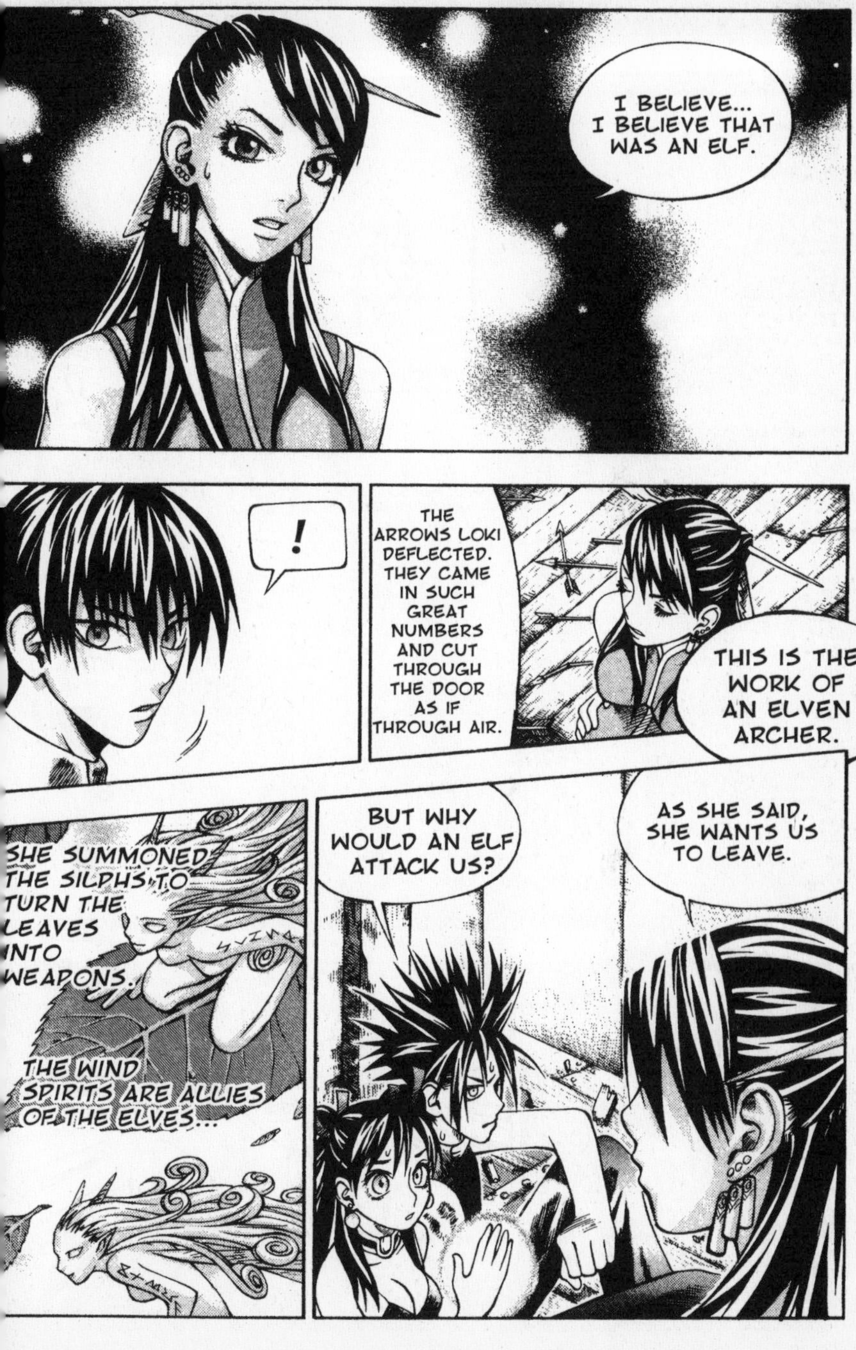
I BELIEVE... I BELIEVE THAT WAS AN ELF.
!
THE ARROWS LOKI DEFLECTED. THEY CAME IN SUCH GREAT NUMBERS AND CUT THROUGH THE DOOR AS IF THROUGH AIR.
THIS IS THE WORK OF AN ELVEN ARCHER.
SHE SUMMONED THE SILPHS TO TURN THE LEAVES INTO WEAPONS.
THE WIND SPIRITS ARE ALLIES OF THE ELVES...
BUT WHY WOULD AN ELF ATTACK US?
AS SHE SAID, SHE WANTS US TO LEAVE.

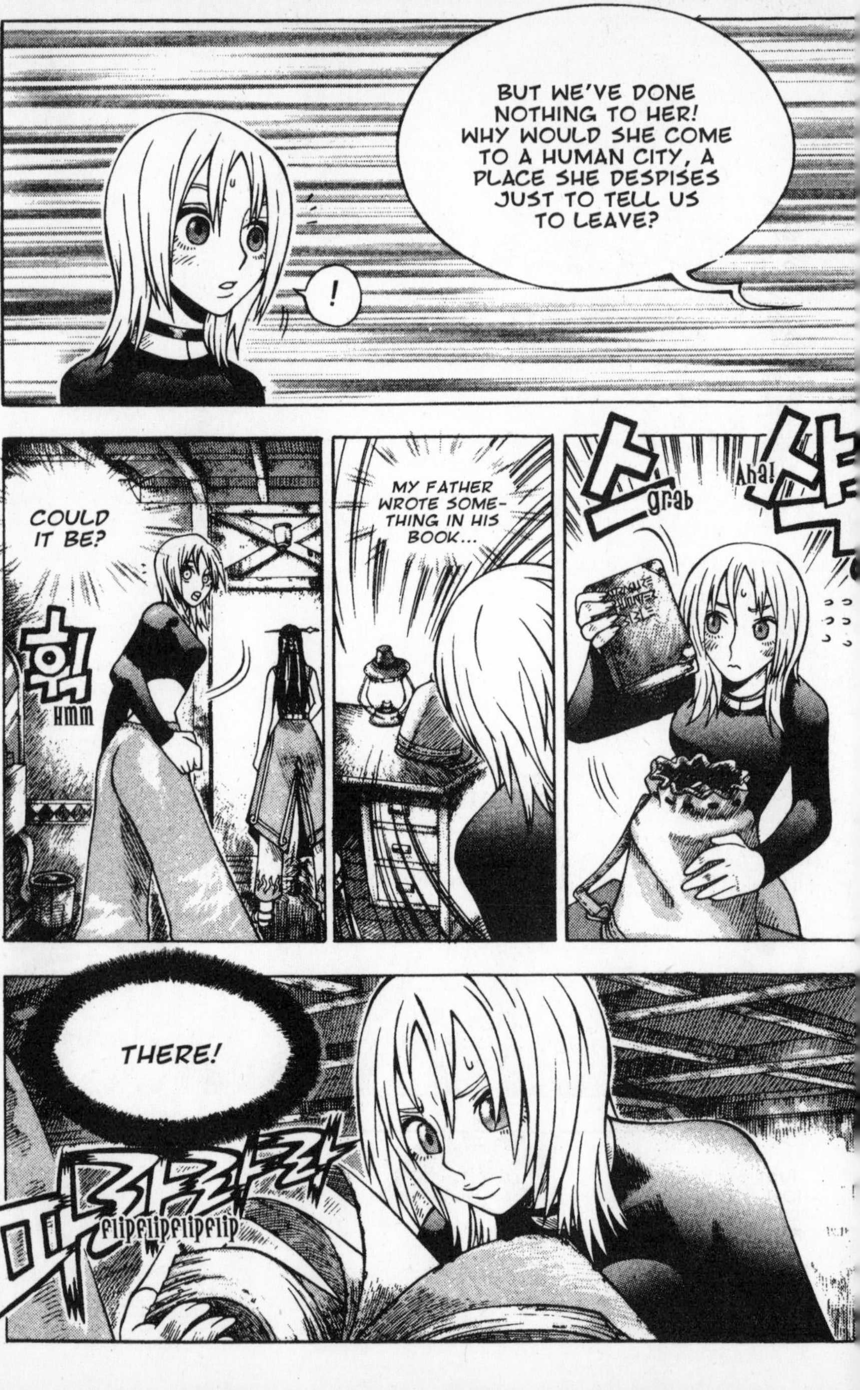
BUT WE'VE DONE NOTHING TO HER! WHY WOULD SHE COME TO A HUMAN CITY, A PLACE SHE DESPISES JUST TO TELL US TO LEAVE?
!
COULD IT BE?
HMM
MY FATHER WROTE SOME-THING IN HIS BOOK...
grab
Aha!
THERE!
flipflipflipflip

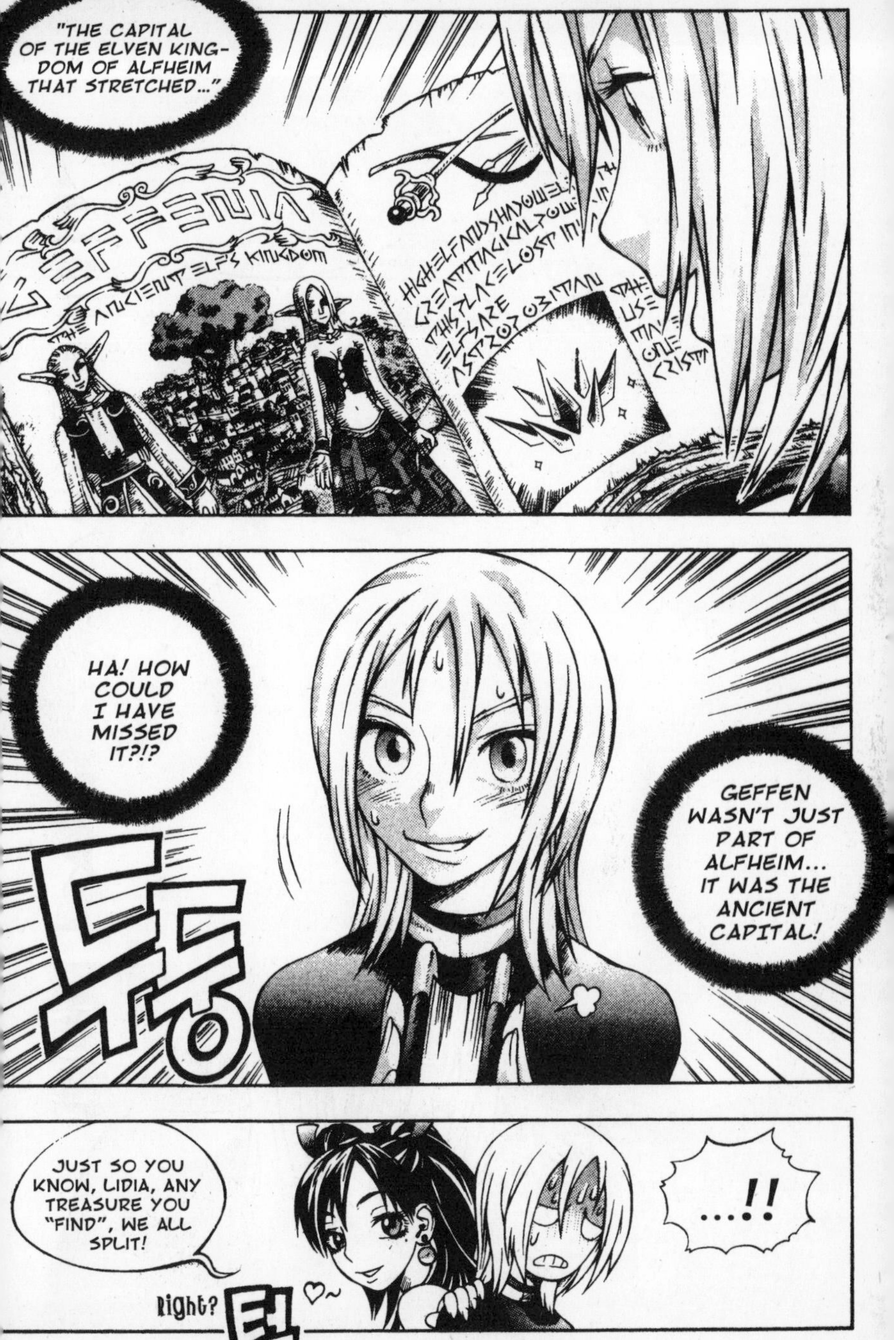
"THE CAPITAL OF THE ELVEN KINGDOM OF ALFHEIM THAT STRETCHED..."
GEFFENIA
THE ANCIENT ELF'S KINGDOM
HA! HOW COULD I HAVE MISSED IT?!?
GEFFEN WASN'T JUST PART OF ALFHEIM... IT WAS THE ANCIENT CAPITAL!
JUST SO YOU KNOW, LIDIA, ANY TREASURE YOU "FIND", WE ALL SPLIT!
Right?
...!!

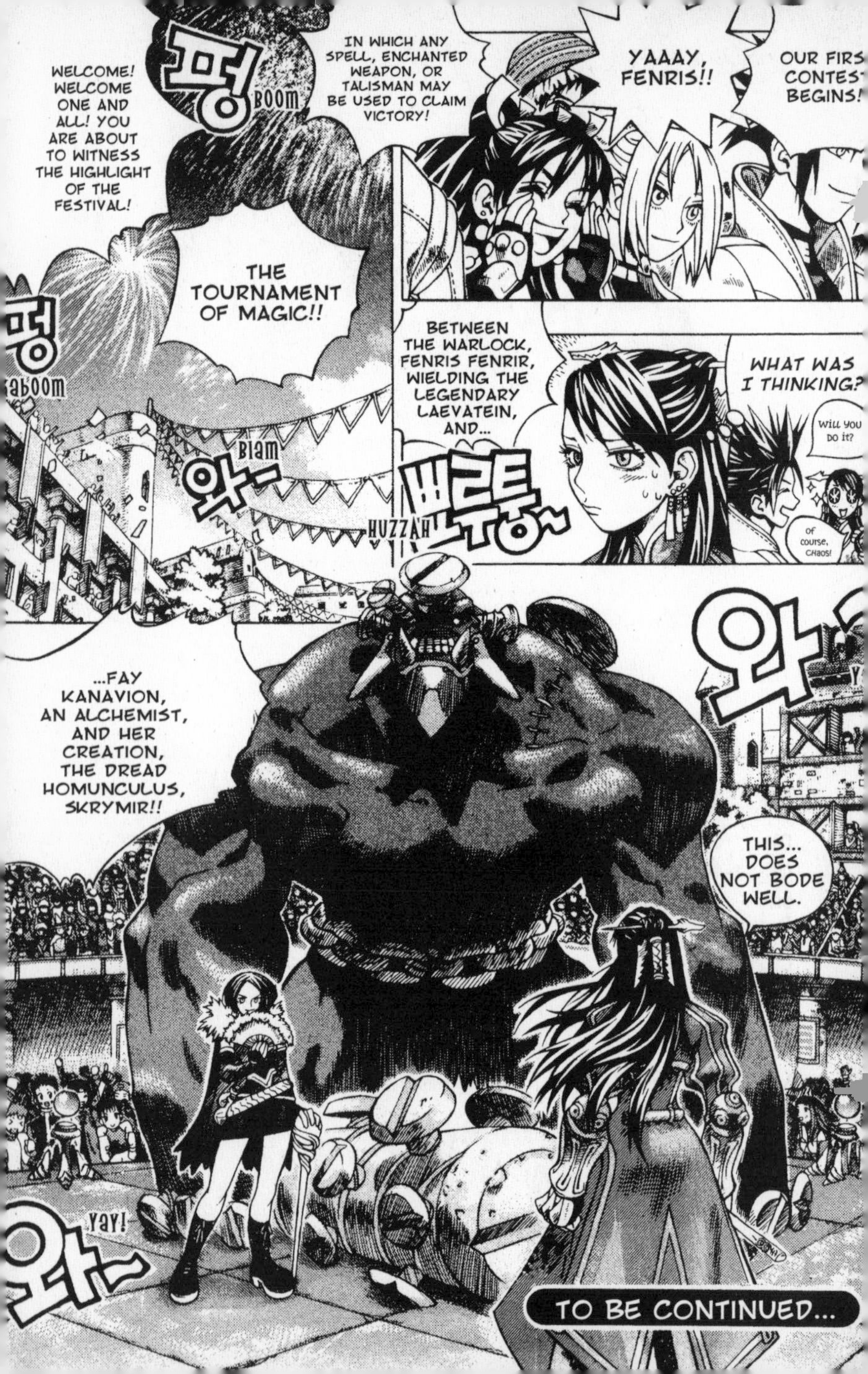
WELCOME! WELCOME ONE AND ALL! YOU ARE ABOUT TO WITNESS THE HIGHLIGHT OF THE FESTIVAL!
BOOM
THE TOURNAMENT OF MAGIC!!
IN WHICH ANY SPELL, ENCHANTED WEAPON, OR TALISMAN MAY BE USED TO CLAIM VICTORY!
YAAAY, FENRIS!!
OUR FIRST CONTEST BEGINS!
HUZZAH
BETWEEN THE WARLOCK, FENRIS FENRIR, WIELDING THE LEGENDARY LAEVATEIN, AND...
WHAT WAS I THINKING?
Will you do it?
Of course, Chaos!
...FAY KANAVION, AN ALCHEMIST, AND HER CREATION, THE DREAD HOMUNCULUS, SKRYMIR!!
THIS... DOES NOT BODE WELL.
YAY!
TO BE CONTINUED...

RAGNARÖK

The city of Geffen is built upon the ruins of the ancient Elven kingdom of Alfheim. What ancient secrets does this magical metropolis conceal? The Elven archer Reina is one of the last of her kind, and when her people's legacy is threatened, she'll do whatever it takes to protect it—even if it means fighting those who fight for good. And what of Skurai? The cursed swordsman has returned with arms open, but can a damned man be trusted?

New allies, new enemies. Ragnarok Volume 9: Legacy of the Vanar, available January 2004.

9

By Myung-Jin Lee

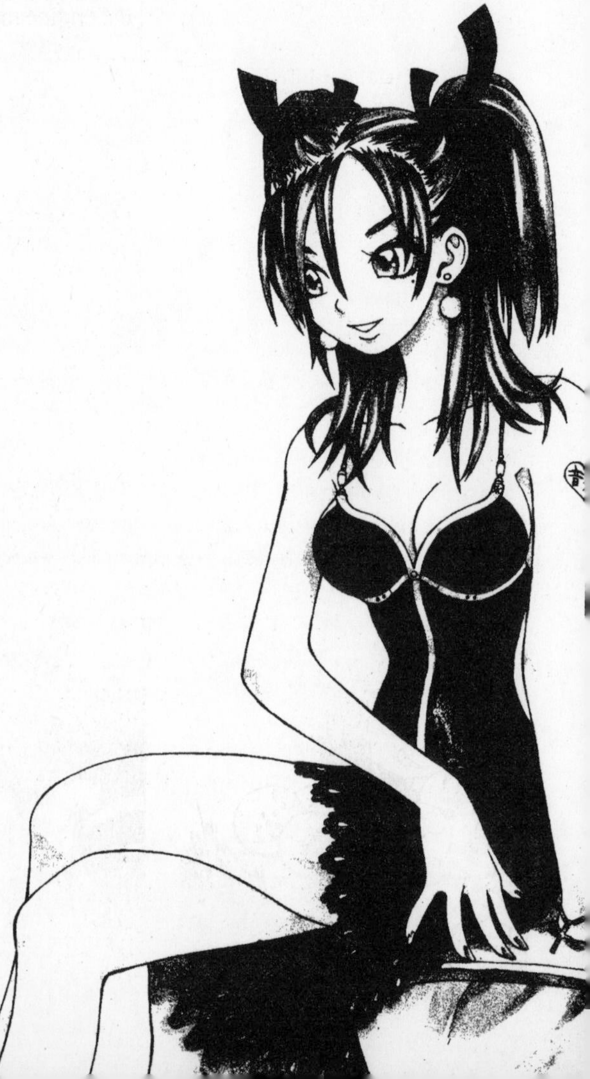

RAGNAROK

Bonus 4-panel strips!

My four assistants at DIVE TO DREAM SEA studio created these four gag comics. I hope you'll enjoy them!

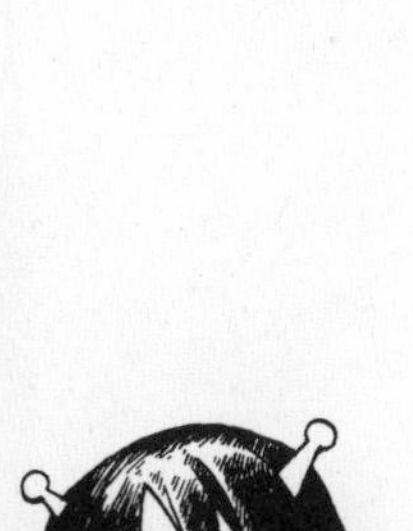

KAHO

HTTP:// lolitacookie.com
HTTP:// www.RAGNAROK.CO.KR
HTTP:// theRagnarok.com

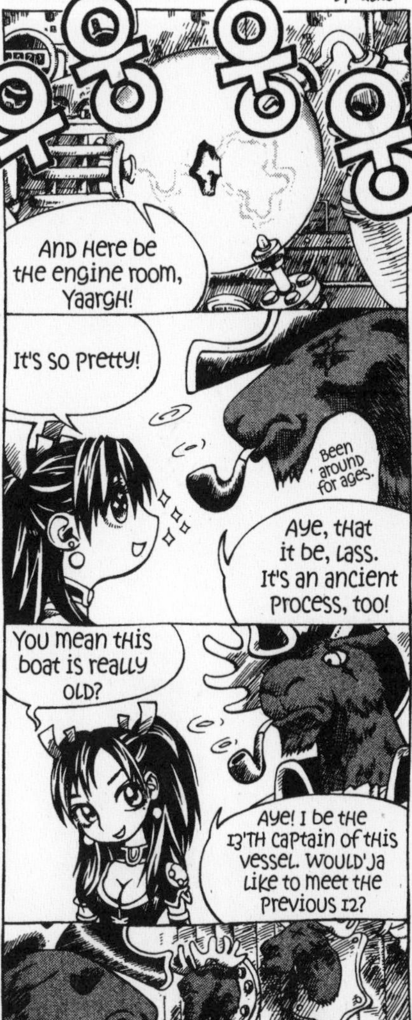
......
by kaho
And here be the engine room, Yaargh!
It's so pretty!
Been around for ages.
Aye, that it be, lass. It's an ancient process, too!
You mean this boat is really old?
Aye! I be the 13'th captain of this vessel. Would'ja like to meet the previous 12?
헉
Okay, pay attention. Starting from the left we have the first captain, Franken Alzheimer III. Then we have... 3rd...4th...5th...

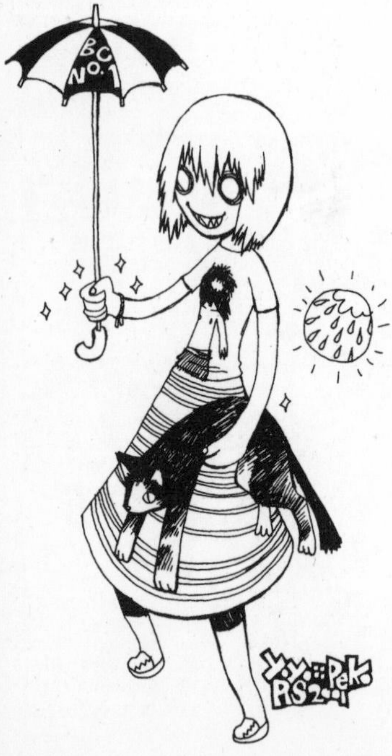
BC
No.1

FENRIS'S END

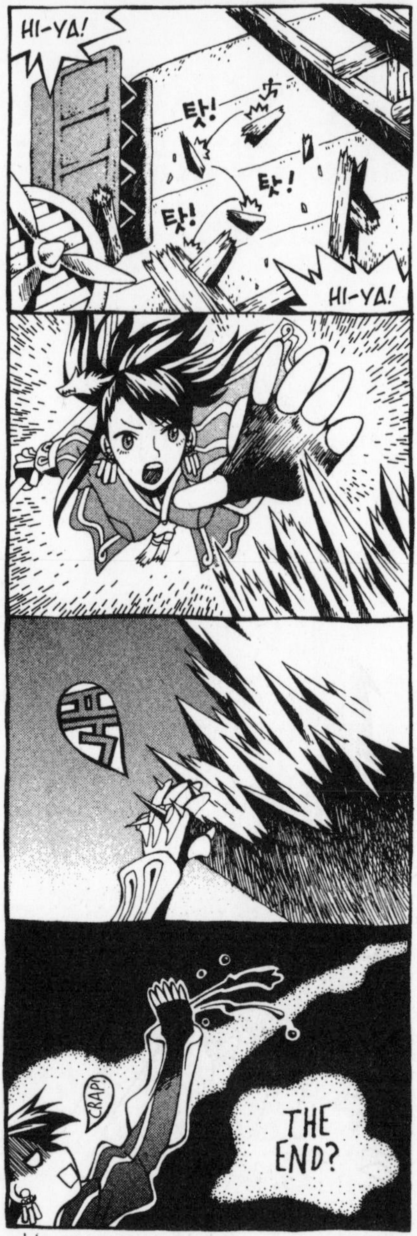
HI-YA!
탓!
탓!
탓!
HI-YA!
CRAP!
THE END?

http:// lolitacookie .com/yoyo

SKURAI KNOWS! -coma.-

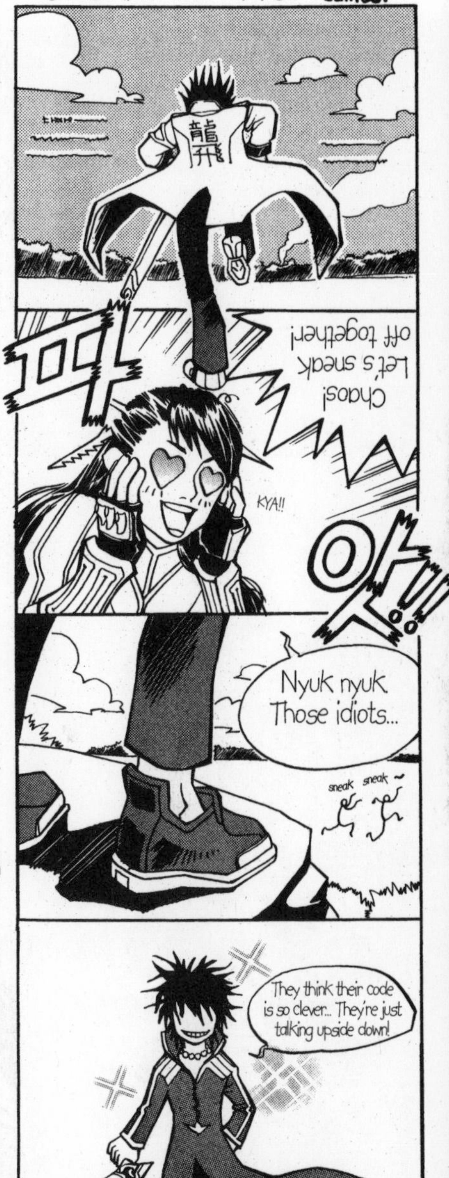

Chaos! Let's sneak off together!
KYA!!
OK!!
Nyuk nyuk. Those idiots...
sneak sneak ~
They think their code is so clever... They're just talking upside down!

coma0505@Lycos.co.kr (No web page -_-;;)

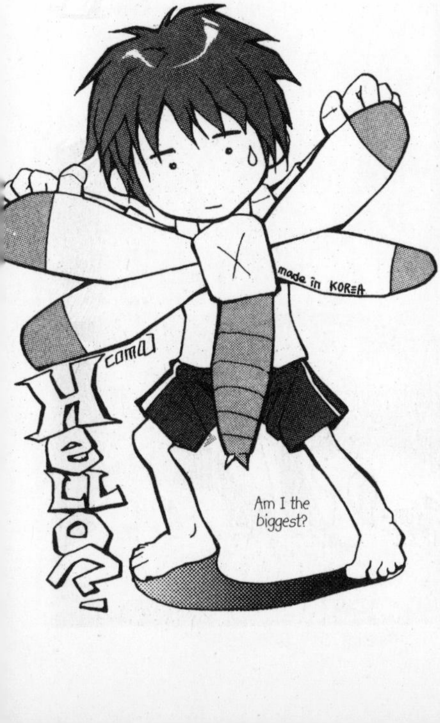

made in KOREA
coma
Hello?
Am I the biggest?

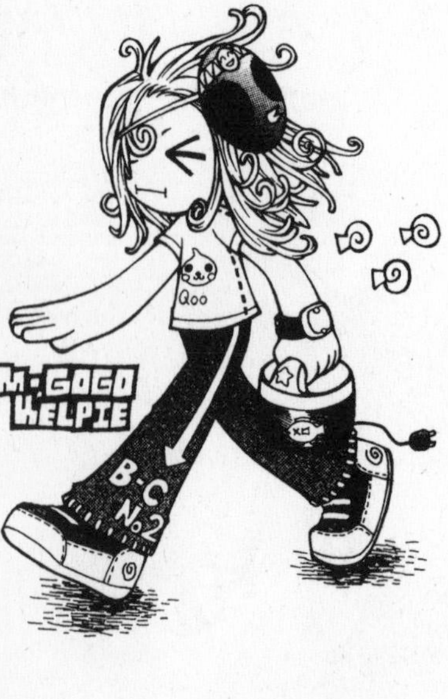
M-GOGO KELPIE
Qoo
B-C No.2

Arkana's Circus!

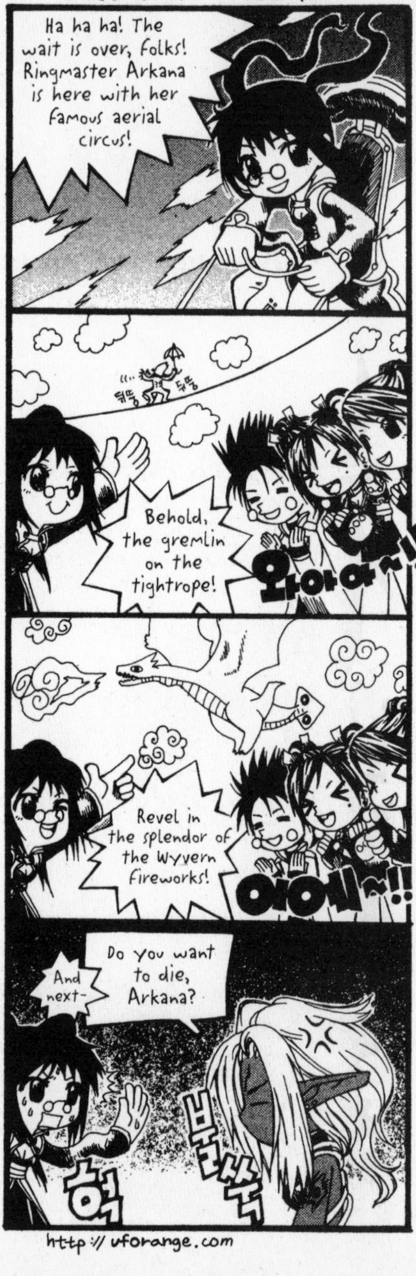
Ha ha ha! The wait is over, folks! Ringmaster Arkana is here with her famous aerial circus!
Behold, the gremlin on the tightrope!
와아아~!!
Revel in the splendor of the Wyvern fireworks!
와아~!!
And next-
Do you want to die, Arkana?
헉

http :// uforange.com

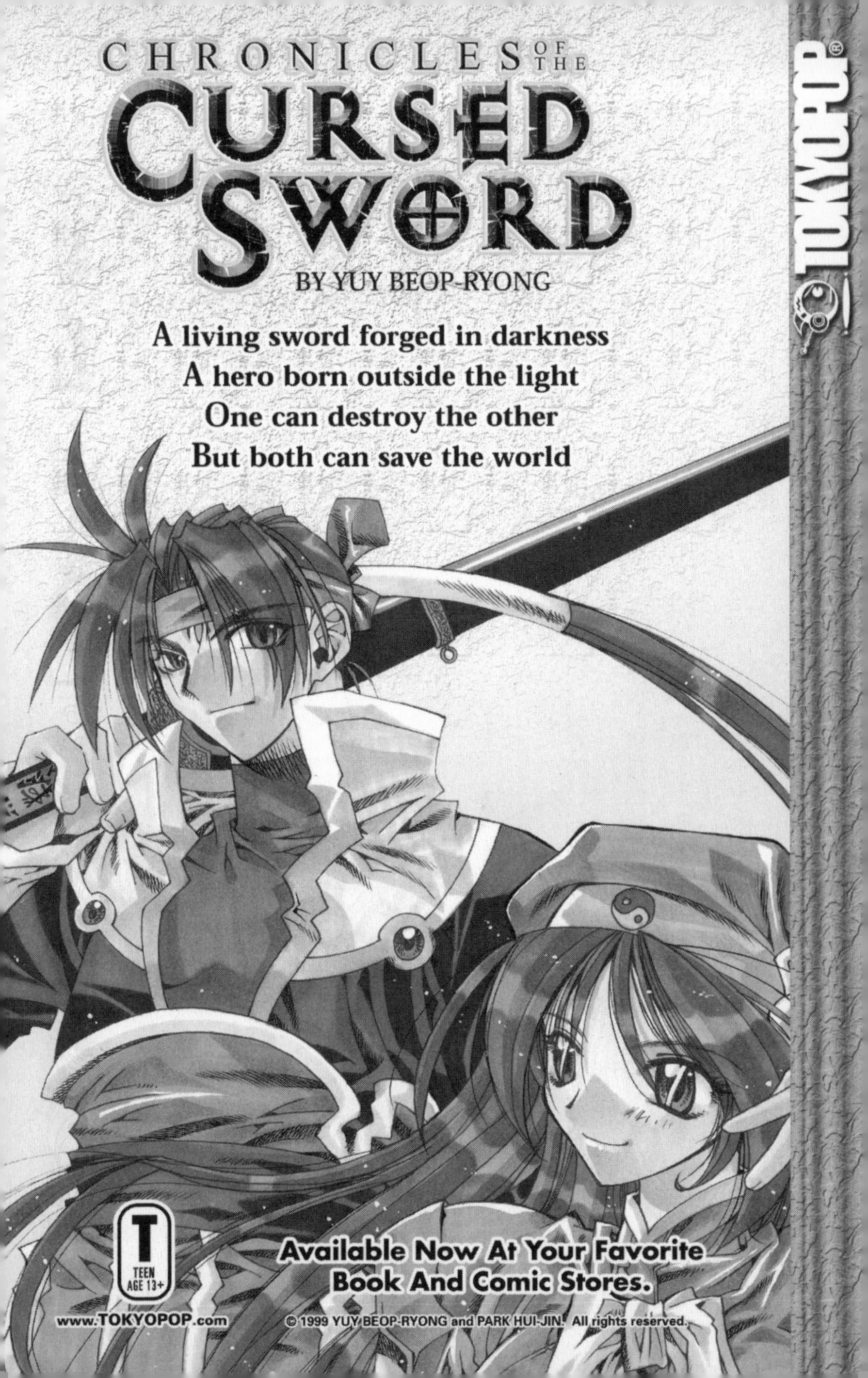
CHRONICLES OF THE
CURSED SWORD
BY YUY BEOP-RYONG
A living sword forged in darkness
A hero born outside the light
One can destroy the other
But both can save the world
TOKYOPOP
T
TEEN
AGE 13+
Available Now At Your Favorite
Book And Comic Stores.
www.TOKYOPOP.com
© 1999 YUY BEOP-RYONG and PARK HUI-JIN. All rights reserved.

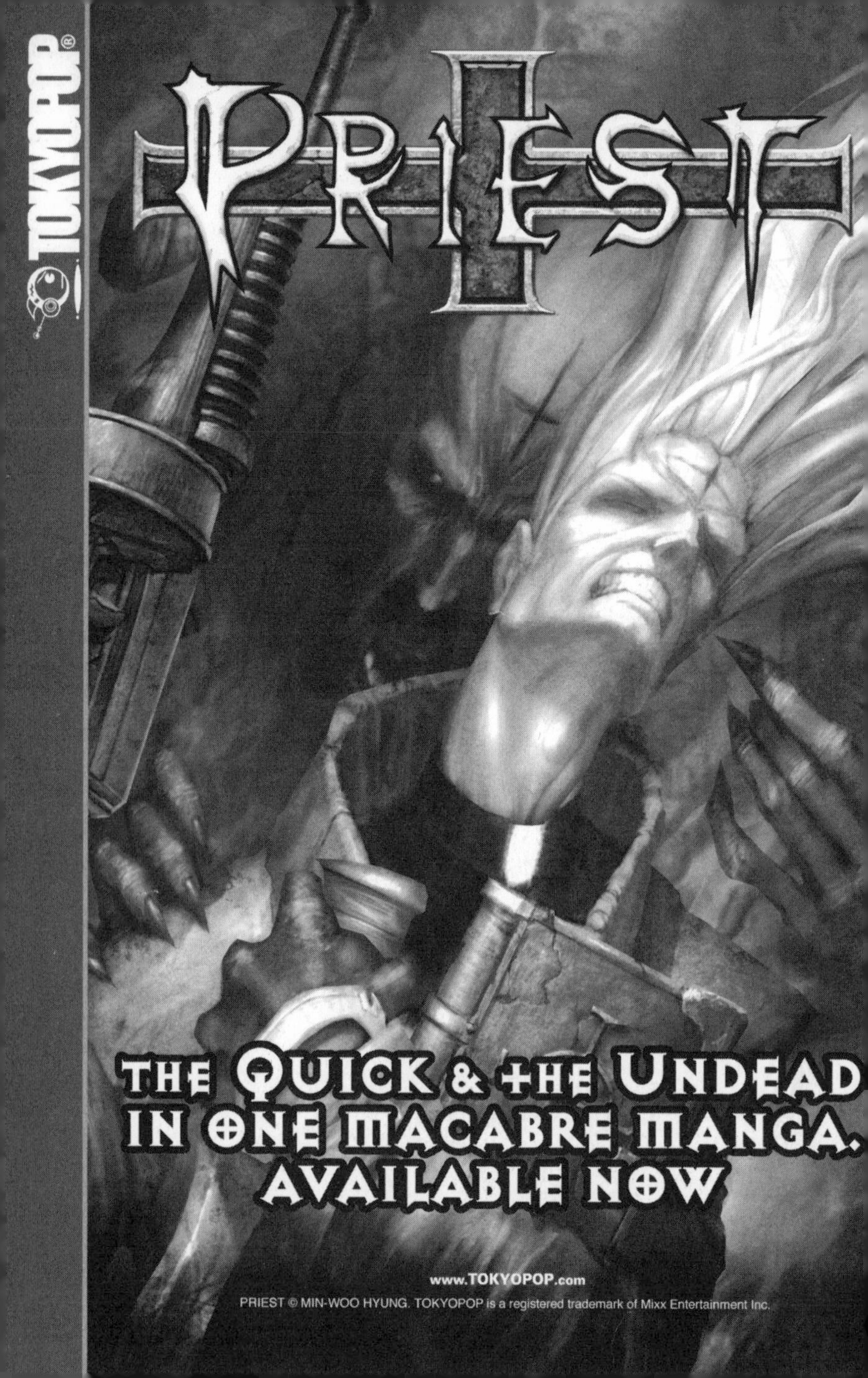
TOKYOPOP
PRIEST
THE QUICK & THE UNDEAD
IN ONE MACABRE MANGA.
AVAILABLE NOW
www.TOKYOPOP.com
PRIEST © MIN-WOO HYUNG. TOKYOPOP is a registered trademark of Mixx Entertainment Inc.

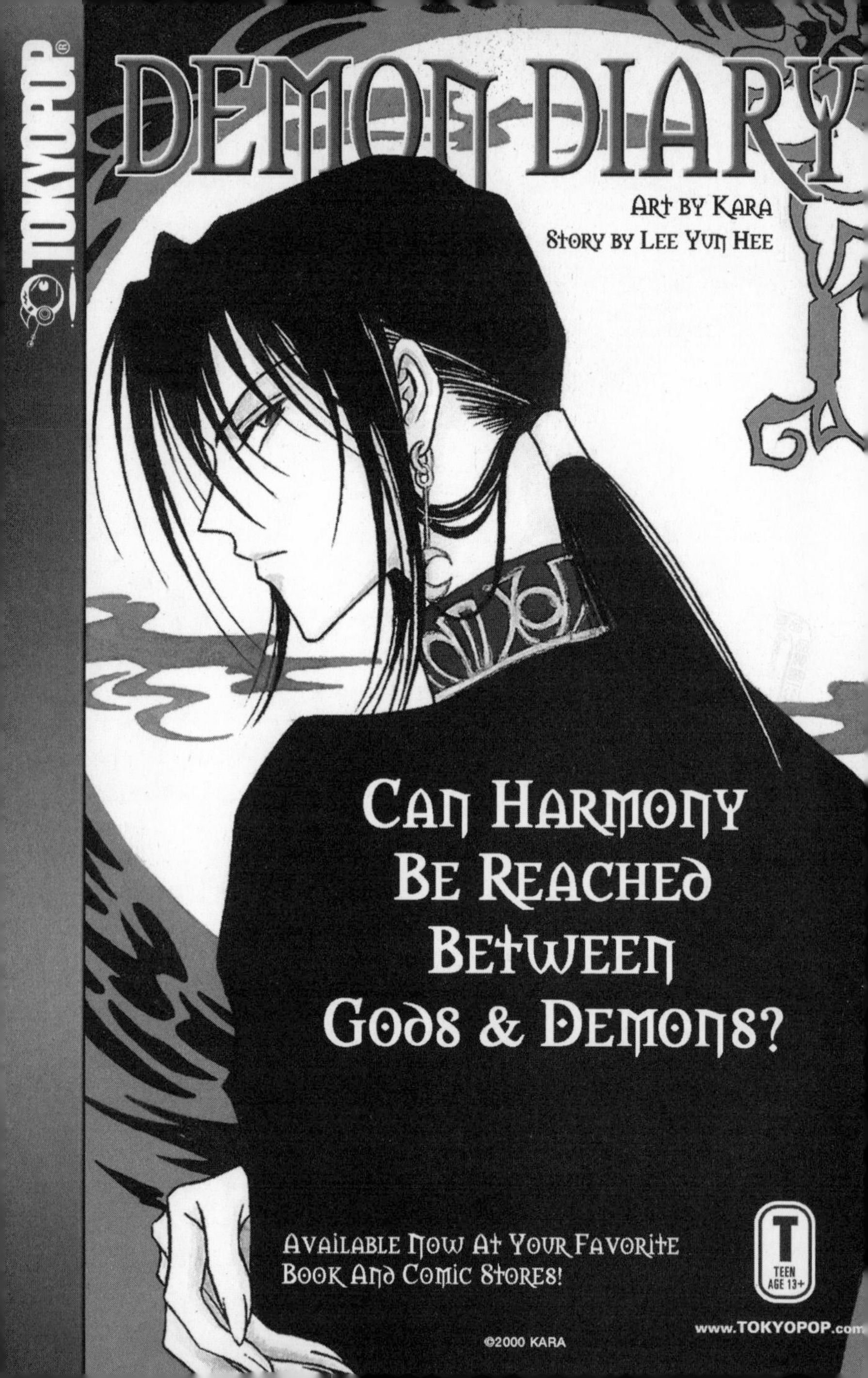
TOKYOPOP
DEMON DIARY
Art by Kara
Story by Lee Yun Hee
Can Harmony Be Reached Between Gods & Demons?
Available Now At Your Favorite Book And Comic Stores!
T
TEEN AGE 13+
www.TOKYOPOP.com
©2000 KARA